Spon's Landscape Handbook

SPECIFICATIONS AND PRICES

Spon's Landscape Handbook

SPECIFICATIONS AND PRICES

Edited by
DEREK LOVEJOY AND PARTNERS
Architects Planning Consultants Landscape Architects

E. & F. N. SPON LTD
LONDON

*First published 1972
by E. & F. N. Spon Ltd
11 New Fetter Lane, London EC4P 4EE*

© 1972 E. & F. N. Spon Ltd

*Typeset by
Santype Ltd (Coldtype Division)
Salisbury, Wiltshire
and printed in Great Britain by
T. & A. Constable Ltd, Edinburgh*

SBN 419 10660 X

*All rights reserved. No part of this book
may be reprinted, or reproduced
or utilized in any form or by any
electronic, mechanical or other means,
now known or hereafter invented, including
photocopying and recording, or in any information
storage and retrieval system, without permission
in writing from the Publisher.*

Published in the U.S.A.
by Halsted Press, a Division
of John Wiley & Sons, Inc.
New York

Preface

ACKNOWLEDGEMENTS

The editors wish to put on record their gratitude for the advice and collaboration of the following firms of Chartered Quantity Surveyors, with particular reference to Chapters 5 and 7.

Widnell & Trollope,
Davis House,
129 Wilton Road,
London S.W.1.

J. G. N. Horsefield,
Walter House,
418 The Strand,
London W.C.2.

The editors are also grateful to the British Standards Institution of 2, Park Street, London W.1. and the Cement and Concrete Association of 52, Grosvenor Gardens, London S.W.1. for their kind permission to reproduce portions of their publications, as noted in the appropriate places in the text.

Acknowledgement is also accorded to all those listed below who responded to the editors' requests for advice and information.

Countryside Commission
Department of the Environment
Forestry Commission
Institute of Landscape Architects
National Playing Fields Association
Royal Institute of British Architects
Royal Institution of Chartered Surveyors
Royal Town Planning Institute
J. St. Bodfan Gruffydd, PPILA
Hal Moggridge, AILA., ARIBA., AAdip.
Mary Mitchell, FILA.
J. A. C. Higgins, FILA., of Department of the Environment
I. C. Laurie, FILA., of University of Manchester
Chief Architect, Redditch Development Corporation
Chief Architect, Runcorn Development Corporation
Chief Architect, Telford Development Corporation
City Architect, Birmingham City Architects Department
County Architect, Lancashire County Council

County Planning Officer, Durham County Council
Landscape Architect, Basildon Development Corporation
Ministry of Development, Northern Ireland
J. H. Berry
Clifton Nurseries
En-Tout-Cas Ltd
Gavin Jones Nurseries Limited
V.E.B. Limited

The editors wish also to acknowledge with gratitude the research work and proof reading by Judy Firth, the typing by Melanie Martin and the drawing up of all the illustrations by Colin Ellis.

DEREK LOVEJOY AND PARTNERS

April 1972

STOP PRESS

REVISION TO RATES – CHAPTER 7

Building Industry Wages Settlement, 14 September 1972, England, Scotland and Wales

The settlement of the wages dispute resulted in increases in the rates used in Chapter 7 as calculated in February, 1972.

The effect of the increases will vary depending on the type of work. In general the increases on soft landscaping rates will be higher than on hard landscaping due to the higher labour content.

On soft landscaping as given in Chapter 7 sections 1, 2, 4, 5 and 13, an addition of 18% should be made to all rates; on hard landscaping as given in sections 3, 6, 7, 8, 9, 10, 11 and 12 an addition of 14% should be made.

To take account of the further increases in wage rates on 25 June 1973 for work executed after that date a total addition of 25% should be made to all soft landscaping rates and an addition of 20% to all hard landscaping rates.

The above percentage increases will not apply to those items quoted as 'supply only'.

On certain items with a high material content such as street furniture, playground equipment and semi-mature trees the percentage increase should be reduced accordingly.

No account has been taken of the further wage increases due in October 1973 and June 1974.

No account has been taken of any increase in the cost of materials in the above percentage increases.

Under the terms of the settlement the standard basic rates of wages will be as follows with effect on and from the dates shown:

Standard basic wage rate per 40 hour week		*Guaranteed minimum bonus payment*	*Guaranteed minimum weekly earnings*
Scotland & Grade A	London & Liverpool		
18 September 1972			
Craftsmen			
£26.00	£26.20	–	–
Labourers			
£22.20	£22.40	–	–
25 June 1973			
Craftsmen			
£27.00	£27.20	£2.60	£29.60
Labourers			
£23.00	£23.20	£2.20	£25.20
10 June 1974			
Craftsmen			
£29.00	£29.20	£3.00	£32.00
Labourers			
£24.60	£24.80	£2.60	£27.20

From 1 October 1973 basic wage rates will be subject to adjustment on the basis of any percentage net rise above 8½% in the retail price index between the figures published in August 1972 and August 1973. The adjustment shall be an extra £0.20 per week to the rates of both craftsmen and labourers for each full 0.75 per cent rise in the index over 8½%. Any adjustment will continue to be paid with the rates effective from 10 June 1974.

The payment of a guaranteed minimum bonus is conditional on the operative meeting the conditions of availability for work prescribed in N.W.R. 2A.1., and
(1) Where a bonus or productivity scheme is in operation, bonus earnings having fallen below the level of the guaranteed minimum for reasons outside the operatives control.
or
(2) Where no such scheme is in operation there has been no interruption of normal working within the operatives control.

Building and Civil Engineering Industry Northern Ireland
With effect from Monday 5 June 1972 the standard rates of wages are craftsmen £0.56½ per hour, labourers £0.48 per hour. These rates to remain unchanged until the first pay week in June 1973.

Contents

PREFACE

Acknowledgements *page* v

1 INTRODUCTION

1.1 Aims and objectives 1

2 LEGISLATION AND LEGAL CONSIDERATIONS

2.1 Planning permission 3
2.2 The principal planning acts 3
2.3 The Civic Amenities Act 1967 4
2.4 The National Parks and Access to the Countryside Act 1949 and the subsequent Countryside Acts 5
2.5 The Agriculture Act 1947 7
2.6 The Forestry Acts 1919-1967 7
2.7 The Woodland Dedication Scheme 8
2.8 Tree Preservation Orders 9
2.9 Derelict land reclamation 10
2.10 Caravan sites 13

3 FEES

3.1 Introduction 15
3.2 Landscape Architects' fees 15
    Preface 15
    General conditions 15
    Remuneration on a time basis 18
    Remuneration on a percentage basis 19
    Other bases of remuneration 23
    Consultancy, management and occasional visits 24
    Additional services 25
    Expenses 26
    Mode and time of payment 26
    Work overseas 28
    Appendix 1 29

Contents

3.3	Architects' fees	30
	General	30
	Remuneration. Consultants. Responsibilities. Specialist subcontractors and suppliers. Copyright. Inspection. Delay and changes in instructions.	
	Normal services	33
	Work stages. Development studies. Development plans. Sites and buildings. Constructional research. Negotiations. Special drawings. Furnishings and works of art. Approvals in the normal services.	
	Fees for the normal services	36
	Total construction cost. New works. Works to existing buildings. Repetition. Partial services. Mode and time of payment. Percentage fees for the normal services.	
	Other services	41
	Town planning. Quantity surveying, valuing and surveying. Garden and landscape design. Building surveys and structural investigations. Separate trades contracts. Interior design, shopfitting and furniture design. Building systems and components. Litigation and arbitration. Consultancy.	
	Time charges	43
	Hourly rates. Travelling time.	
	Out-of-pocket expenses	44
	Drawings and documents. Hotel and travelling expenses. Disbursements. Compounding of expenses.	
	Abandoned works and interpretation	45
	Abandoned works. Resumed commissions. Interpretation. Disputes. Arbitration.	
3.4	Quantity Surveyors' Fees. Scale 36.	47
3.5	Quantity Surveyors' Fees. Scale 37.	52
	General	52
	Lump sum contracts: pre-contract services.	52
	Lump sum contracts: post-contract services.	57
	Contracts based on bills of approximate quantities: pre-contract and post-contract services.	61
	Contracts based on schedules of prices: pre-contract services.	64
	Contracts based on schedules of prices: post-contract services.	64
	Prime cost contracts: pre-contract and post-contract services.	65
	Time charges.	67
	Litigation and arbitration.	67

4 DRAWING OFFICE PRACTICE AND CONTRACT PROCEDURE

4.1	Introduction	68
4.2	Working drawings and planting plans	68
4.3	Description of works/specification	69
4.4	Bills of quantities	70
4.5	Contracts – introduction	71
4.6	Selection of tenderers	71
4.7	Tendering procedures	72
4.8	Negotiated contracts	73
4.9	Acceptance of tenders	73
4.10	Form of contract	74
4.11	Sub-contracts	74
4.12	Contract management and supervision	76
4.13	Instructions and variations	76
4.14	Certificates and payments	77
4.15	Completion and handovers	77
4.16	Making good of defects and permanent after-care	79
4.17	Final account procedure	79

5 SPECIFICATION

5.0	Introduction	80
5.1	Preparatory operations	81
	5.1.1 Introduction	81
	5.1.2 B.S. 4428:1969 Recommendations on preparatory operations	85
5.2	Groundworks	88
	5.2.1 Introduction	88
	5.2.2 B.S. 3882:1965 Recommendations and classification for topsoil	92
	5.2.3 B.S. 4428:1969 Groundworks	96
5.3	Drainage	105
	5.3.1 Introduction	105
	5.3.2 B.S. 4428:1969 Drainage	105
	5.3.3 Code of Practice 303:1952	109
	5.3.4 Specification items	109
5.4	Seeding of grass areas	116
	5.4.1 Introduction	116
	5.4.2 B.S. 4428:1969 Seeding of grass areas	117
	5.4.3 Typical seed mixes	119

5.4	Seeding of grass areas (*continued*)		
	5.4.4	Alternative items (not in B.S. 4428:1969)	122
	5.4.5	Hydro-seeding	123
5.5	Turf and turfing		124
	5.5.1	Introduction	124
	5.5.2	B.S. 3969:1965 Recommendations for turf for general landscape purposes	125
	5.5.3	Alternative items on turf (not in B.S. 3969:1965)	126
	5.5.4	B.S. 4428:1969 Turfing	127
	5.5.5	Alternative items on turfing (not in B.S. 4428:1969)	129
5.6	Plants and planting including semi-mature trees		131
	5.6.1	Introduction	131
	5.6.2	B.S. 3936:Part 1:1965 Nursery stock, trees and shrubs	133
	5.6.3	B.S. 3936:Part 4:1966 Nursery stock, forest trees	136
	5.6.4	B.S. 4428:1969 Individual tree planting	137
	5.6.5	B.S. 4428:1969 Planting of shrubs, hedges, climbers, herbaceous plants and bulbs	139
	5.6.6	B.S. 4428:1969 Forestry planting for amenity purposes	143
	5.6.7	B.S. 4043:1966 Recommendations for transplanting semi-mature trees	147
5.7	Enclosure		158
	5.7.1	Introduction	158
	5.7.2	Screen walls	158
	5.7.3	Retaining walls	158
	5.7.4	Traffic barriers and pedestrian rails	159
	5.7.5	Fences	161
5.8	Hard ground finishes		166
	5.8.1	Introduction	166
	5.8.2	Preparatory items	166
	5.8.3	Kerbs and edgings	168
	5.8.4	Flexible surfaces	170
	5.8.5	Rigid paving	180
	5.8.6	Unit paving	188
	5.8.7	Driveways	195
	5.8.8	Steps	195
5.9	Recreation and sports facilities		196
	5.9.1	Layouts	196
	5.9.2	Artificial surfaces and finishes	196
5.10	Playground equipment		199
	5.10.1	Introduction	199
	5.10.2	Selected typical equipment	199

5.11	Water features		203
	5.11.1 Lakes and ponds		203
	5.11.2 Ornamental pools		203
	5.11.3 Swimming pools		203
	5.11.4 Fountains		204
5.12	Street furniture		205
	5.12.1 Introduction		205
	5.12.2 Amenity lighting		205
	5.12.3 Litter bins		208
	5.12.4 Outdoor seats		209
	5.12.5 Plant containers		210
	5.12.6 Cycle stands		210
5.13	Maintenance		211
	5.13.1 Introduction		211
	5.13.2 B.S. 3998:1966 Recommendations for tree work		211
	5.13.3 Grass maintenance		220
	5.13.4 Shrub bed maintenance		220

6 DRAWINGS

Institute of Landscape Architects' Fees	225
Planting plans	226
Enclosure	228
Copings	228
Low rails	230
Fences	233
Gates	239
Hard ground finishes	240
Path edgings	240
Channels	242
Mowing margins	243
Typical parking layouts	244
Paths	245
Tree grids	249
Concrete driveways	250
Steps	252
Recreation and sports facilities	254
Lacrosse	254
Association Football	254
Hockey	254
Rugby Union	255
Rugby League	255

Recreation and sports facilities (*continued*)
- Bowling green — 255
- Cricket — 255
- Athletics — 256
- High jump — 256
- Shot putt — 256
- Long jump — 256
- Pole vault — 256
- Javelin — 256
- Triple jump — 256
- Discus and hammer — 256
- Netball — 256
- Basketball — 256
- Tennis — 256

7 PRICING

7.0	Introduction	257
7.1	Preparatory operations	258
7.2	Groundworks	261
7.3	Drainage	265
7.4	Seeding of grass areas	274
7.5	Turf and turfing	277
7.6	Plants and planting including semi-mature trees	279
7.7	Enclosure	295
7.8	Hard ground finishes	309
7.9	Recreation and sports facilities	320
7.10	Playground equipment	322
7.11	Water features	335
7.12	Street furniture	338
7.13	Maintenance	345

8 MACHINERY AND EQUIPMENT: ROUND-UP OF RECENT INNOVATIONS

8.1	Introduction	346
8.2	Aerators and scarifiers	346
8.3	Graders	347
8.4	Mowers	347
8.5	Sprayers	353
8.6	Sweepers	354

9	**RESEARCH REPORT**	
9.1	Sources of information on research	356

BIBLIOGRAPHY

Books referred to in the text or useful for additional information	358
Publications	360

APPENDIX

Professional bodies and associations concerned with the environment	374

INDEX 380

Index to Advertisers	397

1 Introduction

1.1 AIMS AND OBJECTIVES

1.1.1 This volume follows in part, the traditional pattern of a price book but also aims to widen the range into a handbook containing much additional information related to the making of the external environment. This information is not otherwise available in one place at present.

1.1.2 There are many differences between landscape, and building or engineering work. For instance, normal landscape bills of quantities have far fewer items than do bills for a building. For this and other reasons the number of individual priced items in this book is at present relatively small. This leaves scope therefore to cover other related subjects which should be a useful additional aid to all professional and contracting personnel who need to refer to the description of work/ specification and pricing sections. Because detailed landscape specification is not yet commonly used, special attention has been given to detailed clauses.

1.1.3 In many cases comprehensive information cannot, for reasons of space, be provided and it would be inappropriate in a publication of this kind to provide information which should be sought in the relevant detailed technical books. Wherever possible, reference is made to such sources. There are a number of instances where prices and dimensions may be thought open to question and this is often inevitable when dealing with landscape work. It is seldom necessary to obtain in soft landscape work the degree of precision associated with building and civil engineering construction, although a reasonable degree of accuracy is desirable, even with the setting out of plant material and grass areas.

1.1.4 As major elements of landscape work are of an organic growing nature some items never have a completely static size or specification. It is, therefore, clear that landscape specification is bound to be substantially different from building work specification. The differences are enhanced when climatic conditions and considerations of ecology and other sciences are taken into account.

1.1.5 The role of the landscape architect is growing steadily. Nowadays it often embraces regional planning and land use designation. The range of activities which it is intended to cover in this book is fairly wide but primary importance is given to items of work related to general landscape contracts, hard and soft. Nevertheless, a number of more specialized items have been included; for instance sections covering:

1.1.5 (cont'd)	reclamation, forestry, sports grounds, maintenance, after-care or general landscape management. As the range of landscape work continues to widen, these subjects may, in the future, justify far more space in revised editions.
1.1.6	Some subjects are covered more fully than others. If this produces an inbalance, this is something that should be corrected in future revised editions in the light of comments and experience. With a first attempt at such a publication it is obvious that some minor or unavoidable errors or omissions will occur and in order that everyone may gain by corrections of future editions, the authors would welcome detailed and constructive comments which the users may care to contribute. Problems also arise from preparing the book entirely in metric units, though many of these will resolve themselves as we all become more accustomed to working in the new measurements.

2 Legislation and legal considerations

2.1 PLANNING PERMISSION

2.1.1 Increasingly landscape work requires consultations with statutory and local authorities. In many cases, planning permission is granted for a major development, subject to a satisfactory landscape design being submitted for approval. In many cases full detailed planting plans are required for submission before a development can start on the ground, even though landscape work may not be possible until the very end of the project and after several years. Unfortunately, at present, some planning authorities who ask for such information, lack the staff qualified to appraise in detail the landscape schemes submitted; few authorities appear to be able to re-check thoroughly on the ground, at a later date, to ensure that the scheme was carried out wholly in accordance with the plans submitted or is being maintained correctly by the developer or his successor. If a landscape submission has to be made, it should be discussed in draft, provided the client agrees, with the planning department concerned, before a formal application is made. Such action will help to ensure that the planting scheme not only suits the client's brief but also takes into account the particular reason (if any) for a landscape condition having been required by the planning authority.

2.1.2 In some large scale mineral operations, such as sand and gravel extraction, the planning authority may require details of a long term phased working, restoration and planting scheme. Such a scheme may be required to indicate pits which will be re-filled, pits which which will remain water-filled; and the intended arrangements for disposal of waste material. Such plans may also need to give information on the future land-use of the restored areas; whether this be for recreation, building development or a return to woodland, forestry or agriculture. Extensive landscape planning of this kind inevitably involves the employment of landscape architects.

2.2 THE PRINCIPAL PLANNING ACTS

2.2.1 The Town and Country Planning Act of 1962 consolidated the Act of 1947 and its subsequent amending Acts. The Town and Country Planning Act of 1968 introduced further amendments with particular reference to structure plans for towns.

4 *Legislation and legal considerations*

2.2.2 Together, these acts establish a comprehensive control over land use in England and Wales and make it necessary to obtain planning permission for all 'development'. Development is defined as the 'carrying out of building, engineering, mining or other operations in, on, over or under land, or the making of any material change in the use of any building or other land.' Appeals against refusals of planning permission in England and Wales are heard by inspectors appointed by the Secretary of State for the Environment. Although the Minister bases his decisions on the inspector's report, its recommendations are not binding and may be rejected.

2.2.3 In relation to the landscape and site layout it is clear that in many instances planning permission must be applied for, even though no building operations may be involved. The 1947 Act introduced Tree Preservation Orders and Building Preservation Orders. Most subsequent Acts, especially the Civic Amenities Act of 1967, have strengthened this portion of the previous legislation. By the Town and Country Planning (Landscape Areas Special Development) Order 1950, the automatic planning permission granted by delegated legislation to enable agricultural and forestry and building works to be carried out was made subject to a condition that notification of such a development is to be made to the local planning authority. The authority has fourteen days in which to make objections, and the development can be implemented after this period, if no objection has been made.

2.2.4 The Town and Country Planning Act of 1947 does not apply to Northern Ireland.

2.2.5 The corresponding act in Scotland is the Town and Country Planning (Scotland) Act of 1947, amended by the Acts of 1954, 1959 and 1969. Scottish planning legislation has not yet been consolidated, though it is expected that this will implemented in 1972. Appeals against refusals of planning permission are heard at local public enquiries before a 'reporter' appointed by the Secretary of State for Scotland. Automatic planning permission for agricultural and forestry building and works is covered by the Town and Country Planning (General Development) (Scotland) Order of 1950.

2.3 THE CIVIC AMENITIES ACT 1967

2.3.1 The preamble to this Act summarizes its aims as: 'An Act to make further provision for the protection of buildings of architectural or historical interest and of the character of areas of such interest; for the preservation and planting of trees; and for the orderly disposal of disused vehicles and equipment and other rubbish.' Part 1 of the Act is concerned with historic buildings and in particular makes it a duty of local authorities to identify and designate 'Conservation Areas'. These will often contain buildings which lack sufficient quality to justify individual preservation orders but have architectural merit as a group.

Legislation and legal considerations

2.3.1 (cont'd) This provision protects vital areas of townscape, squares and terraces where the whole ensemble contributes to the environment and where piece-meal demolition of individual buildings could be detrimental to the character of the area.

2.3.2 Part 2 covers the planting and preservation of trees. A duty is placed upon local authorities, when granting planning permission, to lay down conditions on the planting of new trees and the retention of existing trees as part of the proposed development. These conditions are binding and permanent. As a result of this Act a tree covered by a Tree Preservation Order, must be replaced by the owner if it is removed or dies. The replacement will automatically be protected by an Order. The penalties for cutting down or lopping trees without permission were increased to be more in accord with current money values and to act as a more definite deterrent than in the past. It is also possible to impose instant Orders on trees in immediate danger as is the case with buildings. Such an Order becomes effective immediately it is issued but must be confirmed by the Minister within six months to give it permanent validity.

2.3.3 Part 3 makes provision for the orderly disposal of the abandoned vehicles and bulky refuse which now disfigures so much countryside and so many public open spaces. Local authorities are required to provide refuse dumps, where unwanted bulky rubbish may be taken for disposal. The powers for removing abandoned vehicles from roads and open spaces were strengthened to make removal quicker and simpler. Local authorities also gained the power, but not the duty, to remove bulky refuse left anywhere in the open air. Such removal may be charged to the owner, if he can be traced. Penalties for dumping cars and refuse illegally were made more severe.

2.3.4 This act does not apply to Northern Ireland but does cover Scotland where the Secretary of State for Scotland holds the same powers as the Secretary of State for the Environment in England and Wales.

2.4 THE NATIONAL PARKS AND ACCESS TO THE COUNTRYSIDE ACT 1949 AND THE SUBSEQUENT COUNTRYSIDE ACTS

2.4.1 The 1949 Act established the National Parks Commission with powers to formulate proposals for the establishment of National Parks and to advise on the preservation and enhancement of natural beauty throughout England and Wales. There are no National Parks in Scotland.

2.4.2 The Amenity Lands Act (Northern Ireland), 1965, made legislative provision for National Parks in Northern Ireland.

Legislation and legal considerations

2.4.3　Responsibility for a National Park rests with the County Council if the whole of the park is within its county. In other cases a planning board or a joint advisory committee is established. The board, instead of the County Council, is then the local planning authority for its area.

2.4.4　Control of development is exercised under the general powers of the town and country planning acts, but the park authority is specifically instructed to have regard to the needs of agriculture and forestry. The park authorities have powers to provide accommodation, meals, camping sites and car parks possibly with government grants. They may improve waterways for amenity, and restrict traffic on roads in conjunction with the Department of the Environment. The park authority may supply information about the park to the public by means of publications and information centres.

2.4.5　The Act enables the local planning authority in a National Park or elsewhere to enter into access agreements with owners of open country. In default of agreement it may enforce Access Orders to enable the public to enjoy these areas for recreation. A warden service may be established to assist visitors and to enforce bye-laws which ensure proper standards of behaviour. Other powers available throughout the country under the Act enable authorities to plant and improve areas of derelict land. Areas not suitable for designation as National Parks may be designated as Areas of Outstanding Natural Beauty. There are no special administrative arrangements for such areas, but strict control over development is maintained and special grants are available. The powers to provide accommodation etc. are not available. The Act enables the Nature Conservancy and local authorities to establish Nature Reserves.

2.4.6　The Act provided for a survey of public rights of way, for the settlement of disputes over such rights and for the compilation and periodic revision of definitive maps of rights of way. New rights of way may be created, by compulsion if necessary. Paths may be diverted and obsolete paths closed. The National Parks Commission, now the Countryside Commission, has powers to propose long-distance routes for walking or horse riding. Subject to the approval of the Secretary of State for the Environment or the Secretary of State for Wales, local authorities are responsible for carrying out the work of creating and maintaining rights of way with the aid of government grants. The Countryside Commission is required to prepare annual reports, which are valuable accounts of progress.

2.4.7　The Countryside Act of 1968 established the Countryside Commission which replaced the National Parks Commission. The main additional result of this Act was that local authorities gained new powers to set up, equip and manage country parks and picnic sites. In some instances this involves the creation of brand new parks, in others, the conversion or improvement of existing facilities in parks or other areas already open to public access. Grants are available for up to 75% of expenditure

2.4.7 (cont'd) approved for this purpose on the recommendation of the Commission. Scotland has a separate Countryside Commission set up under the Countryside (Scotland) Act 1967 with similar powers and functions.

2.5 THE AGRICULTURE ACT 1947

2.5.1 Under this Act the National Agricultural Advisory Service was established. The free technical advice and information which it supplied was of considerable value to the landscape architect undertaking large scale landscape surveys and dealing with landscape and planning problems in the countryside. In order to improve regional organisation, the Agricultural Development and Advisory Service came into being on March 1st 1971 replacing the National Agricultural Advisory Service. This new body combines the Ministry's professional, scientific and technical services. Some advice can be obtained free but a charge is made for services such as testing and analysis.

2.6 THE FORESTRY ACTS 1919-1967

2.6.1 The Forestry Act of 1919 established the Forestry Commission and charged it with the general duty of promoting the interests of forestry, the development of afforestation and the production and supply of timber in the United Kingdom. The Act empowered the Commissioners to make advances by way of grants or loans for the purpose of the afforestation or replanting of land, to establish or assist in the promotion of woodland industries, to collect and publish statistics relating to forestry, to promote and develop education in forestry, to carry out forestry research and experiments and to make, or aid in making, such enquiries as they think necessary for the purpose of securing an adequate supply of timber in the United Kingdom.

2.6.2 The Forestry Act of 1945 changed the constitutional status of the Forestry Commission. Forestry policy became the direct responsibility of the Minister of Agriculture, Fisheries and Food and the Secretary of State for Scotland. The exercise of the main functions of the Commissioners became subject to the direction of these Ministers and the powers of the Commissioners to acquire land were transferred to them. The land vested in the Commissioners at the date of the Act was transferred to the Ministers, who manage and use any land vested in or acquired by them which they have not placed at the disposal of the Commissioners. The land in the possession of the Commissioners at the date of the Act was to remain at the disposal of the Commissioners until the Ministers directed otherwise. The Commissioners' powers under the Forestry Act of 1919 in respect of forestry operations, education, research and grants were unaffected.

8   *Legislation and legal considerations*

2.6.3   The Forestry Act of 1947 provided for the dedication of land to forestry purposes, the enforcement of forestry dedication covenants (in England and Wales) and of dedication agreements (in Scotland), and empowered certain classes of owners to enter into such covenants or agreements.

2.6.4   The Forestry Act of 1951 dealt with the licensing of the felling of growing trees and made permanent the control previously operated as a temporary measure under Defence Regulation No. 68. The Forestry Commission took over this control from the Board of Trade in January 1950.

2.6.5   The Forestry Act of 1967 consolidated the various Forestry Acts from 1919 to 1963. In 1965 the forestry functions of the Ministry of Agriculture in Wales were transferred to the Secretary of State for Wales. The Secretary of State for Scotland is still responsible for forestry in Scotland.

2.7   THE WOODLAND DEDICATION SCHEME

2.7.1   This scheme, which provides comprehensive assistance from the Forestry Commission, has already been adopted by 4,000 estates, involving 480,000 hectares (1,200,000 acres) of woodland. The owner enters into a covenant or agreement with the Forestry Commission, under which he undertakes to manage his woodlands for the main purpose of timber production in accordance with an agreed plan of operations, and agrees to ensure skilled supervision. In return he receives, under the Basis II provisions:—

2.7.1.1   PLANTING GRANT: currently £57.27 per hectare (£23.17 per acre) for every hectare satisfactorily planted, replanted, or otherwise restocked.

2.7.1.2   ANNUAL MANAGEMENT GRANT: to cover replanting and extensions in all managed woodlands, which for this purpose include those existing at the date of dedication, plus in most cases a further area determined by the agreed plan of operations. The amount of grant is currently at the rates of £2.62 per hectare (£1.06 per acre) for the first 40.47 hectares (100 acres), £1.76 per hectare (£0.71 per acre) for the second 40.47 hectares (100 acres) and £1.08 (£0.44 per acre) for the remainder, on any one estate.

2.7.2   Alternatively, an owner may elect, at the outset, to receive assistance under the Basis 1 arrangement. He will then receive 25% of the approved net annual expenditure on the dedicated woodlands, until they become self-supporting. If he adopts this basis, he must keep accounts in a prescribed form.

2.7.3 An owner who dedicates his woodlands binds himself and his successors in title not to use the lands so dedicated for any purposes other than forestry. Provision is however made for a relaxation of this requirement should exceptional circumstances arise. When a dedicated estate changes hands, the successor in title is invited to continue to manage the woods under the approved plan of operations, and if he undertakes to do so he becomes entitled to the appropriate grants.

2.8 TREE PRESERVATION ORDERS

2.8.1 As a result of the Town & Country Planning Act of 1947 (see 2.2.1) a planning authority has statutory powers to impose Tree Preservation Orders in the area under its jurisdiction on individual trees, groups of trees or woodlands which it regards as worth preserving. This applies particularly in cities, towns and suburbs well endowed with trees, but subject to pressures for re-development, where the planning authority wishes to ensure that re-building does not involve loss of the best trees in the area. Preservation orders may sometimes be placed on newly planted trees if a special situation requires it and if new trees might otherwise not survive.

2.8.2 Orders can only be served on private owners of property. No trees on land owned by local authorities, government departments, institutions, statutory bodies and nationalised industries are eligible for this type of protection.

2.8.3 Once an Order has been served on the owner of a property, the specified trees (shown on plans and a typed schedule) may not be cut down or lopped without the prior consent of the planning authority. A fine can be imposed for non-compliance. The Civic Amenities Act of 1967 increased the powers of enforcement and the speed of implementation. Details of the main clauses of this Act are given in 2.3.

2.8.4 If a landscape architect or any other professional person is involved in the planning of a scheme containing trees protected by Tree Preservation Orders, he will often find that a flexible attitude will be adopted by the planning authority and that some trees which inhibit the building layout can be removed if the final project will provide new trees sufficient in number and size to produce a reasonable degree of replacement for the loss.

2.8.5 Tree Preservation Orders should be applied to sites before planning applications are submitted as there is considerable doubt about the validity of placing such an Order on a site where the planning permission granted implies the acceptance of the felling of some existing trees. Anyone served with a Tree Preservation Order may appeal to the Minister against confirmation of the Order.

2.9 DERELICT LAND RECLAMATION

DEFINITION

2.9.1 There is no statutory definition of derelict, neglected or unsightly land but for grant purposes the Department of the Environment have adopted the following (Ministry of Housing and Local Government Circular 68/65). 'Derelict land means land so damaged by industrial or other development that it is incapable of beneficial use without reinstatement. This definition includes sites such as disused spoil heaps, worked out mineral excavations, abandoned industrial installations and land damaged by mining subsidence. It *excludes* land which may be regarded as derelict from natural causes such as marsh land and neglected woodland.'

LEGISLATION

2.9.2 The main legislation dealing with derelict land is the Local Employment Act of 1970. This Act gave the then Minister of Technology the power to specify by order as derelict land a locality where the economic situation was such that it would be particularly appropriate to exercise the powers conferred by section 25 of the Industrial Development Act of 1966. The Local Employment Act also gave the then Minister for Housing and Local Government the power to pay grants to local authorities towards the cost of acquiring and improving derelict land where the Minister of Technology was satisfied that the work would contribute to the development of industry in the area.

LOCAL AUTHORITIES POWERS TO CLEAR DERELICTION

2.9.3 Local Act powers apart, the only specific power enabling local authorities to clear derelict land is contained in Section 89(2) of the National Parks and Access to the Countryside Act of 1949 as amended and extended by Section 6(1) of the Local Authorities (Land) Act of 1963. These Acts enable any local authority to plant trees or carry out such work as appears to them to be expedient for the purpose of restoring or improving the appearance of 'derelict land in their area which in the opinion of the local authority is in any way unsightly.'

GRANTS

2.9.4 Grant for works on derelict, neglected or unsightly land carried out by a local authority may be payable under the following provisions:

	Act	Area to which Act applies	Rate of grant
2.9.4.1 (a)	Industrial Development Act 1966	Development areas	85%
(b)	Industrial Development Act 1966 and Local Employment Act 1970	Derelict land clearance areas and intermediate areas	75%
(c)	Local Government Act 1966	Everywhere in England and Wales	50%
(d)	Section 97 (1) (c) National Parks and Access to the Countryside Act 1949	National parks and areas of outstanding natural beauty	75% on work carried out under Section 6 (1)/1963

2.9.4.2   The payment of the grant under (a) and (b) is subject to the agreement of the Department of Trade and Industry that the schemes will contribute directly or indirectly to the development of industry in the area.

2.9.4.3   With the exception of (d), the grant is not tied to any specific executive power. Local authorities may use either Section 6/1963 or any other suitable development power appropriate to the end use envisaged to carry out the work of reclamation.

2.9.4.4   Development areas are defined in Statutory Instrument 1966-1032; details are available from the Department of Trade and Industry.

2.9.4.5   Derelict land clearance areas and intermediate areas are specified by an order by the Minister of Technology dated 26 February 1970. They are listed in the Ministry of Housing & Local Government Circular 17/70. The areas specified under the Order are:—
   The Yorkshire and Humberside Derelict Land Clearance Area.
   The North West Derelict Land Clearance Area.
   The North Midland Derelict Land Clearance Area.

2.9.4.6   Subject to the approval of the Department of the Environment, the grants payable to local authorities cover or contribute towards the acquisition of the land, the fees of consultants employed to design the reclamation scheme, and the cost of the necessary reclamation works. From this sum is deducted the improved after-value of the site. The costs of basic works necessary to reclaim the site, but not the costs of development improvements, are covered by the grant. For example earthmoving, some drainage, cultivation and grass seeding, would be

2.9.4.6 (cont'd) covered, as would the provision of paths for access or maintenance. Tree planting and fencing would be eligible under some circumstances, but items such as railings, seats, litter bins and hard paving would not be allowed for grant. However it should be noted that the Countryside Commission has the power, under the Countryside Act of 1968, to recommend a grant in respect of certain development if the land is within a designated national park or country park or is in an approved picnic area.

2.9.4.7 The amount of grant is calculated on the loss incurred by the local authority in carrying out the scheme—that is, the difference between the cost of the scheme (including land acquisition) and the value of the land after the work has been completed (the 'after value'). In the case of land which is to be used for public open space the after value is deemed to be nil, so that the whole of the approved cost is eligible for grant.

APPLICATIONS AND APPROVALS

2.9.5 Applications for the approval of schemes on land specified as derelict and for the payment of grants should now be made by local authorities to the regional office of the Department of the Environment. Applications should be accompanied by maps or drawings of the proposed scheme, an outline specification/description of work and a cost estimate. The usual practice is to discuss prospective schemes with the regional office of the Department before application is made. The examination of applications for grant and especially the preliminary discussions with local authorities, are carried out as part of the normal planning work by small administrative and technical teams in the regional offices of the Department of the Environment. As reclamation is only part of the revitalisation of the whole environment, it must be considered in that wider context.

2.9.6 Apart from this general consideration the main questions arising on grant applications are:

2.9.6.1 Is the land at present derelict? If it is not already designated as such, is it needed for the reclamation of adjoining derelict land?

2.9.6.2 What is the proposed after use of the land?

2.9.6.3 What is the cost in relation to the benefit and the after-use value, if any?

2.9.6.4 What is the distinction and ratio of reclamation works to development works?

2.10 CARAVAN SITES

2.10.1 Caravan sites are controlled under the Caravan Sites and Control of Development Act of 1960, and the Public Health Act of 1936. Camping sites for tents, etc., are controlled under the Town and Country Planning Acts. Generally, a person intending to operate a caravan site must obtain planning permission from the local planning authority and a site licence from the local authority. The licence must be prominently displayed on the site. Local authorities may themselves provide caravan sites.

2.10.2 Planning permission and a site licence are not required if the caravan is used in conjunction with a dwelling house, if it is on the site for less than 28 days in a year and used only casually, if it is under the auspices of an approved recreational organisation, or if it is used in connection with building or agricultural operations or by travelling showmen.

2.10.3 The Secretary of State for the Environment is empowered to specify model standards for caravan sites. The standards laid down in 1960 can be summarised as follows.

2.10.4 PERMANENT RESIDENTIAL CARAVAN SITES

2.10.4.1 Caravans should be at least 6.100 m (20 ft.) apart and no less than 3.050 m (10 ft.) from a carriageway. The density should not exceed 50 caravans per hectare. (20 per acre).

2.10.4.2 Roads should be at least 3.960 m (13 ft.) wide, 2.740 m (9 ft.) if part of a one way traffic system. Footpaths should be at least 762 mm (2 ft. 6 ins) wide.

2.10.4.3 No caravan or toilet block should be more than 45.720 m (150 ft.) from a road. Each caravan should have a hard-standing.

2.10.4.4 The provisions for fire-fighting equipment, water supply, drainage, sanitation and washing facilities should be as specified.

2.10.4.5 Each caravan should have a refuse bin.

2.10.4.6 Lockable covered storage space, at least 2.800 m^2 (30 sq. ft.) per caravan, should be provided not less than 4.570 m (15 ft.) from any other caravan, but separate from the caravan served.

2.10.4.7 Properly surfaced parking space for a minimum of one car per three caravan standings should be provided. Other spaces, not necessarily surfaced, should bring the provision up to one parking space per caravan.

2.10.4.8 An area equivalent to one-tenth of the site area should be devoted to recreational purposes.

2.10.5   HOLIDAY CARAVAN SITES

(sites in regular use, except during the winter)

2.10.5.1   The density should not exceed 60-75 caravans per hectare (25 per acre).

2.10.5.2   The standards for water supply, drainage, washing facilities, paving, footpaths, storage facilities and hard standings are less demanding than those specified for residential sites.

2.10.5.3   Where densities are 30 to the hectare (12 per acre) or less, no standing should be more than 54.860 m (180 ft.) from a water stand pipe.

3 Fees

3.1 INTRODUCTION

3.1.1 PROFESSIONAL FEES

3.1.1.1 The current fee scales of the Institute of Landscape Architects, Royal Institute of British Architects and the Royal Institute of Chartered Surveyors are given in this chapter. As fee scales are subject to alteration from time to time, it is advisable to check with the relevant Institute to see whether amendments have been made since this book was published. In order to avoid any confusion for those used to using certain paragraph numbers in the scales, the numbering of each fee scale and its sub-sections is exactly as in the current publications and has not been changed to fit in with the system followed in this book.

3.2 LANDSCAPE ARCHITECTS' FEES

The Conditions of Engagement and Scale of Professional Charges issued by the Institute of Landscape Architects.

LAST REVISED APRIL 1972.

PREFACE

0.1 Members of the Institute of Landscape Architects are governed by the Code of Conduct of the Institute. This determines their relationship both inter se and with the public.

0.2 Members are remunerated solely by fees and charges paid to them by the client in consideration of services rendered to the client. No other source of remuneration is recognised or tolerated by the Institute.

0.3 The Profession is dedicated to improvement of the human environment wherever and whenever the services of its members are invited. These conditions are framed to enable them to act effectively.

1. GENERAL CONDITIONS

1.1 The work of the landscape architect is to study the requirements of the client, and of the site. He will advise upon, and agree with the client a course of action suitable to the situation. He will prepare for, by means of drawings and specifications, and direct a contract for the physical execution of the work on the site, and act as the agent of his client in the direction and supervision of the work and settle the financial account between the client and the contractor, acting as arbitrator if necessary in any area of dispute.

1.2   He may advise on the need for consultants or other specialist services, and on the need for specialist suppliers of goods or services, and in the latter cases for their work to be embodied into a contract or contracts and directed and supervised on site as before.

1.3   He shall have authority to give instructions for the work on behalf of the client and to make such variations to the contract as may be found in the course of the work to be necessary or desirable to achieve the prime object subject always to his duty to advise his client of the financial implications of any course of action at all times.

1.4   He, or a deputy nominated by him, shall give such periodic supervision of the work as normally may be required for its proper completion. Constant supervision does not form part of the normal service.

1.5   A Clerk of Works may be appointed. He shall be nominated or approved by the Landscape Architect and work under his direction, but he shall be appointed and paid by the client unless reimbursement is agreed to be made to the Landscape Architect for his services.

1.6   The Landscape Architect shall not make any material deviation from the client's instructions and must have his client's authority before undertaking work or proceeding to another stage of the work.

1.7   The Landscape Architect shall examine the work executed by the contractor and check the valuation of the work made for the purpose of securing payments to the contractor. While the Landscape Architect shall exercise due care in examining the work and the accounts prior to certifying he shall in no case be liable for work by the contractor which may be either improperly executed or in breach of the terms of the contract; such liability in every case to remain with the contractor. The Landscape Architect will be impartial in dealing with such matters between client and contractor.

1.8   The fees and charges hereinafter described are the minimum, and shall be taken to apply unless higher fees and charges shall have been agreed between the Landscape Architect and his client before any work is begun.

1.9   Members of the Institute of Landscape Architects do not compete with one another in respect of fees or charges, and estimates of fees may not be given individually to a prospective client who is considering the appointment of one out of a number of firms, though

be nominated at the request of either party by the President of the Institute of Arbitrators.

1.16 Fees may be charged in any one or in any combination of the following ways as shall be agreed between the Landscape Architect and his client:

2. REMUNERATION ON A TIME BASIS

2.1 The type of work for which this scale is appropriate includes all classes of work for which a landscape architect may be engaged. It is particularly suitable for consultancy and advisory work of some magnitude (but see also 5.2); for alteration works; for work which is partly consultative, and partly executive; for intermittent work spread over a period of several months or years; and for work in collaboration with other professions, (but see 3.9.7).

2.2 To charge on this basis the landscape architect must keep a full record of time (which shall include travelling time, see 2.9) spent by himself and his staff on the project.

2.3 Principals shall be defined as professionally qualified persons acting alone, in group practice, or as partners, who take direct responsibility for their acts. Principals' rates may, by prior agreement, be applied to persons who are not principals. (i.e. Associates or other senior members who have responsibility for certain projects, control over staff, and who share a proportion of the overheads incurred by non-chargeable staff such as secretaries, librarians, etc.) Any such agreement must not result in a lower total remuneration than would have been received by the normal application of the 'Principal' and 'Staff' parts of the scale.

2.4 The rate charged by Principals is not solely remuneration for the personal time given by them to the project, but includes their managerial capacity and a proportion of the cost of overheads.

2.5 **The rates charged for Principals' time begin at £3.50 per hour**

2.6 The actual rates charged will be based on several factors which shall include:—
(a) Professional standing of the landscape architect;
(b) Length of experience;
(c) Specialisation in particular aspects of the work;
(d) The size of the office and the number of staff being supervised.
The commencing rate of £3.50 per hour is that which might be charged by a newly qualified professional practicing alone.

2.6.1 Rates in the order of £4 to £6 per hour are likely to be charged by Principals:—

Fees

the members may agree between themselves an order of cost
the prospective client in making an appointment. (See 8.7.1)
Landscape Architects whose appointments have been confir
give estimates of the order of cost of their services by q
appropriate percentage or by estimating the time charges wh
involved, provided it is fully understood that all such estima
subject to revision in accordance with the actual costs of t
executed or the time actually spent on the work. (See 8.7.2

1.10 No agreement between the Landscape Architect a
shall preclude the possibility of revision at any time durin
of engagement, and particularly in the light of unforesee
circumstances. The possibility of such revision will
relevant where long term engagements are entered into or
occur which are beyond the control of the Landscape Arc

1.11 The Landscape Architect will keep his client ap
progress of the work. Any new instructions either directl
from the client which have the effect of rendering inv
already completed or in hand by the Landscape
immediately be notified to the client as such and shall
These shall be assessed by the Landscape Architect havi
magnitude of the variation and agreed afresh with t
proceeding.

1.12 Where a Landscape Architect is employed as
other professions (e.g. an Architect) these fees and
apply equally. In such cases where the Landscape A
instructions are received from the other profession an
arise within the team which are beyond the control
Architect, extra fees for such work shall be cha
foregoing paragraph. The Landscape Architect s
situation to the notice of all parties concerned at the

1.13 All drawings, specifications, and documen
Landscape Architect shall remain his property, t
same being reserved to him.

1.14 Termination of an engagement may be at
expiry of reasonable notice by either party,
Landscape Architect shall be entitled to such
appropriate under Section 8 Mode and Time of Pa

1.15 Any differences or disputes may be, by a
parties, submitted to the Institute of Landscape
In such a case there should be a statement of u
and submitted to reduce the area of dispute t
parties agree to accept the ruling as final.

Alternatively, any dispute may be referred to th
person to be agreed between the parties or faili

—with several years experience;
—having charge of a group of professional staff, backed by a comprehensive office service.

2.6.2 Rates of £6 per hour and above are likely to be charged by principals with long experience, with a large staff, and by those who have uncommon specialised knowledge of a particular aspect of the subject.

2.7 **Staff shall be charged at an hourly rate of 0.15% of salary***

2.8 Qualifying clauses:

2.8.1 Compounded rates
By agreement an hourly rate can be compounded to a daily rate on the basis of a 7 hour day.

2.8.2 Resident Staff
For staff wholly resident on one job, the rate can be compounded to a daily or even weekly rate + lodging and meal expenses etc.

2.9 Travelling Time
Travelling time is chargeable at the same hourly rate as other work. The charging of travelling time outside of office hours is normal, but on projects involving a great deal of travelling, is subject to negotiation.

2.10 The work of each member in practice in his own right or as a member of a firm, whether principal or assistant shall be charged at the appropriate rate in the above scale irrespective of the type of work (e.g. management, design, draughtsmanship, specification, supervision) on which he is engaged at any time.

3. REMUNERATION ON A PERCENTAGE BASIS

3.1 The type of work for which this scale is appropriate includes that where the landscape architect is in charge of a contract which includes all the elements for which he has prepared designs, and which is separate from (but may be a sub-contract of) any building or civil engineering contract. The principle on which this scale is based is that there must be a clearly defined cost of work against which a percentage fee is set. It cannot, therefore, be applied to projects or parts of projects in which the landscape architect advises on, or prepares designs for, work which is an integral part of a building or civil engineering contract.

3.2 The percentage scale has to cover works which may differ widely in their intricacy. For this reason the scale is expressed as a graph,

*i.e. £0.15 per hour for each £100 of gross annual salary.

which shows the 'normal' fee, but which is qualified by coefficients, varying according to the type and size of job, and the class of contract.

3.3   In the early stages of the work the percentage will be calculated on the landscape architect's preliminary *estimate* of the cost of the work. This percentage will be adjusted as more precise information on costs becomes available at revised estimate stage, tender stage, contract stage, and will be finally adjusted at the completion of the work when the actual cost is known. (See 8.4)

3.4   **The percentage scale is only applied to a contract costing £2,000 or over. Below this figure the fee will be agreed by negotiation between landscape architect and client.**

3.5   The work to be covered by the percentage charge, includes the following:
(a) Consultations with the client (but see 5.1)
(b) Appraisal of site conditions
(c) Preparation of preliminary sketch plans and approximate estimates for the client's approval: except that where the client or his representative makes or causes material variations from the original instructions, the work involved in preparing new sketch plans shall be charged for in addition on the time basis.
(d) Preparation of all drawings and specifications (other than those for which a consultant is employed) required for the execution of the work.
(e) Preparation of contract documents (other than Bills of Quantities); obtaining and advising on tenders.
(f) General supervision of work in progress (but see 3.9.2)
(g) Checking and certifying accounts, but not measurement and valuation of the work.
(h) Submission of plans for necessary approvals by public bodies.

3.6   Explanation of Calculations

3.6.1 The scale for percentage fee is to be calculated from two components. **The first is a variable percentage figure read off from the attached graph on the basis of the cost of the project. This is the 'norm'—the line in the centre of the graph.**

The second component is a coefficient which alters the 'norm' and is based on one or more variables, i.e.
(a) type of job (and therefore its complexity)
(b) form of contract.
These coefficients are found in the table 3.8

3.6.2 **Where two variables apply, the coefficients must be compounded by multiplying them before applying.**

3.6.3 Example

Contract value	£40,000
Percentage fee, read off NORM line on graph	7%
Coefficients:	
Contract coefficient: Work is for hard and soft works and is main contract, unencumbered:	0.9
Job coefficient: Project is for an industrial estate:	0.9
Compounded coefficient (multiply)	0.81
True percentage (0.81 x 7% = 5.67%) i.e.	$5\tfrac{2}{3}\%$
Fee to be charged	£2,267

3.7 Graph (see drawing 6.3.1 in Chapter 6.)

3.8 Tables of coefficients

3.8.1 *Contractual differentials*

Normal work including both 'hard' and 'soft' in a sub-contract (i.e. to a building or engineering main contract)	1.0
Work including both hard and soft works but in a main contract, unencumbered	0.9
Contract for predominantly soft works:	
(a) as a main contract, unencumbered	1.1
(b) as a sub-contract	1.2

3.8.2 *Type of work differentials*

1.2 Private gardens

1.1 Housing

1.0 College and university sites
1.0 Urban offices and commercial properties
1.0 Hospital sites
1.0 School sites
1.0 Barracks
1.0 Urban recreation areas and public parks
1.0 Urban parking areas; parking areas attached to major recreational projects
1.0 Caravan sites
1.0 Cemeteries and crematoria

0.9 Industrial sites
0.9 Marinas
0.9 Reclamation of dereliction
0.9 Gravel and other mineral workings

0.8 Sports stadia and playing fields
0.8 Golf courses
0.8 Landscape of roads

0.8 Coastal defence schemes
0.8 Rural parking areas

0.7 Agricultural improvement
0.7 Afforestation, shelter belt planting, and simple rural seeding or planting schemes
0.7 Rural recreation and camping areas

3.8.3 Where a project is partly of one type and partly of another, also where a project is of a type which does not fall clearly into any one of the above categories, interpolation between the coefficients should be made.

> 'Predominantly soft works' shall be taken to mean all works of a horticultural nature including land drainage, with pipes up to 375 mm diameter, but not including excavation into the subsoil layers. All other works shall be regarded as 'hard works'.
> A commission where the 'hard works' element exceeds 50% of the contract value shall be classed as being 'hard and soft' in nature.
> Where the 'hard works' element is less than 50% of the contract value the commission shall be classed as being 'predominantly soft' in nature.

3.9 Qualifying clauses:

3.9.1 Limited stages only.
Professional work which it has been agreed shall cover only a certain stage or stages of the contract will only attract a proportion of the fees. These are expressed as a percentage of the total fee and are listed in 8.3.

3.9.2 Supervision
As at 3.9.1 above, the whole of the supervision of the works can, by prior agreement, be omitted from percentage scale calculations (i.e. by ref to 8.3). Supervision should then be charged for on a time basis, and the frequency of visits will be a matter for agreement between landscape architect and client.

3.9.3 Extension or reduction of contract
Any contract can be substantially extended by the introduction of additional work. Where this work is sufficient to alter the position of the contract on the graph to a lower percentage the landscape architect shall then charge the *additional* work at the rate shown at the new point on the graph. He shall not be expected to reduce his remuneration for the earlier work to the same percentage. Where new work is added to a project and in consequence a new contract for execution is called for, the additional work shall be treated as a new project and charged accordingly. Similarly where, after the sketch plan stage, a project is so reduced that the fee scale falls on to a *lower* point on the graph, the landscape architect's fees for that part of the work already carried out, shall *not* be thereby reduced.

3.9.4 Phased contracts
Where a project is phased so that each phase is the subject of a separate contract, additional fees will be merited.

3.9.5 Abandoned Work
The landscape architect shall be paid for the work done. That is, he shall be paid the appropriate proportion of the fee up to the stage reached, and on a pro-rata basis for any preparatory work for the next stage. The normal 'stages' are those defined under 'Modes and Time of Payment' (Section 8.3).

3.9.6 Delayed Work
Where the preparatory work on execution of a contract has been delayed for reasons beyond the control of the landscape architect so that it fails to reach an agreed stage at which fees would become due, the landscape architect is entitled to ask for a proportion to be paid on account.

3.9.7 Architects as clients
Where the landscape architect is engaged by an Architect to carry out part of the work in his commission, the landscape architect shall be entitled to receive a remuneration of not less than 92½% of the fees received for this work by the Architect.

3.9.8 Repetitive Work
Landscape work does not lend itself to the repetitive use of a single design. In the exceptional case where a landscape design is used in whole or part for more than one site, the fees may be, by prior written agreement reduced by an amount not exceeding 15%.

4. OTHER BASES OF REMUNERATION

4.1 Lump Sum
By prior agreement **The fees due on a project may be compounded into a lump sum**, payable in whole or by periodic instalments. The calculation of such a lump sum should be based—as far as can be ascertained—on the fees which would have been charged on a time or percentage basis.

4.2 Ceiling Figure
By agreement a lump sum may be adopted as a ceiling figure up to which the landscape architect will calculate his fees on a time basis, giving the client adequate warning when the agreed sum is about to be expended. Any further work shall then be done on a time basis, or shall be the subject of further negotiation. The ceiling can be changed at intervals by forward forecasting.

4.3 The principle on which the lump sum scale is based is that of giving the client the convenience of knowing his commitment in the early stages of the project; it shall not be operated to offer a reduced fee nor as a competitive estimate.

4.4 Retainers
The client who wishes to retain the services of a landscape architect or firm of landscape architects for a period, during which all work arising will be carried out by the named professional(s) may do so on payment of a retainer fee. This may take several forms:
(a) A nominal sum over and above normal fees
(b) A payment based on an estimated time commitment
(c) A payment based on a percentage fee for estimated contract work.
It may, by prior agreement, be allowed to stand in full, irrespective of the amount of work involved, or it may be re-calculated on a monthly, quarterly or yearly basis according to the actual commitments. In the latter situation the amended fees should be based on one or other of the recognised scales.

5. CONSULTANCY, MANAGEMENT AND OCCASIONAL VISITS

5.1 Advisory work, consultations, and attendance at committees or working parties concerned with special aspects of a project such as research and development will normally be charged on the Time Basis (section 2).

5.2 Where the work is of a minor nature, un-connected with any large project or contract, or where one only, or a series, of short but un-connected consultations are called for, **The landscape architect shall charge, for his own time, a minimum fee of £10 for the first hour, dropping thereafter to the scale listed in section 2.6.**

5.3 Where a landscape architect is empowered by his client to engage the services of a specialist consultant on some aspect of the work not within the landscape architect's professional work, e.g. mechanical or structural or civil engineering, architecture, town planning, hydraulics, geology, ecology, botanical or soil classification or similar, the cost of the fees of such a specialist shall be added to the landscape architect's own fees. **Furthermore he shall be entitled to add to his own fees an amount equal to 7½% of such specialist fees as remuneration for the overheads incurred in the management and processing of the specialist work.**

5.4 Where such specialist advice contributes to a contract (which is being charged on the percentage scale: Section 3 herein) to the extent of providing drawings and specifications which can be incorporated in the contract, **The landscape architect's fee in respect of that work only shall be reduced by 50%. The fee for overheads (5.3 above) shall still apply.**

6. ADDITIONAL SERVICES

6.1 Specifically excluded from the services provided within the normal percentage fee are the following: Quantity Surveying, Site Surveying, soil surveys, designs for furniture and ornaments, personal selection of plant material. Any such services which are required shall be charged additionally.

6.2 Quantity Surveying. Where Bills of Quantities, detailed estimates, measurements and valuation of work in progress or similar services are required, either a Quantity Surveyor shall be appointed and paid by the client, or appointed and paid by the Landscape Architect who shall be reimbursed as to his fees by the client, or **Where the work of a Quantity Surveyor is done by the Landscape Architect extra fees shall be charged for the service in accordance with the scales of professional charges of the Royal Institution of Chartered Surveyors.** (*Bills of Quantities — normally Category C.*)

6.3 **Site surveys shall be charged for on a time basis or on a negotiated sum based on an assessment by the landscape architect of the staff time likely to be involved, and upon the intricacy of the work.**

6.4 Services of a preliminary nature, such as advising on the selection of sites, making site inspections, undertaking feasibility studies, preparing development plans or programmes for long term projects, and investigating the relationship of land to local or county planning proposals, all where not linked immediately to an actual contract, are charged on a time basis.

6.5 By prior agreement a rebatement of percentage scale fees for sketch plans may be made against work already done on master plans or development programmes which contribute directly to the final plans for the project. This rebatement shall never exceed *half* the fees due for sketch plans.

6.6 Where a Landscape Architect is asked to prepare a report on the feasibility of a project, or on the method of tackling a problem, before being commissioned, the Landscape Architect and client should reach a prior understanding on the amount of work to be done on such a report, and whether the report is of such a nature that it would justify fees, in which case the appropriate fee should be agreed beforehand.

6.7 Visits to nurseries and other places for the selection of plants and materials; special designs for garden furniture and ornaments and other items not part of the general construction; negotiations with public bodies beyond the statutory deposition of plans for approval; and any other items not included in (a) to (h) of 3.5 shall be charged on a time basis.

6.8 Where a Landscape Architect is qualified in other professional disciplines (e.g. architect, planner, engineer, etc.) and is engaged to carry out work appropriate to such disciplines, either in conjunction with, or separately from a landscape project, he may, at his own discretion, charge work in accordance with the scales of the appropriate Professional Institution.

7. EXPENSES

7.1 **In addition to the fees shown in any other part of these conditions, the landscape architect shall be reimbursed for all out of pocket expenses actually and properly incurred** in carrying out the commission. They shall include the following:

7.2 Hotel and travelling expenses, cost of meals, gratuities, and other similar disbursements for principals and staff. In the absence of other agreed scale, for mileage rate of cars, the rates quoted by the motoring organisations AA/RAC, shall be charged.

7.3 The cost of printing, reproduction or purchase of all plans, drawings, maps, photographs, and other documents used in the preparation for, and execution of the job, including the cost of all drawings which the Landscape Architect is obligated to supply to client, QS, consultants and contractors.

7.4 Expenses incurred in advertising for tenders, advertising for Clerks of Works and resident site staff.

7.5 Expenses can be compounded by agreement in whole or part, into a lump sum fee, or quarterly or monthly payment, or into an increase of the percentage fee. When so compounded, the sum shall be based on a calculation of the expenses reasonably expected to be incurred.

7.6 Normal postal and telephone charges shall *not* be charged to the client. However, where the cost of long distance and overseas telephone calls are likely to be a significantly large proportion of the expenses of a commission, these may be charged, by prior agreement.

8. MODE AND TIME OF PAYMENT

8.1 The principle on which these conditions are laid down is that a Landscape Architect is performing a continuing service for his client, during the period of his engagement, and is entitled to regular payment for these services, as and when they are performed.

8.2 Where the time scale is employed (Section 2) the parties should agree the intervals (e.g. weekly, monthly, or quarterly) at which detailed accounts shall be submitted. These shall be due for payment within fourteen days of receipt.

8.3 Where the percentage scale is employed (Section 3) the appropriate proportion of the percentage charge, shall be due for payment at each stage of the office and contract procedure. The normal stages are:

Up to: Inception, client's briefing, site appraisal and advice on the suitability of the site . . . 15%*
Sketch design and rough estimate of cost . . 30%
Final design drawings and outline specification, estimate of cost and programme of work . . 40%
Detail design, planting details, working drawings, schedules and specification sufficient for preparation of tender documents 70%
Obtaining tenders, supervising the work and final account 100%
(*These figures may also be applied as coefficients e.g. 0.15, 0.30, 0.40, 0.70, 1.00.)

In contracts over the value of £10,000 the stages are likely to be long, and the Landscape Architect is then entitled to ask for interim payments between the major stages as above. During the supervision period he may include a request for a proportion of his own outstanding fees at each issue of a certificate to the contractor.

8.4 As stated in 3.3 the amount of fees due on a percentage basis shall be re-calculated at the time of the final certificate.

8.5 Lump sum fees may be paid in one sum, or—by prior agreement—in instalments at intervals during the course of the work.

8.6 Requests for repayment of expenses, with supporting evidence shall, unless otherwise agreed, be submitted at the same time as accounts for fees, and shall be in respect of the same period.

8.7 Estimates of Professional Fees.

8.7.1 Members of the Institute must not, under the Code of Conduct, compete with each other in respect of fees. Where a prospective client asks for an estimate of fees, or time charges (or even time-estimates which would be converted to a fee estimate) from a number of firms, the members must decline to give such an estimate until their appointment has been confirmed.

Nevertheless a landscape architect may give a prospective client an 'order of cost' for budgeting purposes. To avoid misunderstanding this should be submitted in the form of the Institute's proforma (see Appendix; see also 1.9). This proforma will state that the 'order of cost' is in no way to be regarded as a competitive estimate. Where there is any doubt regarding the possible use of estimates by a client in a competitive way, the case should be referred to the President of the Institute of Landscape Architects who may, at his discretion, quote a common fee.

8.7.2 Members or firms whose appointment has been confirmed may give estimates of their fees based on the appropriate percentage costs, from the best known information, or on a time basis, quoting separately for principals and staff at various salary levels. The services to be included in such estimates are to be clearly stated.

8.7.3 Furthermore, it must be clearly understood between the Landscape Architect and his client, that any estimates of fees are not 'lump-sum' quotations, but are to be amended in accordance with either a percentage of the actual contract sum (if under Section 3) or the actual time spent (if under Section 2) or the finally agreed lump sum (if under Section 4).

8.7.4 Estimates for expenses shall be similarly given.

9. WORK OVERSEAS

9.1 The Scale of Fees included in these Conditions are normally for work by members of the I.L.A. in Great Britain and Northern Ireland. Where these same Conditions are recognised outside these territories the scales should be applied.

9.2 In countries where there is a local association of Landscape Architects the I.L.A. members may adopt the local scale of conditions. In doing so they should ensure that, after making appropriate allowances for rate of exchange and cost of living, they are not charging less than the appropriate I.L.A. scale for these conditions. In this connection para 8.7.1 must be strictly applied.

9.3 In all other conditions, members are free to make their own determination of fees, taking note of the following points:

9.3.1 Percentage fees are difficult to apply in view of the lack of contracting organisations in many countries, and the prevalence of direct labour contracts.

9.3.2 Due to the use of unskilled labour, a higher degree of supervision is often required.

9.3.3 The establishment of a local office, or at least the engagement of resident staff, may be necessary.

9.3.4 There may be restrictions in force relating to the exchange rates of currency, the taking of money out of the country, or the payment of local taxes, which will affect the genuine remuneration received.

APPENDIX 1.

Clients requesting an estimate of fees from a number of firms
The following is the form of words which members of the Institute must use in giving to clients an estimate of fees (see 8.7 et seq.) when they know, or suspect, that several firms have been approached competitively.

". . . Under the Code of Conduct of the Institute of Landscape Architects, I/we are unable to give an accurate estimate of fees until the decision has been made to appoint one firm of landscape architects for this commission. I/we are pleased, however, to give an 'order of cost' for budgeting purposes, which should not be regarded either as a competitive estimate, or as a 'lump sum' fee. Actual fees would be computed on the appropriate scale of fees in the I.L.A. CONDITIONS OF ENGAGEMENT AND SCALE OF PROFESSIONAL CHARGES. I/we consider that the professional services for the . . . project* would be charged on a percentage/time/lump sum basis, and that an order of expenditure of £ . . . to £ . . . would be involved, over a period of . . . months/years . . ."

Note (1) Where a client has *not* been given a copy of the Institute's CONDITIONS OF ENGAGEMENT AND SCALE OF PROFESSIONAL CHARGES, a copy of para. 8.7.1 should be included with the reply.

*Note (2) In order to make even such a rough estimate, the landscape architect will need to know roughly the size and scope or capital cost of the project. The client may have no idea of his needs at this early stage, and it will therefore be necessary for the landscape architect to define exactly what is to be included in his 'order of cost'.

In some cases it may be desirable to offer only a site appraisal and report which would enable an estimate of capital cost to be prepared on which a further estimate of fees could be based.

3.3 ARCHITECTS' FEES

Extracts from the Conditions of Engagement issued by the Royal Institute of British Architects.

LAST REVISED NOVEMBER 1971

PART 1: GENERAL

1.00 This part deals with general conditions of engagement and will apply irrespective of the nature or extent of services to be provided.

1.1 Remuneration

1.10 The services normally provided by an architect in studying his client's needs, advising him, preparing, directing and co-ordinating design and inspecting work executed under a building contract are described in Part 2: Normal Services. Other services that an architect may provide are described in Part 4: Other Services.

1.11 The Normal Services for a building project are divided into a sequence of Work Stages A to H through which the architect's work progresses, augmented by services which vary widely in nature and extent with the circumstances of the project.

1.12 Fees for Work Stages C to H are generally calculated as a percentage of the total construction cost of the works, as described in Part 3 of these conditions.

1.13 Fees for Work Stages A and B and for those other services which are likely to vary widely in nature and extent are charged additionally on a time basis, as described in Part 5 of these Conditions.

1.14 In exceptional circumstances, any service normally charged on a percentage fee may, by prior written agreement between architect and client, be charged on a time basis, in which case the architect shall notify the RIBA.

1.15 The minimum fees and charges described in these Conditions may not be sufficient in all circumstances, in which case higher fees and charges may be agreed between the client and architect when the architect is commissioned.

1.2 Consultants

1.20 Normal services do not include quantity surveying, town planning, civil, structural, mechanical, electrical or heating and ventilating engineering or similar consultants' services. Where the provision of such services is within the competence of the architect's own office or where they are provided by consultants in association with the architect, fees shall be in accordance with the scale of fees of the appropriate professional bodies, but all time charges shall be in accordance with Part 5 of these Conditions.

1.21 Where the services of more than one profession are provided by a single firm or consortium, fees shall be the sum of the appropriate fees for the individual professional services rendered.

1.22 The architect will advise on the need for independent consultants and will be responsible for the direction and integration of their work but not for the detailed design, inspection and performance of the work entrusted to them.

1.23 Independent consultants and quantity surveyors should be nominated or approved by the architect in agreement with the client. They should be appointed and paid by the client.

1.3 Responsibilities

1.30 The architect must have the authority of his client before initiating any service or Work Stage.

1.31 The architect shall not make any material alteration, addition to or omission from the approved design without the knowledge and consent of the client, except if found necessary during construction for constructional reasons in which case he shall inform the client without delay.

1.32 The architect shall inform the client if he has reason to believe the total authorised expenditure or contract period are likely to be materially varied.

1.33 The architect shall advise on the selection and appointment of the contractor and shall make such periodic visits to the site as he considers necessary to inspect generally the progress and quality of the work and to determine in general if the work is proceeding in accordance with the contract documents.

1.34 The architect shall not be responsible for the contractor's operational methods, techniques, sequences or procedures, nor for safety precautions in connection with the work, nor shall he be responsible for any failure by the contractor to carry out and complete the work in accordance with the terms of the building contract between the client and the contractor.

1.4 Specialist sub-contractors and suppliers

1.40 The architect may recommend that specialist sub-contractors and suppliers should design and execute any part of the work. He will be responsible for the direction and integration of their design, and for general inspection of their work in accordance with Stage H of the Normal Services, but not for the detailed design or performance of the work entrusted to them.

1.5 Copyright

1.50 The provisions of this Section shall apply without prejudice to the architect's lien on drawings against unpaid fees.

1.51 In accordance with the provisions of the Copyright Act 1956, copyright in all drawings and in the work executed from them, except drawings and works for the Crown, will remain the property of the architect unless otherwise agreed.

1.52 Where an architect has completed Stage D or where an architect provides detail design in Stage EFG the client unless otherwise agreed shall, on payment or tender of any fees due to the architect, be entitled to reproduce the design by proceeding to execute the project, but only on the site to which the design relates.

1.53 Where an architect has not completed Stage D or where he and his client have agreed that Clause 1.52 shall not apply, the client may not reproduce the design by proceeding to execute the project without the consent of the architect and payment of any additional fee that may be agreed in exchange for the architect's consent.

1.54 The architect shall not unreasonably withhold his consent under Clause 1.53 but where his services are limited to making and negotiating Town Planning consents he may withhold his consent unless otherwise determined by an arbitrator appointed in accordance with Clause 7.50.

1.6 Inspection

1.60 During his on-site inspections made in accordance with Clause 1.33 the architect shall endeavour to guard the client against defects and deficiencies in the work of the contractor, but shall not be required to make exhaustive or continuous inspections to check the quality or quantity of the work.

1.61 Where frequent or constant inspection is required a clerk or clerks of works should be employed. He shall be nominated or approved by the architect and be under the architect's direction and control. He may be appointed and paid by the client or employed by the architect.

Fees

1.62 Where the need for frequent or constant on-site inspection by the architect is agreed to be necessary, a resident architect shall be appointed by the architect.

1.63 Where the architect employs a resident architect or a clerk or clerks of works he shall be reimbursed by the client in accordance with either Part 5 or Part 6 of these Conditions.

1.7 Delay and changes in instructions

1.70 Extra work and expense caused in any Stage resulting from delay in receiving instructions, delays in building operations, changes in the client's instructions, phased contracts, bankruptcy or liquidation of the contractor or any other cause beyond the control of the architect, shall be additionally charged on a time basis.

PART 2: NORMAL SERVICES

2.00 This part describes the services normally provided by an architect for a building project. The fees for Work Stages C to H are generally charged on a percentage basis as described in Part 3 of these Conditions. Stage C begins where the architect's brief has been determined in sufficient detail. Fees otherwise, including work in Stages A and B to determine the architect's brief, are charged additionally on a time basis as described in Part 5 of these Conditions. Initial consultations may be given free of charge.

2.1 Work Stages

2.10 Work Stages charged on a **time** basis:

A Inception
Receiving an initial statement of requirements, outlining possible courses of action, and advising on the need for a quantity surveyor and consultants. Determining the brief in sufficient detail for subsequent Stages to begin.

B Feasibility studies
Undertaking a preliminary technical appraisal of a project sufficient to enable the client to decide whether and in what form to proceed, and making town planning inquiries or application for outline town planning approval. Such an appraisal may include an approximation of the cost of meeting the client's requirements, a statement on the need for consultants, an outline timetable and a suggested contract procedure.

2.11 Work stages normally charged on a **percentage** basis:

C Outline proposals
Analysing the client's requirements and where necessary instructing the quantity surveyor and consultants. Preparing, describing and illustrating outline proposals, including an approximation of the cost of meeting them. Informing the client of any major decisions which are needed and receiving any amended instructions.

D Scheme design
Preparing in collaboration with the quantity surveyor, and consultants if appropriate, a scheme design consisting of drawings, and outline specification sufficient to indicate spatial arrangements, materials and appearance. Presenting a report on the scheme, the estimated cost and timetable for the project, for the client's approval.

E F G Detail design, production information, bills of quantities
Completing a detailed design and specification as necessary, incorporating any design work done by consultants and nominated subcontractors and suppliers. Obtaining estimates and other information from nominated subcontractors and suppliers. Preparing information necessary for the preparation of bills of quantities, if any, by the quantity surveyor, carrying out cost checks as necessary and preparing production drawings.

H Tender action to completion
Obtaining and advising on tenders and preparing and advising on the contract and the appointment of the contractor. Supplying information to the contractor, arranging for him to take possession of the site and examining his programme. Making periodic visits to the site as described in Clause 1.33; issuing certificates and other administrative duties under the contract. Accepting the building on behalf of the client, providing scale drawings showing the main lines of drainage and obtaining drawings of other services as executed, and giving initial guidance on maintenance.

2.2 Development studies
To be charged on a time basis

2.20 Services where a client's initial statement of requirements in Stage A requires a special service (such as operational research) before consideration of the brief and development of outline proposals as described in Stage C can begin.

2.3 Development plans
To be charged on a time basis

2.30 Preparing development plans for any large building or complex of buildings which will be carried out in phases over a number of years.

2.31 Preparing a layout only, or preparing a layout for a greater area than that which is to be developed immediately.

2.4 Sites and buildings
To be charged on a time basis

2.40 Advising on the selection and suitability of sites, conducting negotiations concerned with sites or buildings, making measured surveys, taking levels and preparing plans of sites and buildings or existing buildings.

2.41 Making inspections, preparing reports or giving general advice on the condition of premises.

2.42 Work in connection with soil investigations.

2.5 Constructional research
To be charged on a time basis

2.50 Research where the development of a scheme design in Stage D involves special constructional research, including the design, construction or testing of prototype buildings or models.

2.6 Negotiations
To be charged on a time basis

2.60 Exceptional negotiations such as those arising from applications for Town Planning, Building Byelaw, Building Act or Building Regulations approvals.

2.61 Providing information, making all applications other than those covered by the Normal Services, such as those including applications for licences, negotiations in connection with party walls and grant aids.

2.62 Submission to the Royal Fine Art Commission and town planning appeals.

2.7 Special drawings
To be charged on a time basis

2.70 Preparing any special drawings, models or technical information specially for the use of the client, or for Town Planning, Byelaw and Building Regulations approvals; for negotiations with ground landlords, adjoining owners, public authorities, licensing authorities, mortgagors and others.

2.8 Furnishings and works of art
To be charged on a time basis

2.80 Advising on the selection and suitability of loose furniture, fittings and soft furnishings, on the commissioning or selection of works of art, obtaining tenders and supervising their installation.

2.9   Approvals in the Normal Services

2.90 Except in Scotland, Stages C to E F G of the Normal Services include the duty of making and negotiating applications for Town Planning consents, Building Byelaw, Building Act and Building Regulations approvals, as appropriate. All work in connection with these applications will not necessarily be included in any particular Stage.

2.91 In Scotland, the Normal Services cover the duty of preparing drawings and technical information necessary for submission of applications for licences, Town Planning and Building (Scotland) Act approvals as appropriate. The actual completion of the application and its presentation to the appropriate Court is not part of the architect's responsibility.

PART 3: FEES FOR THE NORMAL SERVICES

3.00 This part describes how the percentage fees for the Normal Services are calculated and may be varied, and when they and other charges are due. Percentage fees are based on the total construction cost of the works and on the issue of the final certificate shall be re-calculated on the actual total construction cost.

3.1   Total construction cost

3.10 The total construction cost shall be the cost, as certified by the architect, of all works (including site works) executed under his direction, subject to the following conditions:

3.101 The total construction cost shall include the cost of all work designed or supervised by consultants which the architect is responsible for directing and co-ordinating in accordance with Clause 1.22, irrespective of whether such work is carried out under separate building contracts for which the architect may not be responsible. The architect shall be informed of the cost of any such separate contracts.

3.102 The total construction cost shall not include nominated subcontractors' design fees for work on which consultants would otherwise have been employed. Where such fees are not known, the architect shall estimate a reduction from the total construction cost.

3.103 For the purpose of calculating the appropriate fees, the total construction cost shall include the actual or estimated cost of any work executed which is excluded from the contract but otherwise designed by the architect.

3.104 The total construction cost shall include the cost of built-in furniture and equipment. Where the cost of any special equipment is excluded from the total construction cost, the architect shall charge for work in connection with such items on a time basis.

3.105 Where appropriate the cost of old materials used in the work shall be calculated as if they were new.

3.106 Where any material, labour or carriage are supplied by a client who is not the builder, the cost shall be estimated by the architect as if they were supplied by the builder and included in the total cost.

3.107 Where the client is the builder, a statement of the ascertained gross cost of the works may be used in calculating the total construction cost of the works. In the absence of such a statement, the architect's own estimate shall be used. In either the statement of the ascertained gross cost or the architect's estimate there shall be included an allowance for the builder's profit and overheads.

3.11 The fee for any part of the work omitted on the client's instruction shall be calculated in accordance with Section 3.5 of these Conditions.

3.2 New works

3.20 Fees for new works generally are shown in Table 1.

3.3 Works to existing buildings

3.30 Higher percentages are chargeable for works to existing buildings and are shown in Table 2.

3.31 The percentage in Table 2 will not necessarily be sufficient for alterations to all buildings, especially those of historic importance, and higher fees may be appropriate.

3.32 Where extensions to existing buildings are substantially independent, fees may be as for new works, but the fee for those sections of works which marry existing buildings to the new shall be charged on the higher scale at the fee applicable to an independent commission of similar value.

3.4 Repetition

3.40 Where a building is repeated for the same client fees for the superstructures excluding all work below the top of ground floor slabs or joists may be reduced as follows:

3.401 On all except the first three of any houses of the same design.

3.402 On all except the first of any other buildings to the same design.

Fees

3.41 Where a single building incorporates a number of identical compartments such as floors in multi-storey or complete structural bays in single-storey buildings, fees may be reduced on all identical compartments in excess of 10 provided that the building does not otherwise attract fee reductions and that it is completed in a single contract.

3.42 Reductions shall not be made for repeated individual dwelling units in multi-storey housing schemes but such schemes may qualify for fee reductions under Sub-clause 3.402 or Clause 3.41.

3.43 Reductions in accordance with Clauses 3.40 and 3.41 shall be made by waiving either the fee for Stages D and E F G of the Normal Services where a complete design can be re-used without modification other than the handling of plans, or for Stage E F G where a complete design can be re-used with only minor modification other than the handling of plans.

3.44 The total construction cost of the works shall be taken first and the fee for normal or partial services calculated thereon. The appropriate reduction shall then be applied to the cost of the repeated superstructures or sections and the result deducted from the full fee.

3.45 Screen walls and outbuildings and garages shall be excluded from the construction cost of works on which fees are waived unless they are included in the type drawings and specifications.

3.46 The fees for work in Stage H of the Normal Services shall not be reduced for repetitive works or repeated buildings, and any additional work arising out of repetition shall be charged on a time basis.

3.5 Partial services

3.50 Where for any reason the architect provides only part of the Normal Services described in Part 2 of these Conditions he shall be entitled to commensurate remuneration, and his fees and charges shall be calculated as follows:

3.501 Where an architect completes the work described in any of Stages C to E F G he shall be entitled to the appropriate proportion of the full percentage fee for the service in accordance with Table 3.

3.502 Where an architect is commissioned to undertake only the work described in Stage H, whether in whole or part, fees shall be on a time basis.

3.503 Where an architect originally engaged to provide the Normal Services does part only of the work described in Stage H, he shall be entitled to not less than the percentage fee otherwise due to him under Clause 3.61.

3.504 Where an architect provides part only of the services described in Stages C to E F G fees for service in any Stage which is incomplete shall be on a time basis, except by prior written agreement in accordance with Clause 3.53.

3.51 Where work done by a client results in the omission of part of Stages C to H described in Part 2 of these Conditions or a sponsored constructional method is used, a commensurate reduction in fees may be made by prior written agreement, provided each such agreement specifies in sufficient detail the work to be done by the client which would otherwise have formed part of the Stages provided by the architect, and is either made in accordance with the RIBA Memorandum on the application of this Clause or is approved by the RIBA.

3.52 All percentage fees for partial service shall be based on the architect's current estimate of the total construction cost of the work. Such estimates may be based on an accepted tender or, subject to Clause 3.53, on the lowest of unaccepted tenders.

3.53 Where partial service is provided in respect of works for which the executed cost is not known and no tender has been accepted, percentage fees shall be based either on the architect's estimated total construction cost or the most recent cost limit agreed with the client, whichever is the lower.

3.6 Mode and time of payment

3.60 On completion of each Stage of Stages C to H of the Normal Services described in Part 2 of these Conditions, the appropriate proportion of the full percentage fee calculated on the current estimated construction cost of the works, plus any other fee and out of pocket expenses which have accrued, shall be due for payment.

3.61 Notwithstanding Clause 3.60, fees in respect of Stages E F G and H shall be due for payment in instalments proportionate to the drawings and other work completed or value of the works certified from time to time.

3.62 Alternatively, the architect and client may arrange for interim payment of fees and charges during all Stages of the work, including payment during Stage H by instalments other than those related to the value of the works certified from time to time.

3.63 On the issue of the final certificate the final instalment of all fees and other charges shall then be due for payment.

Percentage fees for the Normal Services

Minimum charges are laid down in Tables 1 and 2 so that a fee shall not be less than the fee for works having a lower construction cost.

Fees

Table 1: New works

Total construction cost	Minimum % rate	Minimum charges for completed Work Stages:			
		H	EFG	D	C
Up to £2,500	10.0	–	–	–	–
£2,500–£8,000	8.5	£250	£187.50	£87.50	£37.50
£8,000–£14,000	7.5	£680	£510.00	£238.00	£102.00
£14,000–£25,000	6.5	£1,050	£787.50	£367.50	£157.50
£25,000 and over	6.0	£1,625	£1,218.75	£568.75	£243.75

For works for which the fee has not been reduced for repetition as provided in Section 3.4, the minimum fees shown in Table 1 shall be reduced as follows:

Total construction cost	Minimum % rate	Minimum charge
£750,000–£1,750,000	5.75	£45,000
£1,750,000 and over	5.5	£100,625

except that for certain hospitals, defined as 'hospital projects let as a single commission by a client representing a University and a Hospital Board' with a total construction cost of £7,000,000 or more, the minimum fee shall be 6%.

Table 2: Works to existing buildings

Total construction cost	Minimum % rate	Minimum charges for completed Work Stages:			
		H	EFG	D	C
Up to £2,500	13.0	–	–	–	–
£2,500–£8,000	12.5	£325	£243.75	£113.75	£48.75
£8,000–£14,000	12.0	£1,000	£750.00	£350.00	£150.00
£14,000–£25,000	11.0	£1,680	£1,260.00	£588.00	£252.00
£25,000 and over	10.0	£2,750	£2,062.50	£962.50	£412.50

Table 3: Apportionment of fees between stages of service

On completion of each Stage of the Normal Services described in Part 2 of these Conditions, the following proportions of the cumulative fee shown in Tables 1 and 2 are payable:

Work stage	Proportion of fee	Cumulative total
C	15%	15%
D	20%	35%
E F G	40%	75%
H	25%	100%

PART 4: OTHER SERVICES

4.00 This part describes other services which may be provided by the architect. Unless otherwise stated fees for these services shall be on a time basis.

4.1 Town planning

4.10 Fees for town planning work shall be in accordance with the Professional Charges of the Town Planning Institute, except that all layouts shall be charged on a time basis and all time charges shall be in accordance with Part 5 of these Conditions.

4.2 Quantity surveying, valuing and surveying

4.20 Fees for preparing bills of quantities, valuing works executed where no quantity surveyor is employed, valuation of properties and other surveying work not described elsewhere in these Conditions, shall be in accordance with the Professional Charges of the Royal Institution of Chartered Surveyors.

4.3 Garden and landscape design

4.30 Fees for garden and landscape design executed under separate landscape contracts shall be in accordance with the Scale of Professional Charges of the Institute of Landscape Architects.

4.4 Building surveys and structural investigations

4.40 Preparing schedules of dilapidations and negotiating them on behalf of landlords or tenants; taking particulars on site, preparing specifications for repairs or restoration work, inspecting their execution.

4.41 Making structural investigations, the limits of which shall be clearly defined and agreed in writing, such as are necessary to ascertain whether or not there are defects in the walls, roof, floors and drains of a building which may materially affect its life and value.

4.5 Separate trades contracts

4.50 Where there are separate contracts for each trade the fees shall be determined by prior written agreement and shall not be less than 20 per cent higher than the fee for Stages C to H of the Normal Services.

4.6 Interior design, shopfitting and furniture design

4.60 Fees may be charged on a percentage or time basis for the following work. Where percentage fees are charged, rates up to double those shown in Table 1 will normally be appropriate:

4.601 Special services, including the provision of special sketch studies, detailed advice on the selection of furniture, fittings and soft furnishings and inspection of making up such furnishings for interior design work executed under a special building contract or subcontract or a contract separate from that for other works on which the architect may be employed.

4.602 Works of a special quality, such as special shopfitting, fronts and interiors, exhibition design and similar works, including both the remodelling of existing shops and the design of new units, both independently and within the shell of an existing building, irrespective of whether the architect is employed for shopfitting design only or the work forms part of a general building contract.

4.61 Where all shopfitting drawings are provided by specialist sub-contractors the fee shall be as for the Normal Services described in Part 2 of these Conditions.

4.62 For the design of special items of furniture and fittings for limited production only, i.e. not more than 49 off, the percentage fee shall be either 15 per cent of the total production cost or calculated on a time basis.

4.63 Payment for the design of mass-produced items of furniture may be by royalty, or by time charges and sale of copyright. Fees for the design of prototypes shall be either on a time basis or an advance on royalties.

4.7 Building systems and components

4.70 For the development of building systems, percentage fees on the total production cost may be agreed specially. Otherwise, fees shall be either on a time basis or an advance on royalties.

4.71 Payment for the design of mass-produced building components may be by royalty, or by time charges and sale of copyright. Fees for development work in connection with the design of prototypes shall be either on a time basis or an advance on royalties.

Fees

4.72 Where an architect recommends to an independent client the use of a building system or components on which he is receiving royalties, the client shall be so informed. The total construction cost shall not be reduced but the architect may reduce his fees to the extent of the royalties received.

4.8 Litigation and arbitration

4.80 For qualifying to give evidence, setting proofs, conferences with solicitors and counsel, attendance in court or at arbitrations or town planning inquiries, or before other tribunals, for services in connection with litigation, and for arbitration, fees shall be on a time basis.

4.81 Time charges shall be in accordance with Part 5 except that the time rate for arbitrators shall be not less than £6 per hour with a minimum fee of £30.

4.9 Consultancy

4.90 For acting as consultant architect, fees shall be on a time basis.

4.91 Where an architect is retained to provide consultancy or other services on a regular or intermittent basis, annual retention fees may be charged, and where appropriate may be merged with subsequent percentage fees or time charges.

PART 5: TIME CHARGES

5.00 Time charges are based on a minimum hourly rate for principals and other operational staff. In assessing the rate at which time should be charged, all relevant factors should be considered, including the complexity of the work, the qualifications, experience and responsibility of the architect, and the charcter of any negotiations.

5.1 Hourly rates

5.10 The minimum hourly rate for principals shall be £5 per hour.

5.11 The minimum hourly rate for architectural and other operational staff, including resident architects and clerks of works not appointed and paid direct by the client, shall be 15 pence per hour for each £100 of gross annual salary, which shall include bonus payments and the employer's share of other overheads such as national insurance and occupational pension schemes.

5.2 Travelling time

5.20 Where work is being charged on a time basis, travelling time shall be charged in accordance with Section 5.1 of these Conditions.

5.21 Where work charged on a percentage fee is at such a distance that an exceptional amount of time is spent in travelling, additional charges may be made by prior written agreement.

PART 6: OUT OF POCKET EXPENSES

6.00 In addition to the fees under any other part of these Conditions, the architect shall be reimbursed for all reasonable out of pocket expenses actually and properly incurred in connection with the commission. Such expenses include the following:

6.1 Drawings and documents

6.10 Printing, reproduction or purchase costs of all documents, drawings, maps, models, photographs, and other records, including all those used in communication between architect, client, quantity surveyor, consultants and contractors, and for enquiries to contractors, sub-contractors and suppliers, notwithstanding any obligation on the part of the architect to supply such documents to those concerned, except that contractors and suppliers will pay for any prints additional to those to which they are entitled under the contract.

6.2 Hotel and travelling expenses

6.20 Hotel and travelling expenses, including mileage allowances for cars at recognised rates, and other similar disbursements.

6.3 Disbursements

6.30 All payments made on behalf of the client, including expenses incurred in advertising for tenders, clerks of works, and other resident site staff, including the time and expenses of interviewers and reasonable expenses for interviewees.

6.31 Fees and other charges for specialist professional advice, including legal advice, which have been incurred by the architect with the specific authority of the client.

6.32 Postage and telephone charges incurred by the architect may be charged by prior written agreement.

6.4 Compounding of expenses

6.40 By prior written agreement, expenses may be estimated or standardised in whole or part, or compounded for an increase in the percentage fee.

PART 7: ABANDONED WORKS AND INTERPRETATION

7.00 An engagement entered into between the architect and the client may be terminated at any time by either party on the expiry of reasonable notice, when the architect shall be entitled to remuneration in accordance with Section 3.5.

7.1 Abandoned works

7.10 Where the construction of works is cancelled or postponed on the client's instructions, or the architect is instructed to stop work indefinitely at any time, the commission may be deemed to be abandoned and fees for partial service shall be due.

7.11 Notwithstanding Clause 7.10, if instructions necessary for the architect to continue work are not received from the client six months after such instructions were requested, the commission shall be deemed to have been abandoned.

7.12 Where a commission is abandoned or any part of the works is omitted at any time before completion, fees for partial service in respect of the whole or part of the works shall be charged for all service provided with due authority.

7.2 Resumed commissions

7.20 If a commission which has been abandoned is resumed without substantial alteration within two years, any fees paid under Section 7.1 shall rank solely as payments on account toward the total fees payable on the execution of the works and calculated on their total construction cost.

7.21 Where a commission which has been abandoned is resumed at any time with substantial alteration or is resumed after two years, any fees paid under Section 7.1 above shall be regarded as final payment for the service originally rendered. The resumed commission shall then be deemed separate, and fees charged in accordance with Section 3.5 of these Conditions.

7.22 All additional work arising out of a commission which is resumed in accordance with Clause 7.20 shall be charged on a time basis.

7.3 Interpretation

7.30 Any question arising out of these Conditions may be referred in writing by architect or client to the RIBA for advice provided always that any difference or dispute between them is determined in accordance with either Clause 7.40 or 7.50.

7.4 Disputes

7.40 Any difference or dispute on the application of these Conditions to fees charged by a member of the RIBA may by agreement between the parties be referred to the RIBA for an opinion, provided always that such opinion is sought on a joint statement of undisputed facts and the parties undertake to accept it as final.

7.5 Arbitration

7.50 Where any difference or dispute arising out of these Conditions cannot be resolved in accordance with Clause 7.40, it shall be referred to the arbitration of a person to be agreed between the parties, or, failing agreement within 14 days after either party has given to the other a written request to concur in the appointment of an arbitrator, a person to be nominated at the request of either party by the President of the Institute of Arbitrators, except that in a difference or dispute arising out of the provisions of Section 1.5 the arbitrator shall, unless otherwise agreed, be a chartered architect.

3.4 QUANTITY SURVEYORS' FEES: SCALE 36

Scale 36 Inclusive Scale of Professional Charges for quantity surveying services for building works.

ISSUED JULY 1969

Note: This scale of professional charges is not intended to apply to work in Scotland for which the Scales of the Scottish Branch of the R.I.C.S. provide. The Scales may be obtained from the Scottish Branch Secretary, 7 Manor Place, Edinburgh 3.

Works

1. This scale of professional charges is for use when an inclusive scale of charges on building works over £200,000 in value is considered to be appropriate by mutual agreement between the building owner and the quantity surveyor. It is not intended for use when alterations form a significant part of the work, nor when partial services only are required; in such cases Scale No. 37 would apply.

2. This scale does not apply to civil engineering works (see Scale No. 38) nor to housing schemes for local authorities for which separate scales of fees have been agreed.

3. The fees set out below cover all quantity surveying services as may be required in connection with a building project irrespective of the type of contract from initial appointment to final certification of the contractor's account such as
(a) Budget estimating; cost planning and advice on tendering procedures and contract arrangements.
(b) Preparation of tendering documents for main contract and specialist sub-contracts; checking tenders received and reporting thereon or negotiating tenders and pricing with a selected contractor and/or sub-contractors.
(c) Preparing recommendations for interim payments on account to the contractor; preparing periodic assessments of the anticipated final cost of the works and reporting thereon; measurement of work and adjustment of variations in accordance with the terms of the contract and preparing final account, pricing same and agreeing total with the contractor.
(d) Providing a reasonable number of copies of bills of quantities and other documents; normal travelling and out-of-pocket expenses. Additional copies of documents, abnormal travelling and out-of-pocket expenses (e.g. in remote areas or overseas) and salaries of site checkers if required may be charged in addition by prior agreement with the building owner.

4. Copyright in the bills of quantities and other documents prepared by the quantity surveyor is reserved.

5. The fees for the services outlined in paragraph 3 shall be as follows, subject to paragraph 6:—

(a) CATEGORY A: Banks; chapels; churches; council offices; courthouses; houses; libraries; old people's homes; public houses and inns; petrol service stations; police stations; sports pavilions; synagogues; teaching laboratories and industrial laboratories of a like nature; town halls; university buildings other than halls of residence and hostels; and the like.

Value of Work	Category A Fee
£	£
Up to 300,000	4.0% (Minimum Fee £8,000)
300,000– 600,000	12,000 + 3.0% on balance over 300,000
600,000–1,200,000	21,000 + 2.8% on balance over 600,000
1,200,000–2,400,000	37,800 + 2.4% on balance over 1,200,000
Over 2,400,000	66,600 + 2.3% on balance over 2,400,000

(b) CATEGORY B. Abattoirs; canteens; church halls; cinemas; community centres; departmental stores; enclosed swimming baths; fire stations; halls of residence; hospitals; hostels; industrial laboratories, other than those included in Category A; offices, other than those included in Categories A and C; railway stations; residential hotels; restaurants; schools; shops and the like being works of a simpler character than those in Category A or works with some element of repetition.

Value of Work	Category B Fee
£	£
Up to 300,000	3.6% (Minimum Fee £7,200)
300,000– 600,000	10,800 + 2.5% on balance over 300,000
600,000–1,200,000	18,300 + 2.3% on balance over 600,000
1,200,000–2,400,000	32,100 + 2.1% on balance over 1,200,000
Over 2,400,000	57,300 + 1.9% on balance over 2,400,000

(c) CATEGORY C. Blocks of flats and maisonettes; factories; garages; offices with open floor space to be finished to tenants' requirements (tenants requirements to be Category A); open air swimming baths; warehouses and the like, being works containing little internal detail or works with a large amount of repetition.

Fees 49

Value of Work	Category C Fee
£	£ £
Up to 300,000	3.2% (Minimum Fee £6,400)
300,000– 600,000	9,600 + 2.3% on balance over 300,000
600,000–1,200,000	16,500 + 2.1% on balance over 600,000
1,200,000–2,400,000	29,100 + 1.7% on balance over 1,200,000
Over 2,400,000	49,500 + 1.5% on balance over 2,400,000

(d) The above fees shall be calculated upon the total of the final account for the whole of the work including all nominated sub-contractors' and nominated suppliers' accounts. When work normally included in a completed building is the subject of a separate contract for which the quantity surveyor has not been paid fees under any other clause hereof, the value of such work shall be included in the amount upon which fees are charged.

(e) If any of the materials used in the works are supplied by the building owner, the estimated or actual value thereof shall be included in the amounts upon which fees are to be calculated.

(f) When a contract comprises buildings which fall into more than one category the fee shall be calculated as follows:—

(i) The amount upon which fees are chargeable shall be allocated to the categories of work applicable and the amounts so allocated expressed as percentages of the amount upon which fees are chargeable.

(ii) Fees shall then be calculated for each category on the total amount upon which fees are chargeable.

(iii) The actual fee chargeable shall then be calculated by applying the percentages of work in each category to the appropriate total fee and adding the resultant amounts.

(iv) If both the building owner and the quantity surveyor so desire a consolidated percentage fee applicable to the total value of the work may be agreed. Such a percentage shall be based on this scale and on the estimated cost of the various sections of the works and calculated in accordance with the principles stated above.

6. (a) If bills of quantities are prepared by the quantity surveyor for the heating, ventilating and electrical services (or for any part of such services) there shall be a fee on the amount of such bills of quantities for these services in addition to the fee calculated in accordance with

Fees

paragraphs 5(a) to (f) as follows:—

Value of Work	Additional Fee
£	£ £
Up to 500,000	1.5%
Over 500,000	7,500 + 1.25% on balance over 500,000

(b) The values of all such services, whether the subject of separate contracts or not, shall be aggregated and the total value of work so obtained used for the purpose of calculating the additional fee chargeable in accordance with this paragraph. Except that when more than one firm of consulting engineers are engaged on the design of these services, then the separate values of the various contracts for which each such firm is responsible shall be aggregated and the additional fees charged shall be calculated independently on each such total value so obtained.

(c) If final accounts are prepared by the quantity surveyor for the heating, ventilating and electrical services (or for any part of such services), there shall be a fee of 1.5% on the amount of measured work (i.e. measured additions, measured omissions or complete remeasurement) in such accounts for these in addition to the fee calculated in accordance with paragraphs 5(a) to (f).

7. In the absence of agreement to the contrary, fees shall be paid by instalments as follows:—

(a) Upon acceptance by the building owner of a tender for the works, one half of the fee calculated on the amount of the accepted tender.

(b) The balance by instalments at intervals to be agreed between the date of the first certificate and one month after final certification of the contractor's account.

8. (a) In the event of no tender being accepted, one half of the fee shall be paid within six months of completion of the tender documents. The fee shall be calculated on the amount of the lowest original *bona fide* tender received. If no such tender has been received, the fee shall be calculated upon a reasonable valuation of the work, based upon the tender documents.

(b) In the event of the project being abandoned at any stage other than those covered by the foregoing, the proportion of fee payable shall be by agreement between the building owner and the quantity surveyor.

Fees

9. If the works are substantially varied at any stage or if the quantity surveyor is involved in an excessive amount of abortive work, then the fees shall be adjusted by agreement between the building owner and the quantity surveyor.

10. The foregoing scale of fees is exclusive of any services in connection with litigation and arbitration.

3.5 QUANTITY SURVEYORS' FEES: SCALE 37

Scale 37 Itemised Scale of Professional Charges for quantity surveying services for building works.

LAST REVISED FEBRUARY 1971

Note: This Scale of Professional Charges is not intended to apply to work in Scotland for which the Scales of the Scottish Branch of the R.I.C.S. provide. The Scales may be obtained from the Scottish Branch Secretary, 7 Manor Place, Edinburgh 3.

GENERAL

1. The fees are in all cases exclusive of travelling and of other expenses (for which the actual disbursement is recoverable unless there is some special prior arrangement for such charges), and cost of reproduction of bills of quantities and other documents, which are chargeable in addition at net cost.

2. Copyright in bills of quantities and other documents prepared by the quantity surveyor is reserved.

3. If any of the materials used in the works are supplied by the building owner, then the estimated or actual value thereof shall be included in the amounts upon which fees are to be calculated.

4. This scale does not apply to civil engineering works (see Scale No. 38) nor to housing schemes for local authorities for which separate scales of fees have been agreed.

LUMP SUM CONTRACTS: PRE-CONTRACT SERVICES

Bills of quantities

5. *Basic Scale*. For preparing bills of quantities:

    (a) CATEGORY A. Banks; chapels; churches; council offices; court-houses; houses; libraries; old people's homes; public houses and inns; petrol service stations; police stations; sports pavilions; synagogues; teaching laboratories and industrial laboratories of a like nature; town halls; university buildings, other than halls of residence and hostels; and the like.

Fees

Value of Work	Category A Fee
£	£ £
Up to 30,000	3.0% (Minimum Fee £150)
30,000– 60,000	900 + 2.5% on balance over 30,000
60,000– 120,000	1,650 + 1.8% on balance over 60,000
120,000– 600,000	2,730 + 1.4% on balance over 120,000
600,000–1,200,000	9,450 + 1.2% on balance over 600,000
Over 1,200,000	16,650 + 1.0% on balance over 1,200,000

(b) CATEGORY B. Abattoirs; canteens; church halls; cinemas; community centres; departmental stores; enclosed swimming baths; fire stations; halls of residence; hospitals; hostels; industrial laboratories, other than those included in Category A; offices, other than those included in Categories A and C; railway stations; residential hotels; restaurants; schools; shops; and the like, being works of a simpler character than those in Category A or works with some element of repetition.

Value of Work	Category B Fee
£	£ £
Up to 30,000	2.8% (Minimum Fee £140)
30,000– 60,000	840 + 2.3% on balance over 30,000
60,000– 120,000	1,530 + 1.5% on balance over 60,000
120,000– 600,000	2,430 + 1.1% on balance over 120,000
600,000–1,200,000	7,710 + 1.0% on balance over 600,000
Over 1,200,000	13,710 + 0.8% on balance over 1,200,000

(c) CATEGORY C. Blocks of flats and maisonettes; factories; garages; offices with open floor space to be finished to tenants' requirements (tenants' requirements to be Category A); open air swimming baths; warehouses; and the like, being works containing little internal detail or works with a large amount of repetition.

Value of Work	Category C Fee
£	£ £
Up to 30,000	2.5% (Minimum Fee £125)
30,000– 60,000	750 + 2.0% on balance over 30,000
60,000– 120,000	1,350 + 1.3% on balance over 60,000
120,000– 600,000	2,130 + 0.9% on balance over 120,000
600,000–1,200,000	6,450 + 0.8% on balance over 600,000
Over 1,200,000	11,250 + 0.6% on balance over 1,200,000

(d) The scales of fees for preparing bills of quantities (paragraphs 5(a) to (c)) are overall scales based upon the inclusion of all provisional and prime cost items, subject to the provision of paragraph 5(g). When work normally included in a completed building is the subject of a separate contract for which the quantity surveyor has not been paid fees under any other clause hereof, the value of such work shall be included in the amount upon which fees are charged.

(e) Fees shall be calculated upon the basis of the accepted tender for the whole of the work subject to the provisions of paragraph 10. In the event of no tender being accepted, fees shall be calculated upon the basis of the lowest original *bona fide* tender received. In the event of no such tender being received, the fees shall be calculated upon a reasonable valuation of the works based upon the original bills of quantities.

(f) In calculating the amount on which fees are charged the total of any credits and the total of any alternative bills shall be added to the amount described above. The value of any omission or addition forming part of an alternative bill shall not be added unless measurement or abstraction from the original dimension sheets was necessary.

(g) If the value of the heating, ventilating and electrical services together exceeds 25% of the amount calculated as described in paragraphs 5(d) and (e), then, subject to the provisions of paragraph 6, no fee is chargeable on the amount by which the value of these services exceeds the said 25%.

(h) When a contract comprises buildings which fall into more than one category, the fee shall be calculated as follows:—

(i) The amount upon which fees are chargeable shall be allocated to the categories of work applicable and the amounts so allocated expressed as percentages of the total amount upon which fees are chargeable.

(ii) Fees shall then be calculated for each category on the total amount upon which fees are chargeable.

(iii) The actual fee chargeable shall then be calculated by applying the percentages of work in each category to the appropriate total fee and adding the resultant amounts.

(j) When a project is the subject of a number of contracts then, for the purpose of calculating fees, the values of such contracts shall not be aggregated but each contract shall be taken separately and the scale of charges (paragraphs 5(a) to (h)) applied as appropriate.

6. *Heating, Ventilating and Electrical Services*

(a) If bills of quantities are prepared by the quantity surveyor for the heating, ventilating and electrical services (or for any part of such services) there shall be a fee on the amount of such bills of quantities for these services in addition to the fee calculated in accordance with paragraphs 5(a) to (j) as follows:

Value of Work		Additional Fee
	£	£
Up to	500,000	1.5%
Over	500,000	7,500 + 1.25% on balance over 500,000

(b) The values of all such services, whether the subject of separate contracts or not, shall be aggregated and the total value of work so obtained used for the purpose of calculating the additional fee chargeable in accordance with this paragraph. Except that when more than one firm of consulting engineers are engaged on the design of these services, then the separate values of the various contracts for which each such firm is responsible shall be aggregated and the additional fees charged shall be calculated independently on each such total value so obtained.

7. *Works of Alterations*

On works of alteration or repair, or on those sections of the works which are mainly works of alteration or repair, there shall be a fee of 1% in addition to the fee calculated in accordance with paragraphs 5(a) to (j) and 6.

8. *Works of Redecoration and Associated Minor Repairs*

On works of redecoration and associated minor repairs, there shall be a fee of 1.5% in addition to the fee calculated in accordance with paragraphs 5(a) to (j) and 6.

9. *Bills of Quantities Prepared in Special Forms*

Fees calculated in accordance with paragraphs 5(a) to (j), 6, 7, and 8, include for the preparation of bills of quantities on a normal trade basis. If the building owner requires additional information to be provided in the bills of quantities (e.g. annotations) or the bills to be prepared in an elemental, operational or similar form, then the fee may be adjusted by agreement between the building owner and the quantity surveyor.

10. *Reduction of Tenders*

(a) If a tender, when received, is reduced before acceptance, fees are to be calculated upon the unreduced amount of such tender. When the preparation of bills of reductions is required, a fee is chargeable for preparing such bills of reduction as follows:—

(i) 1.5% upon the gross amount of all omissions requiring measurement or abstraction from original dimension sheets.

(ii) 2.5% upon the gross amount of all additions requiring measurement.

(iii) 0.5% upon the total of all remaining additions.

Note: The above scale for the preparation of bills of reductions applies to work in all categories.

(b) If the reductions are not necessitated by amended instructions of the building owner or by the inclusion in the bills of quantities of items which the quantity surveyor has indicated could not be contained within the approved estimate and if a cost planning service has been requested by the building owner and is chargeable in accordance with paragraph 11, then in such a case no charge shall be made by the quantity surveyor for the preparation of bills of reductions and the fee for the preparation of the bills of quantities shall be based on the reduced amount of the tender.

Cost Planning and Approximate Estimates

11. (a) The fee for providing a cost planning service or for preparing an approximate estimate calculated by measurement other than as described in paragraph 11 (b) shall be based on the time involved (see paragraphs 37 and 38). Alternatively, the fee may be on a lump sum or percentage basis agreed between the building owner and the quantity surveyor.

(b) No charge shall be made for preparing approximate estimates on a cubic foot, superficial foot or similar basis.

Pricing Bills of Quantities

12. (a) For pricing bills of quantities, negotiating and agreeing prices with a contractor:

Value of Work	Fee
£	£ £
Up to 30,000	0.5% (Minimum Fee £25)
30,000– 120,000	150 + 0.3% on balance over 30,000
120,000– 240,000	420 + 0.2% on balance over 120,000
Over 24,000	660 + 0.1% on balance over 240,000

(b) The fees shall be calculated on the total value of the works as defined in paragraphs 5(d), (f), (g) and (j).

(c) For pricing bills of quantities, if instructed, to provide an estimate comparable with tenders the fee shall be ONE-THIRD (33⅓%) of the fee for pricing bills of quantities, negotiating and agreeing prices with a contractor calculated in accordance with paragraphs 12(a) and (b).

(d) For pricing bills of quantities for heating, ventilating, and electrical installations, negotiating and agreeing prices with a contractor, there shall be a separate fee as paragraph 12(a) calculated on the amount of such bills of quantities valued in accordance with paragraph 6(b).

(e) For pricing bills of quantities, if instructed, for heating, ventilating and electrical installations, the fee shall be ONE-THIRD (33⅓%) of the fee calculated in accordance with paragraph 12(d).

LUMP SUM CONTRACTS: POST-CONTRACT SERVICES

Alternative scales (I and II) for post-contract services are set out below, to be used at the quantity surveyor's discretion in prior agreement with the building owner.

Alternative I

Overall scale of charges for complete post-contract services.

13. *Basic Scale.* For surveying works in progress, taking particulars and reporting for interim certificates for payments on account to the contractor, preparing periodic assessments of anticipated final cost and reporting thereon, measuring and making up bills of variations including pricing and agreeing totals with the contractor, and adjusting fluctuations in the cost of labour and materials if required by the contract:

(a) CATEGORY A: Banks; chapels; churches; council offices; courthouses; houses; libraries; old people's homes; public houses and inns; petrol service stations; police stations; sports pavilions; synagogues; teaching laboratories and industrial laboratories of a like nature; town halls; university buildings, other than halls of residence and hostels; and the like.

Value of Work	Category A Fee
£	£ £
Up to 30,000	2.0% (Minimum Fee £100)
30,000– 60,000	600 + 1.8% on balance over 30,000
60,000– 120,000	1,140 + 1.6% on balance over 60,000
120,000– 600,000	2,100 + 1.4% on balance over 120,000
600,000–1,200,000	8,820 + 1.1% on balance over 600,000
Over 1,200,000	15,420 + 1.0% on balance over 1,200,000

(b) CATEGORY B. Abattoirs; canteens; church halls; cinemas; community centres; departmental stores; enclosed swimming baths; fire stations; halls of residence; hospitals; hostels; industrial laboratories, other than those included in Category A; offices, other than those included in Categories A and C; railway stations; residential hotels; restaurants; schools; shops; and the like, being works of a simpler character than those in Category A or works with some element of repetition.

Value of Work	Category B Fee
£	£ £
Up to 30,000	2.0% (Minimum Fee £100)
30,000– 60,000	600 + 1.8% on balance over 30,000
60,000– 120,000	1,140 + 1.6% on balance over 60,000
120,000– 600,000	2,100 + 1.1% on balance over 120,000
600,000–1,200,000	7,380 + 0.9% on balance over 600,000
Over 1,200,000	12,780 + 0.8% on balance over 1,200,000

(c) CATEGORY C. Blocks of flats and maisonettes; factories; garages; offices with open floor space to be finished to tenants' requirements (tenants' requirements to be Category A); open air swimming baths; warehouses; and the like, being works containing little internal detail or works with a large amount of repetition.

Value of Work	Category C Fee
£	£ £
Up to 120,000	1.6% (Minimum Fee £80)
120,000– 600,000	1,920 + 1.1% on balance over 120,000
600,000–1,200,000	7,200 + 0.8% on balance over 600,000
Over 1,200,000	12,000 + 0.7% on balance over 1,200,000

(d) Fees are to be calculated upon the basis of the account for the whole of the work, subject to the provisions of paragraph 13(g).

(e) The scales of fees for post-contract services (paragraphs 13(a) to (c)) are overall scales based upon the inclusion of all nominated sub-contractors' and nominated suppliers' accounts, subject to the provision of paragraph 14. When work normally included in a completed building is the subject of a separate contract for which the quantity surveyor has not been paid fees under any other clause hereof, the value of such work shall be included in the amount on which fees are charged.

(f) In calculating the amount on which fees are charged the total of any credits is to be added to the amount described above.

(g) If the value of the heating, ventilating and electrical services together exceed 25% of the amount calculated as described in paragraphs 13(d) and (e) above, then subject to the provisions of paragraph 14, no fee is chargeable on the amount by which the value of these services exceeds the said 25%.

(h) When a contract comprises buildings which fall into more than one category, the fee shall be calculated as follows:—

(i) The amount upon which fees are chargeable shall be allocated to the categories of work applicable and the amounts so allocated expressed as percentages of the total amount upon which fees are chargeable.

(ii) Fees shall then be calculated for each category on the total amount upon which fees are chargeable.

(iii) The actual fee chargeable shall then be calculated by applying the percentages of work in each category to the appropriate total fee and adding the resultant amounts.

(j) When a project is the subject of a number of contracts then, for the purposes of calculating fees, the values of such contracts shall not be aggregated but each contract shall be taken separately and the scale of charges (paragraphs 13(a) to (h)) applied as appropriate.

(k) The above overall scales of charges for post-contract services assume normal conditions when the bills of quantities are based on drawings accurately depicting the building work the building owner requires. If the works are materially varied by the building owner to the extent that substantial remeasurement is necessary then the fee for post-contract services should be adjusted by agreement between the building owner and the surveyor.

14. *Heating, Ventilating and Electrical Services*

If final accounts are prepared by the quantity surveyor for the heating, ventilating and electrical services (or for any part of such services), there shall be a fee of 1.5% on the amount of measured work (i.e. measured additions, measured omissions or complete remeasurement) in such accounts for these services in addition to the fee calculated in accordance with paragraphs 13(a) to (j).

Alternative II

Scale of charges for separate stages of post-contract services.

Note: The scales of fees in paragraphs 15 and 16 apply to work in all categories.

Valuations for interim certificates

15. For surveying works in progress, taking particulars and reporting valuations for interim certificates for payments on account to the

contractor:

Total of Valuations	Fee
£	£ £
Up to 60,000	0.5%
60,000– 240,000	300 + 0.4% on balance over 60,000
240,000–1,200,000	1,020 + 0.3% on balance over 240,000
Over 1,200,000	3,900 + 0.2% on balance over 1,200,000

Note: When consulting engineers are engaged in supervising the installation of heating, ventilating and electrical services and their duties include reporting valuations for inclusion in interim certificates for payments on account in respect of such services, then valuations so reported shall be excluded from any total amount of valuations used for calculating fees.

Preparing accounts of variations upon contracts

16. For measuring and making up bills of variations including pricing and agreeing totals with the contractor:—

(a) 1.5% upon the gross amount of all omissions requiring measurement or abstraction from the original dimension sheets.

(b) 2.5% upon the gross amount of the additions requiring measurement and upon dayworks.

(c) 0.5% upon the gross amount of all remaining additions, except as provided for in the following paragraph.

(d) 2.5% upon the aggregate of the amounts of the increases and/or decreases in the cost of labour and materials in accordance with any fluctuations clause in the conditions of contract.

Note: When consulting engineers are engaged in supervising the installation of heating, ventilating and electrical services and their duties include for the adjustment of accounts and pricing and agreeing totals with the sub-contractors for inclusion in the measured account, then any totals so agreed shall be excluded from any amounts used for calculating fees.

Cost control services

17. The fee for providing cost control services (e.g. preparing periodic assessments of anticipated final cost and reporting thereon) shall be based on the time involved (see paragraphs 37 and 38). Alternatively, the fee may be on a lump sum or percentage basis agreed between the building owner and the quantity surveyor.

CONTRACTS BASED ON BILLS OF APPROXIMATE QUANTITIES: PRE-CONTRACT AND POST-CONTRACT SERVICES

Bills of Approximate Quantities, Interim Certificates and Final Accounts

18. *Basic Scale.* For preparing bills of approximate quantities suitable for obtaining competitive tenders which will provide a schedule of prices and a reasonably close forecast of the cost of the works, but subject to complete remeasurement, surveying works in progress, taking particulars and reporting for interim certificates for payments on account to the contractor, preparing periodic assessments of anticipated final cost and reporting thereon, measuring and preparing final account, including pricing and agreeing totals with the contractor and adjusting fluctuations in the cost of labour and materials if required by the contract:

(a) CATEGORY A. Banks; chapels; churches; council offices; courthouses; houses; libraries; old people's homes; public houses and inns; petrol service stations; police stations; sports pavilions; synagogues; teaching laboratories and industrial laboratories of a like nature; town halls; university buildings, other than halls of residence and hostels; and the like.

Value of Work	Category A Fee
£	£ £
Up to 30,000	5.0% (Minimum Fee £250)
30,000– 60,000	1,500 + 4.3% on balance over 30,000
60,000– 120,000	2,790 + 3.4% on balance over 60,000
120,000– 600,000	4,830 + 2.8% on balance over 120,000
600,000–1,200,000	18,270 + 2.3% on balance over 600,000
Over 1,200,000	32,070 + 2.0% on balance over 1,200,000

(b) CATEGORY B. Abattoirs; canteens; church halls; cinemas; community centres; departmental stores; enclosed swimming baths; fire stations; halls of residence; hospitals; hostels; industrial laboratories; other than those included in Category A; offices, other than those included in Categories A and C; railway stations; residential hotels; restaurants; schools; shops; and the like, being works of a simpler character than those in Category A or works with some element of repetition.

Value of Work	Category B Fee
£	£ £
Up to 30,000	4.8% (Minimum Fee £240)
30,000– 60,000	1,440 + 4.1% on balance over 30,000
60,000– 120,000	2,670 + 3.1% on balance over 60,000
120,000– 600,000	4,530 + 2.2% on balance over 120,000
600,000–1,200,000	15,090 + 1.9% on balance over 600,000
Over 1,200,000	26,490 + 1.6% on balance over 1,200,000

(c) CATEGORY C. Blocks of flats and maisonettes; factories; garages; offices with open floor space to be finished to tenants' requirements (tenants' requirements to be Category A); open air swimming baths; warehouses; and the like, being works containing little internal detail or works with a large amount of repetition.

Value of Work	Category C Fee	
£	£	£
Up to 30,000	4.1% (Minimum Fee £205)	
30,000– 60,000	1,230 + 3.6% on balance over	30,000
60,000– 120,000	2,310 + 2.9% on balance over	60,000
120,000– 600,000	4,050 + 2.0% on balance over	120,000
600,000–1,200,000	13,650 + 1.6% on balance over	600,000
Over 1,200,000	23,250 + 1.3% on balance over	1,200,000

(d) The scales of fees for pre-contract and post-contract services (paragraphs 18(a) to (c)) are overall scales based upon the inclusion of all nominated suppliers' and nominated sub-contractors' accounts subject to the provision of paragraph 18(g).

When work normally included in a completed building is the subject of a separate contract for which the quantity surveyor has not been paid fees under any other clause hereof, the value of such work shall be included in the amount on which fees are charged.

(e) Fees shall be calculated upon the basis of the account for the whole of the work, subject to the provisions of paragraph 19.

(f) In calculating the amount on which fees are charged the total of any credits is to be added to the amount described above.

(g) If the value of the heating, ventilating and electrical services together exceeds 25% of the amount calculated as described in paragraphs 18(d) and (e), then, subject to the provisions of paragraph 19, no fee is chargeable on the amount by which the value of these services exceeds the said 25%.

(h) When a contract comprises buildings which fall into more than one category, the fee shall be calculated as follows:

(i) The amount upon which fees are chargeable shall be allocated to the categories of work applicable and the amounts so allocated expressed as percentages of the total amount upon which fees are chargeable.

(ii) Fees shall then be calculated for each category on the total amount upon which fees are chargeable.

(iii) The actual fee chargeable shall then be calculated by applying the percentages of work in each category to the appropriate total fee and adding the resultant amounts.

(j) When a project is the subject of a number of contracts then, for the purposes of calculating fees, the values of such contracts shall not be aggregated but each contract shall be taken separately and the scale of charges (paragraphs 18(a) to (h) applied as appropriate.

19. *Heating, Ventilating and Electrical Services*

(a) If bills of approximate quantities are prepared by the quantity surveyor for the heating, ventilating and electrical services (or for any part of such services) there shall be an additional fee equal to ONE-HALF (50%) of the fee calculated in accordance with paragraphs 6(a) and (b).

(b) If final accounts are prepared by the quantity surveyor for the heating, ventilating and electrical services (or for any part of such services), there shall be a fee of 1.5% on the amount of measured work (i.e. measured additions, measured omissions or complete remeasurement) in such accounts for these services in addition to the fee calculated in accordance with paragraphs 18(a) to (j).

20. *Works of Alterations*
On works of alteration or repair, or on those sections of the work which are mainly works of alterations or repair, there shall be a fee of 1% in addition to the fee calculated in accordance with paragraphs 18(a) to (j) and 19.

21. *Works of Redecoration and Associated Minor Repairs*
On works of redecoration and associated minor repairs, there shall be a fee of 1.5% in addition to the fee calculated in accordance with paragraphs 18(a) to (j) and 19.

22. *Final Accounts Prepared in Special Forms*
Fees calculated in accordance with paragraphs 18(a) to (j), 19, 20 and 21 include for the preparation of final accounts on a normal trade basis. If the building owner requires additional information to be provided in the final accounts or the accounts to be prepared in an elemental, operational or similar form, then the fee may be adjusted by agreement between the building owner and the quantity surveyor.

Cost Planning and Approximate Estimates

23. (a) The fee for providing a cost planned service or for preparing an approximate estimate calculated by measurement other than as described in paragraph 23(b) shall be based on the time involved (see paragraphs 37 and 38). Alternatively, the fee may be on a lump sum or percentage basis agreed between the building owner and the quantity surveyor.

(b) No charge shall be made for preparing approximate estimates on a cubic foot, superficial foot or similar basis.

Pricing Bills of Approximate Quantities

24. The fees for pricing bills of approximate quantities, negotiating and agreeing prices with a contractor and for pricing bills of approximate quantities, if instructed, to provide an estimate comparable with tenders shall be the same as for the corresponding services in paragraphs 12(a) to (e).

Instalment Payments

25. The quantity surveyor shall be paid from time to time the appropriate fees and expenses for completed stages of his services or otherwise by prior agreement between the building owner and the quantity surveyor. In the case of the preparation of the bills of approximate quantities the fee shall be the equivalent of forty per cent (40%) of the fees calculated in accordance with the appropriate sections of paragraphs 18 to 22 and based on the total value of the bills of approximate quantities.

CONTRACTS BASED ON SCHEDULES OF PRICES: PRE-CONTRACT SERVICES

Schedules of Prices

26. The fee for preparing, pricing and agreeing schedules of prices shall be based on the time involved (see paragraphs 37 and 38). Alternatively, the fee may be on a lump sum basis agreed between the building owner and the quantity surveyor.

Cost Planning and Approximate Estimates

27. (a) The fee for providing a cost planning service or for preparing an approximate estimate calculated by measurement other than as described in paragraph 27(b) shall be based on the time involved (see paragraphs 37 and 38). Alternatively, the fee may be on a lump sum or percentage basis agreed between the building owner and the quantity surveyor.

(b) No charge shall be made for preparing approximate estimates on a cubic foot, superficial foot or similar basis.

CONTRACTS BASED ON SCHEDULES OF PRICES: POST-CONTRACT SERVICES

Final Accounts

28. *Basic Scale* for surveying works in progress, taking particulars and reporting for interim certificates for payments on account to the

contractor, preparing periodic assessments of anticipated final cost and reporting thereon, measuring and preparing final account including pricing and agreeing totals with the contractor, and adjusting fluctuations in the cost of labour and materials if required by the contract, the fee shall be SIXTY PER CENT (60%) of the fee for preparing bills of approximate quantities, interim certificates and final accounts calculated in accordance with paragraphs 18(a) to (j).

Heating, Ventilating and Electrical Services
29. If final accounts are prepared by the quantity surveyor for the heating, ventilating and electrical services (or for any part of such services), there shall be a fee of 1.5% on the amount of measured work (i.e. measured additions, measured omissions or complete remeasurement) in such accounts for these services in addition to the fee calculated in accordance with paragraph 28.

Works of Alteration
30. On works of alteration or repair or on those sections of the work which are mainly works of alteration or repair, there shall be a fee of 1% in addition to the fee calculated in accordance with paragraphs 28 and 29.

Works of Redecoration and Associated Minor Repairs
31. On works of redecoration and associated minor repairs, there shall be a fee of 1.5% in addition to the fee calculated in accordance with paragraphs 28 and 29.

Final Accounts in Special Forms
32. Fees calculated in accordance with paragraphs 28, 29, 30 and 31 include for the preparation of final accounts on a normal trade basis. If the building owner requires additional information to be provided in the final accounts or the accounts to be prepared in an elemental, operational or similar form, then the fee may be adjusted by agreement between the building owner and the quantity surveyor.

PRIME COST CONTRACTS: PRE-CONTRACT AND POST-CONTRACT SERVICES

Cost Planning

33. The fee for providing a cost planning service shall be based on the time involved (see paragraphs 37 and 38). Alternatively, the fee may be on a lump sum or percentage basis agreed between the building owner and the quantity surveyor.

Estimates of Cost

34. (a) For preparing an approximate estimate calculated by measurement, other than described in paragraph 34(c), of the cost of work and,

if required under the terms of the contract, negotiating, adjusting and agreeing the estimate:

Value of Work	Fee
£	£ £
Up to 6,000	1.25% (Minimum Fee £25)
6,000– 30,000	75 + 1.0% on balance over 6,000
30,000– 120,000	315 + 0.75% on balance over 30,000
Over 120,000	990 + 0.5% on balance over 120,000

(b) The fee shall be calculated upon the total of the approved estimates.

(c) No charge shall be made for preparing approximate estimates on a cubic foot, superficial foot or similar basis.

Final Accounts

35. (a) For checking prime costs, reporting for interim certificates for payments on account to the contractor and preparing final accounts:

Value of Work	Fee
£	£ £
Up to 6,000	2.5% (Minimum Fee £50)
6,000– 30,000	150 + 2.0% on balance over 6,000
30,000– 120,000	630 + 1.5% on balance over 30,000
Over 120,000	1,980 + 1.25% on balance over 120,000

(b) The fee shall be calculated upon the total of the final account less the value of any work charged for in accordance with paragraph 35(c).

(c) On the value of any work to be paid for on a measured basis, the fee shall be 3%.

(d) The above charges do not include the provision of checkers on the site. If the surveyor is required to provide such checkers an additional charge shall be made by arrangement.

Cost Control Services

36. The fee for providing cost control services (e.g., preparing periodic assessments of anticipated final cost and reporting thereon) shall be based on the time involved (see paragraphs 37 and 38). Alternatively, the fee may be on a lump sum or percentage basis agreed between the building owner and the quantity surveyor.

TIME CHARGES

37. (a) For any services the charges for which are to be based on the time involved such charges shall be calculated on the hourly cost of the staff involved (excluding clerical staff) plus 125% to cover overheads and principals' remuneration.

(b) The hourly cost shall be calculated by taking the sum of the annual cost of the employee conerned of

(i) Salary and bonus but excluding expenses.

(ii) Employer's contributions payable under Pension and Life Assurance Schemes; and

(iii) Employer's contributions made under the National Insurance Acts, the Redundancy Payments Act and any other payments made in respect of the employee by virtue of any statutory requirements; and dividing by 1750.

38. If particular circumstances require a principal to undertake work which would normally be done by an employee then a charge shall be made for the principal's time at the rate which would be chargeable if such work had been done by a senior assistant in the firm.

39 Paragraphs 37 and 38 do not apply to principals engaged in litigation and arbitration.

LITIGATION AND ABRITRATION

40. For qualifying to give evidence; settling proofs; conferences with solicitors and counsel; attendance in the courts or before arbitrators, or other tribunals; and for similar services:

(i) In the case of a principal, a fee by arrangement according to the circumstances, including the professional status and qualifications of the quantity surveyor.

(ii) In the case of a member of staff, a fee based on the time involved (see paragraphs 37 and 38).

4 Drawing office practice and contract procedure

4.1 INTRODUCTION

4.1.1 Although most contractual procedures are the same in landscape work as in building and engineering schemes there are a number of differences of detail which need to be appreciated. This chapter summarises the various stages, from the production of working drawings to the final account and pinpoints, as far as possible, the landscape considerations to be borne in mind.

4.2 WORKING DRAWINGS AND PLANTING PLANS

4.2.1 To ensure a maximum degree of accuracy, all working drawings should be set out direct from the survey and grid, if available, and not from the sketch plan design drawings. Working drawings for all constructional details should follow, as far as is practical, current architectural practice of presentation and notation and the British Standard for drawing office practice (a British Standard for landscape drawing office practice is in course of preparation). Drawings for large site work may have to follow civil engineering practice in showing sections and relating plans to grid or chainage lines. All drawings should now be in metric dimensions and to recognised metric scales. For very large sites a map notation may be necessary and on most sites it is essential to have a key master plan which indicates areas with special detailing, covered separately on drawings at a larger scale. All key plans, site plans and part site plans should have the north point clearly indicated, as orientation is of particular relevance in landscape work. Working drawings for planting plans must show clearly what is intended by having a plant list on each plan. The scale of the plan should be large enough to show the actual names (or key numbers) and positions of individual plants or groups of plants. This will allow the contractor to follow the plan and site the plants without any difficulty. The scale should be determined in relation to the nature of the work. For example, a plan for a simple tree planting scheme could be to a much smaller scale than would be possible or appropriate for a complex shrub area. It is a great help on site if the actual names of plants can be put on the appropriate tree of shrub group on larger scale drawings, although this does entail much more lettering work in the drawing office. On small scale plans a key system should be used with key numbers (T.1., S.1. etc.) placed against each plant species (see illustration in chapter

Drawing office practice and contract procedure

4.2.1 (cont'd) 6). The plant list must be on the planting plan and not on a separate sheet and should be written in a format similar to an extract from bills of quantities. This must include the key number, the quantity, the Latin generic name, planting size and any vital specification notes such as: 'feathered,' 'balled,' 'pot grown.' The ultimate size of plants is sometimes shown on planting lists but this can be misleading and should be avoided unless clear notes are added concerning time span and the effect on plant growth of maintenance, drainage, micro-climate, pollution and other influential factors. In addition the common name may be shown if the drawing is to be used by the client or others to whom this may be helpful. However, common nomenclature is so non-standardised in the nursery trade at present that its use on working drawings can cause further confusion and should be avoided if possible.

4.2.2 All working drawings should be fully dimensioned, although the setting out of the plants can be approximate, subject to staking out by the contractor and checking on site by the landscape architect immediately prior to planting. If this is the case however, the procedure to be followed must be clearly stated so that the contractor fully appreciates that this checking of staking out must be done before tree holes are dug.

4.3 DESCRIPTION OF WORK/SPECIFICATION

4.3.1 All tender and contract documentation must include a complete description of work/specification. Where bills of quantities are used the description of work is incorporated in the bills. Although there are many ways of setting out a description of work/specification it is usually divided into a series of main sections.

4.3.2 *General conditions of contract and preliminaries:* This sets out in detail the general aspects of the contract and covers all the items of administration and overheads which must be allowed for in pricing the contract.

4.3.3 *Materials:* All materials to be used must be described and where appropriate the source of supply and name of manufacturer stated. The quality of materials is to be laid down, with reference to British Standard Specifications where applicable (see Bibliography). Detailed specifications are covered in Chapter 5.

4.3.4 *Workmanship:* This section should describe the specific procedure and methods of construction. References to British Standards Codes of Practice are to be stated where applicable.

4.3.5 *Maintenance and defects/liability:* This section should define the maintenance to be included under the contract, showing clearly what work is required in this respect both during the construction

Drawing office practice and contract procedure

4.3.5
(cont'd)
period and after practical completion. It must also include clarification of the guarantee on materials and plant replacements during the defects liability period. The defects liability period may vary depending on the time of year that the contract is carried out but is usually 12 months, which ensures coverage of one complete growing and one dormant season. For semi-mature trees and forestry planting 2 years should be the minimum period. Confusion is often caused by the use of the description 'maintenance period,' especially as under building contracts no physical maintenance is required by the contractor after practical completion (except for making good of inherent defects). In landscape work, because of the use of growing materials, a requirement should be written into the contract for physical maintenance to take place throughout the *'defects liability period.'* If this latter phrase is always used, *'maintenance'* is then seen to refer only to physical maintenance operations: i.e. mowing, weeding and watering.

4.4 BILLS OF QUANTITIES

4.4.1   All contracts, except the very smallest, should have bills of quantities. This is particularly necessary on those put out to tender, since it ensures that all contractors tender on an equal basis and simplifies the pricing of variations. Even where a scheme is negotiated, bills of quantities are desirable, as most landscape contracts, by their very nature, are prone to additions and omissions as the work progresses. Part of the bill will incorporate the plant schedule and its details as referred to in the foregoing description of planting plans (4.2). For many contracts a quantity surveyor should be engaged to prepare bills and to give a full service from preliminary cost plan exercises to settlement of the final account.

4.4.2   There are several ways of setting out the planting section of the bills. Normal practice among quantity surveyors is to itemise and price each labour separately. As a result, variations can be made and are easy to calculate with the additional cost of each item, such as more excavation, extra ties, longer stakes. Alternatively there may be some advantages in arranging for the price of each plant to include the complete cost of supply and planting operation. For trees this will include digging the hole, providing soil for the tree pit, planting the tree, staking, tying and mulching and a guarantee. By putting all these items of work into one unit price a simple method of pricing is obtained and many landscape contractors are used to tendering on this basis. If the items are set out separately for pricing the bill can become rather long.

4.4.3   On some contracts there are advantages in having bills divided not only by trades or materials but also by physical areas of the site (e.g. courtyard A, boiler house area, tree belt, car park). This is essential on large contracts where work may be phased and practical completion

Drawing office practice and contract procedure

4.4.3
(cont'd) dates placed on each section as it is finished. Phasing may be over a period of months or even years. Similarly variations in design can be controlled more easily by separate areas than by one bill covering all planting and all paving. Although this separation may be more complex for the contractor to price, it does allow for special rates for differing circumstances, such as access to difficult internal courtyards. A breakdown into areas can also make it easier for the contractor to organize the ordering of materials related to a phased programme.

4.4.4 At the end of the bills of quantities, a page should be added to the usual schedules of rates and materials on which a schedule of substitutions can be made by each tenderer. It will then be easy to find a list of the species, variety or size of all plants, which the tenderer wishes or needs to substitute for those specified, owing to supply difficulties.

4.5 CONTRACTS — INTRODUCTION

4.5.1 The two parties to a contract are the employer and the contractor. The landscape architect acts as the representative or agent for the client and where necessary he must be the arbiter of what can be expected under the contract from the contractor. Where a quantity surveyor is used, his powers and duties are as laid down in the conditions in the form of contract. Except where stated otherwise all references to contracts mean the I.L.A. standard form.

4.6 SELECTION OF TENDERERS

4.6.1 For competitive tendering a list of firms to be invited should be agreed with the employer by the landscape architect, before contractors are asked whether they wish to tender for the work in question.

4.6.2 All government departments and many local authorities are governed by regulations or standing orders which control methods of tender invitation. Some authorities and organisations have lists of approved firms from which all tenderers must be chosen. Standing orders sometimes make it necessary to invite open tenders from all contractors who wish to submit a price. This system has considerable disadvantages and selected lists are becoming the more normal procedure. In some cases an authority may advertise a project and ask for firms wishing to be placed on a tender list to write in with details. This stills leads to a selected list.

4.6.3 Wherever possible an indication of willingness to tender should be obtained from each firm on the agreed list before tender documents are despatched.

Drawing office practice and contract procedure

4.6.4   Lists of firms from which a selection can be made may be obtained from the following trade associations:—

British Association of Sportsground and Landscape
Contractors Ltd.,
140 Bensham Lane,
Thornton Heath, Surrey.   01-684 2973

Association of British Tree Surgeons and Arborists,
Pembroke Cottage
11 Wings Road,
Upper Hale,
Farnham, Surrey.   025-13-5924

Association of Tree Transplanters,
c/o Civic Trees Ltd.,
91A High Street,
Great Missenden, Bucks.   Great Missenden 3661

National Association of Agricultural Contractors,
(Garden Section),
140 Bensham Lane,
Thornton Heath, Surrey.   01-684 2973

Association of Swimming Pool Contractors,
140 Bensham Lane,
Thornton Heath, Surrey.   01-684 0665

British Association of Landscape Industries,
North Lane Gardens,
Roundhay,
Leeds LS8 2QT.   Leeds 659147

4.6.5   Other associations should be approached for various specialist activities. For work having no soft landscape content a whole range of building and engineering contractors could be appropriate.

4.6.6   Many specialist contractors advertise in *Landscape Design* obtainable from the Institute of Landscape Architects, 12 Carlton House Terrace, London S.W.1. 01-839-4044.

4.7   TENDERING PROCEDURES

4.7.1   The usual number of tenderers varies from 3 to 6 and the larger the project the greater the number necessary. Each tenderer must be sent the tender documents in duplicate, consisting of a description of work/specification, bills of quantities, a comprehensive set of working drawings, the form of tender and a special envelope. The tender and priced bills of quantities must be returned in the envelope provided

Drawing office practice and contract procedure 73

4.7.1 (*cont'd*) which is opened only at the specified date and time, often in the presence of the client. At least two full working weeks must be allowed for tendering; for complex contracts the period should be longer. This is particularly important on schemes containing large quantities of plants, where tenderers will need to contact several suppliers to locate the required material before they can work out accurate prices.

4.7.2 A note should have been added to the planting sections of bills requiring tenderers to state alternative species, varieties or heights for which they are pricing, if they are unable to obtain those specified. These substitutions will be summarised in the schedule referred to in 4.4.4. Proper attention to this item can be particularly important in close competitive tendering where the lowest tenderer may be offering many substitutions or plants below the size required. If this is clearly shown in the tenderer's priced bill, misunderstanding at a later date is avoided. The differences between the tenderers' offers should be considered when the client is being advised on which tender to accept. Because of a persistent supply problem, the checking of landscape tenders by a landscape architect or someone with sound horticultural knowledge who understands the consequences of the proposed substitutions is essential if problems are to be avoided.

4.8 NEGOTIATED CONTRACTS

4.8.1 In certain circumstances it is possible to negotiate a contract price with a selected contractor without inviting competitive tenders. This usually takes place for private clients with high class projects where a contractor suitable for the type of work envisaged is selected on the basis of his reputation for similar work. Even in these circumstances the usual formalities of description of work/specification, bills of quantities and contract must be adhered to in order to ensure that the best value for money is obtained and to give a degree of legal protection to both parties.

4.9 ACCEPTANCE OF TENDERS

4.9.1 It is usual practice for the lowest tender received to be accepted but if good reasons exist (for example see the schedule for substitutions in 4.4.4) the second lowest or another higher tender may be accepted. The right of the employer not to accept the lowest tender, or any tender, must be clearly written into the tender documents, so that tenderers are aware of this fact. Nevertheless acceptance of other than the lowest tender on frequent occasions could bring the system of competitive tendering into disrepute. It should be recognised, however, that a contractor who submits a very keen tender may well try to restore his profit margin by claims for extras during the construction and at the end of the contract.

4.9.1 (cont'd) Acceptance or rejection of tenders should be decided upon without undue delay. All tenderers should be informed in writing of the results as soon as a contract is signed with the successful firm.

4.10 FORM OF CONTRACT

4.10.1 The successful contractor and employer should enter into a formal agreement on an I.L.A. Agreement and Conditions of Contract form (1969 edition) although some bodies still insist on using the R.I.B.A. Standard Form of Contract (1963 edition: July 1971 revision) even on pure landscape work. In many instances large firms, government departments and local authorities have their own standard form of contract which must be used. In all cases, the type of contract to be used must be stated clearly at the time of tendering.

4.11 SUB-CONTRACTS

4.11.1 In many instances landscape work forms a sub-contract to a main building or civil engineering contract. In these circumstances there must be no conflict between the conditions and terms of payment in the sub-contract and main contract. Most building and civil engineering contracts state that prices must allow for a cash discount (normally 2½%) which the general contractor is entitled to receive on the value of all sub-contracts. The landscape contractor then becomes a 'nominated sub-contractor' (nominated by the landscape architect but with an order placed directly with him by the main contractor.)

4.11.2 An alternative procedure is to measure all landscape work in the main bill and allow the general contractor to sub-let or otherwise arrange for the implementation of the work. This is a reasonable method for the landscape element in a contract which includes a high proportion of earth moving, paving and constructional items (such as retaining walls), which may be somewhat beyond the experience of the average landscape contractor. The general contractor should be required to have the planting work done by a specialist. This can be ensured by writing into the main contract a carefully selected short-list of landscape contractors from which the general contractor must choose his specialist sub-contractor for a clearly defined section of the work.

4.11.3 On sites where there is existing landscape work being maintained by a contractor or maintenance department, that contractor or department may be nominated as the sub-contractor for the new specialist work. As the sub-contractor will have to maintain the finished product, such arrangements often result in a high standard of workmanship.

4.11.4 The advantage of having the landscape element sub-let within the main contract is that its programming and dovetailing with the building work is under the direction of a general contractor, as are all sub-contracts.

4.11.4 (cont'd) However, care must be taken to ensure that the general contractor fully accepts his responsibility. In practice he is often reluctant to do so, especially since much landscape work is carried out at the end of the contract when everyone is thinking about the next job. It is particularly important to emphasise to general contractors the seasonal nature of landscape work, since it is seldom fully understood by a building contractor that a few weeks lost on the construction programme may result in a full season's postponement of the landscape sub-contract with ensuing financial problems and other difficulties.

4.11.5 Given the opportunity, the main contractor may soon disclaim the specialist skill needed for general or detailed organisation of landscape work and unreasonably divert the supervision and programming responsibility in its entirety to the landscape architect.

4.11.6 One disadvantage of the sub-contract procedure is that the settlement of the final account of the building or civil engineering contract may be delayed until the defects liability period of the landscape sub-contract has expired, usually at a much later date than the end of the building maintenance period. Nevertheless, this can be an extra incentive for the general contractor to see that the work is properly programmed and completed on time. As soft landscape work is largely seasonal, it is almost inevitable that it is not finished until many months after the main building work. Added to this is the problem of the defects liability period. This period is normally 6 months on a construction contract but for landscape work it must be at least 12 months. The completion of the sub-contract is thus extended until even further beyond the end of the main contract.

4.11.7 There is a satisfactory way round this situation. The main contractor has his final account settled by the employer at the end of his defects liability period and from this he also pays the landscape sub-contractor who has previously entered into a written indemnity or financial bond direct with the employer to cover the remainder of the sub-contract defects liability period. This can be taken a stage further by the sub-contractor signing a contract with the main contractor which includes a 6 months defects liability period and then signing another contract direct with the employer for a further 6 months. This becomes particularly useful if the contract includes for the sub-contractor to carry out physical maintenance (not just give a defects guarantee) for the whole of the defects liability period.

4.11.8 Difficulties can also occur over the delays in payment which may result when the landscape sub-contractor is paid through the main contractor instead of directly by the employer.

4.11.9 It must be clearly stated that the sub-contractor is not permitted to sub-let any part of the work without the prior written agreement of the landscape architect. This clause must be enforced, difficult though it is, if standards are to be kept under control.

4.12 CONTRACT MANAGEMENT AND SUPERVISION

4.12.1 Where a landscape architect is appointed, site visits will be required reasonably regularly during the course of the contract. Although impromptu visits can have advantages and the possibility of them occurring at any time may have a salutary effect on some contractors, it is better for site visits to be arranged in advance with the contractor. In this way the contractor's representative can be present to answer queries, to raise points requiring site decision and to give any necessary directions to operatives. On large schemes it is particularly desirable to have a competent clerk of works capable of supervising landscape work. Unless this is the case, the landscape architect can be burdened with an unreasonable degree of day to day supervision.

4.12.2 Where the landscape work is a sub-contract it is important that the clerk of works for the construction contract is briefed on the standards which need to be achieved on the landscape element. In many cases, the landscaping takes place when the main contractor's work is finished; by then the clerk of works may have left the site, leaving the sub-contractor without day-to-day supervision. Where the landscape element justifies it a landscape clerk of works should also be appointed.

4.12.3 With sub-contract work, special supervision arrangements need to be made. The landscape architect and specialist sub-contractor may have an informal working arrangement, acting directly and keeping the architect and general contractor informed of decisions made. Nevertheless formal contract responsibility for giving instructions will be vested with the architect or engineer to whom the landscape architect will be acting as consultant. The formal instructions must be given by the architect or engineer direct to the general contractor who must then instruct his sub-contractor without delay. The general contractor needs to be informed of the seasonal implications of landscape work and the serious consequences which can result at certain times of year if instructions are delayed on their way to the landscape sub-contractor. It can be seen that if the formal channels are used, a considerable period can elapse between a landscape architect advising the architect on the need for an instruction and that instruction being received by the operative on site. This emphasises the need for direct informal arrangements, wherever possible, mutually agreed by all the parties concerned. In some landscape work, weather and ground conditions can affect the standard which can reasonably be expected under the terms of the contract and judgement must be used on the standard to be required.

4.13 INSTRUCTIONS AND VARIATIONS

4.13.1 All instructions, including verbal site instructions, must be confirmed in writing immediately. It is desirable to use a standard instruction form (usually I.L.A. or R.I.B.A.) so that all instructions to the contractor

Drawing office practice and contract procedure

4.13.1 (cont'd) during the period of the contract are in a file of quick reference sheets. This eliminates the need for looking through correspondence files for information on instructions issued. Copies of the instruction forms will also go to the quantity surveyor who may not receive copies of all letters; the system will therefore speed up the pricing of variations and facilitate cost control and calculation of the final account.

4.13.2 Instructions should clarify a point or tell the contractor to proceed with some particular portion of the contract and should not involve any alteration in the contents or the price of the contract. An instruction which is also a variation order will instruct the contractor to omit, add or substitute some item and make the necessary financial adjustment.

4.13.3 Where appropriate, variations should refer to the original clause number in the bills of quantities or description of work/specification. It is useful for office purposes to note on the file copy the reason for the variation if it is not self-apparent. The file copy should also show whether the client needs to be informed if he is not on the regular circulation list. The pricing of all variations should be determined and agreed upon when the order is issued to avoid undue problems at the final account stage. Where a variation cannot be related to bill rates the extra work price should be agreed with the contractor and confirmed in a written quotation before the instruction is issued. This quotation should then be referred to in the instruction.

4.14 CERTIFICATES AND PAYMENTS

4.14.1 Interim certificates should be issued on a valuation based on the quantity surveyor's recommendation using the standard I.L.A. form or another certificate appropriate to the contract being used. On interim certificates there is normally a retention of 10% maximum, up to the limit of the retention fund, with half being released at the point of practical completion and the remainder when defects have been made good at the end of the defect liability period. The minimum sum for interim certificates is to be agreed between the parties.

4.15 COMPLETION AND HANDOVERS

4.15.1 When the contractor finishes all his work an inspection must take place so that a practical completion date can be ascertained and a formal notification issued by the landscape architect. This then allows for the release of half the retention monies and also establishes the date from which the defects liability period commences. In cases where the contractor is required under the contract to maintain his work physically throughout the defects liability period, the final handover to the employer does not take place until the clearance of defects has been carried out at the end of that period (usually not less than 12 months).

4.15.1 If, on the other hand, the contract includes only a guarantee during the
(*cont'd*) defects liability period and not full physical maintenance, (e.g. mowing, weeding, watering) then the final handover to the employer or his maintenance representative must take place when practical completion is achieved. In some cases the period of physical maintenance can be 2 or 3 years to ensure that the employer is handed a fully established scheme.

4.15.2 Handovers can be done by means of a letter but a full site inspection by all parties concerned is usually necessary so that a complete understanding of responsibilities is established. As landscape work is growing and organic and never static, delays in handover can cause difficult problems. Any such delay at the height of the growing season can result in lawns becoming hay fields and shrub beds being smothered with weeds.

4.15.3 Because of the seasonal nature of the work it is most convenient to time the handover in Autumn or Spring. However, there are many occasions when handovers cannot be simple clear-cut operations. The employer may, for instance, have to take over grassed areas after the contractor's first cut but before the tree planting specified in the contract has taken place. If at all possible, this sort of arrangement should be avoided so that divided or overlapping responsibilities do not occur. On large sites, especially those associated with extensive or phased building complexes (particularly housing schemes) there may be staged completions and handovers of buildings and landscaping. In these cases, where considerable complications may occur, it is vital that all the parties concerned: architect, main contractor, landscape subcontractor (where applicable), employer and maintenance staff, should be advised by the landscape architect, in writing, of the up-to-date division of maintenance responsibilities after each phased handover. The use of marked-up drawings is the best way of avoiding misunderstandings or demarcation disputes. In all cases, the parcels of land for handover should be as large as possible with all elements complete in each area. Where possible, they should be defined by physical boundaries or features. In some instances a reduction in the number of phased handovers can be achieved by the method of agreeing an 'average' date for practical completion. For instance a contract may have had the first areas completed six months before the last phase. If a practical completion date is set half-way through this period of time, at the end of 12 months defect liability period some portions will have been complete for 15 months and the rest for 9 months. If proper judgement is exercised this 'averaging system' can reduce the administrative work of everyone concerned and lead to a single clear-cut handover, without any loss of quality in the end product.

4.16 MAKING GOOD OF DEFECTS AND PERMANENT AFTER-CARE

4.16.1 Although inspections usually occur throughout the defects liability period a final inspection must take place at the end of the period. At this point the contractor will be instructed to remedy any final defects and replace any dead or unsatisfactory plants, unless these failures are the result of action by others, such as vandals. This remedial work, including plant replacements and re-seeding, will be undertaken at the contractor's own expense, as allowed in the contract.

4.16.2 Once this remedial work has been carried out satisfactorily and the employer has taken over the completed scheme, all maintenance and replacement work thereafter is the sole responsibility of the employer and his maintenance staff, unless he retains the contractor, after the handover, on a separate maintenance contract. This course of action is to be recommended since the constant need for good maintenance and after-care is not fully appreciated by many clients, including some local authorities. Their attention needs to be drawn to this critical aspect, if it is to be ensured that the newly planted scheme does not suffer from neglect after hand-over. Such neglect can result in large numbers of plant casualties, decline in grass quality and the eventual gradual disintegration of the design concept. Few clients realise the particular importance of watering and weeding in the first few years until plants are sufficiently established to withstand droughts and compete with and smother weeds.

4.17 FINAL ACCOUNT PROCEDURE

4.17.1 If a file of instruction orders (as mentioned in 4.13.1) has been kept throughout the course of the contract, the final account should be a simple matter of adding up the priced amendments on these forms and adjusting the original contract figure accordingly.

4.17.2 Adjustments in prime cost and provisional sums, dayworks and other such items will be settled by the quantity surveyor at this point. Any outstanding claims should also be considered and settled. Settlement will be made much easier for the quantity surveyor if the procedures recommended in 4.13.1-3 have been followed during the course of the contract.

4.17.3 When the final account has been agreed by the quantity surveyor, the contractor must sign it, confirming his acceptance and stating that he has no further claim under the contract. On receipt of the final account the landscape architect will issue a final certificate.

5 Specification

5.0 **INTRODUCTION**

5.0.1 Extracts from British Standards, as noted in the appropriate sub-sections, are reproduced by kind permission of the British Standards Institution from whom copies of the complete standards may be purchased. (B.S.I. 2 Park Street, London W1A 2BS.)

5.0.2 The British Standards and the other specification information are up to date at the time of going to press but where applicable a check should be made with the British Standards Institution or the relevant organisation or manufacturer on subsequent modifications.

5.0.3 The metric S.I. method of dimensioning is used throughout and where necessary, British Standards, manufacturers technical data and other sources of information have been converted to this system. It is anticipated that B.S.I. may revise B.S. 4428 to use centimetres in accordance with current continental horticultural practice but as this has not happened so far this book keeps consistently to the more satisfactory S.I. method.

5.1 PREPARATORY OPERATIONS

5.1.1 INTRODUCTION

5.1.1.1 The British Standard recommendations for preparatory operations are contained in B.S.4428:1969. The main part of this section of the standard is quoted here in full by kind permission of B.S.I. The quantities and dimensions have been converted to rounded metric equivalents; the clauses and paragraphs have been renumbered and the footnotes have been omitted.

5.1.1.2 The pricing of preliminary clauses varies from contract to contract and therefore it is not possible to provide meaningful figures against every item covered by the standard detailed later in this section. For this reason the pricing portion of Section 5.1 in Chapter 7 is very limited.

5.1.1.3 In certain circumstances where the British Standard recommendations may be thought to be insufficiently detailed, the specification/description of work can be amended to include some of the following alternative or additional items:

Site enclosure

Temporary fencing

5.1.1.4 Allow for providing temporary fencing if required to enclose any portion of the site during the carrying of the work with gates in same, as necessary; alter and adapt from time to time and remove at completion.

Existing Services

5.1.1.5 Notwithstanding any information which the landscape architect may make available to the contractor, either verbally or by the production of record plans purporting to show the position of existing water, gas, re-diffusion, electricity and Post Office mains, service connections, private pipelines, etc., it shall be the responsibility of the contractor to satisfy himself by his own independent observations and enquiries as to any omission from or the accuracy or otherwise of the information provided, in so far as it affects his contract area.

5.1.1.6 The contractor shall make all the necessary arrangements for the diversion, if necessary, of any such existing services required for the purpose of the contract or otherwise, and shall allow for upholding and temporarily supporting, repairing and maintaining any such services, if and as encountered during the progress of the works, pending the decision of the employer concerned as to their diversion or otherwise as may be appropriate. No scaffolding, props, staging, ropes, supports other than required for the temporary support of such services, shall be fixed or attached to them and the contractor

Specification—Preparatory operations

5.1.1.6 **Existing Services** *continued*
(*cont'd*) shall accept responsibility arising from the presence of such mains, cables, etc.

5.1.1.7 Any damage to services caused by the contractor or his sub-contractors in the course or in consequence of the contract operations shall be made good at the expense of the contractor.

5.1.1.8 In the event of existing works being disturbed through any cause whatsoever, the contractor shall immediately draw the landscape architect's attention, verbally, and subsequently in writing, to the nature of this disturbance in order that the employer may be informed forthwith.

Temporary Works

5.1.1.9 The contractor shall provide, maintain and remove on completion of the works all temporary works necessary for carrying out the contract, including roadways, sleeper tracks, stagings, etc., over roads, footpaths, cycle tracks, streams or unstable ground, fencing, hoardings, footways, guard rails, barriers, gantries and the like and shall make them safe and suitable in every respect to carry all plant required for the work or for providing access and to secure adequate protection of the public in their legal use of the adjacent paths, roads, pavements and buildings and to comply with the applicable by-laws, regulations or instructions of any authority concerned. All temporary works shall be constructed and maintained to the satisfaction of the landscape architect.

General protection and reinstatement

5.1.1.10 The contractor shall allow for safeguarding and protecting against damage due to the carrying out of the contract all existing and completed works (by others) on the site such as fences and gates, pavings, manhole covers and kerbs. In this connection the contractor should particularly note, when visiting the site, the width and construction of any existing carriageways and the nature and construction of any other existing works. The contractor will be held responsible for maintaining the nature of the existing verges, embankments, cuttings, terraces and the like. Should any damage or loss be caused to any existing or completed works due to or arising from the performance of the contract then the contractor will be required to reinstate and make good such damage or loss at his own expense and to the satisfaction of the landscape architect.

5.1.1.11 All fences, walls, footpaths, or other routes which may be injured during the execution of the work shall be properly restored to the satisfaction of the landscape architect, at the expense of the contractor.

5.1.1.12 The contractor shall avoid nuisance to neighbouring owners and occupiers by keeping the amount of noise to a minimum and confining it to reasonable hours. He shall also reduce the amount of

Specification—Preparatory operations

5.1.1.12 (cont'd) **General protection and reinstatement** *continued* dust by suitable timing of his operations and/or by keeping the site watered, as and when necessary.

5.1.1.13 Wherever ground is temporarily disturbed by the contractor during the course of his contract operations it shall be restored by him to its original state and form, or to such other appropriate state and form as shall be approved by the landscape architect.

Existing vegetation

Protection

5.1.1.14 No existing trees, shrubs or other plants shall be removed or cut without specific instructions. The landscape contractor shall take all precautions to protect, in the course of his work, all existing plant materials from malicious or accidental damage and shall ensure that no branches shall be lopped and no roots over 50 mm diameter shall be severed from growing trees, without express prior permission.

5.1.1.15 No soil, spoil, constructional materials or rubbish shall be stored or tipped within the spread of existing trees, shrubs or hedges and no bonfires shall be lit in any situation where they can cause damage to existing trees, shrubs or hedges. The landscape contractor must cover up and/or protect from injury from any cause, all new work, materials and plants. He must also supply any other requisite protection for the whole of the works executed, whether by himself or special tradesmen or sub-contractors and any damage caused must be made good by the landscape contractor at his own expense.

Remedial work and liability to damage

5.1.1.16 Should any tree which it is intended to preserve be uprooted, destroyed, or in the opinion of the landscape architect be damaged beyond reasonable chance of survival in its original shape due to the contractor's negligence, then the contractor shall without charge to the employer provide and plant suitable replacement trees or shrubs of a similar type and age. If such replacement trees or shrubs are not obtainable other trees or shrubs, selected by the landscape architect, shall be provided and planted. The contractor's liability shall continue until the replacement trees and shrubs have survived the winter following the planting and have completed satisfactorily the following summer's growth.

Vegetation to be cleared

5.1.1.17 When burning of vegetation is not permitted, all material is to be carried away to a tip provided by the contractor.

5.1.1.18 Felling shall be the complete removal of a tree, including the removal of the stump to a specified depth below ground by hand or machine hacking, grubbing out, or (in exceptional circumstances and with prior permission) burning. It shall include the chemical killing

5.1.1.18 (cont'd) **Vegetation to be cleared** continued
of any stump or roots remaining. It shall include the careful taking down in sections of any large trees in confined spaces, or near to buildings or to other trees which are to be retained.

5.1.1.19 Grubbing shall include the complete removal of tree stumps and roots over 100 mm dia. by hand or machine excavation, winching or other means. It shall include the chemical killing of any stump or roots which require such treatment.

5.1.1.20 Scrub clearance shall be the removal of scrub, bushes, undergrowth, saplings and seedlings from a specified area of the site by hand or mechanical means. It shall include the grubbing up of all stumps and root runs which can be taken out without undue removal of top soil. It shall be taken to include also the partial clearance of an area in which selected saplings, bushes, shrubs are to be retained. In such cases the selected plants to be preserved shall have been clearly marked or otherwise indicated on site.

Soil stripping
(see groundworks section for pricing of this operation)

5.1.1.21 Topsoil and sub-soil shall be stripped to a total depth of 900 mm and each stacked separately in the area directed by the landscape architect.

5.1.1.22 Topsoil shall be stacked in spoil heaps not more than 1.250 m high and shall not remain unused for more than 12 months unless work is undertaken to turn the soil over to prevent it becoming stale. Weed growth on topsoil heaps shall be controlled by mechanical or approved chemical means, to prevent soil becoming polluted with weed seeds.

Existing artifacts

Preservation of features

5.1.1.23 The contractor shall allow for taking all reasonable and necessary precautions to safeguard existing features. He shall make good at his own expense and reinstate or restore to the satisfaction of the landscape architect, any damage done to existing structures, paths, fences and natural features on or off the site, in the course of executing the contract.

Materials for possible re-use

5.1.1.24 Any stone, brick, clay paviors, granite setts or other surfacing materials shall be taken up, wheeled and stacked on site for possible re-use. No such materials, at whatever stage they are found, shall be removed from the site without written permission from the landscape architect.

Materials arising from site works

5.1.1.25 Should suitable sand, gravel, hardcore or aggregate be found in the excavations, the landscape architect may require the contractor to use the same in the works in substitution for materials the contractor would otherwise have provided. In this event the material shall be paid for by the contractor at an agreed price.

5.1.1.26 The employer reserves the right to dispose of any surplus sand, gravel, hardcore, aggregate or topsoil in any way he wishes, or to direct the contractor to deal with it as ordinary excavated material for disposal on site.

Rubbish

5.1.1.27 All rubbish including that of sub-contractors and special tradesmen, is to be immediately cleared and carted away as it accumulates during the progress of the contract. At completion the site is to be left in a clean and tidy condition. All materials condemned by the landscape architect are to be removed immediately at the contractor's own expense.

5.1.1.28 The contractor shall be responsible for providing a temporary tip and for meeting all costs arising therefrom.

5.1.1.29 No temporary spoil or rubbish heaps are to be formed over the rooting area of trees or shrubs.

5.1.1.30 The location and timing of the burning of rubbish in bonfires shall be subject to the landscape architect's approval. Bonfires shall not be situated on the windward side of trees nor any closer than 18.000 m to the outmost spread of tree branches.

5.1.2 B.S.4428:1969 RECOMMENDATIONS ON PREPARATORY OPERATIONS

Site enclosure

5.1.2.1 All fencing should be maintained in good and effective condition until the work is completed. The type of fencing used will depend on a number of factors, e.g. the location of the site, the likelihood of trespass and pilfering by children or others, and the degree of danger to persons accidentally trespassing. Urban sites are more likely to need protection than rural ones, and in some cases the latter may not need fencing at all. The following types of fence are considered suitable:

(A) 1.200 m to 1.800 m cleft chestnut fencing complying with B.S.1722, Part 4.

(B) 1.200 m to 2.100 chain link fencing complying with B.S.1722, Part 1.

Specification—Preparatory operations

Existing services

5.1.2.2 The location of all service runs, such as water supply, gas, electricity (overhead or underground), telephones and drainage should be ascertained before work is started and marked upon a plan, giving position, size and depth. Where they will be affected by excavation, or where machines may be working nearby, they should be carefully sealed off, protected or diverted. In most cases it will be necessary to obtain the approval and assistance of the statutory undertakings and local authorities concerned.

Existing vegetation

Protection

5.1.2.3 Where work is carried out near existing vegetation whch is to be retained it should be protected from damage with 1.200 m cleft chestnut fencing or similar. This should be maintained in good and effective condition until the work is completed. Fencing to protect trees should coincide, as far as is practicable, with the spread of the branches, or in the case of fastigate trees with a radius of half the height of the tree. Materials should never be stacked within the root spread of trees. Normal maintenance should be carried out within fenced areas during the execution of the work. Areas of grass to be cut for turf should be treated during the growing period with weed-killer and should be kept well mown before lifting. Where work is done by contract, a penalty clause should be inserted to cover damage done to trees and shrubs.

Remedial work

5.1.2.4 Existing plants and grass included in the landscape plan which have been neglected, should be restored to a healthy condition, and shapely habit. Accidental damage which occurs during the execution of the work should be carefully repaired. Tree work is described in B.S.3998.

Preparation for moving

5.1.2.5 Trees and large shrubs which are to be transplanted normally require preparation some time in advance. Advice on this subject is given in B.S.4043. Turf to be stripped for use elsewhere should be left in situ and not lifted until the site on which it is to be laid has been prepared; the area of turf to be lifted should be divided into parallel strips 300 mm wide with a half-moon edging iron or turf racer. Each strip is then divided in the same way into suitable lengths (usually 1.000 m) for lifting with a turf lifting iron. Alternatively, for larger areas, turf may be cut with a turf cutting machine. The aim should be to produce a turf 25 mm or 40 mm thick, and of even thickness throughout. If hand lifting, it is better to take up a thicker turf which can subsequently be reduced in thickness in a turf gauge box. The turves can then be rolled or folded and stacked ready for moving.

Vegetation to be cleared

5.1.2.6 Long grass and weeds should be cut, and trees, hedges and other plants not required should be cleared and the roots grubbed out. The material

Specification—Preparatory operations

5.1.2.6 **Vegetation to be cleared** *continued*
(*cont'd*) arising should be burned clear of existing trees and the ash spread on site, or carted away if burning is not permitted (or practicable). Clearance of tree stumps is described in B.S.3998.

Stripping
5.1.2.7 In certain cases it is necessary to strip the topsoil. This will occur when the area is to be occupied by buildings, roads or other hard surfaces, when major changes of level are required, or when the soil is likely to suffer damage from building or engineering activities. In such cases the full depth of topsoil should be carefully stripped and strict precautions taken to prevent it becoming mixed with subsoil or other deleterious materials. While topsoil is stacked, measures should be taken to ensure that weed control by spraying with total or appropriate selective weedkillers is carried out during the growing season to prevent weeds seeding. Alternatively the appearance of the heap may be improved, and weeds suppressed by sowing a short term crop of Italian rye grass. (See groundworks section for pricing of soil stripping).

Existing artifacts

To be retained
5.1.2.8 If work is to be undertaken close to existing buildings, paved areas and special structures to be retained, they should be protected from damage with 1.200 m cleft chestnut fencing complying with B.S.1722 Part 4.

Materials for re-use
5.1.2.9 Before starting demolition, any stone, brick, clay tiles, paving slabs, granite setts or other materials suitable for re-use should be carefully taken up and stacked on site until required or removed by agreement.

Demolition
5.1.2.10 Buildings, walls, roads, foundations, disused drains, manholes and any other construction not required should then be demolished and removed to the following minimum depths below finished levels:

Grass areas	450 mm
Ground cover perennial planting areas	450 mm
Shrub planting areas	600 mm
Tree planting (within 2.000 m of tree station)	900 mm

All unwanted material should be carted off the site. Below the depths given, concrete slabs or other impervious layers should be broken up to allow free drainage. When subsoiling and drainage operations are to be carried out involving depths below those mentioned above, then consideration should be given to the need to demolish to lower levels.

Rubbish
5.1.2.11 All rubbish should be collected and disposed of either by burning 10.000 m clear of the spread of existing trees or any areas to be grassed down, or by carting off site.

5.2 GROUNDWORKS

5.2.1 INTRODUCTION

5.2.1.1 The British Standard recommendations for topsoil are contained in B.S.3882:1965 and the recommendations for groundworks in B.S.4428:1969. The main sections of both these standards are quoted here in full by kind permission of B.S.I. The quantities and dimensions have been converted to rounded metric equivalents, the clauses and paragraphs have been renumbered and footnotes and diagrams have been omitted.

5.2.1.2 The British Standard on topsoil is preceded by a number of clauses related to topsoil and groundworks which, in certain circumstances, might be used as alternatives or as additions to the B.S. clauses quoted later in this section. All parts of this section which can be priced are covered in the relevant part of Chapter 7. Additional or alternative clauses follow:

Excavations

Records and preparations

5.2.1.3 Before any excavations are commenced the contractor shall carry out and record a check level grid of the site and shall agree with the landscape architect the existing ground levels. These levels shall be marked on a plan and signed by the landscape architect and contractor before the work is commenced.

5.2.1.4 The contractor must satisfy himself as to the nature of the ground to be excavated and the conditions of the site, as prices for excavation are deemed to include for digging in any sub-soil, with the exception of hard rock which can only be removed by means of explosives, compressed air plant or wedges.

5.2.1.5 Claims in respect of excavations through brick, stone, or concrete foundations or rock will be considered when they occur in bulk, but claims in respect of loose intermittent quantities of less volume than 0.5 m^3 will not be allowed, and allowance must be made in the rates for normal excavation for grubbing up same and also for grubbing up redundant sewers, drains, debris, rubble, etc.

5.2.1.6 Rates for excavation are to include for the breaking up, as necessary, and the removal by either hand or machine, for all necessary planking and strutting and for keeping all excavation free from water and falling soil.

Running silt or sand

5.2.1.7 Additional payment for excavating in running silt or running sand and for planking and strutting extending into running silt or running

Specification–Groundworks

5.2.1.7
(cont'd)
Running silt or sand continued
sand shall only be made where the ground conditions are such that material from the sides of the excavation runs in, or but for the planking and strutting would run in, as the excavation work is being carried out. No payment will be made where ground conditions have deteriorated as a result of excavations being left open.

Rock

5.2.1.8
Additional payment for excavating in rock shall be made only in respect of rock found in ledges or masses in its original position which would normally have to be loosened either by blasting or by pneumatic tools or if excavated by hand, by wedges and sledge hammers. All solid boulders or detached pieces of rock exceeding 100 mm^3 in size in trenches or exceeding 200 mm^3 in size in general excavation, but not otherwise shall be regarded as rock.

Blasting

5.2.1.9
Blasting shall not be allowed without written permission from the landscape architect, who shall be fully informed by the contractor as to the steps taken to safeguard the surrounding property, and the contractor shall take all responsibility for any damage or annoyance caused by reason of blasting and give all notices etc., required to the Police and any other Statutory Authorities.

Bulking

5.2.1.10
The contractor's attention is drawn to the fact that all measurement of excavation and subsequent disposal are net measurements and he shall allow in his prices for increase in bulk and for transporting excavated material to and from temporary spoil heaps as may be necessary.

Grading

5.2.1.11
The contractor is to grade and cross grade over site, (on areas filled by others) to achieve final grades. All finished gradients are to be smooth-flowing marrying with all existing levels, eliminating all abrupt angles and changes of levels. All earth shaping works are to be carried out in consultation with the landscape architect on site. Minor fillings and excavations are to be made as necessary to bring the grass and planting areas into running levels between paths and kerbs.

5.2.1.12
The landscape contractor shall grade the site to levels and contours in accordance with the grading and contour drawings and shall be responsible for setting up correct level pegs and profiles.

5.2.1.13
The landscape contractor shall include for loading and depositing surplus sub-soil on site, or importing approved fill to be spread in layers not exceeding 150 mm consolidated. The grading shall be

5.2.1.13 (cont'd)	**Grading** continued evenly carried out to 100 mm below finished level to all falls and gradients eliminating all depressions and mounds by using machinery suitable to the physical condition of the existing soil.
5.2.1.14	**Topsoil & topsoiling** Topsoil shall be clean and the contractor must allow for removing all stones and alien materials, perennial weeds, roots and any other plant matter. Imported topsoil to be from an approved source obtained from top 150 mm of ground. It shall be fertile with a humus and fibre content and be of medium texture, and approved by the landscape architect before use.
5.2.1.15	As topsoiling proceeds all consolidated wheel tracks shall be forked over.
5.2.1.16	Any topsoil brought on to site without approval will be deemed to have been brought in at the contractor's risk and he will be instructed to cart such topsoil off the site at his own expense unless instructions to the contrary be given in writing.
5.2.1.17	Final grading of the top 150 mm is to be carried out to ensure a true specified level and slope and to avoid dishing or other depressions where water may collect. The use of a heavy roller to roll out humps will not be permitted and any area that becomes unduly compacted during the grading operation shall be loosened by forking or harrowing.
5.2.1.18	Following blade grading apply soil ameliorants as directed. These shall be separately and evenly applied and shall be thoroughly worked in the topsoil.
5.2.1.19	The level of the topsoil is to be at least 50 mm above all paved areas to allow for shrinkage and/or settlement.
5.2.1.20	**Cultivation** Over all landscape areas shown as grass and planting, the contractor is to cultivate the ground to a minimum depth of 150 mm, bring to a fine tilth and regulate to evenly running levels. Clear out all weeds, large stones, broken brick, concrete, perennial weeds and weed roots, etc., and cart to shoot.
5.2.1.21	All planting areas are to be cultivated by hand digging to a minimum depth of 300 mm and cleaned free of weeds and rubbish. Any excessive hand excavation found to be necessary shall be measured and agreed by the landscape architect or his representative at the time.
5.2.1.22	The contractor shall include in his tender price for carrying out any necessary cultivation from time to time, as and when instructed by

Specification—Groundworks

5.2.1.22
(cont'd)
Cultivation *continued*
the landscape architect, to destroy all weed growth if, owing to the time of year, weather, or other causes, there is a period of waiting between completion of the topsoiling works as specified and the actual seeding or planting operations.

Stone picking

5.2.1.23 Clear from surface all stones with one dimension greater than 38 mm. Load into lorries and haul to tip provided by contractor.

Peat

5.2.1.24 All peat used as an additive to the soil or as a mulch shall conform to B.S.4156:1967. It shall be procured from an approved source, be dark brown in colour, free from rubbish and, when requested, the landscape contractor shall retain for the landscape architect's inspection a marked package or bale container.

Manure and compost

5.2.1.25 All manure or compost used as an additive to the soil or as a mulch shall be procured from an approved source and the landscape contractor shall notify the landscape architect of the material content he proposes to use before carting to the site.

5.2.1.26 Manure shall be farmyard cow manure with a minimum admixture of straw. Compost shall consist of decomposed and semi-decomposed herbaceous and deciduous vegetation. Each must have been conditioned in storage piles for not less than 2 years, be moderately moist but not water-logged and of a short texture. No compost to be used which has a grass clipping content exceeding 25%.

5.2.1.27 Spent mushroom compost may be used as a mulch or as a topsoil admix at the discretion of the landscape architect. Poultry manure, however, will not be allowed.

Chemical fertilizers and sprays

5.2.1.28 Chemical fertilizers and sprays are to be used only where specified and measured. They shall conform in every respect to the mixture required and be applied strictly in accordance with the manufacturers' instructions. All chemicals are to be used and distributed under the direct supervision of the foreman and it is to be understood that any damage caused by excess or drift will be made good at the contractors' expense.

5.2.1.29 All chemicals used shall be non-toxic to human beings, birds and animals under normal use and only chemicals on the 'Agricultural Chemicals Approval Scheme' current list of approved products may be used.

Chemical fertilizers and sprays *continued*

5.2.1.30 Apply fertiliser at the rate of 70 g per m^2 and incorporate into the ground by roughly raking.

5.2.2 B.S.3882:1965, RECOMMENDATIONS AND CLASSIFICATION FOR TOPSOIL

Scope

5.2.2.1 This British Standard describes some of the requirements for topsoil for general landscape work purposes. It also classifies topsoil in relation to three particular characteristics, texture, reaction (lime content) and stone content, which it may sometimes be desirable to specify fairly closely. It is primarily concerned with topsoil as dug which is to be imported on to a site.

Appendix A gives notes on some relevant methods of test for topsoil. Appendix B lists the information to be given for the purpose of an order or an enquiry.

Definitions

5.2.2.2 For the purposes of this British Standard the definitions given in B.S.3975 apply.

In addition for the purposes of this British Standard the following definition applies:

Stone. Any hard inorganic particle larger than 2 mm that cannot be readily broken down by washing with water.

Description of topsoil

5.2.2.3 Topsoil is the original surface layer of grassland or cultivated land. It does not generally include soil from woodland, heathland, moorland, bog or other special areas such as land impaired by industrial activity. It should not contain an excessive amount of weed seeds or roots of perennial weeds.

It is usually a darker shade of brown, grey or red than the subsoil that lies immediately beneath it, because it contains organic matter intimately mixed with the mineral matter. Adequate organic matter is essential to the fertility of a soil. Topsoil tends to be friable and shows some degree of porosity. It should be free from subsoil.

Such soil should be a suitable material for growing the ordinary range of grasses and cultivated plants under satisfactory conditions of management. It should be borne in mind, however, that an inherently favourable topsoil may be deficient in one or more of the essential elements of plant food but that this can usually be easily corrected by the use of appropriate fertilizers.

For certain specialized purposes, or for cultivation of a more intensive nature, it may be desirable to specify the topsoil more precisely. It will normally be sufficient to do this for three important characteristics—the texture, the lime content and the stone content.

Texture
5.2.2.4 The texture of topsoil, that is to say its lightness (coarseness) or heaviness (fineness) depends upon the proportions of particles of different sizes which it contains. It will be governed by the proportion of clay, silt and sand, and by the proportions of particles of different sizes in the silt and sand fractions. Topsoil complying with the description in Clause 5.2.2.3 may be classified according to its texture as follows:

Light
5.2.2.5 Topsoil containing a high proportion of sand. It may be possible to mould it when moist, but it will lack cohesion and fall apart easily.

Medium
5.2.2.6 Topsoil containing a high proportion of loamy material. It can be easily moulded when moist, but is not very sticky and does not leave a smooth polished surface when smeared.

Heavy
5.2.2.7 Topsoil containing a high proportion of clay. It is sticky when moist and leaves a smooth, polished surface when smeared.

Soil reaction
5.2.2.8 The pH of a soil is a convenient measure of its reaction, which is related to the presence or absence of calcium carbonate (lime). It gives a measure of the acidity or alkalinity of the soil.

5.2.2.9 Topsoil complying with the description in Clause 5.2.2.3 may be classified according to its reaction as follows:

	pH
Acid	less than 6.0
Slightly acid to neutral	6.0−7.0
Slightly alkaline	7.0−7.5
Alkaline	more than 7.5

Under exceptional circumstances topsoils occur of such extreme acidity that even normally calcifuge plants fail upon them; even for these plants it is unwise to use a topsoil with a pH of lower than 4.0. A number of plants suffer from the deficiency of iron, manganese and other elements in calcareous soil, but there are many others that grow perfectly healthily in such soil.

Stone content
5.2.2.10 In many localities the soils are stony and it is not easy to obtain topsoil free from stones. Stones are generally inert (although fragments of chalk or soft limestone may not be) so provided they are not present in excessive quantity, they will not be harmful to most plants (some root vegetables must be grown in relatively stone-free soils); large stones may, however, be damaging to implements and machinery, and may

Specification—Groundworks

5.2.2.10 (cont'd) **Stone content** *continued*
also be undesirable on playing fields. It is important to bear in mind that any plants to be grown upon the topsoil will obtain their living from the material in which the stones occur; the texture and other characteristics of this material must receive the same scrutiny as it would if there were no stones present.

Normally, up to 20 per cent of stones by dry weight is acceptable. Even on playing fields a well-managed grass sward will soon bury stones.

5.2.2.11 Topsoil complying with the description in Clause 5.2.2.3 may be classified according to its stone content as follows:

Classification	Percentage of stones by dry weight
Stone-free	less than 1
Slightly stony	1—5
Stony	5—20
Very stony	20—50
Extremely stony	Over 50

Size of stones

5.2.2.12 For ordinary purposes stones of a size up to 50 mm in any dimension are acceptable. Topsoil containing many stones of a larger size will involve the labour of picking up those at the surface.

Appendix A: Notes on methods of test for topsoil

A.1. Sampling for texture and lime content

5.2.2.13 In nature the undisturbed soil may in some places show a great deal of variation in character within very short distances; topsoil imported to a site may therefore vary likewise. This means that samples collected for examination must be carefully taken and must be adequate in number, if serious errors are to be avoided.

The method of sampling generally practised in the field is to take twenty-five cores, 25 mm in diameter, with a screw auger to a depth of 150 mm, or to the bottom of the layer of cultivation, whichever is less, and to mix these together thoroughly to make the sample. In no circumstances should one sample refer to an area greater than 4 hectares, while, if there is any visible variation in the nature of the topsoil of different parts of the site, it may be desirable to sample each separately. Naturally, if consignments of topsoil are to be sampled after their removal from their place of occurrence, the method employed must be dictated by the circumstances. The difficulty of defining soil-sampling procedure is well recognized and is referred to in paragraph 3.1 on page 28 of the 'Official Methods of Analysis of the Association of Official Agricultural Chemists', 8th Edition, 1955.

A2. Determination of texture

5.2.2.14 A simple procedure for the assessment of the texture of topsoil is described in Clauses 5.2.2.4-7. Where further information is required it

Specification–Groundworks

5.2.2.14 **A2. Determination of texture** continued
(cont'd) will be necessary to resort to a laboratory method; in this case Test 6 (C): Standard method of fine analysis (pipette method), of B.S. 1377 is recommended.

A3. Determination of soil reaction
5.2.2.15 A precise determination of the reaction of topsoil requires the use of an electrometric method in the laboratory. The method described in Test 9 (A): Standard method (electrometric), in Section Three: Determination of the pH value of soil, of B.S. 1377 is recommended.

Test 9 (B) of B.S. 1377 describes a colorimetric method which gives a rough indication of the reaction of topsoil.

A4. Sampling for stone content
5.2.2.16 The proportion of stones in topsoil may vary very greatly within very short distances; it is therefore essential that an adequate number of samples should be subjected to examination. The size of the individual stones and the texture of the topsoil must have a considerable bearing upon the weight of sample to be taken.

A5. Determination of stone content
5.2.2.17 The stone content of topsoil may be determined by the method described in Test 6 (A): Standard method of coarse analysis by wet sieving, in Section Six: Determination of the particle size distribution in soils, of B.S. 1377.

The method described in Test 6 (B): Standard method of coarse analysis by dry sieving, of B.S. 1377 may be used where the sample to be tested does not contain an appreciable amount of clay, i.e. where the sample is light topsoil as described in Clause 5.2.2.5.

Appendix B

Information to be supplied with an enquiry or order for topsoil
5.2.2.18 For the purpose of an enquiry or an order for topsoil, the following information should be given:
(a) Quantity required in cubic metres or tonnes.
(b) The number of this British Standard, i.e. B.S. 3882.
(c) Class of texture, if required.
(d) Class of acidity or alkalinity (lime content), if required.
(e) Acceptable classes of stone content, if required.
(f) Any requirements as to the maximum size of stones.

For example: 100 m^3 of medium, slightly acid, not more than stony, topsoil B.S. 3882.

Specification—Groundworks

5.2.3 B.S. 4428:1969 GROUNDWORKS
(from Recommendations for general landscape operations)

Synopsis of operations required

5.2.3.1 Depending on circumstances one of the following categories of groundworks will be necessary:
Category A. Surface cultivations only.
Category B. Surface cultivations, and regulating by minor grading within the topsoil depth.
Category C. Minor grading involving adjustment of local high and low spots.
Category D. Major grading after removal of all topsoil.

Gradients desirable

5.2.3.2 Maximum gradients are often limited by soil type, but where there is freedom to design, the following should be considered.

In ground shaping and modelling

5.2.3.3 When grass cutting on banks it is essential that the operators should be fully experienced.

Maximum gradient for hand maintenance	1:1 (45°)
,, ,, ,, small machines	1:1½ (33°)
,, ,, ,, special bank machines	1:2 (27°)
,, ,, ,, suitable tractor-drawn mowers	1:3 (18°)

In sports fields

5.2.3.4 For general playing pitches an absolutely horizontal area is not necessary and indeed may lead to serious drainage difficulties. A uniform fall of 1:80 (0°43') is perhaps ideal but gradients of up to 1:50 need not be adjusted provided they are even. In hilly or rocky districts even steeper gradients may be inevitable, though it should be recognised that a reasonable standard of play without undue fatigue will not be possible with a gradient which exceeds 1:40 (1°25').

Site investigations before operations

5.2.3.5 Before carrying out any physical investigation consult:
(A) Geological and/or soil survey maps for a general indication of the drift or soil type.
(B) All statutory undertakings and local authorities for the presence of underground apparatus.

Topsoil

5.2.3.6 The following enquiries and investigations are desirable:
(A) Ascertain depths over entire site, e.g. by setting out a grid at, say, 30.000 m centres and determining depths by hand auger or spade.
(B) Carry out tests for pH, chemical, physical and biological conditions. The facilities of the Agricultural Development and Advisory Service, local Farm Institutes, the Sports Turf Research Institute and private consultants should be used to pinpoint deficiencies, if they appear to exist.

Subsoil

5.2.3.7 Inspection should be carried out to 750 mm below the level of lowest excavation by one or more of the following methods:

(A) Hand auger: In moist clays and soils free from stones, auger sizes 37 mm to 225 mm diameter (depths below about 4.500 m in the larger auger sizes are difficult).

(B) Tractor-mounted diggers: Tractor-mounted diggers can excavate open pit inspection pits down to 4.800 m, in all soils except rock.

(C) Mounted mechanical augers: Mounted mechanical augers may be used for samples down to 9.000 m in soils free from rock and boulders, though with some difficulty in dry, sandy soils; auger sizes 225 mm to 900 mm diameter.

(D) Mechanical drilling rigs: mechanical drilling rigs are used by specialist firms especially for samples below 10.000 m.

(E) Hand excavations: Compared to the above mechanical methods, hand digging, especially below 1.500 m, is very expensive.

It is generally unnecessary to examine the subsoil at the same intervals as the topsoil if conditions are expected to be uniform. Special techniques are required when undisturbed samples are required. Methods of testing are described in B.S. 1377.

Recording

5.2.3.8 Results of investigation into the soil should be logged by means of a vertical diagram, giving:
(A) Ground level to Ordnance Datum.
(B) Depth and description of usable topsoil.
(C) Depths and types of subsoil layers.
(D) Level of water table or zone of saturation.

Drainage investigations
(see 5.3)

Other investigations

5.2.3.9 The proportion of sand, soil and clay at about 700 mm should be determined by mechanical analysis and the results should be shown as described in B.S. 1377.

5.2.3.10 Areas of rock should be plotted as far as possible by additional trial borings.

5.2.3.11 An estimate should be made of the proportion of stone in the topsoil. (see B.S. 3882)

5.2.3.12 Observations and tests may be necessary to determine the permeability of the soil and subsoil for drainage purposes.

5.2.3.13 Access for heavy machinery (especially those which are on tracks) and low loaders must be determined; temporary roads on the site should be marked.

Other investigations *continued*

5.2.3.14 The position and depth of all underground apparatus on the site should be verified, marked and, if necessary, exposed.

Work near trees

5.2.3.15 Ploughing and ripping should not be carried out within the branch spread of trees to be retained.

Category A; land requiring surface cultivation only

5.2.3.16 Generally all land which is to be maintained by mowing machinery should be surface graded either by hand raking or by graders as described in this section. Where the surface is to be left rough and not mown, as in agricultural conditions, the following methods of work are applicable; however, precise cultivations cannot be recommended for all sites.

Methods of work

5.2.3.17 Grub out unwanted trees and scrub and where land is covered with a thick sward, break up the soil by ploughing to the full depth of the topsoil, using an implement with a digger-type body to turn and break the furrow slice.

5.2.3.18 Where ground is hard, break up with ripper; the same implement may be used to expose large roots and boulders.

5.2.3.19 Where land has been in arable cultivation and contains few weeds and no sward, it may conveniently be disc-ploughed or rotary cultivated, provided the implement is capable of reaching the full depth of topsoil.

5.2.3.20 Cultivate topsoil with rigid tine cultivator and fixed tine harrow to break up furrow slices.

5.2.3.21 Thereafter harrow with rigid tooth implements to further break down the soil.

5.2.3.22 Where trees and scrub have been cleared, cultivate with root rake as required to remove roots.

5.2.3.23 Rake out tufts of grass and rubbish with harrows and collect and burn them.

5.2.3.24 Where there is evidence of impeded drainage, the desirability of sub-soiling should be considered. It is normally most economical to draw the sub-soiler at centres equal to twice the depth of cultivation, e.g. at 1.200 m centres to a depth of 600 mm.

5.2.3.25 Remove large stones, spread soil ameliorants and additives.

Specification—Groundworks

Category B; minor grading or regulating

Definition

5.2.3.26 Minor grading or regulating may be defined as the formation of true running contours by blade grading and movement of soil within the depth of topsoil. It is important to gauge the depth of the topsoil on high places beforehand; cover may be as little as 75 mm to 100 mm and minor grading is not practicable unless some 150 mm of soil or more is available. Hollows should preferably be filled with soil by tipping.

Methods of work

5.2.3.27 After removing scrub and trees, break up turf or sward by plough or disc-harrow (or in hard conditions by ripper) and where trees have been removed pass a root rake through the soil to collect roots.

5.2.3.28 Fill and reconsolidate hollows preparatory to grading.

5.2.3.29 Reduce topsoil throughout a suitable depth (at least 150 mm) to a tilth suitable for blade grading, by cultivations with discs and rotary cultivator, rigid tine cultivators, clod crushers or scrubbers. The resultant soil condition to be such that the particles are small and dry enough (from dust to about 10 mm) to run freely with the blade grader.

5.2.3.30 For areas 0.2 hectares and over, blade grade with one of the following types of rigid blade graders, adjustable for tilt, pitch and angle.
(A) Grader trailed or hydraulically controlled from wheeled or crawler tractors.
(B) Motor road grader, fixed unit.
(C) Earth levelling blade to wheeled tractor, rear mounted.

Category C; minor grading involving adjustment of local high and low spots.

5.2.3.31 To discover the extent of work required it is essential to use boring rods between satisfactory points and areas, and to plot the high and low spots to determine their extent and estimate volumes.

5.2.3.32 Proceed with cultivations if required as in Category A until the topsoil is in a condition to be removed.

5.2.3.33 Strip off topsoil from areas to be adjusted and set aside.

5.2.3.34 Reduce high areas and fill low areas using machinery as specified in Category D.

5.2.3.35 Return topsoil to stripped areas.

5.2.3.36 Subsoil if necessary. Grade and cultivate as described in 5.2.3.24.

5.2.3.37 Grade and cultivate as described.

Category D; major grading

Definition

5.2.3.38 Major grading is defined as a method of adjusting contours when final levels can only be obtained by removal of topsoil and grading/regulating/excavating into the sub-soil beneath.

Calculations of earth works

5.2.3.39 In the interests of economy the quantities of earth to be moved must be calculated. This is necessary for:
   (A) Arriving at accurate finished levels.
   (B) Deciding, in the light of the amounts, the type of machinery to be used.
   (C) Avoiding unnecessary removal or importation of soil.

5.2.3.40 Drawings for major ground works should show spot levels on a grid system as well as 300 mm contours (shown by dotted lines); grids can be from 6.000 m to 30.000 m centres.

5.2.3.41 Calculations should generally be made on quantities measured in the solid excluding bulking, particularly if earth is to be moved and laid down as mentioned below by tractor-drawn scrapers, as the weight of such machines is generally sufficient to return most soils to about their original volume. If earth is tipped and left to consolidate, the bulking factor could be considerable for cohesive soil dug dry, and subsequent sinkage should be taken into account. For material such as hard chalk and other rock, the volume increase should be investigated and allowed for.

5.2.3.42 Careful calculations in the balance of cut and fill will ensure that there is no surplus or deficit of material. It has generally been found possible to arrive at the finished levels to within 75 mm of the calculated level, but much depends upon the moisture content and consolidation of the fill. It is recommended that measurements for groundworks should be calculated in the solid from the drawing. Any excess or deficit of soil, due to bulking, can usually be accommodated by raising or lowering the finished levels by an equal amount over the whole area, thus maintaining the same gradients. If precise formation levels (closer than 75 mm) are required, they should be so specified.

Methods of work

5.2.3.43 Provide catchment drains or ditches to collect excessive run-off and prevent water entering from adjacent land.

5.2.3.44 Remove scrub as well as top growth by cutting and burning. Flail or swipe mowers can be used.

5.2.3.45 Where turf is excessively thick, plough, disc harrow, and reduce vegetative content by weathering and cultivations.

Specification—Groundworks

Methods of work *continued*

5.2.3.46 When soil is in a condition for stacking, remove all topsoil to its full depth (in contract work this must be specified by depth) and place it in heaps either off site in a convenient position, or on the neutral line of cut and fill. Strict precautions are essential to prevent loss or admixture with sub-soil.

Soil heaps should be formed in positions which facilitate eventual respreading, reduce travel to a minimum and will not result in interference with subsequent major levelling and/or grading operations.

While topsoil is stacked measures should be taken to ensure that weed control by spraying with total or appropriate selective weedkillers is carried out during the growing season to prevent weeds seeding. Alternatively heaps may be sown with a short term crop of Italian rye grass.

5.2.3.47 Set out convenient profiles for contours and finished levels.

Major excavation by earth-moving machines

5.2.3.48 Track-laying tractor and scraper. A track-laying tractor and scraper is capable of both excavating and transporting the material, and can in certain materials, and where suitably routed, give a considerable degree of compaction in the fill without the use of any other compacting equipment. It is suitable for use in the softer materials, but can be used for harder materials if the material to be excavated is first scarified or broken up with a rooter, or with the help of a booster. It may become uneconomic to use this type of tractor and scraper for lengths of haul over about 540.000 m. (graph from the original B.S. omitted).

5.2.3.49 Wheeled tractor and scraper. A wheeled tractor and scraper is capable of excavating the same material as the track-laying tractor and scraper, but may require a booster for loading as the wheeled tractor may be unable to load its scraper without the help of a track-laying tractor pushing behind. The wheeled tractor and scraper travels very much more quickly and can therefore be used for distances greater than those which are economic for the track-laying tractor and scraper. Generally, it is economic for distances of up to about two miles, provided that the transport route is suitably maintained for wheeled vehicles. Scrapers, whether operated by track-laying or wheeled tractors are capable of producing a reasonably smooth finish to the bottom of the excavations.

5.2.3.50 Bulldozer and angle dozer. Bulldozers and angle dozers are primarily designed for spreading and levelling operations, but are also used for back filling and excavating shallow cuttings. They will work satisfactorily in soft or loose materials, provided the tracks will grip. The usual length of push does not normally exceed 30.000 m to 60.000 m. (Bulldozer capacity diagram omitted).

5.2.3.51 Lorries/dumpers and other rubber-tyred vehicles. Lorries/dumpers and other rubber-tyred vehicles fed by one of the following:
  (A) General purpose excavator   (C) Dragline
  (B) Face shovel   (D) Back acting or drag shovel

Major excavation by earth-moving machines continued

5.2.3.52 The use of heavy rubber tyred vehicles should be governed by weather conditions. Compaction of soil beneath wheels during excessively wet conditions can have a deleterious effect upon soil structure which it may not be possible to correct. Tracked vehicles exert less compaction and are to be preferred. For effect of compaction upon subsequent drainage see section 5.3.

Consolidation

5.2.3.53 Sub-soil should be placed in layers not exceeding 150 mm thick; consolidation of fill may be accomplished by the use of special compacting machinery or by running over it with the next load; filling by tipping over an exposed face is not recommended because of the difficulty of consolidation. Where consolidation is difficult and critical, refer to CP 2003.

Banks

5.2.3.54 Recommendations concerning the angles at which safe slopes may be cut and embankments formed in rock are set out in CP 2003.

5.2.3.55 Recommendations concerning the angles at which non-cohesive and cohesive soils are safe are described in CP 2003

5.2.3.56 It is important to consider during the design stage the effect of water on banks both in cuttings and embankments; drainage is specifically referred to in section 5.3.

5.2.3.57 Before work is begun, profiles should be established showing the angles to be worked to, in order to avoid overfilling or overcutting; cuttings should be made from profiles, and banks should be firmed by placing successive layers not more than 150 mm thick up to the profile line.

5.2.3.58 Slopes at which banks should be cut or formed for ease of maintenance are described in 5.2.2.3.

5.2.3.59 It is recommended that the top and toe of banks should be rounded off. The curve to be followed should be described by a drawing, and should be such that machine maintenance is possible.

5.2.3.60 For ease of maintenance, a verge at least 1.000 m wide is desirable between a bank edge and boundary.

Disposal of rubbish with excavated material

5.2.3.61 The opportunity should be taken at the beginning of major earthworks to dispose of unwanted inorganic material at the bottom of tipping areas after the topsoil has been removed, so that a clear distance of 1.000 m is available on top of it after filling.

Material which will leave cavities after rotting, such as grass, leaves, roots and timber, must be excluded. Metal containers should be

5.2.3.61 **Disposal of rubbish with excavated material** continued
(cont'd) flattened under the tracks of heavy machinery and large objects cut up.
Stone, slabs, rocks and hardcore should be placed so that voids are not formed.
The use of household refuse in tipped areas should be the subject of a separate study, and is not dealt with in these recommendations.

Rock
5.2.3.62 If the presence of rock is suspected from trial holes and/or from geological maps, it is necessary to determine:
(A) Whether normal earth-moving machinery can cut without rippers.
(B) What type of additional rippers may be required.
(C) If explosives and/or compressors will be required.

The storage and use of explosives is controlled by Statutory Regulations. Sufficient insurance cover should be taken out to cover possible claims. Explosives should not be used except by trained personnel and preferably under the supervision of a competent qualified civil engineer. Local police must be informed beforehand of operations.

Sub-soil cultivations
5.2.3.63 After completion of sub-soil moving, the formation level should be graded with the box scraper to even, running contours and then, depending upon the soil texture and degree of compaction, loosened with a subsoiler or ripper.
For light, non-cohesive soils a 3-tine ripper may be adequate if drawn up to 300 mm deep with spacings up to 600 mm centres.
For stiff clays and other cohesive soils a single-tine ripper, driven 450 mm deep at 1.000 m centres, and drawn by a crawler tractor, may be necessary.
For chalk and similar rock-like material, deep ripping to bring up large blocks of material and flints should be avoided, but means should always be found, by drawing an implement, to loosen the surface to avoid a pan and ensure free drainage.

Spreading topsoil
5.2.3.64 Topsoil should be spread evenly on formation levels to the following depths (topsoil depths diagram omitted):
(A) Banks: 75 mm to 100 mm.
(B) Grass areas: 100 mm minimum after firming.
(C) Sports fields: 150 mm minimum after firming.
(D) Shrub areas: 400 mm minimum after firming.
(E) Tree pits: 600 mm minimum after firming.
When shrub beds and tree pits occur in large areas requiring major grading, formation levels are usually prepared at the specified depth for grass over the whole area to facilitate the use of larger machines. Further excavation is subsequently carried out to the additional depth for shrub and tree planting.

5.2.3.64 **Spreading topsoil** continued
(cont'd) In all cases where excavation is necessary to obtain adequate depth for shrub beds and tree pits, existing topsoil which is suitable for re-use should be kept separate from subsoil and other excavated material.

5.2.3.65 After spreading, the soil should be cultivated to crumb size by implements as in 5.2.2.29 to a condition suitable for blade grading. Large stones and unwanted material 75 mm size and over should be picked off and carted away. Areas should then be graded with a rigid blade grader to true, flowing contours; the degree of acceptable accuracy determined by boring rods or a straightedge (as applicable) after firming will depend upon the use of the land.

If material to improve soil structure and texture is used, it should be applied before the last cultivations prior to seeding.

Fallow period
5.2.3.66 If possible, freshly prepared areas should be cleaned by allowing them to lie fallow for a period of several months, preferably in late spring or summer. During this period weeds should not be allowed to seed, and growing weeds should be eliminated by alternate cultivation and chemical control. (A table on the accuracy of contours and the maximum permitted deviations has been omitted here).

5.3 DRAINAGE

5.3.1 INTRODUCTION

5.3.1.1 This chapter contains only items associated with subsoil drainage, normally referred to as field or land drainage, and ditching. The British Standard recommendations for this type of drainage are contained within B.S. 4428, General Landscape Operations, and B.S. Code of Practice 303:1952 superceeded by C.P. 301:1971 Building Drainage. The drainage section of B.S. 4428 and certain definitions from C.P. 303, not covered by B.S. 4428, are quoted in full in this chapter, by kind permission of B.S.I. The quantities and dimensions have been converted into rounded metric units, the clauses and paragraphs have been renumbered and tables, footnotes, and diagrams have been omitted.

5.3.1.2 All specification items in this chapter are in accordance with those in B.S. 4428 where appropriate, but they have been expanded in certain respects in detail and range. Where applicable, prices for these items, together with some alternatives, are given in Chapter 7, section 3.

5.3.2 B.S. 4428:1969: DRAINAGE (from Recommendations for general landscape operations)

Drainage

5.3.2.1 In landscape work, drainage is required:
    (A) To prevent water from higher ground flowing to the site over the surface or below the ground.
    (B) To prevent erosion and damage to new works, especially banks.
    (C) To prevent damage by discharge from site, especially during construction.
    (D) To lead away surface water, especially when falls to the land are small.
    (E) To lower a high water table.
    (F) To drain ponds and divert or pipe ditches and water-courses.
    (G) To carry away the outflow of springs.

Information required for design

5.3.2.2 Investigations into site conditions should determine:
    (A) Position, size and depth of useful water sewer/s.
    (B) Availability of adjacent ponds, ditches and water-courses for outlets.
    (C) Whether the ground is capable of soaking (and, if possible, at what rate) to accommodate soakaways or bore holes.
    (D) Annual rainfall.
Intensity of rainfall, for use in calculations of run-off.
    (E) The proportion of clay in the subsoil. This should be carried out by mechanical analysis of subsoil at about 700 mm depth to determine the proportion of clay.

Specification—Drainage

5.3.2.2 **Information required for design** continued
(cont'd)   (F) The history of previous field drainage and ditching. (Information may be available, particularly if the schemes have been grant aided, at the local offices of the Land Drainage Division of the Ministry of Agriculture, Fisheries and Food).
A visual inspection often reveals the lines of old drainage systems under grass where the line of drain is a different colour from its surroundings, particularly during dry periods: such lines should be investigated by trial holes and the results plotted on to a plan.

Design

5.3.2.3   Detailed design of comprehensive land and field drainage is outside the scope of these recommendations, but the general considerations fall under two main headings.

5.3.2.4   (A) Those in respect of the period of construction and immediately (up to 2-3 years) after.
Such drainage problems arise because of the vulnerable nature of the works, and because of the slow return to optimum permeable soil conditions after radical disturbance of the soil structure by compaction during earth moving and cultivations. Particular care must be taken with soils having high proportions of silt and clay to avoid compaction, and if it does occur to minimize its effects by ripping and subsoiling.
It is also necessary to prevent the formation of, or to break up, crusts which form on some soils and give rise to quick run-off. To guard against damage by swift sheet run-off which may form gully erosion and cause damage to adjacent property, it is often necessary to install cut-off drains either in the form of ditches or french drains at the top of cuttings when the higher land has low permeability; at the foot of cuttings when seepage is likely through the cutting; at the top edge of embankments, as these are the most vulnerable features in earth works; and at the lower edges to collect run-off and prevent damage to the toe of the filling. The need for some of these remedies often diminishes considerably with time, being greatly influenced by the growth to maturity of ground vegetation.

5.3.2.5   (B) Those which affect permanent drainage of the land, which are: means of lowering a water table in zones of permanent or intermittent saturation; drainage to tap the outflow of springs or permeable layers; means of dealing with surplus water in the topsoil and subsoil arising from direct precipitation. For these purposes it may be necessary to install forms of subsoil drainage such as by the installation of agricultural tiles (or other pipes), or by mole ploughing, or by a combination of both methods.

Workmanship and materials

5.3.2.6   General recommendations as to workmanship and materials, ditching, bridges and culverts, subsoil drainage, together with diagrams of chambers, outfalls and pipe inlets may be found in 'Technical notes' published by the Ministry of Agriculture, Fisheries and Food.

Outlets

5.3.2.7 It is essential to make adequate provision for the disposal of water from landscape operations. Such water may be channelled:
(A) To public surface water sewers. The approval of the local authority is required. This may be granted on terms which may include the provision of silt traps; calculations as to estimated flow may be required.
(B) To neighbouring ditches and watercourses. The consent of adjoining land owners may be required and legal easements may be necessary; drainage boards or local authorities may exercise jurisdiction over position and construction of outfall.
(C) To soakaways or deep boreholes. Some knowledge as to the permeability of the underlying strata is essential; works in the gathering grounds of Water Boards may require their consent. Expert advice should be sought.

5.3.2.8 Size and capacity of outlet pipes should be calculated having regard to the catchment area drained, and the possible inclination of the pipe.
As a guide to determine the quantity of water likely to arrive at the outlet, the tables (omitted here) in the original British Standard may be used, but it is essential to select the drainage coefficient appropriate to the soil and rainfall (12.5 mm in 24 hours is frequently used; other standards are 8 mm per day when mean annual rainfall is up to 875 mm and 6 mm above it). It is important to consider in addition the effect of quick run-off (over the surface) from intense storms, particularly during the construction stages, and cut-off drains with their outlets at the lower edges of large areas should be designed on engineering principles especially in urban surroundings where flooding can affect adjacent property (storms of intensity of 37 mm per hour are not uncommon).

Subsoil drainage

5.3.2.9 Subsoil drainage is a method of drainage of soils by the insertion of pipes, or the forming of channels, below ground in such positions that they will gather water from the soil, at depths chosen on the basis of soil, crop and climate; they are required when it is necessary to:
(A) Lower a water table to a depth that will enable optimum root penetration in zones of intermittent or permanent saturation; and/or
(B) Gather water, arriving by direct precipitation, from zones of non-saturation and so assist in drying the topsoil and upper layers of the ground.
Because of the variables in vegetation and climate (especially rainfall and evaporation) and the variability of soils there is much controversy about the depth at which water tables should be maintained (and consequently the depth and distance apart of subsoil drainage) to suit local conditions. There is some evidence that a depth of about 550 mm from the surface is the level at which the water table should be controlled for grass and a depth of 1.000 m to 1.300 m would be more appropriate for shrubs and trees.

Subsoil drainage *continued*

5.3.2.10   Systems of subsoil drainage are:

(A) 'Tile' systems, which include the use of clayware, plastics, or concrete pipes. Such systems, if properly installed and maintained, last indefinitely.

(B) 'Mole' drainage, a system of draining heavy (clay) land by drawing an implement through the subsoil to form a channel at a predetermined depth, which receives water from a vertical slit in the soil made by the passage of the implement, as well as from cracks in the soil itself. This system has only a short life, dependent upon the nature of the subsoil, but in some circumstances can be repeated at intervals of time, in established turf, provided proper care is taken as to soil conditions and that the implements are adequate; it has the great advantage of low initial cost. Connections should be made to a skeleton tile system (diagram omitted).

Special features of drainage for landscape work

5.3.2.11   In landscape operations the following are of considerable importance.

(A) In trenching operations topsoil should be separated from subsoil and the latter carted away and particularly not spread on areas subject to foot traffic.

(B) Where it is necessary to remove water from the surface and from the topsoil, trenches should be kept as narrow as practicable and pipes filled over with permeable material such as clinker stone of a size 40 mm down to 4 mm and reasonably free from dust.

(C) Not less than 150 mm of topsoil should be placed at the top of trenches.

(D) Junctions between mains and laterals should be of clayware and purpose-made, either 'Y' or oblique, as appropriate (they need not be saltglazed).

(E) Inspection chambers should be incorporated at intervals and at points of junctions of mains, to facilitate cleaning and so avoid excavations in established grounds.

(F) Mains adjacent to large trees should be of sealed pipes.

(G) Large scale drainage operations are more economically carried out by contractors using specially constructed trench cutting and pipe laying machinery; diggers and machinery which have no means of maintaining an accurate level should be avoided.

(H) Arrangements for drainage should be as simple as possible to avoid if possible multiplicity of junctions; complicated short run herringbone systems should be avoided, and consideration in placing lines should be given to the requirements of machine operations. A pattern in the form of a gridiron has these advantages.

Footnote

5.3.2.12   (At the end of the British Standards section on drainage are drawings showing arrangements of tile and mole drains and a table giving the relationship between soil permeability and subsoil drainage).

5.3.3 CODE OF PRACTICE; 303: 1952
(superceded by C.P. 301 1971. since going to press.)

Field drains

Methods of laying

5.3.3.1   (A) Natural: The pipes are laid to follow the natural depressions or valleys of the site, branches discharging into the main, as tributaries do into a river.

(B) Herringbone: A system consisting of a number of main drains into which discharge, from both sides, smaller subsidiary branches parallel to each other but at an angle to the mains, forming a series of herringbone patterns. Normally these subsidiaries should not exceed 30 m in length.

(C) Grid: A main or mains near the boundaries of a site, into which branches discharge from one side only.

(D) Fan shaped: The drains are laid converging to a single outlet at one point on the boundary of a site, without the use of a main (or collecting) drain.

(E) Moat or cut-off system: Sometimes drains are laid on one or more sides of a building to intercept the flow of subsoil water and thereby protect the foundations.

(Although not mentioned specifically in C.P. 303 this definition has a more general application to landscape work i.e. for the protection of soft areas from surface run-off and from subsoil water problems.)

5.3.4 SPECIFICATION ITEMS
(not necessarily in British Standards of Code of Practice)

'Tile' Drainage

General

5.3.4.1   Install drainage system in herringbone (or grid) fashion, shown on drawing, working from outlets. All lateral and main drains shall be laid at a minimum depth of 450 mm to invert with steady fall of the land along their line except as indicated on drawing. Laterals shall be spaced at 4.000 m intervals and laid at an angle to flow of the main drains of 60°, connected by approved 60° angled junctions. No drain shall be laid to less fall than 1 in 200 (or 1:300) or greater than 1:80.

Work to include carting away surplus subsoil, backfilling trenches or cuts with gravel rejects, as specified, and replacing 150 mm depth of topsoil over trenches.

5.3.4.2   The drainage system as described would normally be installed with one of the following types of drain either laid by hand or machine using pipe laying attachment or chute.

General *continued*

5.3.4.3 Clayware (to B.S. 1196) or porous concrete (to B.S. 1194) drains: 75 mm for laterals and 100 mm for mains, laid by hand or chute in 150 mm and 300 mm wide trenches.

5.3.4.4 Rigid plastic perforated drains: 50 mm for laterals, laid in 125 mm wide trench by chute, and 63 mm for mains, laid by hand in 300 mm wide trench.

5.3.4.5 Flexible plastic perforated drains: 70 mm for laterals, laid in 70 mm cut by mole plough, and 110 mm for mains, laid in 110 mm cut by mole plough.
(Rigid plastic perforated drains are manufactured under the trade name 'Pipaway' and flexible plastic perforated drains under the trade name 'Lamflex'.)

Preliminaries

5.3.4.6 Any existing drains or water courses which are damaged, cut through or interfered with in the construction work must be pointed out to the landscape architect or his representative. They must either be restored as nearly as possible to their original directions and levels, or connected to the new drainage system at an opportune time, or diverted, all to the satisfaction of the landscape architect.

5.3.4.7 All pipes and fittings shall be of 'British Standard' quality.

5.3.4.8 Tile drain pipes to B.S. 1196 and of sizes shown on drawing shall be used. All connections between laterals and mains shall be formed using clayware (or stoneware) angled junctions of appropriate sizes.

5.3.4.9 Clayware tile drains which have been exposed to frost shall not be used unless approved by the landscape architect.

5.3.4.10 Drains must be kept free from earth, debris, superfluous cement and any other obstructions throughout the contract and shall be handed over in clean condition.

Excavation

5.3.4.11 Drain trenches shall be excavated by one of the following types of machine as approved, and described in B.S. 2468:
- rotary wheel trencher
- back-acter trencher
- endless bucket trencher
- plough-type trencher
- back-acter excavator

5.3.4.12 Excavate drain trenches by first carefully removing true topsoil this being preserved to one side of trench for replacement.

5.3.4.13 Excavate subsoil to required depth and cart away as work proceeds. Subsoil shall not be left lying by side of trenches or lost by spreading

Specification—Drainage

5.3.4.13 **Excavation** continued
(cont'd) over site but shall be removed before the next stage of drainage is done, e.g. before the pipes are laid and/or at the end of each working day whichever is the earlier.

The subsoil shall be used as filling in areas agreed to. In completing this filling the subsoil shall be spread in layers not exceeding 250 mm deep and shall be adequately firmed, the finished surface being left smooth to receive the topsoil.

Allow for replacing topsoil stripped from agreed areas for receiving subsoil.

5.3.4.14 Trenches shall be as wide as necessary at ground level to allow easy laying of pipes, and to avoid subsidence. For hand laid drains the trench bottoms shall be at least 100 mm wider than the outside diameter of pipes.

Laying
5.3.4.15 Lay drains to true lines and steady falls.

5.3.4.16 Pipes shall be laid either on graded, crumb free, bed of trench or on 25 mm bed of fine ash or sand.

5.3.4.17 Clayware pipes shall be laid as instructed (either with a 10 mm gap between each pipe, or closely butted together, or butted together with a loose clayware tile over each joint.)

5.3.4.18 The end pipe of each drain shall be sealed with a broken pipe.

Testing
5.3.4.19 Bone and test all drain runs for line and gradient before filling in.

Filling
5.3.4.20 Filling shall not commence until drains have been inspected and approved by the landscape architect.

5.3.4.21 Samples of materials thought suitable for use in backfilling drain trenches shall be submitted to the landscape architect for approval before bulk purchase is made.

5.3.4.22 Backfill drain trenches to within 150 mm of finished surface (or up to formation level) using approved clean aggregate of 75 mm to 20 mm gauge, (e.g. graded clinker, gravel rejects, or crushed slag or stone) adequately firmed and brought to a level surface. Allowance shall be made for final 25 mm cover of approved, fine, hard, ash before topsoil replacement.

5.3.4.23 All filling shall be carried out carefully to avoid displacement or damage of pipes. Approved backfilling shall be carefully introduced by shovel or chute.

Filling continued

5.3.4.24 Topsoil must be replaced carefully over the above backfilling and consolidated to prevent subsequent depressions.

Catchwater drains

5.3.4.25 Catchwater drains shall be the same as subsoil tile drains except that they shall be filled to within 50 mm of finished ground level with approved aggregate (75 mm to 20 mm gauge) adequately firmed and levelled, and topped with 40 mm depth of fine hard ash. Back filling materials should be free from soil, silt, dust or detrimental organic material, and maintained as such.

Silt pits and inspection chambers

5.3.4.26 Excavate and build silt pits or inspection chambers with 225 mm brick walls either of engineering bricks (B.S. 1031 Class B) bedded in cement mortar (1:3), or common bricks bedded in cement/lime mortar (1:1:6) with inside faces rendered with 15 mm waterproof cement sand mix (1:3). Bottoms shall be 150 mm thick concrete (1:3:6 mix 40 mm aggregate). Tops shall be 100 mm thick reinforced concrete (1:2:4 mix 20 mm aggregate) either in sections (2, 3, or 4 according to size) with rebated joints and countersunk galvanised lifting ring, with tops set 150 mm below ground level, or set 230 mm below ground level and fitted with 600 mm x 450 mm medium duty galvanised (or bitumen coated) cast iron manhole (to B.S. 497) bedded in cement mortar on brick upstand and cover set in thick grease. Allowance shall be made for building in inlet and outlet pipes in salt glazed ware and necessary strutting, planking, filling and ramming. Disposal of sub-soil shall be as specified for drain trenches.

5.3.4.27 Silt pits shall be constructed with internal dimensions 900 mm x 600 mm and depth of 300 mm below outlet pipe.

5.3.4.28 Inspection chambers shall be constructed with internal dimensions of 600 mm x 600 mm and depth the same as outlet pipe. Glazed invert channels to same diameter as outlet pipe will be provided with necessary curved channels and tapers. Channels shall be benched up with concrete (1:2:4 mix, 20 mm aggregate) average 250 mm thick, shaped to sides, worked round channels and finished smooth in cement, rounded off.

Outlets

5.3.4.29 Break through side of existing manhole, insert 150 mm salt glazed outlet pipe, build in and connect to new tile drain including necessary excavation.

5.3.4.30 Excavate for and construct outfall in 100 mm thick reinforced concrete (1:3:6 mix, 40 mm aggregate) with vertical headwall 900 mm high x 600 mm wide, splayed base 600 mm wide at back and 900 mm wide at

Specification—Drainage

5.3.4.30 **Outlets** continued
(cont'd) front with distance from back to front of 1.050 m and fall of 75 mm to the front, and triangular flank walls 900 mm high x 1.050 m base length.

During construction provide and set in position 150 mm diameter oulet pipe in saltglazed ware. Provide and fit over outlet a 300 mm x 300 mm galvanised mild steel grating of not more than 25 mm mesh.

Include for all necessary damming, pumping, formwork and part returning excavations, making firm the ground all round the structure to the satisfaction of the landscape architect.

Surplus excavations shall be disposed of as for drain trenches.

Soakaways

5.3.4.31 Dimensions of soakaways shall be as indicated on drawing or varied, as approved, according to the rate of run off and permeability of subsoil.

5.3.4.32 Excavate for and construct soakaway of concrete pipes, (to B.S. 556 or B.S. 1194) perforated for depth below drain inlet, with 50 mm diameter holes at approx. 500 mm centres horizontally and 230 mm vertically, staggered, including 300 mm base of approved clean, compacted, hardcore and 150 x 300 mm concrete foundation to pipe circumference. Backfill around outside face of pipe, up to level of inlet drain, with 200 mm minimum width of approved hardcore. Provide light or heavy duty concrete chamber (to B.S. 556) set 250 mm below ground level with concrete slab over circular opening or with galvanized (or bitumen coated) circular manhold cover and frame (to B.S.497 grade B) for 560 mm opening, bedded in cement mortar and set in thick grease, flush with ground level.

Allowance shall be made for building in inlet pipe in salt-glazed ware, necessary strutting planking, filling, ramming and removal of suplus fill.

5.3.4.33 Excavate for and construct soakaway with 225 mm brick walls of common bricks laid bonded with dry joints (without mortar) on 600 mm x 150 mm concrete foundation, including 300 mm base of approved clean, compacted hardcore. Backfill around outside face of walls, up to invert level of inlet pipe, with 200 mm minimum width of approved hardcore and provide 100 mm thick reinforced concrete (1:2:4 mix, 20 mm aggregate) cover in sections (2, 3, or 4 according to size) each with rebated joints and countersunk galvanised lifting ring, set 200 mm below ground level.

Allowance shall be made for building in inlet pipe in salt-glazed ware, necessary planking, filling, ramming and removal of surplus subsoil.

5.3.4.34 Excavate pit and fill with approved clean compacted hardcore to within 500 mm of ground level including necessary back filling, ramming and removal of surplus subsoil.

'Mole' drainage

5.3.4.35 Mole channels shall be formed over grid or peripheral tile drain system which shall intercept mole channels at 45.000 m maximum intervals. Tile drains shall be 100 mm diameter at 600 mm minimum depth with porous fill to trenches, as specified under tile drains.

5.3.4.36 Drain by approved mole plough set at depth of 450 mm in parallel runs at 1.200 m centres using 50 mm (or 75 mm) diameter mole. Gradient for mole channels shall be between 1:100 and 1:200.

Ditches

Excavation

5.3.4.37 Ditches shall be excavated or trimmed by one of the following types of machine as approved, and described in B.S. 2468:
   drag-line excavator with side-arm attachment and taper-sided bucket,
   ditcher,
   gripper,
   drainage plough.

5.3.4.38 Unless otherwise specified excavated material shall be deposited to one side of ditch, as instructed, to form bank of regular and stable profile.

Boundary ditches

5.3.4.39 All new ditches shall be properly trimmed to the maximum uniform gradients permitted by the general configuration of the ground, or to the definite levels indicated.

5.3.4.40 Any existing ditches shall be cleaned and trimmed as described in item 5.3.4.39

5.3.4.41 Permanent ditches are to be formed to the boundaries of the site and fields where indicated. They are to have a bed width of 600 mm (or as required) and depth of average 600 mm below finished ground level (or as required). Side slopes are to be battered to a 45° slope.

Piped ditches

5.3.4.42 Piped ditches shall be laid to falls as shown on the drawings.

5.3.4.43 Trenches shall be 300 mm wider than the external diameter of the pipes, with side slopes sufficient to avoid subsidence.

5.3.4.44 Pipes shall be 'Ogee' concrete pipes (to B.S. 4101) laid with 15 mm open joints, or stoneware with open joints, as required, on the prepared bed of trench to falls, with each pipe lined up to the adjoining pipe.

5.3.4.45 Trenches shall be backfilled with 40 mm to 75 mm graded broken stone permeable filling material or gravel rejects up to within 250 mm of

Specification—Drainage

5.3.4.45 **Piped ditches** *continued*
(*cont'd*) adjoining ground level, the sides of the trench above the stone shall be trimmed to 45° forming an open ditch above the drain, the level of the stone being lowered where necessary to give a longitudinal fall to the open ditch.

Culverts

5.3.4.46 Where indicated crossings are to be formed over ditches by the insertion of 300 mm diameter spun concrete drain pipes (to B.S. 4101) set and surrounded in concrete 150 mm thick. The pipes shall be jointed with yarn to quarter the depth of socket and cement mortar extending outside joint to form 45° fillet.

Allowance should be made for all necessary excavation, back filling and ramming.

5.4 SEEDING OF GRASS AREAS

5.4.1 INTRODUCTION

5.4.1.1 The British Standard recommendations for seed and seeding of grass areas are contained in B.S. 4428:1969. The main sections of this part of this standard are quoted here in full by kind permission of B.S.I. The quantities and dimensions have been converted to rounded metric equivalents, the clauses and paragraphs have been renumbered and the footnotes have been omitted.

5.4.1.2 In Chapter 7 the standard prices given, using various seed mixes, are based on compliance with the British Standard quoted above. In addition a number of extra items which might be desirable for differing circumstances and higher quality work are described after the British Standard and then priced separately in Chapter 7.

5.4.1.3 In certain circumstances the British Standard recommendations might not be thought sufficiently detailed and a specification/description of work could probably also include some of the following items:

Seeding of grass areas

Preparation

5.4.1.4 During any fallow period prior to sowing seed, the tilth shall be maintained free from weeds.

5.4.1.5 Protect seed from damp and vermin until required and return any unused seed to the seed merchant for holding until required on site.

5.4.1.6 No seed to be sown until the cultivation and preparatory work have been approved by the landscape architect.

Germination

5.4.1.7 No payment for re-seeding shall be made to the contractor if the seed fails, due to any cause whatsoever. He shall be required to make good the soiling and repeat the seeding until a good sward is obtained.

5.4.1.8 Grass areas will only be accepted as reaching practical completion when germination has proved satisfactory and all weeds have been removed.

Maintenance and defects liability

5.4.1.9 Damage, failure or dying back of grass due to neglect of watering, expecially for seeding out of normal season shall be the responsibility of the contractor.

5.4.1.10 Any shrinkage below the specified levels during the contract or defects liability period shall be rectified at the contractor's expense.

Specification—Seeding of grass areas

Maintenance and defects liability *continued*

5.4.1.11 The contractor is to exercise care in the use of rotary cultivator and mowing machines to reduce to a minimum the hazards of flying stones and brickbats. All rotary mowing machines are to be fitted with safety guards.

5.4.2 B.S. 4428:1969 SEEDING OF GRASS AREAS

(from Recommendations for general landscape operations)

Fertilizing

5.4.2.1 An appropriate pre-germination fertilizer to stimulate new growth should be applied where necessary at the prescribed rates.

Final raking or harrowing

5.4.2.2 In preparation for sowing, the surface should be lightly and uniformly firmed and reduced to a fine tilth up to 25 mm in depth by raking or harrowing with a spike and chain harrow. All large stones (for general areas, stones more than 50 mm in any dimension) should be removed from the surface.

Seed

5.4.2.3 The seed mixture should be selected according to the soil type, light conditions, the climate, and also the intended use of the area. The germination capacity of each constituent of the mixture should be not less than 80%, and the purity of the mixture not less than 90%. Total weed seed content should not be more than 0.5% and the total content of other crop seeds should not be more than 1%. These minimum germination figures should be related to annual tests commencing on 1st August each year, and should be considered valid for up to 14 months, covering supplies of seed in the following August and September.

Where seeds are required for a first class ornamental lawn, the use of a non-ryegrass mixture is specified. The seed should be free of perennial ryegrass and cocksfoot in a purity test of a 50 g sample.

Seed should be obtained at least 21 days before sowing and, if required by the purchaser, samples should be taken from sealed bags after delivery with a Cambridge type seed sampler and tested for composition, purity and germination at an official seed testing station before sowing. Samples of seed should be taken from each bag of the consignment and mixed together to form a representative bulk sample, of at least 110 g.

Note: It is intended that these recommendations should be superceded by whatsoever details appear under any regulations governing amenity grasses made in due course under the Plant Varieties & Seeds Act.

Turf edging to seeded area

5.4.2.4 In areas where initial appearance is important, turves may be laid to provide a neat edge to seeded lawns. After preparation of the seed bed,

5.4.2.4 (cont'd) **Turf edging to seeded area** continued
a 300 mm wide margin should be raked back and a single row of turves laid end to end round the perimeter. The level of the seed bed should be married-in to the turf. As far as possible turves should be selected to match the mixture of grasses being sown. Watering may be required to prevent turf drying out before it becomes established.

Sowing
5.4.2.5 Although in some areas and on some soils sowing may be undertaken at all seasons, providing a satisfactory tilth can be obtained, sowing from the end of July to mid October is recommended.

Sowing should be carried out during suitable calm weather conditions at a rate of 45 g/m^2 for small areas and fine lawns, and from 130-200 kg/hectare for large sports areas, where an efficient broadcast machine should be used. The operation should be carried out in equal sowings in transverse directions.

After sowing, the ground should be raked or chain-harrowed; on light soils the surface should be rolled and cross-rolled with a lightweight roller.

Seeding on steep banks
5.4.2.6 On steep banks and other inaccessible areas, where normal seeding operations are not practicable, consideration should be given to the use of a hydro-seeding process, or control of erosion by bitumen emulsion or latex.

Pre-emergent weedkiller
5.4.2.7 Where fallowing has not been possible a pre-emergent weedkiller may be applied, after sowing, in accordance with the manufacturer's instructions.

Initial cut (topping)
5.4.2.8 About 48 hours before topping, large stones (more than 50 mm in any dimension) should be removed and all areas rolled with a light roller to firm grass and press in remaining stones.

When the grass is established and from 40 mm to 75 mm high, according to the seed mixture, it should be topped with a roto-scythe so as to leave from 25 mm to 50 mm of growth, to cut weeds, to control the growth of coarser grass and to encourage tillering. Where mowing without a box produces a swathe, this should be spread evenly to prevent damage to the growing grass beneath. This applies particularly to grass cut during periods of dull or wet weather.

There are 3 good reasons why you should contact Nickersons first when you start thinking about grass mixtures...

... p.t.o.

1 Specially bred varieties

Improved varieties of grasses, the result of Nickerson's own breeding work and from the world's leading grass breeders, are vigorously tested by Nickersons in Britain under British conditions.

This means that the seed Nickersons sell contains varieties which have passed through assessments of performance, persistence and suitability, and that this seed is superior to mixtures containing older, less suitable varieties.

2 Specially blended

Grass mixtures used for different purposes require grass varieties in different combinations. Nickersons are continuously conducting large scale trials in conjunction with leading County Councils, CIRIA (the Construction Industry Research and Information Association), and the Sports Turf Research Institute at Bingley in order to ensure that varieties are blended in the correct proportions for each use. This means that Nickersons will always give you the right mixture for your requirements.

3 Proven in Practice

The exclusive Nickersons Seal Grass Blends have been widely used in major landscape developments, and in many leisure and sports grounds throughout the country — the Home Pierpont National Watersports Centre at Nottingham. — The large seaside marina at Crosby, Lancs. — The New Chadderton Park at Derby.

Nickersons Seal Grass Blends containing specially bred varieties blended in the correct proportions have been proven in practice. They can give you reduced maintenance costs and a fine attractive hard wearing turf that will last for many years. That's why you get best value for money with Seal Grass Blends.

NICKERSONS of ROTHWELL | scientific seedsmen

Find out how these unique mixtures can help you. Contact Nickersons of Rothwell, Field House, Grimsby, Lincolnshire. Tel: Grimsby 58021. Telex: 52261.

5.4.3 TYPICAL SEED MIXES

Maxwell Hart mixtures

Non-Ryegrass

5.4.3.1 Hart Sea Marsh Mixture; Superfine turf:
70% Chewings Fescue, Oregon.
20% Cumberland Marsh Fescue.
10% Browntop, Agrostis tenuis, Oregon.

5.4.3.2 Hart No. 1; Superfine turf:
80% Chewings Fescue, Dutch or Oregon.
20% Browntop, Agrostis tenuis, Oregon.

5.4.3.3 Hart No. 2; Cricket, tennis & tees;
Dwarf grass turf:
10% Chewings Fescue, Oregon.
5% Browntop, Agrostis tenuis, Oregon.
10% Crested Dogstail, New Zealand.
45% Creeping Red Fescue, Canadian/Dutch.
30% Smooth-stalked Meadow-grass, Prato/Arista.

5.4.3.4 Harts Economy; Superfine turf:
90% Canadian/Dutch Creeping Red Fescue.
10% Oregon Browntop.

5.4.3.5 Hart 3x; Dwarf grass turf:
5% Browntop, Agrostis tenuis, Oregon.
60% Creeping Red Fescue, Canadian/Dutch.
5% Rough-stalked Meadow-grass, Poa trivialis.
30% Smooth-stalked Meadow-grass, Poa pratensis.

5.4.3.6 Hart No. 7; Fine turf for shade:
10% Browntop, Agrostis tenuis, Oregon.
10% Creeping Red Fescue, Canadian/Dutch.
10% Fine Leafed Sheeps Fescue.
10% Rough-stalked Meadow-grass, Poa pratensis.
20% Smooth-stalked Meadow-grass, Poa pratensis.
30% Wood Meadow-grass, Poa nemoralis.
10% Wavy Hairgrass, Aira flexuosa.

5.4.3.7 D.C. 'Arista'; Dense carpet turf:
60% 'Agio' Creeping Red Fescue.
30% 'Arista' Poa pratensis.
10% 'Highland' Browntop.

Specification—Seeding of grass areas

Ryegrass

5.4.3.8   Hart No. 4; Pedigree strain:
2½% Timothy Olympia.
5% Browntop, Agrostis tenuis, Oregon.
37½ Creeping Red Fescue, Danish.
25% Smooth-stalked Meadow-grass, Poa pratensis.
10% Perennial Ryegrass, Certified S.23.
10% Perennial Ryegrass, Certified S.321.
10% Perennial Ryegrass, New Zealand Ruanui.

5.4.3.9   Hart No. 5; Leafy strain (light soil):
5% Browntop, Agrostis tenuis, Oregon.
20% Creeping Red Fescue, Danish.
20% Smooth-stalked Meadow-grass, Poa pratensis.
10% Perennial Ryegrass, Certified S.23.
40% Perennial Ryegrass, Certified S.321.
5% Crested Dogstail.

5.4.3.10 Hart No. 6; Recreation Ground (heavy soil):
2½% Timothy Olympia.
15% Creeping Red Rescue, Danish.
5% Rough-stalked Meadow-grass, Poa trivialis.
10% Perennial Ryegrass, Pajbjerg, Verna.
10% Perennial Ryegrass, Compas.
45% Perennial Ryegrass, S.321.
12½% Smooth-stalked Meadow-grass.

5.4.3.11 Hart No. 8; Hardwearing:
10% Creeping Red Fescue, Danish.
10% Smooth-stalked Meadow-grass, Poa pratensis.
80% Perennial Ryegrass, Certified S. 321.

5.4.3.12 Hart No. 9; Road verge:
10% Creeping Red Fescue, Danish.
90% Perennial Ryegrass, Irish.

5.4.3.13 Hart No. 12; Reservoir and steep banks:
15% Creeping Red Fescue, Danish.
10% Smooth-stalked Meadow-grass, Poa pratensis.
10% Hungarian Forage Grass, Bromus inermis.
50% Perennial Ryegrass, Certified S.321.
2½% Yarrow.
10% Alta (Tall) Fescue.
2½% Wild White Clover.

5.4.3.14 D.F. 'Pelo'; Very hardwearing:
70% 'Pelo' Hardwearing leafy perennial Ryegrass.
30% 'Dawson' Creeping Red Fescue.

Specification—Seeding of grass areas

5.4.3.15 *Ryegrass continued*
R.G.1 Aberystwyth; Very hardwearing:
70% Perennial Ryegrass, Certified S.23.
30% Creeping Red Fescue, Certified S.59.

5.4.3.16 D.E. 'Compas'; Very hardwearing:
70% 'Compas' Hardwearing leafy perennial Ryegrass.
30% 'Agio' Creeping Red Fescue.

The En-Tout-Cas Co. Ltd. (Johnsons) Mixtures

5.4.3.17 Super A; (without Ryegrass): Bowling greens, cricket squares, putting greens:
60% Chewings Fescue.
20% Creeping Red Fescue, Canadian.
10% Cumberland Marsh Fescue.
10% Agrostis tenuis Browntop.

5.4.3.18 B; (without Ryegrass): Grass tennis courts, lawns, fairways:
15% Chewings Fescue.
10% Fine Leafed Sheep's Fescue.
55% Creeping Red Fescue, Canadian.
10% Agrostis tenuis Browntop.
10% Poa pratensis (Smooth-stalked Meadow-grass).

5.4.3.19 C; All sports ground areas:
40% Creeping Red Fescue, Canadian.
10% Agrostis tenuis Browntop.
35% Perennial Ryegrass Certified New Zealand.
15% Perennial Ryegrass Certified S.23.

5.4.3.20 D; Hardwearing, low price sports ground mixture:
20% Creeping Red Fescue, Canadian.
80% Perennial Ryegrass.

5.4.3.21 'Dawson'; Bowling greens (without Ryegrass):
40% Chewings Fescue.
40% Dawson Red Fescue.
20% Agrostis tenuis Browntop.

5.4.3.22 'Prato'; Cricket outfields (without Ryegrass):
15% Chewings Fescue.
40% Creeping Red Fescue, Canadian.
15% Agrostis tenuis Browntop.
30% Poa pratensis Prato.

5.4.3.23 'Pelo': For general sports grounds. (with Ryegrass):
25% Chewings Fescue.
30% Creeping Red Fescue, Canadian.
10% Agrostis tenuis Browntop.
35% Perennial Ryegrass Pelo.

The En-Tout-Cas Co. Ltd. (Johnsons) Mixtures *continued*

5.4.3.24 'King'; For playing fields; includes King Timothy. (with Ryegrass):
30% Creeping Red Fescue, Canadian.
10% Agrostis tenuis Browntop.
10% Poa trivialis.
35% Perennial Ryegrass Pelo.
15% King Timothy.

5.4.3.25 'C/W'; For cricket wickets:
50% Chewings Fescue.
10% Agrostis tenuis Browntop.
40% Crested Dogstail.

5.4.3.26 'F'; For shade:
40% Creeping Red Fescue, Canadian.
10% Agrostis tenuis Browntop.
30% Poa trivialis.
10% Deschampsia flexuosa (Wavy Hairgrass).
10% Poa nemoralis.

5.4.4 ALTERNATIVE ITEMS (NOT IN B.S. 4428:1969)

Fertilizing

5.4.4.1 Three to five days before seeding, fertilizer is to be worked into the top 50 mm of soil as the final tilth is reached. A mixture of two fertilizers is to be used, each at 70 g per m^2 and applied in transverse directions and worked into the final tilth:

(A) containing superphosphate with minimum 18% Phosphoric acid (water soluble).

(B) containing sulphate of amonia with minimum 20% nitrogen.

Protection of seeded areas

5.4.4.2 The contractor shall protect newly grassed areas at all vulnerable points to prevent damage by pedestrians. For this purpose he shall provide and fix a fence of 3 strands of wire supported on wooden posts 900 mm out of the ground at approximately 1.800 m centres. These fences shall be maintained by the contractor and when the grass is established shall be removed and cleared away and the ground reinstated. Any damage to the grass shall be made good until the areas are handed over.

Maintenance

5.4.4.3 Top dress with fish meal fertilizer at the rate of 70 g per m^2 after the second mowing.

5.4.4.4 Maintenance shall consist of watering, weeding, cutting, repair of all erosion and settlement and reseeding as necessary to establish a uniform and healthy stand of the specified grasses and shall continue until acceptance by the landscape architect (10 cuts in one season).

Landscape Developments
Sports Ground Construction...

G. S. DANIELS
(Contracts)
LIMITED

6, Stewart House, Sycamore Avenue,
Chandler's Ford, Eastleigh, Hants
042-15 66655

102 New Walk, Leicester
0533 22178

387 Winchester Road, Southampton
0703 68956

For Landscaping,
Soil Improvement,
Hydraulic Seeding etc.
specify **BRITISH PEAT**
from
L & P Peat Ltd. Carlisle

Available in Bulk, Press Pack and Sacks from our works in Mid Scotland, Cumberland and Lancashire

LSD offer a complete service for

HYDRO-SEEDING
LANDSCAPING
SPORTS FACILITIES
TURFING
SEEDING
PLANTING
LAND RECLAMATION
SOIL STABILISATION

LANDSCAPE & SPORTSGROUND DEVELOPMENT LTD.

HEAD OFFICE: HIGHAM, ROCHESTER, KENT. MEDWAY 79888
AND AT
6A MARKET STREET, EBBW VALE, MON. EBBW VALE 2650.

Specification—Seeding of grass areas

Maintenance *continued*

5.4.4.5 Pernicious weeds to be treated with selective weedkiller applied 12 weeks after seeding if the grass was sown in the spring. Grass sown in the autumn to be similarly treated at the end of May the following year. Weedkiller to be ICI 'Weedkiller for new grass,' or May & Baker 'Actrilawn.'

5.4.5 HYDRO-SEEDING

5.4.5.1 There are a number of different methods of hydro-seeding with grass or seeds of woody material. These vary considerably in their composition and method of application. No prices or specifications are included in this section or in 7.4, as costs vary considerably depending on the size of the job, water supply, accessibility for machinery and other relevant factors. Each such case therefore requires its own individual specification and costing, according to the conditions prevalent.

5.5 TURF AND TURFING

5.5.1 INTRODUCTION

5.5.1.1   The British Standard recommendations for turf are in B.S. 3969:1965 and the recommendations for turfing are contained in B.S. 4428:1969. The main sections of both these standards are quoted here in full by kind permission of B.S.I. The quantities and dimensions have been converted to rounded metric equivalents, the clauses and paragraphs have been renumbered and the footnotes and diagrams have been omitted.

5.5.1.2   In Chapter 7 the standard price given for turf and turfing is for compliance with these two British Standards. In addition a number of extra items which might be desirable for differing circumstances and higher quality work are described after the British Standards and priced separately in Chapter 7.

5.5.1.3   In certain circumstances the British Standard recommendations might not be thought sufficiently detailed and a specification/description of work could probably also include some of the following items:

Turf

Delivery

5.5.1.4   The contractor shall supply a sample of the turf he proposes using for the approval of the landscape architect and shall ensure that all turves are similar to the approved sample.

5.5.1.5   The contractor shall inform the landscape architect of the location of the supply, so that turves can be inspected prior to lifting.

Turfing

Laying

5.5.1.6   Any turf brought on the site or laid prior to the approval of the landscape architect, will be deemed to have been brought on or laid at the landscape contractor's risk, and he will be instructed to lift and/or cart away such turf off the site and replace and/or relay at his own expense, unless instruction in writing to the contrary be given by the landscape architect.

Laying around trees

5.5.1.7   Turf shall not be laid to within 300 mm of any tree trunk.

5.5.1.8   Turves adjacent to trees to be trimmed exactly to stem and stake of tree to cover soil completely.

Specification—Turf and turfing

5.5.1.9 *Laying around trees* continued
Turf areas adjoining buildings, boundary walls or fences to be taken to the faces of the structure to give complete soil cover.

5.5.1.10 *Watering*
Damage or failure due to neglect of watering shall be the responsibility of the contractor. The landscape sub-contractor shall be responsible for the replacement of any areas of scorched turf at his own expense.

5.5.2 B.S. 3969:1965, RECOMMENDATIONS FOR TURF FOR GENERAL LANDSCAPE PURPOSES

5.5.2.1 For the purposes of this British Standard, the following are the common and botanical names of the grasses and perennial weeds referred to:
Agrostis (*Agrostis* species)
Annual Meadow-grass (*Poa annua* L.)
Cocksfoot (*Dactylis glomerata* L.)
Creeping Soft-grass (*Holcus mollis* L.)
Crested Dogstail (*Cynosurus cristatus* L.)
Fescues (*Festuca* species)
Meadow Barley (*Hordeum secalinum* Schreb.)
Perennial Ryegrass (*Lolium perenne* L.)
Sea Meadow-grass (*Puccinellia maritima* (Huds.) Parl.)
Smooth-stalked Meadow-grass (*Poa pratensis* L.)
Sweet Vernal-grass (*Anthoxanthum odoratum* L.)
Timothy (*Phleum nodosum* L.)
Wall Barley (*Hordeum murinum* L.)
Yorkshire Fog (*Holcus lanatus* L.)

Clover (*Trifolium* species)
Pearlwort (*Sagina procumbens* L. and *Sagina apetala* Ard.)
Yarrow (*Achillea millefolium* L.)

Grasses

5.5.2.2 *Desirable grasses*
The constituent grasses of the turf should include not less than 60 per cent dwarf-growing Agrostis and Fescues, Smooth-stalked Meadow-grasses, Crested Dogstail and Timothy, and not more than 40 per cent dwarf leafy Perennial Ryegrass. The purchaser may stipulate that the constituent grasses should not include Ryegrass.

5.5.2.3 *Undesirable grasses and weeds*
It is undesirable that the turf should contain weed grasses such as Annual Meadow-grass, Cocksfoot, Creeping Soft-grass, Meadow Barley, Sea Meadow-grass, Sweet Vernal-grass, Wall Barley or

5.5.2.3 (cont'd) **Undesirable grasses and weeds** continued
Yorkshire Fog, or perennial weeds such as Clover, Moss, Pearlwort or Yarrow.

5.5.2.4 **Soil**
The soil of the turf should be of a loamy nature and free from stones over 15 mm gauge. Soil may vary from heavy to light loam but should be consistent in character for the whole of each requirement.

5.5.2.5 **Condition**
The grass should be of close texture, of even density and green in colour. The turf should be sufficiently fibrous for turves to hold together when handled, but excess fibre or mat is undesirable. The grass should have been closely mown and should not exceed 25 mm in height. It should not be visibly affected by pest or disease.

5.5.2.6 **Dimensions**
Turves should be of rectangular shape and of uniform thickness. Unless otherwise agreed, they should have a minimum thickness of soil of 25 mm and a width of 300 mm.

5.5.2.7 **Delivery**
Turves should not be lifted in frosty weather, or when water-logged. They should be packed to avoid drying out in transit and should be rolled or laid flat but not folded.

Turf should ordinarily be delivered to the site within 36 hours of lifting and should be off-loaded by hand, unless arranged on pallets for mechanical handling.

If stacked, turves should be placed grass to grass. If kept for any period the turves should be laid out and maintained as for turfed areas.

5.5.3 ALTERNATIVE ITEMS ON TURF (NOT IN B.S. 3969:1965)

5.5.3.1 **Conditions**
The turf shall be treated with selective weedkiller not less than four weeks prior to lifting.

5.5.3.2
The turf shall be extra quality meadow turf (pc of £15.00 per 100 m^2)

5.5.3.3
The turf shall be good quality Cumberland (the size is normally 300 x 300 mm) (pc. of £20.00 per 100 m^2).

5.5.4 B.S. 4428:1969 TURFING
(from Recommendations for general landscape operations)

Final preparation
5.5.4.1 The surface should be lightly and uniformly firmed and reduced to a fine tilth up to 25 mm in depth. All large stones should be removed from the surface.

Where indicated by an analysis of soil structure and fertilizer content, a dressing of organic matter of fertilizer may be applied.

Turf laying

Season
5.5.4.2 The turf may be laid when weather and soil conditions are suitable and, where possible, preference should be given to autumn and early winter operations. (No turf should be laid in exceptionally dry or frosty weather or in other unsuitable weather conditions.)

Delivery and stacking
5.5.4.3 For large areas it is advisable that supplies of turves should be delivered at appropriate intervals throughout the work so as to avoid as far as possible stacking turves for long periods. Where it is not possible, they should be unloaded and conveniently stacked on cleared ground to a maximum height of 1.000 m unless arranged on pallets for mechanical handling. After four days stacked turves should be inspected at frequent intervals; any which show signs of deterioration should be used without delay, or laid out.

Laying
5.5.4.4 No turf should be laid until the topsoiling in whole or in part has been satisfactorily completed by being brought to an even tilth and firmness.

Turves from the stack should be wheeled to turf layers on planks laid closely side by side. Adequate timber planks should be used to support workmen and barrows and provide access.

The turves should be laid on the prepared soil bed and firmed into position in consecutive rows with broken joints (as in stretcher bond brickwork), closely butted and to the correct levels. The turf should be laid off planks working over turves previously laid. Where necessary, the turves should be lightly and evenly firmed with wooden beaters, the bottom of the beaters being frequently scraped clean of accumulated soil or mud. A dressing of finely sifted topsoil (complying with B.S. 3882) or fine peat should be applied and well brushed into the joints. Any inequalities in finished levels owing to variation in turf thickness or uneven consolidation of soil should be adjusted by raking and/or packing fine soil under the turf. A roller should not normally be used. The finished level of the turf should conform to the levels indicated, allowing for final settlement. Turf edges and margins should be laid with whole turves (for illustration see original British Standards publication.)

Turfing to banks exceeding 30°

5.5.4.5 Stability, and the retention of soil and seed may be a problem when turfing to banks with a gradient exceeding 30°. Information concerning the construction of such banks, grading and drainage, is given in the section of the British Standard on groundworks and the section on drainage. No topsoiling or turfing should be undertaken until the bank has been satisfactorily graded and any necessary cut-off drains completed.

Turf

5.5.4.6 Turves should comply with the requirements of B.S. 3969:1965. It is particularly important that turves to be used on banks should be sufficiently fibrous to withstand difficult handling conditions.

Season

5.5.4.7 Turfing to banks should preferably be carried out during the autumn or early winter. The spring should normally be avoided because of the harmful effects of prolonged dry weather and drying winds at that time of year.

Formation level

5.5.4.8 If the normal preparation of the formation level would result in subsoil slipping down the slope it should be omitted. However, it is essential that the smooth, polished surfaces produced by excavation in certain soils should be loosened. This will assist in retaining topsoil on the slope, prevent water running down the impervious surface and encourage the penetration of stabilising root growth.

Topsoiling

5.5.4.9 A 75 mm to 100 mm layer of topsoil will normally be sufficient. On steeper slopes, where there are practical difficulties in retaining topsoil on the gradient, it will be necessary to soil in narrow strips across the bank, starting from the bottom, and laying two or three rows of turves before proceeding with the next strip.

Turf laying

5.5.4.10 Sufficient timber planks and ladders should be used to ensure safe and efficient working. The turves may be laid diagonally or horizontally. They should be laid to stretcher bond pattern, butt-jointed, firmed and secured by stout wooden pegs 200 mm in length, or by 4 mm 8 SWG galvanized wire pins, bent or hairpin pattern, at least 200 mm long.

Finely sifted topsoil should be worked well into the joints. On the very steep banks or where stability is a major problem, netting should be laid over the turf and pegged down. Where necessary, the wire netting should be reinforced at the top and bottom, and intermediately with stout wire cable threaded through the mesh.

Alternative method

5.5.4.11 An alternative method for use on very steep slopes is to lay two layers of turf. The first is inverted and laid diagonally across the slope, with

5.5.4.11 **Alternative method** *continued*
(*cont'd*) each turf secured as described above. The exposed underside is scarified and the upper layer laid diagonally, at right angles to the first. This should also be secured with pegs long enough to penetrate into the formation level. Finely sifted topsoil should be worked into the joints of each layer of turf.

Watering
5.5.4.12 All necessary watering should be carried out with sprinklers or oscillating sprays so as not to wash soil out of the joints. If shrinkage occurs and the joints open, fine topsoil or compost should be brushed in and well watered. Special care is needed on banks.

5.5.5 ALTERNATIVE ITEMS ON TURFING (NOT IN B.S. 4428:1969)

Final preparation for turfing
5.5.5.1 All areas to be turfed are to be cultivated to a depth of at least 100 mm, cleared free of weeds and rubbish and brought to a very fine tilth.

5.5.5.2 Before turfing, Fisons 'PS5' pre-turfing fertilizer (used in accordance with the manufacturers' instructions) is to be worked into the top 50 mm of soil as the final tilth is reached.

5.5.5.3 Before turfing I.C.I. 'Garden Plus' pre-turfing fertilizer (used in accordance with the manufacturers' instructions) is to be worked into the top 50 mm of soil as the final tilth is reached.

5.5.5.4 A mixture of two fertilizers is to be used each at 70 g per m^2 and applied in transverse directions and worked into the final tilth. The two fertilizers shall be made up as follows:
   (A) Containing Superphosphate with minimum 18% Phosphoric acid (water soluble).
   (B) Containing sulphate of ammonia with minimum of 20% nitrogen.

Insecticide
5.5.5.5 After completion, all turf areas to be dressed with I.C.I. 'Sydol' (benzene hexachloride) insecticide in accordance with the manufacturers' instructions. The dressing is to be evenly distributed over the whole of the turfed areas.

Top dressing
5.5.5.6 On completion of laying, the whole of the turfed areas to be top dressed to a depth of 10 mm with fine sifted soil well brushed in.

Maintenance after practical completion date
5.5.5.7 The contractor shall carry out the initial cut on newly turfed areas when first growth is apparent; blades set 20 mm above ground. Continue

Specification—Turf and turfing

5.5.5.7 **Maintenance after practical completion date** *continued*
(*cont'd*) cutting at appropriate intervals during the growing season and maintain 40 mm high sward until the grass areas are handed over for regular maintenance. Price to be on the basis of 10 cuts during one growing season.

5.5.5.8 Top dress with fish meal fertilizer at rate of 70 g per m^2 after second mowing. Further maintenance shall consist of watering, weeding, cutting, repair of all erosion and settlement and re-seeding as necessary to establish a uniform and healthy stand of the specified grasses and shall continue until acceptance as agreed by the landscape architect.

5.5.5.9 The turf after complete establishment shall be treated with Fisons 'Mecodex' selective weedkiller, applied in accordance with the manufacturer's instructions (note should be taken of the manufacturer's recommendations on period to elapse before application).

5.5.5.10 The turf after complete establishment shall be treated with Fisons 'Cambadex' selective weedkiller, applied in accordance with the manufacturer's instructions (note should be taken of the manufacturer's recommendations on period to elapse before application is made).

5.5.5.11 The turf after laying shall be treated with I.C.I. 'Weedkiller for New Grass' selective weedkiller, applied in accordance with the manufacturer's instructions. (Small areas only).

5.6 PLANTS AND PLANTING INCLUDING SEMI-MATURE TREES

5.6.1 INTRODUCTION

5.6.1.1 The British Standard recommendations for Nursery Stock are in B.S. 3936. Part 1 (1965) covers trees and shrubs, Part 4 (1966) deals with forest trees. Not quoted in this publication are Part 2 (Roses), Part 3 (Fruit), Part 5 (Poplars and willows for timber production), Part 7 (Bedding plants grown in boxes), Part 9 (Bulbs, corms and tubers), and the following yet to be published: Part 6 (Herbaceous perennials and alpines), Part 8 (Bedding plants grown in pots), Part 10 (Dahlias), Part 11 (Chrysanthemums), Part 12 (Root stocks). Planting of trees, shrubs and forestry is covered by the appropriate section of B.S. 4428:1969. Transplanting semi-mature trees is covered by B.S. 4043:1966. The main sections of the above-mentioned standards are quoted here in full by kind permission of B.S.I. The quantities and dimensions have been converted to rounded metric equivalents, the clauses and paragraphs have been renumbered and footnotes, diagrams and tables have been omitted.

5.6.1.2 In Chapter 7 prices for various plants are given, based on compliance with these British Standards.

5.6.1.3 The plants listed in plant schedules should be varieties which are grown commercially in reasonable numbers, and a requirement that stock should be from a nursery close to the site, although theoretically desirable, is often unreasonable in practice and impossible to enforce when plant material availability tends to be so erratic. Plants from Common Market countries would be barred, if the above requirement was enforced.

5.6.1.4 In certain circumstances the British Standard recommendations might not be considered to be sufficiently detailed for certain circumstances and a specification/description of work would probably also include some of the following items:

Trees

Orientation
5.6.1.5 Before lifting is started a mark should be made on the stem to indicate the approximate north side so that the tree may be final-planted with the same orientation as that when growing in the nursery.

Plant material

Supply and substitution
5.6.1.6 Upon submission of evidence that certain materials including plant materials are not available at time of contract, the contractor shall

Specification—Plants and planting including semi-mature trees

5.6.1.6 **Supply and substitution** *continued*
(*cont'd*) be permitted to substitute other material and plants, with an equitable adjustment of price. All substitutions shall be of the nearest equivalent species and variety to the original specified and shall be subject to the approval of the landscape architect.

Planting

5.6.1.7 No tree pits shall be dug until final tree positions have been pegged out for approval by the landscape architect.

5.6.1.8 All plants should be refirmed into the ground, if lifted by frost during the landscape contract period.

Watering

5.6.1.9 The landscape contractor shall allow for the adequate watering in of all newly planted trees and shrubs immediately after planting (particularly when planting takes place in the spring) and he shall, during the following growing season, keep the plant material well watered.

5.6.1.10 All shrubs which are supplied with their roots balled or pot grown, shall be well soaked prior to planting, particularly evergreens and conifers.

5.6.1.11 Watering in and subsequent frequent watering of summer-planted container-grown plants is essential.

Maintenance

5.6.1.12 The landscape contractor shall maintain all planted areas within the landscape contract boundaries until the area is handed over in whole or in phases. Maintenance shall include watering, weeding, cultivating, control of insects, fungus and other diseases by means of spraying with an approved insecticide or fungicide, pruning adjustment and repair of anchors and wire, repair of minor washouts and other horticultural operations necessary for the proper growth of the plants and for keeping the landscape sub-contract area neat in appearance.

Pruning and repairs

5.6.1.13 Upon completion of planting work on the landscape sub-contract all trees should be pruned and all injuries repaired where necessary. The amount of pruning shall be limited to the minimum necessary to remove dead or injured twigs and branches and to compensate for the loss of roots and the result of transplanting operations. Pruning shall be done in such a manner as not to change the natural habit or special shape of the trees. All cuts should be made flush leaving no stubs. On all cuts over 75 mm diameter and on bruises or scars on the bark, the injured cambium shall be traced back to living tissue and removed. Wounds shall be smoothed so as not to retain water and the treated area shall be coated with Shellac or an approved treewound paint, all in accordance with B.S. 3998. (Tree work).

5.6.2 B.S. 3936: Part 1: 1965 NURSERY STOCK, TREES AND SHRUBS

Specification: general requirements

Scope

5.6.2.1 This part of this British Standard specifies some requirements for trees and shrubs, including conifers and woody climbing plants, which are suitable to be transplanted and grown for amenity.

Definitions

5.6.2.2 For the purposes of this British Standard, the following definitions apply:

Tree. A woody perennial with a distinct stem.

Shrub. A woody perennial, usually of less size than a tree, with several stems from or near ground level.

Conifer. Trees and shrubs of the order Coniferales, together with Ginkgo.

Otherwise the definitions in B.S. 3975, 'Glossary of terms for landscape work' apply. Note especially Part 4, 'Plant description'.

Compliance

5.6.2.3 (A) Trees. A tree, other than a conifer, shall comply with the requirements of this section on General Requirements and, according to its form, with the requirements of one of the clauses under Specific Requirements 5.6.2.10-16.

(B) Shrubs. A shrub, other than a conifer, shall comply with the requirements of both this section and clause 5.6.2.17.

(C) Conifers. A conifer shall comply with the requirements of both this section and clause 5.6.2.18.

Origin

5.6.2.4 Trees and shrubs shall be true to name. Those which are normally propagated vegetatively shall, if grown from seed, be stated to have been so produced.

If subjects have been budded or grafted this shall be stated, and the name of the root stock shall be supplied if requested by the purchaser.

If high-worked this shall be stated.

Root system

5.6.2.5 The root system shall be conducive to successful transplantation. Where necessary, the root-ball shall be preserved by support with hessian or other suitable material. On soils where retention of a good ball is not possible, the roots should be suitably protected in some other way.

Condition

5.6.2.6 Trees and shrubs shall be substantially free from pest and disease, and shall be materially undamaged. Torn or lacerated roots shall be pruned before dispatch. No roots shall be subjected to adverse conditions, such

5.6.2.6 (cont'd) Condition *continued*
as prolonged exposure to drying winds or subjection to water-logging, between lifting and delivery.

The root-ball shall be free from pernicious perennial weeds.

Dimensions
5.6.2.7 Trees and shrubs shall be of the size stated.

Packaging
5.6.2.8 Packaging shall be adequate for the protection of the plants and such as to avoid heating or drying out.

Marking
5.6.2.9 Each specimen of tree and shrub, or each bundle, shall be legibly labelled with the following particulars:
(A) Its name.
(B) The name of the supplier, unless otherwise agreed.
(C) The number of this British Standard.

Specification: specific requirements

Bush tree
5.6.2.10 A bush tree shall have a leg of 300 mm to 750 mm and a well-balanced branching head.

Half standard
5.6.2.11 A half standard shall have a sturdy reasonably straight stem 1.100 m to 1.400 m in height from ground level to the lowest branch, and a minimum diameter of 20 mm when measured between 600 and 900 mm from the ground. It shall have a well-balanced branching head.

Three-quarter standard
5.6.2.12 A three-quarter standard shall have a sturdy, reasonably straight stem 1.450 m to 1.600 m in height from ground level to the lowest branch, and a minimum diameter of 20 mm when measured between 600 and 900 mm from the ground. It shall have a well-balanced branching head.

Standard
5.6.2.13 A standard shall have a sturdy reasonably straight stem 1.700 m – 1.850 m in height from ground level to the lowest branch, and a minimum diameter of 20 mm when measured between 600 and 900 mm from the ground. It shall, according to the species and the intended use, have either a well-balanced branching head or a well-defined, straight and upright central leader with the branches growing out from the stem with reasonable symmetry.

Tall standard
5.6.2.14 A tall standard shall have a sturdy reasonably straight stem 1.850 m to 2.150 m in height from ground level to the lowest branch and a minimum diameter of 25 mm when measured between 600 and

Specification—Plants and planting including semi-mature trees

5.6.2.14 **Tall standard** *continued*
(*cont'd*) 900 mm from the ground. It shall, according to the species and the intended use, have either a well-balanced branching head or a well-defined, straight and upright central leader with the branches growing out from the stem with reasonable symmetry.

Weeping standard
5.6.2.15 A weeping standard shall have a sturdy, reasonably straight stem with a minimum height of 1.700 m from ground level to the lowest branch and a minimum diameter of 20 mm when measured between 600 mm and 900 mm from the ground. It shall have a well-balanced branching head.

Feathered tree
5.6.2.16 A feathered tree shall have a defined, straight and upright leader and its stem shall be well-furnished with lateral shoots. The height shall be stated.

Shrub
5.6.2.17   (A) General. The height of shrubs shall be stated, if requested. This height shall be measured from ground level, excluding the root-ball or any container.
(B) Open-ground shrub. An open-ground shrub, other than a shrub for a hedge, shall have been transplanted and, according to species, cut back or trimmed to encourage bushiness.
(C) Shrubs for hedges. Shrubs for hedges shall have been transplanted, slacked or undercut and, according to species, cut back or trimmed to encourage bushiness. They shall be graded for size.
(D) Pot-grown shrub. A shrub which is pot-grown or container-grown may, according to species, be cut back or trimmed to encourage bushiness. The size of the pot shall be stated. Climbers shall be adequately staked.

Conifer
5.6.2.18 A conifer shall be well-furnished, according to species. The size shall be stated.

General notes
5.6.2.19 The original British Standards publication then follows with an appendix listing forms and sizes of trees and shrubs normally supplied. It also indicates those plants which should be pot-grown for ease and safety in transplanting.

5.6.2.20 This is followed by an appendix listing sizes of conifers normally supplied, with information on those which should have a single central leader and those which should be root-balled or pot-grown.

5.6.2.21 An illustration is then given showing the normal form of standard, bush and feathered trees.

Specification—Plants and planting including semi-mature trees

5.6.3   B.S. 3936: Part 4:1966: NURSERY STOCK, FOREST TREES

Specification

Scope

5.6.3.1   This part of this British Standard specifies some requirements for forest tree stock, to be grown for timber production, of the species specified in Table 1 (not included here).

It includes requirements as to origin, dimensions, root and shoot, description, condition and packaging.

Definitions

5.6.3.2   For the purposes of this British Standard the definitions in B.S. 3975 apply, together with the following specific definitions:

Seedling. Any plant grown from seed and remaining undisturbed since sowing.

Transplant. Any plant which has been transplanted one or more times in the nursery.

Undercutting. The severing of the roots of seedlings or transplants at a regulated depth in the bed, such plants being subsequently described as undercut seedlings or transplants, as appropriate.

Height. The distance measured from the root collar to the tip of the bud of the leading shoot, when the latter is supported in a vertical position.

Stem diameter. The diameter of the main stem at the root collar.

Origins

5.6.3.3   The origin of seed shall be stated with as much detailed information as possible.

Dimensions

5.6.3.4   (A) Plants for forest use. The minimum dimensions of plants for forest use shall be in accordance with Table 2 (not shown here).

(B) Plants for nursery use. The minimum height of plants for use in the nursery shall be 40 mm for conifers and 75 mm for broadleaved species. At this stage it is not possible to relate height to stem diameter.

Tables

5.6.3.5   (In the original British Standard, tables are then provided which give scientific names of a range of forest trees with preferred and deprecated common names, followed by a table of minimum dimensions for a range of common species).

Root and shoot

5.6.3.6   The root systems of plants shall contain a reasonable proportion of fine fibrous rootlets, and shall be adequate for the age and size of the plants.

Plants shall have a vigorous leading shoot and shall be appropriately furnished with laterals, according to species and age.

Evergreen species shall carry at least the current year's foliage.

Specification—Plants and planting including semi-mature trees 137

Description and condition
5.6.3.7 Description
(A) Type: All plants shall be described as seedlings or transplants as appropriate; if they have been undercut, this shall be stated.
(B) Age: Plants for forest use, except *Abies*, shall be not more than four years old. Plants for nursery use shall be not more than three years old.
If requested, the age of plants shall be stated. It shall be expressed by indicating separately the time spent in the seed bed and the transplant lines. Each transplanting shall be indicated by a + sign, and undercutting by the letter 'u', e.g.:
1 + 0   2 + 1
1 + 1   2 + 2
1 u 1   2 + 1 + 1
No plants shall remain for more than two years in either seed beds or transplant lines without undercutting or transplanting.
(C) Height: Heights of individual plants in any quoted height range shall be reasonably evenly distributed throughout that range.

5.6.3.8 Condition. Plants shall be substantially free from pests, disease, discoloration and deformity, and shall be materially undamaged. Precautions must be taken to avoid damage after lifting, e.g. by exposure to drying wind, sun or frost, by subjection to waterlogging or by unsuitable storage conditions.

5.6.3.9 Packaging. Packaging shall be such as to avoid heating and drying out.

5.6.4 B.S. 4428:1969 INDIVIDUAL TREE PLANTING (from Recommendations for general landscape operations)

Nursery stock
5.6.4.1 All trees should comply with the general requirements specified in B.S. 3936 Part 1, and with the specific requirements where applicable.

Season
5.6.4.2 Tree planting is normally carried out between October and April inclusive. Evergreen trees are best moved when the ground is warm enough to encourage rapid root action in autumn or late spring. Exceptions to this rule are specially prepared subjects, either container-grown material or material which has been lifted in season, balled and wrapped and kept on the surface in wood shavings, sand, peat or other suitable material; all subjects moved in warm weather should be subject to proper precautions such as additional overhead spraying with water, mulching, shading and the use of an anti-desiccant.

Protection
5.6.4.3 Trees should be supplied with protection in accordance with the recommendations of B.S. 3936. After delivery, if planting is not to be

Specification—Plants and planting including semi-mature trees

5.6.4.3 **Protection** *continued*
(*cont'd*) carried out immediately, balled plants should be placed cheek to cheek and the ball covered with sand or moist peat to prevent drying out. Bare-rooted plants can be heeled in by placing the roots in a prepared trench and covering them with earth which should be watered in to avoid air pockets round the roots.

Tree pits
5.6.4.4 The tree pit should be excavated to allow adequate clearance between the root ends (when fully spread) or the perimeter of the ball and the side of the pit. The size of the pit should be such as to allow for the provision of not less than 0.500 m^3 of good topsoil for planting. The depth should be at least 75 mm greater than the depth of the root system. The bottom of the hole should be forked to break up the sub-soil. If the depth of topsoil is only a few millimetres some sub-soil may have to be removed from the site. Special care is needed in turfed or newly seeded areas to ensure that soil removed from the pit does not damage the existing grass, and that foot damage is mitigated by the use of planting boards.

Soil
5.6.4.5 It is important to select the species suitable for the soil and conditions. Trees should be planted in an open and friable soil of a high organic content. If this does not exist the soil should be improved by preparing a mixture consisting of 7 parts by volume of topsoil complying with the recommendations of B.S. 3882, 3 parts of moist fibrous peat and 2 parts of sharp river sand. Approximately 200 g of organic fertilizer per tree should be worked into the backfill mixture.

Staking

Requirement
5.6.4.6 Newly planted trees must be held firmly although not rigidly by staking to prevent a pocket forming around the stem and newly formed fibrous roots being broken by mechanical pulling as the tree rocks.

Methods
5.6.4.7 The main methods of staking are:
(A) A single vertical stake, 600 mm to 900 mm longer than the clear stem of the tree, driven 600 mm to 900 mm into the soil.
(B) Two stakes as above driven firmly on either side of the tree with a cross-bar to which the stem is attached. Suitable for bare-rooted or balled material.
(C) A single stake driven in at an angle of 45° and leaning towards the prevailing wind, the stem just below the lowest branch being attached to the stake. Suitable for small bare-rooted or balled material.
(D) For plant material 3.000 m to 4.500 m high, with a single stem a three-wire adjustable guy system may be used in exposed situations.

Specification—Plants and planting including semi-mature trees

5.6.4.7 **Methods** *continued*
(cont'd) Sweet chestnut and peeled larch poles are two examples of the most durable timbers for staking. The end should be pointed and the lower 1.000 m to 1.200 m should be coated with a non-injurious wood preservative (not creosote or tar), allowing at least 150 mm above ground level. Sawn timber, if used, should be pressure treated. The stake should be cut off just below the first crotch after the tree has been planted and burrs removed (Drawings of staking, guying, etc omitted).

Planting

5.6.4.8 It is most important to plant trees at the original soil depth; the soil mark on the stem is an indication of this and it should be maintained on the finished level, allowing for settling of the soil after planting. All plastic and other imperishable containers should be removed before planting. Any broken or damaged roots should be cut to sound growth. The bottom of the planting pit should be covered with 50 mm to 75 mm of soil. Bare roots should be spread evenly in the planting pit; a small mound in the centre of the pit on which the roots are placed will aid an even spread. Soil should be placed around the roots, gently shaking the tree to allow the soil particles to sift into the root system to ensure close contact with all roots and to prevent air pockets. Backfill soil should be firmed as filling proceeds, layer by layer, care being taken to avoid damaging the roots. Organic material should be applied, according to soil requirements.

Tying

5.6.4.9 Each tree should be firmly secured to the stake so as to prevent excessive movement. Abrasion must be avoided by using a buffer, rubber or hessian, between the tree and stake. The tree should be secured at a point just below its lowest branch, and also just above ground level; normally two ties should be used for each tree. These should be adjusted or replaced to allow for growth.

Tree guards

5.6.4.10 Where tree guards are necessary, care should be taken to ensure that they do not impede natural movement or restrict growth.

5.6.5 B.S. 4428:1969 PLANTING OF SHRUBS, HEDGES, CLIMBERS, HERBACEOUS PLANTS AND BULBS (from Recommendations for general landscape operations)

Nursery stock

5.6.5.1 All shrubs, hedging plants, climbers, herbaceous plants and bulbs should comply with the appropriate requirements specified in B.S. 3936 where applicable, and otherwise should be of reasonable size and shape and in healthy condition and follow the general quality and packaging requirements of B.S. 3936.

Specification—Plants and planting including semi-mature trees

5.6.5.1 (cont'd) **Nursery stock** *continued*

Planting should be carried out as soon as possible after reaching site. Where planting must of necessity be delayed, care should be taken to protect the plants from pilfering or damage from people or animals. Plants with bare roots should be heeled-in as soon as received or otherwise protected from drying out, and others set closely together and protected from the wind. If planting is to be delayed for more than a week, packaged plants should be unpacked, the bundles opened up and each group of plants heeled-in separately and clearly labelled. If for any reason the surface of the roots becomes dry the roots should be thoroughly soaked before planting.

Season and weather conditions

Season

5.6.5.2 Most deciduous shrubs to be lifted from open ground should be moved in the dormant period, which is normally between October and April inclusive. Conifers and evergreens should be planted in early autumn or late spring. Herbaceous plants may be moved September to October and March to April.

Weather conditions

5.6.5.3 Frost. Frost and snow need not necessarily prevent planting, provided that the roots are not actually frozen and that the frozen ground or snow is not dug in. Frozen soil and snow should be carefully set aside and replaced on top after planting.

5.6.5.4 Water. Planting should not be carried out in waterlogged soil.

5.6.5.5 Wind. When planting is carried out in periods of persistent wind, especially north or east winds, it is often desirable to provide temporary protection as a wind-break for conifers and evergreen shrubs to prevent the foliage drying out before the roots have time to make new growth. Wind is usually more dangerous to newly planted subjects than frost.

Preparation of ground

5.6.5.6 (See also section on Groundworks.) When shrubs and herbaceous plants are planted in beds, the beds should be pegged out to correspond with the planting plan. Where the site is infested with perennial weeds the ground should, if possible, be allowed to fallow for three to four months in late spring or summer. Throughout this fallowing period steps should be taken to destroy all growing weeds by cultivation and the use of appropriate chemicals, repeated as necessary.

After fallowing, an organic fertilizer, moist peat, or other humus-forming material should be spread and worked-in to make good significant deficiencies disclosed by a soil analysis.

Except in the case of large beds which can be satisfactorily machine cultivated, heavy ground should be double dug if there has not been sufficient soil disturbance during preparatory work.

Specification—Plants and planting including semi-mature trees

Protective fencing
5.6.5.7 According to local environment shrubs may have to be protected adequately from vandalism until established.

Planting
5.6.5.8 All subjects planted in dry weather should be firmed and watered.

Shrubs
5.6.5.9 Tall shrubs may need staking.

Shrubs in beds
5.6.5.10 Positions of shrubs to be planted should be marked out in accordance with the planting plan. When shrubs are set out, precautions should be taken to prevent roots drying. Planting holes should be excavated, about 150 mm wider than the root-spread. Polythene and other non-perishable containers should be removed and any badly damaged roots carefully pruned. The shrubs should then be set in holes so that the soil level, after settlement, will be at the original soil mark on the stem of the shrub. The hole should be backfilled to half its depth and firmed by treading. The remainder of the soil can then be returned and again firmed by treading.

Shrubs in grass
5.6.5.11 When planting isolated shrubs in grass the turf should be removed over a diameter 1.000 m or 150 mm wider than the root spread taking care to protect the surrounding turves; after excavation the turf should be chopped up and forked back into the bottom of the hole and covered with 50 mm of topsoil, before planting as described in 5.6.5.10.

Ground cover shrubs
5.6.5.12 Low growing ground cover shrubs may be planted as for herbaceous plants. If climbers, such as ivy, are used for ground cover planting, the cane which is usually supplied with the plant should be carefully removed and the stems pegged out to encourage growth in the required directions.

Climbers and wall shrubs
5.6.5.13 Unless climbers and wall shrubs are self-clinging kinds, requiring only temporary support, some form of support will need to be constructed before planting is attempted. For example, a wall will require to be wired or have trellis affixed to it. Walls can be wired by fixing galvanised wire 600 mm from the ground and then at 300 mm spacing to the required height, carried through screw eyes spaced at 1.900 m centres, screwed into wall plugs. When trellis is used, this should be affixed to wooden battens or spacing pieces screwed into plugs set in the wall, so that it is set out not less than 12 mm clear from the wall.

142 Specification—Plants and planting including semi-mature trees

Climbers and wall shrubs continued

5.6.5.14 Pits should be excavated at least 300 mm wider than the root spread and 500 mm deep. In all cases, but especially where the plants are to be grown against a wall, the pits should be backfilled with good top spit loam rich in humus-forming materials and necessary fertilizers. After setting out the plants as per planting plan, excavate holes according to the size of the plant. Thoroughly water all dry plants and set in holes so that the old soil mark comes level with the top of the soil after firming. Plants should be at least 150 mm out from the wall, with the roots spread away from the wall. Branches should be lightly secured to trellis or wire to allow for any settlement of the soil. Any superfluous branches may be removed. Many climbers are pot grown and will be tied to canes on arrival on site. In those cases, where plants are too young to reach the wire or trellis when planted, or are of a self-clinging type, the cane should be retained. In the case of larger plants, the cane should be removed, the branches fanned out and separately secured to the supporting wires or trellis.

Herbaceous plants

5.6.5.15 Herbaceous plants should be set out according to the planting plan to ensure correct spacing. Smaller subjects should be planted with a hand trowel, taking care to firm round the roots; larger plants will require a spade to excavate holes, and firming should be done by treading. The depth of planting will depend upon the species.

Bulbs

5.6.5.16 All bulbs and corms should be planted in the appropriate season with a suitable planting tool of appropriate pattern and at the correct depth. The hole formed should be of sufficient diameter to accommodate the bulb or corm which should have its base in contact with the soil at the bottom. In fine turf a plug of turf should be neatly removed and replaced after planting. Bulbs for naturalising should not be planted in rows, but should be scattered by hand over the area allocated to them. They can then be planted where they fall.

Completion

5.6.5.17 On completion, the ground should be forked over and left tidy.

Hedges and screens

Preparation

5.6.5.18 Trenches for hedge planting should be prepared to the same depths and in the same way as for shrub planting (see 5.6.5.10). The width of the trenches depends on size, species and soil condition. The ground should be well prepared by trenching, incorporating organic material according to soil requirements.

Spacing

5.6.5.19 Hedge plants are usually set out between 250 mm and 750 mm apart in a single row or in two rows staggered, depending on the species used,

Specification—Plants and planting including semi-mature trees 143

Spacing *continued*
the size of plants and the ultimate effect required. Taller growing shrubs and trees can be used at wider spacing to form screens, either separately or in combination.

Support
5.6.5.20 Softer plants benefit from some support when young, and this can be achieved with a low post and wire fence. Where some immediate form of enclosure is necessary, the staggered rows may be planted on either side of a cleft chestnut fence.

On exposed sites, protection from prevailing winds, for example by wattle hurdles or low hessian screens, will greatly assist the plants to become established. It is particularly necessary in the case of conifers and evergreens.

Planting
5.6.5.21 Hedging plants should be planted in the way described for shrubs (see 5.6.5.10) or for trees (see 5.6.4).

Cutting back
5.6.5.22 After planting, certain quick-growing species, such as privet or thorn, should be cut back hard to encourage bushy growth from the base. Some other plants, however, such as beech, hornbeam, most evergreens and conifers, should not have the leading shoot cut until it reaches the desired height.

5.6.6 B.S. 4428:1969 FORESTRY PLANTING FOR AMENITY PURPOSES (from Recommendations for general landscape operations)

Planting stock
5.6.6.1 Trees for forestry planting should comply with B.S. 3936, Part 4 or Part 5, as and where applicable. Trees not covered by B.S. 3936, Part 4 should usually be sturdy transplants about 300 mm to 380 mm tall with a balanced root and shoot development, that is, with abundant fibrous roots and not too long a shoot. Small plants 150 mm to 250 mm tall may give better results on exposed sites or on ploughed and turfed ground. Large plants up to 600 mm tall may be more successful on sheltered fertile sites, particularly where heavy weed growth is anticipated.

Preparation of ground

Scrub clearing
5.6.6.2 Scrub may be cleared by hand or machine, or killed by herbicides, depending upon the objects to be achieved and the relative costs on each site. It is not usually necessary to grub out roots. Stump treatment with herbicides to prevent coppicing may be needed.

Scrub clearing continued

5.6.6.3 Complete clearance: Top growth should be cut to ground level. Vigorous re-growth of coppice shoots and weeds may need to be controlled by herbicides. The plantation also may be subject to setbacks from late spring frosts and drought.

5.6.6.4 Partial clearance: Partial clearance to ground level may lead to better survival and quicker establishment of the plantation. Smaller plants may be used, requiring less replacement and reduced weeding. Partial clearance has the important additional advantage of conserving amenity. Treatment will vary with conditions, but the overhead cover will usually be removed in two stages, half after two growing seasons and the remainder after four; it should rarely be retained for more than six growing seasons.

5.6.6.5 Retention of single trees: Thriving, shapely, immature single specimen trees may often be retained to silvicultural and amenity advantage.

Draining

5.6.6.6 All surface water should be removed and the water table lowered far enough to provide a depth of freely drained soil adequate for satisfactory root development. Cut-off drains may be necessary to intercept water flowing on to the area. For maximum effect these should be sited at a slight angle to the contours, and the other main drains should be sited as nearly as possible at right angles to the flow of the water. Their depth, width, shape and spacing will vary with the site. Drains may be formed mechanically (for example, in large scale operations where draining ploughs may be used), but some hand work is usually necessary, particularly in difficult conditions, such as on broken ground or in certain types of woodland.

Cultivation

5.6.6.7 Some form of cultivation, where practicable, is usually beneficial and leads to quicker establishment.

5.6.6.8 Ploughing: Wherever it is practicable, ploughing is the most effective and economical method of cultivating the ground and breaking any pan, or of providing surface drainage and a turf on which to plant, or of assisting in weed suppression. Single furrows may be ploughed at planting spacing or the ground may be ploughed completely. Different types of plough are required for different site conditions. Ploughing depths and direction will also vary. (Draining is a different and separate operation which usually demands a special sort of plough or excavator).

Fencing

5.6.6.9 When there is a risk of damage from deer, stock, sheep, rabbits or the public, the appropriate fences should be erected, selected from B.S. 3854.

Specification—Plants and planting including semi-mature trees

Turf planting
5.6.6.10 On wet or infertile sites trees may be planted on upturned turves at least 380 mm square and 150 mm thick. They may be cut on the planting spot or obtained from a plough furrow or a shallow drain dug for the purpose.

Screefing
5.6.6.11 Clearing the competing surface vegetation from the planting spot with a mattock or spade is the simplest form of cultivation and should be done at the time of planting. Screefing may be the only practicable method in small areas or on steep slopes where machines cannot operate. Alternatively, herbicides may be used in advance of planting to clear a circle of vegetation.

Planting

Spacing
5.6.6.12 In normal forestry practice, trees should be planted at a spacing varying from 1.000 m to 2.500 m depending on species and site conditions. Poplars should be spaced at from 6.000 m to 10.000 m apart. For amenity purposes closer planting or staggered planting may be desirable.

The following list gives the number of forestry plants required per hectare at the spacing shown.

1.000 m x 1.000 m apart	10,000 plants per hectare
1.500 m x 1.500 m apart	4,444 plants per hectare
2.000 m x 2.000 m apart	2,500 plants per hectare
2.500 m x 2.500 m apart	1,600 plants per hectare
6.000 m x 6.000 m apart	278 plants per hectare
8.000 m x 8.000 m apart	156 plants per hectare
10.000 m x 10.000 m apart	100 plants per hectare

Time of planting
5.6.6.13 Planting should normally be carried out when the trees are dormant. Spring planting usually gives the best results with conifers, particularly in exposed areas, but it is a common practice to plant hardwoods in the late autumn. Planting should be stopped during periods of frost or very cold winds.

Handling of plants
5.6.6.14 The two main dangers to avoid are the drying out of the roots and heating in the bundles, either of which may kill the plants, so that the most careful protection is necessary at every stage. Unless packed in polythene bags, the trees should be heeled-in as soon as they arrive on the site in a properly prepared trench and moist soil packed around them. If they are to remain there for more than a few days, the bundles must be opened out, and if the weather is very frosty, they should be

5.6.6.14 **Handling of plants** continued
(cont'd) covered with straw or bracken. Polythene bags are very useful in plant handling but they must not be exposed to direct sunshine. During planting the trees should be carried in waterproof bags to keep the roots moist, and they should only be taken out one at a time as required.

Planting methods

5.6.6.15 Notching: The straight notch and variations, such as L-, T-, and H-shaped notches, are commonly used on mineral soils. Special notching spades are made for this purpose. Properly used, mattocks are good on hard, stony and steep ground. The notch must be vertical and deep enough for the roots to hang freely. The notch should then be closed and the soil well firmed round the roots. The soil should be firmed again in April if frost lift has occurred.

5.6.6.16 Pit planting: This method is uncommon on a forest scale, but may have a limited use for exceptionally large plants on very weedy sites. The tree is planted in a hole sufficiently wide and deep for the roots to assume their natural shape.

5.6.6.17 Planting on turves and ploughed ground: On peats and other wet sites, the tree should be planted through the turf or plough ridge so that its roots reach the layer of rotting vegetation beneath. To avoid drying out, the cut should be made on the side away from the prevailing wind and the tree should always be well firmed-up. Various spades may be used to make the planting notch or to cut out the plug or wedge. On dry heaths, the tree should usually be notch planted low down in the furrow where more moisture is available. If the ground is hard, planting on the ridge (or on the sheltered side of the ridge) may give the roots more scope and increased stability. On some sites it may be important to choose the planting position giving the most freedom from weed competition.

While it is advisable that turves and ploughed ridges should be left to consolidate for a few months before planting, it is essential that planting should be completed within a year if full benefit is to be obtained.

Fertilizers

5.6.6.18 Fertilizers are generally not necessary for establishment on all the commonly planted soils. However, on poor, wet, peaty moorlands and on the poorer dry heaths, a phosphate fertilizer applied in the first season is essential for satisfactory growth. Ground mineral phosphate is the most commonly used form and may be applied at a rate of from 60 to 120 grammes per plant a few weeks after planting. The fertilizer should be placed a few millimetres away from each plant, taking care to avoid the foliage.

Specification—Plants and planting including semi-mature trees 147

Maintenance

General

5.6.6.19 Adequate maintenance is essential for successful establishment. In addition, all fences should be maintained while a risk of damage remains, and it is usually necessary to protect young plantations against fire.

Weeding

5.6.6.20 Vegetation which grows up around young trees must be controlled. In some seasons and in some types of vegetation more than one weeding will be necessary and weeding should be continued each year until the trees are large enough to avoid being smothered. Weeding may be carried out by hand, by machine, by herbicide, or by a combination of all three.

Beating-up

5.6.6.21 The replacement of losses should normally be carried out one year after planting. It is rarely worthwhile to beat-up a young plantation which has less than 20% of dead trees, unless they occur in groups, and it is usually sufficient to plant one tree to replace two or three dead ones.

Drainage

5.6.6.22 It is essential for the future health and stability of the crop that the drains should be cleaned regularly, and occasionally deepened and improved.

5.6.7 B.S. 4043:1966 RECOMMENDATIONS FOR TRANSPLANTING SEMI-MATURE TREES

Scope

5.6.7.1 This British Standard makes recommendations for transplanting semi-mature trees.
Appendix A (not reproduced here) lists trees which are suitable for transplanting in this way. Appendix B recommends root-ball sizes. Appendix C gives examples of guying techniques.

Definition

5.6.7.2 For the purposes of this British Standard, the following definition applies:

Semi-mature trees

5.6.7.3 A tree or shrub at an advanced stage of growth which is to be transplanted with an earth root-ball, or in certain cases bare roots, and is of such combined size and weight that special equipment will be needed to carry out the operation.

Specification—Plants and planting including semi-mature trees

5.6.7.3 (cont'd) *Semi-mature trees continued*
Such trees will generally be between 6.000 m and 15.000 m in height and will weigh between 250 kg and 10 tonne; they also include certain shorter trees and shrubs, which weigh more than 250 kg and need special lifting techniques or equipment because of their spread and weight.

Selection of trees for transplanting

General
5.6.7.4 The choice of semi-mature trees for transplanting is governed by five considerations: objectives; conditions at the planting site; suitability of species for transplanting; availability of species; selection of individual specimens.

Objectives
5.6.7.5 Consideration should be given to the purpose of planting, and whether single trees or group plantings are required. Ultimate size should be taken into account.

Conditions at the planting site
5.6.7.6 Selection of suitable species should then be matched to the natural or possible conditions that can be obtained at the planting site.

Trees suitable for transplanting
5.6.7.7 The selection may then be further modified or restricted to those trees known to respond successfully to transplanting at an advanced stage of growth.

Availability
5.6.7.8 The availability of semi-mature trees of some species is limited.

Selection of individual specimens
5.6.7.9 Trees selected for preparation and eventual transplanting should be vigorous, healthy, undamaged and of good shape.
Ideally they should be nursery-grown isolated specimens, but trees from well-thinned woodland areas and marginal trees beside rides are also suitable when prepared.

Season for transplanting

General
5.6.7.10 All transplanting should normally be carried out during the dormant season for the particular species and in weather conditions suitable for the operation. When it is unavoidable that transplanting be carried out between March and September inclusive, great care and attention to

Specification—Plants and planting including semi-mature trees

5.6.7.10 **General** *continued*
(cont'd) detail are required; additional special techniques will generally need to be employed. Ideal conditions for planting are when the weather is dull and the ground is moist and workable.

Coniferous and other evergreens are best transplanted in autumn. They should not be planted during periods of freezing winds. The object is to prevent excessive transpiration from the foliage without some compensatory action from the root system. An anti-desiccant spray is advised for use on evergreens before transplanting and again after planting. This spray should not be applied during rainy or frosty weather.

Deciduous trees may be transplanted throughout their dormant period.

Transplanting during frosty weather
5.6.7.11 During normal U.K. winters, the cold weather is seldom severe enough to cause damage to roots within, or on the periphery of, prepared earth root-balls, particularly when wrapped. Transplanting semi-mature trees with a balled root at this time can therefore bring the advantages of frost-bound ground, giving excellent conditions for vehicles to operate, of particular importance on sites which are normally soft and rather inaccessible, and the roots in the root-ball may suffer less damage during the operation.

During periods of intense and prolonged frost suitable measures should be taken to protect the bottom and sides of the tree pits, and piles of topsoil, from becoming frozen. The tree pits and piles of topsoil may be covered, for example with boards or tarpaulins; tree pits may be filled with straw.

Preparation by root pruning

General
5.6.7.12 Unless otherwise agreed, all trees should be properly prepared by excavation and root pruning. A sufficient time interval should elapse between initial preparation and transplanting to allow for the development of a new fibrous root system of adequate size and condition appropriate for the size, age, species and condition of the tree and capable of sustaining and developing the continuing growth of the tree on its new site.

Method of preparation
5.6.7.13 A trench should be made around the bole at a suitable distance to give a root-ball of the appropriate size. All protruding roots should be cut cleanly and all root ends over 25 mm in diameter should be painted with a fungicidal sealant.

The trench should be backfilled with a suitable medium and well firmed, and also watered if necessary. Ideally the backfill should be topsoil, complying with the recommendations of B.S. 3882 mixed with

Specification—Plants and planting including semi-mature trees

5.6.7.13 **Method of preparation** continued
(cont'd) humus-forming materials such as moist peat, leaf mould or old, well decayed farmyard manure. The further addition of sharp sand or other gritty materials to heavy soils will be of considerable benefit. The aim should be to provide as nearly as possible the ideal soil for the species being prepared. Where topsoil or other materials are to be imported for backfilling, care should be taken to ensure that they are of appropriate pH values if the tree is intolerant of free lime.

Sometimes it may be necessary to stabilise the tree against wind, either by preparation in at least two stages or by providing support until it is moved.

For coarsely-rooted trees or for some of the more difficult species preparation should be carried out over two or more seasons, by preparing alternate segments in successive years. For the larger and more difficult trees, specialist advice should always be sought.

Tree pits
5.6.7.14 Tree pits should have a diameter at least 600 mm greater than that of the root-ball. Their depth should be at least 225 mm greater than the depth of the root-ball to allow for incorporation of topsoil or other suitable material beneath the root. During the digging operations good topsoil should be stripped first and put to one side for re-use; subsoil and unusable material should be carted away.

The bottoms of the tree pits should be broken up to a depth of at least 225 mm to assist drainage and root penetration. Compacted glazed sides of pits resulting from the use of mechanical diggers in heavy soils should also be roughened. Where the site has been compacted by heavy mechanical equipment, the surrounding area should be cultivated; on heavy or impervious soil, sub-soiling may be necessary.

Shaping the floor of the tree pit to give a slightly raised centre is desirable.

Drainage
5.6.7.15 In heavy or poorly-drained soils the normal preparation of the tree pits recommended in Clause 5.6.7.14 may need some modification, and the addition of artificial drainage may become necessary.

It will be prudent in cases where the drainage of a site is poor to select species most tolerant of such conditions. However, selection of a 'tolerant' species is no substitute for proper drainage. Except in the case of a few species, ill-drained sites will not support healthy tree growth. In exceptional cases, on sites where drainage might be improved later, mound planting may be adopted whereby the tree is planted proud of the natural ground line and the surface is regraded so as to leave the tree growing on a graded mound.

The addition of a layer of gravel, crushed stone, hard-core or other suitable material placed beneath the roots and connected to a system of land drains can give good results. In artificially drained areas care should be taken to divert any existing land drains.

Pre-lifting operations

5.6.7.16 Any low-growing branches which the lifting machine may damage should be tied back, first wrapping delicate subjects with hessian.

If the ground is dry, watering should be carried out at least 24 hours before lifting.

In addition to this normal watering practice, use may be made of anti-desiccant sprays, to reduce transpiration; they should be mixed and applied in accordance with the manufacturer's instructions.

Lifting, loading and transporting

Preparation

5.6.7.17 A trench should be excavated immediately outside the new fibrous roots of the prepared tree, taking care not to disturb the soil around new fibrous roots. The ball should be undermined and freed by excavation, by tilting or by drawing a wire hawser through like a cheese wire. Undercutting should be below the lowest lateral roots, leaving as large an undisturbed root-ball as necessary. Suitable protective wrappings, such as hessian, should be placed around the root-ball and compressive support provided by securely lacing the ball.

Lifting

5.6.7.18 The tree should then be lifted by levering, winching or direct lift, and moved by a machine or other appliance of the appropriate capacity. Self-tightening slings around the bole or branches should not be used. As much support as possible should be given to the root-ball during the lifting process. The machine or the tree, or both, should be suitably padded throughout the lifting and subsequent operations to prevent damage to the tree from bruising, crushing and chafing; additional padding may be necessary in the late spring to protect the bark when the sap is in full flow.

Protection

5.6.7.19 When the root-ball has been lifted free, further supporting and protective wrappings underneath the ball should be used to guard against drying out and possible damage from vibration during transport.

Loading and transporting

5.6.7.20 For long journeys trees should be placed in a horizontal or semi-horizontal position on a suitable vehicle, so that low bridges and other obstacles may be negotiated. The trees should be supported near the point of balance and secured in such a way as to prevent damage to the root-ball by crushing. The heads of all evergreen trees, and of deciduous trees in leaf, should be covered during transit with a light opaque covering to reduce transpiration.

It will normally be necessary to tie in the branches to prevent breakages and avoid overhang. All attachments to the tree should be made with the greatest care, using padding or wrappings so that the bark is not damaged in any way.

Thinning

5.6.7.21 Depending on the ratio of crown to root, some judicious thinning of branches will often be advantageous. Any necessary tree work should be carried out as recommended in B.S. 3998 'Recommendations for tree work'.

Planting

5.6.7.22 Before unloading, the depth and diameter of the root-ball should be measured, so that any adjustment to the hole may be made. The tree should be set in the hole, orientated and planted with the minimum of delay. The tree when finally set, should be at the same depth as in its former position, except as recommended in Clause 5.6.7.14 for heavy or poorly drained land. Some settlement amounting to a few score of millimetres should be expected, and due allowance should be made.

Wrappings should be removed unless any damage is likely to result; it is essential that any impervious materials be completely removed. All damaged roots should be cleanly cut, and the cut surface of those of 25 mm in diameter and over treated with a fungicidal sealant.

Trees with the crowns tied in may have the fastening removed and the branches freed before or after planting, whichever is the more convenient.

Backfilling and mulching

Backfilling

5.6.7.23 The excavation should then be back-filled using topsoil previously saved and/or imported topsoil complying with the recommendations of B.S. 3882, which may be mixed with moist peat, leaf mould or other suitable humus-forming materials. Backfilling should be done in layers of 150-225 mm depth; at each stage the filling should be firmly consolidated to eliminate all air pockets under and around the roots.

If considered necessary at the time of planting, thorough watering should be carried out and any excess water allowed to drain away before completing the filling. The final layer of backfilling should not be consolidated but should be of sufficient depth to allow for settlement.

Mulching

5.6.7.24 Where agreed, a layer of not less than 50 mm of moist peat, leaf mould, grass mowings or other suitable organic material should be spread over the entire surface of the pit on completion of planting to act as a mulch.

Operational damage

5.6.7.25 On completion of planting any broken branches should be pruned, damaged areas of bark should be neatly pared back to sound tissue and all cuts and wounds over 25 mm in diameter should be treated with a fungicidal sealant. See B.S. 3998 (Recommendations for tree work).

Specification—Plants and planting including semi-mature trees

5.6.7.25 **Operational damage** *continued*
(cont'd) The tree should be inspected carefully for less obvious damage, such as bruising and crushing of the bark, which may not become apparent for some months. This damage may be found where the tree and a machine have been in contact and where ropes and other fastenings have been. Here again, the treatment is to pare back neatly to sound tissue and to treat the exposed surfaces. Attention is again drawn to B.S. 3998.

Guying and securing the tree
5.6.7.26 The tree should normally be guyed or secured underground. Relatively small trees may be successfully secured by staking.

Wrapping
5.6.7.27 The trunks and larger, lower branches of newly planted trees may be wrapped, for example with 150 mm wide hessian strips, straw ropes or treated crepe paper. This treatment will considerably reduce drying and will prevent sun scorch. It will generally be necessary on trees with thin bark, on trees planted in paved or other hard surfaced areas where heat may be reflected from the ground surface, and on trees coming from shaded woodland.
    The wrapping should generally be left on until at least the end of the second summer.

Watering and spraying
5.6.7.28 If the soil is dry, trees should be carefully watered in and subsequently maintained in a moist condition. Spraying the crown with water is advantageous during the growing season; it is best done in the evening.

Appendix A
(In the original British Standards publication Appendix A then lists trees suitable for transplanting when semi-mature. It also gives information on what species are easiest to move and the average ultimate sizes under average conditions.)

Appendix B: Notes on size of prepared root systems

General
5.6.7.29 No hard and fast recommendations can be given as to the size of the root system which should be prepared, because of the varying and inter-related factors involved. As a rule of thumb the diameter of the prepared root system should start at 12 times the diameter of the stem measured about 900 mm above the ground, and reduce to 9 times as the size of the tree increases.
    As regards depth of root-ball no firm instructions can be given, but as a guide they will seldom be less than 450 mm in depth even on shallow soils or for young trees, or more than 900 mm in depth for large trees from deep soils. The general advice given in clauses 5.6.7.12-13

154   Specification—Plants and planting including semi-mature trees

5.6.7.29   *General continued*
(*cont'd*)   should be adhered to and the trench dug to the full depth, and slightly below the depth of the lowest lateral roots, and the ball undercut wherever possible.
   The more important factors which effect the choice of size are:
   Species of tree
   Size and habit of growth
   Age and condition
   Natural rooting habit
   Type and depth of soil
   Whether nursery-grown stock or other plant material

Species of tree
5.6.7.30   The adaptability to transplanting at a semi-mature stage is indicated in Appendix A (not given here).

Size and habit of growth
5.6.7.31   There is enormous variation in this factor. The habit of growth will vary from narrow columnar crown types common to certain coniferous species, through to broad spreading crowns typical of many of our native broad leaved species. The important point to consider here is the amount of crown that has to be supported by the reduced root system. In general terms the larger the crown, the larger the root system that should be prepared.

Age and condition
5.6.7.32   The younger and more vigorous a tree is the more readily it can adapt to changed circumstances. It can therefore be generally assumed that a slightly smaller root-ball can be prepared for younger trees than older trees of the same species, although they may be of similar size.

Natural rooting habit
5.6.7.33   The natural rooting habit of a species can have an important bearing on the size of root-balls required and also on the time interval of preparation. The species which have compact fibrous root systems can be cut with smaller diameter root-balls and need a shorter preparation interval than those with a sparse and elongated root system. Species that produce pronounced tap roots generally require a deeper root-ball.

Type and depth of soil
5.6.7.34   Rooting habits are influenced by the texture and composition of the soil. This can vary from sand to clay; in general, sandy loams promote compact fibrous root systems, while clays encourage a sparse and rambling type of system. Rooting depth can be influenced by the depth of topsoil and type of subsoil, also by the presence of hard pan or rock, or again by a persistently high water table.

Specification—Plants and planting including semi-mature trees 155

Period of preparation
5.6.7.35 This is dealt with briefly in 5.6.7.13 (and also in Appendix A — not given here). If a two-year interval or more can be allowed for preparation, a smaller root-ball may be possible.

Whether nursery-grown stock or other plant material
5.6.7.36 If the selected material has been transplanted periodically in its early life or was transplanted at a fairly large size, it is possible that this early inducement to produce a compact fibrous root system may still be evident, particularly in light and medium type soils. If this is so, smaller root-balls may be possible for this material. Trees which have been grown in close canopy will invariably have a more elongated root system than those grown under more open and less competitive conditions.

Appendix C: Four examples of guying and securing techniques

Overhead guying
5.6.7.37 Attach three or four guy wires of 6 mm diameter 7-strand galvanized wire to the tree at approximately two thirds of its height. Loop them around the trunk over the crotch of a branch, and pass through a length of hose to protect the bark. Provide one 150 mm galvanized turnbuckle in each wire, at a height of 450 mm to 900 mm from the ground to give easy adjustment, or higher if necessary so as to be beyond the reach of children. Anchorage may be provided by one or other of the following methods, according to the size of tree and the condition of the ground:

5.6.7.38 Method A: 40 mm wide, 5 mm thick steel angle section stakes, 1.200 m to 1.500 m long, driven 1.050 m into the ground.

5.6.7.39 Method B: Timber 'deadmen' 1.200 m long x 500 mm girth to be sunk into the ground at least 900 mm deep, and placed horizontally at right-angles to the line of pull; the 'deadman' being held in place by two wooden stakes 1.000 m to 1.200 m long x 50 m top diameter, driven into the ground at a suitable angle.

5.6.7.40 In both methods, the stakes and 'deadmen' should be placed in regard to the position of the prevailing wind, and at such a distance from the tree as to give an angle of approximately 60° to the horizontal when the wire is taut, and so that the three wires are equally spaced around the diameter of the tree.

Underground securing; first method
5.6.7.41 Materials

Wooden stakes
  Timber: Oak, Sweet Chestnut or European Larch.
  Length: 1.200—1.400 m
  Diameter: 75—100 mm pointed at one end.

5.6.7.41 **Underground securing; first method** continued
(cont'd) Metal stakes
Angle iron fencing standards
Length: 1.200–1.400 m
Size: 40 x 40 x 5 mm with 10 mm diameter hole at 50–75 mm from top and pointed at other end.
Wire
7-strand galvanized wire, 6–10 mm in diameter according to the height and size of the tree. This can be reinforced by the addition of pig wire or similar coarse meshed material to spread the pull.
Staples
40 mm galvanized wire.
Wooden frame or boards:
Any sound timber will serve.

5.6.7.42 Procedure

Position the tree and partly backfill if required.
Place the stakes in position and partly drive. Place the boards of frame across the root-ball. Cut to length and whip the wires to the stakes, and also join on the cross wires. Drive the stakes until all the wires are taut.
Staples can be lightly driven to keep the wires in place if this is considered necessary. Adjustment is only possible by this method if:
(A) the tops of the stakes are near to the final surface levels, where they may be found again and driven further, or:
(B) by drawing the main wires tighter together by means of the cross wires.

Underground securing; second method
5.6.7.43 Materials

'Deadmen': Logs, railway sleepers or stone.
Species: Preferably Oak, Sweet Chestnut, Elm or European Larch.
Length: 1.800 m or according to size of tree and planting pit.
Diameter: 150 mm approximately.
Wire:
7-strand galvanized wire, 6–10 mm in diameter, according to the height and size of the tree. This can be reinforced by the addition of pig wire or similar coarse meshed material to spread the pull.
Staples
40 mm galvanized wire.
Wooden Frame:
Any sound timber will serve.
Turnbuckles:
200 mm or 250 mm according to size of tree.

Specification—Plants and planting including semi-mature trees 157

Underground securing; second method continued

5.6.7.44 Procedure

Position the tree, then dig in the 'deadmen' either side of the root-ball, or position the 'deadmen' in advance; the depth should be according to the height and size of the tree, but generally 450 mm to 600 mm will suffice. Fix four lengths of wire securely to logs by both whipping and stapling, and firmly ram earth over the 'deadmen'. The lengths of wire should be long enough to meet and join on to the turnbuckles over the root-ball. Bring the soil level up to the top of the root-ball. Next, place the wooden frame over the root-ball. Whip the turnbuckles on to the wires and tighten. Lightly cover the turnbuckles with oil or grease before mulching.

Periodic adjustments are possible by this method to compensate for settlement by merely raking back the mulch and adjusting the turnbuckles.

Illustrations

5.6.7.45 (In the British Standards 8 pages of diagrams and drawings follow showing: methods of preparation by root pruning; examples of wrapping and securing root-ball; planting on normal soil; planting on soil with poor drainage; overhead guying; showing alternative methods of ground anchorage; planting using underground securing [both methods]; wrapping of trunk and larger branches.)

5.7 ENCLOSURE

5.7.1 INTRODUCTION

5.7.1.1 Under the title of this chapter it is possible to group a large number of elements, including screen walls, retaining walls, fences, gates, crash barriers, pedestrian rails and bollards. The book would be put out of balance if all these items were covered in detail, therefore only those items most relevant to landscape work are included in this section.

5.7.1.2 As pricing for walls and other built elements can be found in the 'Architects' and Builders' Price Book,' such information has been omitted from this chapter. On the other hand wall copings can be an important part of landscape 'trim' which is covered in considerable detail in the illustrated portion of the book, (Chapter 6). Consequently drawings covering alternatives for such details are described here and priced out in 7.7.

5.7.1.3 There are many British Standards giving comprehensive coverage to the subject of fences, fencing and gates. There are referred to in this section but are not reproduced in detail. The British Standards reproduced in this chapter are mainly new ones or little known ones applying to soft landscape work. Where they are more commonly used, as in fencing work, it is felt that full details of such specification material are unnecessary. Full details can be obtained from the British Standards Institution.

5.7.2 SCREEN WALLS

Copings to freestanding walls

Drawings of copings
5.7.2.1 As drawings 6.5.7.1–12 in Chapter 6, showing alternative sections, materials and details for capping walls.

5.7.3 RETAINING WALLS

Copings to retaining walls

Drawings of copings
5.7.3.1 As drawings 6.5.7.13–18 in Chapter 6, showing alternative sections, materials and details for copings to brick or concrete retaining walls, sometimes also acting as mowing margins.

5.7.4 TRAFFIC BARRIERS & PEDESTRIAN RAILS

Moveable bollards; for reserved parking

Borer Engineering Company
5.7.4.1 'Borer' collapsible post; 770 mm high, 50 mm diameter galvanised steel tube contained within sealed unit, sunk into ground; post raised by telescopic means and locked upright into position with padlock or chain at top. Fix into ground in 1:2:6 mix concrete base in accordance with manufacturer's instructions.

Le Bas Tube Company Limited
5.7.4.2 'AutopA' collapsible post; 743 mm high, 64 mm diameter galvanised steel tube, hinged at base, with special locking mechanism in vertical position. Fix in accordance with manufacturer's instructions into 1:2:6 mix concrete base.

Fixed bollards

Atlas Stone Company Limited
5.7.4.3 concrete; 150 mm diameter, 330 mm above ground, either with grey granite exposed aggregate finish or white calcined flint and snowcrete.

Bloc Products
5.7.4.4 concrete; 'Gamma'; triangular grey or white concrete, 280 mm at base and 750 mm high.

Concrete Utilities Limited
5.7.4.5 concrete; 'Enfield', reinforced, 838 mm above ground with diameter at top of 152 mm; natural grey colour or exposed aggregate finish.

Mather & Smith Limited
5.7.4.6 cast iron; traditional design; total height 1.525 m including part set in ground.

Mono Concrete Limited
5.7.4.7 concrete; considerable range of types, sizes and finishes available from which the following typical selection is made:
'Bridgford'; 914 mm above ground and 229 mm diameter.
'Truro'; 762 mm above ground and 381 mm diameter.
'Wexham'; 760 mm above ground and 230 mm diameter.
'Wexham Major'; 750 mm above ground and 330 mm diameter.

Crash barriers

Standard safety barrier
5.7.4.8 galvanised sheet steel fender, 2.83 mm thick, 600 mm high with corrugations 90 mm deep and section width of 320 mm bolted at 3.200 m intervals to 150 x 150 mm creosoted or tanalised softwood posts set 300 mm into concrete foundation. Each fender 3.500 m long, overlapped with and bolted to next section by 6 No. high tensile bolts.

Specification–Enclosure

British Aluminium Company Limited

5.7.4.9 'Baco Parapet 1'; aluminium alloy with three horizontal rails; primarily as vehicle guard on bridges over motorways; effective height 1.000 m with spacing of posts at maximum 3.800 m centres.

5.7.4.10 'Baco Parapet 2'; aluminium alloy with three horizontal rails and mesh guard on traffic-side; effective height 1.000 m with spacing of posts at maximum 3.800 m centres.

British Steel Corporation

5.7.4.11 'Group P.1'; rectangular hollow section members in high yield steel with three horizontal rails; effective height 1.050 m with spacing of posts at 2.440 m centres.

Pedestrian guardrails

Abacus Municipal Limited

5.7.4.12 pedestrian barrier; steel, cold rolled section top and bottom rail, rectangular hollow section secondary vertical supports; all to B.S. 3049:1968; height above ground 940 mm with standard panel length of 1.829 m.

Highfield Engineering (Telford) Co. Ltd.

5.7.4.13 pedestrian barrier; steel, square tube top rail and posts with bottom rail and verticals in small rectangular hollow section steel; designed for speedy replacement of damaged panels; height above ground 1.068 m with standard length of panel 1.830 m.

Norman & Sons (Marketing) Limited

5.7.4.14 pedestrian barrier; steel, rectangular hollow section tube for top and bottom rails and posts, with round solid steel infill bars; all to B.S. 3049; height above ground 1.068 m with standard length of panel 1.830 m.

Street Furniture Limited

5.7.4.15 'Dura-Rail X'; aluminium alloy pedestrian guard rail system; height above ground 1.068 m with standard lengths in multiples of 120 mm up to 2.000 m; mill, natural anodized or bronze finish.

Low rails

Drawings of typical softwood timber low rails

5.7.4.16 See drawings 6.5.7.19–22 in Chapter 6 for illustrations of several typical low rails for defining pedestrian routes and protecting plants and grass from undue wear or short-cutting. See Chapter 7 section 7 for the pricing out of these rails.

Specification—Enclosure

5.7.4.17 *Drawings of typical hardwood timber low rails*
See drawings 6.5.7.23–26 in Chapter 6 for illustrations of several typical low rails. See Chapter 7 section 7 for the pricing out of these alternative rails.

5.7.4.18 *Drawings of typical metal low rails*
See drawings 6.5.7.27–34 in Chapter 6 for illustration of various typical low metal rails. See Chapter 7 section 7, for the pricing of these designs.

5.7.5 FENCES

British Standards

5.7.5.1 The relevant specification details can be obtained by reference to the following British Standards publications:

B.S. 1722:Part 1:1963;	Chain Link Fences
B.S. 1722:Part 2:1963;	Woven Wire Fences
B.S. 1722:Part 3:1963;	Strained Wire Fences
B.S. 1722:Part 4:1963;	Cleft Chestnut Pale Fences
B.S. 1722:Part 5:1963;	Close-Boarded Fences including Oak Pale Fences
B.S. 1722:Part 6:1963;	Wooden Palisade Fences
B.S. 1722:Part 7:1963;	Wooden Post and Rail Fences
B.S. 1722:Part 8:1966;	Mild Steel or Wrought Iron Continuous Bar Fences
B.S. 1722:Part 9:1963;	Mild Steel or Wrought Iron Unclimbable Fences with Round or Square Verticals and Flat Standards and Horizontals
B.S. 1722:Part 10:1963;	Anti-intruder Chain Link Fences
B.S. 1722:Part 11:1965;	Woven Wood Fences
B.S. 3854:1965;	Farm Stock Fences

It should be noted that most of the above publications have had revisions subsequent to the initial publication dates recorded above. Consequently a check should be made with the British Standards Institution to ascertain on any particular Standard, the number and date of any amendments.

Typical range of timber and metal fences

5.7.5.2 *Drawings of timber fences*
see drawings 6.5.7.35–43 in Chapter 6 for illustrations of various typical timber fences with specification notes; see Chapter 7 section 7, for the pricing out of these designs

Specification—Enclosure

Drawings of metal fences and railings

5.7.5.3 see drawings 6.5.7.44—47 in Chapter 6 for illustrations of several types of metal fences with specification notes; see Chapter 7 section 7 for the pricing out of these designs.

Drawings of gates

5.7.5.4 see drawings 6.5.7.48—49 in Chapter 6 for illustrations of a typical timber and a typical metal gate with specification notes; see Chapter 7 section 7 for the pricing out of these gates.

Temporary protective fencing

5.7.5.5 See 'Preparatory Operations' section 5.1 for specification of various types of temporary fencing.

Standard fencing (not shown in drawings)

Concrete slab fencing

5.7.5.6 305 x 38 mm slab panels set between twice grooved concrete posts 125 mm square at 1.830 m centres, set in concrete bases; posts 610 mm below ground except for 1.830 m fencing where they should be 760 m below.

Timber picket fence

5.7.5.7 traditional picket fence with 75 x 25 mm softwood vertical palings with pointed tops, screwed to 2 No. 100 x 50 mm horizontal softwood rails, housed into 150 x 100 mm softwood posts with weathered tops at 2.500 m centres and set in concrete base in ground; height of fence and post above 760 mm.

Timber close boarded with concrete posts

5.7.5.8 89 x 19 mm oak pales, lapped 13 mm on 2 No. horizontal rails with concrete setting posts at 2.740 m centres 610 m below ground in concrete base.

5.7.5.9 as above but with 3 No. horizontal rails.

Timber close boarded with timber posts

5.7.5.10 89 x 19 mm oak pales, lapped 13 mm on 2 No. 76 x 38 mm oak rails, 152 x 25 mm gravel board and oak posts at 2.740 m centres set 610 m below ground in concrete base.

5.7.5.11 as above but with 3 No. horizontal oak rails.

Interwoven timber panels; overlap

5.7.5.12 standard panels 1.830 m wide in creosoted softwood or western red cedar fixed to creosoted softwood or oak posts 100 x 100 mm set 915 mm into ground.

Specification–Enclosure

Interwoven timber panels; interlace
5.7.5.13   standard panels 1.830 m wide in creosoted softwood or western red cedar fixed to creosoted softwood or oak posts 100 x 100 mm set 915 mm into ground.

Wrought iron railings
5.7.5.14   traditional pattern; 16 mm diameter verticals at 127 mm intervals with horizontal bars near top and bottom; balusters with spiked tops; 51 x 20 mm standards 520 mm into ground in concrete bases at 2.750 m centres.

5.7.5.15   traditional park type; 16 mm diameter verticals at 80 mm intervals, welded at bottom to 38 x 8 mm flat and slotted through 38 x 8 mm top rail to form hooped top profile; 38 x 15 mm standards 560 mm into ground in concrete bases at 2.750 m centres.

Strained wire; three lines and concrete posts
5.7.5.16   3.25 mm gauge galvanised mild steel line wire with galvanised components and concrete posts and struts; three lines of plain wire threaded through posts and strained with eye bolts; 100 mm square concrete posts at 2.750 m centres set in ground, by 610 mm;

5.7.5.17   125 mm square concrete straining post with 100 x 75 mm concrete strut with post set 915 mm and strut 610 mm below ground.

5.7.5.18   as above but two strut posts to each straining post.

Strained wire; five lines and concrete posts
5.7.5.19   as specification 5.7.5.4 but with five horizontal wires in height of fence.

Chain link fencing on concrete posts
5.7.5.20   3 mm gauge, 51 mm mesh galvanised mild steel chain link with galvanised line wires, tying wires and steel components and concrete posts and struts; line wires threaded through posts and strained with eye bolts; 100 mm square concrete setting posts at 3.000 m centres set into ground 610 mm for 915 mm and 1.220 m fences and 750 mm for 1.830 m high fencing.

5.7.5.21   fencing system with aluminium alloy line and tying wires in place of galvanised steel.

5.7.5.22   125 mm square concrete straining post with one 100 x 75 mm concrete strut with post set 915 mm and strut 610 mm below ground except for 1.830 m fence where post should be 1.000 m and strut 750 mm below ground.

5.7.5.23   as above but two concrete strut posts to each straining post.

Chain link fencing on steel angle posts

5.7.5.24 as specification item 5.7.5.20 but supported on 63 x 63 x 8 mm mild steel angle posts, galvanised finish, in place of concrete.

5.7.5.25 fencing system with aluminium alloy line and tying wires in place of galvanised steel.

5.7.5.26 63 x 63 x 8 mm angle galvanised mild steel straining post with one 44 x 44 x 5 mm angle galvanised mild steel strut, with post set 915 mm and strut 610 mm below ground except for 1.830 mm fence where post should be 1.000 m and strut 750 mm below ground.

5.7.5.27 as above but two angle strut posts to each straining post.

Tennis court surround

5.7.5.28 2 mm gauge 44 mm mesh galvanised mild steel chain link with galvanised steel line wires, tying wires and components; with 44 x 44 x 5 mm galvanised mild steel angle standards, straining posts and struts; gate size 1.070 m x 1.980 m complete with hinges, lock and ironmongery.

Some typical proprietary fencing systems

Concrete

Bell & Webster Limited

5.7.5.29 'Belcon'; reinforced concrete solid panel fence in natural grey finish; posts 127 mm square; panels 51 mm thick, 1.829 m long and in heights of 915 mm to 2.520 m in 229 mm increments.

Ebor Fencing Limited

5.7.5.30 Type PLI; solid panel fence with weatherboard profile; posts at 2.000 m centres and panels 305 mm high giving maximum height of 2.750 m; standard buff sandfaced texture or exposed aggregate on one side (including posts); posts set 750 mm into ground in concrete bases.

Marley Buildings Limited

5.7.5.31 Ranch walling; two, three or four horizontal rails in reinforced concrete; spaced 152 mm apart, with concrete posts at 1.980 m centres; all with exposed aggregate finish on one side and smooth grey face on other; heights are 915 mm for two rail, 1.375 m for three rail and 1.830 m for four rail fences.

P.V.C. Fencing

P. J. P. Trading Limited

5.7.5.32 'Intrad'; horizontal p.v.c. rails, 150 mm deep bolted to concrete or p.v.c. posts at 1.830 m centres; fence heights vary from three rail at 800 mm to eight rail at 1.900 m.

Plastic coated chain link

Colorguard Limited

5.7.5.33 system of vinyl clad chain link fencing in various gauges with stainless steel and hard nylon fasteners to vinyl bonded rectangular hollow section high tensile steel posts; available in five colours with posts and chain link in same colours; posts to suit requirements and can form surrounds to tennis courts and other specialist needs with matching gates; posts are freestanding without the need for struts and gates do not need bracing members; a maintenance free system in normal circumstances.

5.8 HARD GROUND FINISHES

5.8.1 INTRODUCTION

5.8.1.1 The quantity of material available for possible specification writing (until the National Building Specification is available) is very considerable and is at times conflicting on this subject. It has therefore been decided to try and summarise some of the best items available. Whereas the specification sections dealing with soft landscape work in this book are totally comprehensive; in the case of hard paving, reference to more technical publications for particular items may sometimes be necessary. As specifications for paving come from many sources, the sections taken from British Standards by kind permission of B.S.I. are not set out in a separate sub-section but integrated into their appropriate location in the text.

5.8.1.2 The British Standards are quoted in summary form and the quantities and dimensions have been converted to rounded metric equivalents. The clauses have been renumbered to be compatible with the rest of the chapter and footnotes, diagrams and tables have been omitted. Reference to the original British Standard should be made for any specific items not included, where noted.

5.8.1.3 In Chapter 6, drawings of various constructional items are shown including kerbs, mowing margins and various types and layouts of paving. The appropriate references are made in this chapter to these drawings which often include specification notes which are not repeated in all cases in the text.

5.8.1.4 In Chapter 7 the main specification/description of works items in this Chapter plus the relevant drawings in Chapter 6 are priced out.

5.8.1.5 This section is divided into sub-sections covering preparatory items, kerbs and then paving under the three main headings of; flexible surfaces; rigid paving; unit paving. Every paving material on the market is not mentioned but a typical sample has been selected. In future editions the range will probably be extended.

5.8.2 PREPARATORY ITEMS

Typical specification/description of work items

Liability for excavations

5.8.2.1 Notwithstanding any authorisations, approval or direction given by the landscape architect with regard to excavations or any matter connected therewith, the contractor shall be responsible for taking the necessary safety precautions and for the reinstatement or other consequences of any damage arising from the operations.

Specification—Hard ground finishes

Water in excavations

5.8.2.2 The contractor shall keep excavations free from water at all times during the course of the contract.

Excavations generally

5.8.2.3 All excavations shall be opened for inspection in lengths and depths as the landscape architect may direct.

5.8.2.4 The whole of the excavations shall be carried out to the required lines and levels, widths and depths, so that the dimensions of the permanent work shall not be less than shown on the working drawings.

5.8.2.5 Selected and approved materials from excavations suitable for re-use on the contract for hardcore, sand, filling or for forming base to roads or surfacings, shall be kept separate for re-use as instructed, or carted to a tip provided by the contractor.

5.8.2.6 The phasing and method of execution of all foundations for paving shall be to the approval of the landscape architect.

5.8.2.7 Excavate to the appropriate depth for finished levels and fall over the sites of all roads, footpaths, yards etc. as shown on the drawings and well compact the base of the excavation.

5.8.2.8 Break out any old building or wall foundations or other obstructions. Disused drains shall be traced, and shall be taken up or filled with concrete 1:12 as directed by the landscape architect.

5.8.2.9 If any parts of the base are found to be unstable; either excavate further to a firm bed and fill in with suitable hardcore or clinker, or lay down fascines on which the sub-base can be consolidated.

5.8.2.10 The formation areas shall be covered as soon as possible after exposure.

5.8.2.11 Excavations taken wider or deeper than reasonably required to contain the permanent work shall be filled in at the contractor's expense.

5.8.2.12 Excavations taken wider than required shall be filled with selected subsoil material, thoroughly compacted in 150 mm layers.

5.8.2.13 Excavations taken deeper than required shall be filled with mass concrete (1:12).

5.8.2.14 No excavated bottom shall be built upon until approved by the landscape architect.

Hardcore

5.8.2.15 Hardcore shall consist of approved broken brick, concrete, hard stone or quarry waste, which is free from dust and other deleterious or

Specification—Hard ground finishes

Hardcore *continued*

5.8.2.15 (*cont'd*) foreign materials. The hardcore shall contain sufficient fines and be graded and placed as uniformly as possible in layers not exceeding 150 mm thick. Material which will crush under a roller shall not exceed 115 mm in any one direction and that which will not crush shall not exceed 65 mm in any direction. Broken brick, old plaster or other material which will soften or flake in water shall not be used.

5.8.2.16 The top surface of the hardcore shall be thoroughly blinded with well-graded gravel, stone or other approved material and compacted with a roller weighing 8-10 tonne to a firm and even surface, true to line and level.

5.8.2.17 Particular attention shall be paid to the achievement of full compaction around road gullies, in corners, and at other critical junctions, by the use of appropriate plant, which shall be to the approval of the landscape architect. When tested with a 3.000 m straightedge or template, the finished surface shall not show any departure from the true surface of more than 15 mm.

(Note: Sub-base is not normally necessary except on heavy clay or unstable foundations.)

Services under roads, paths etc.

5.8.2.18 All services laid in trenches across roads, paths and paved areas shall, where possible, be completed prior to the construction of the road or paving sub-base.

5.8.3 KERBS AND EDGINGS

Typical specification/description of work items

Precast concrete kerbs

5.8.3.1 Precast concrete kerbs shall be to B.S. 340:1963 which includes the following conditions:
    The cement used shall comply with B.S. 12 or B.S. 146, unless otherwise ordered. The aggregate used, which shall be approved by the purchaser and be of an appropriate size, shall comply with B.S. 882 or B.S. 104.

    Special surface finishes may be agreed. Unless otherwise specified the products shall be supplied in natural colour. If only the surface layer is required to be coloured this shall not be less than 12 mm thick. Pigments used shall comply with B.S. 1014.

Granite and whinstone kerbs

5.8.3.2 Granite and whinstone kerbs shall be to B.S. 435:1931 which includes the following conditions:

Granite and whinstone kerbs continued

5.8.3.2 (cont'd) The kerbs are required to be good, sound and free from defects: worked truly straight or circular, square and out of wind, with the top front and top back edges parallel or concentric to the dimensions specified. Ends should be chisel dressed neatly and accurately square to such depths as may be required to form a close butt joint. The bottom may be left rough.

Sandstone kerbs

5.8.3.3 Sandstone kerbs shall be to B.S. 706:1936 which includes the following conditions:
The stone shall be of a hard, siliceous sandstone from the carboniferous or older geological formation. It must be free from planes of structural weakness. The grains must be angular and closely interlocking and the matrix mainly siliceous. The standard finishes are 'Fine Axed', 'Coarse Axed', 'Rough Punched', 'Sawn Finish'.

Setting of kerbs

5.8.3.4 Kerbs will be laid before the base and surfacing of the road, and path or paving. In the case of concrete roads the kerb will be laid in the road slab.

5.8.3.5 The contractor will be responsible for reinstatement of damage caused by rollers or by heavy lorries etc., and for keeping kerbs clean during surfacing.

5.8.3.6 Kerbs shall be rectangular/splayed/half-battered/half-section kerbs laid on a 10/15 mm layer of cement mortar 1.3 on a concrete foundation 1.2.4 with concrete haunching to both sides, to within 75 mm of the top of the kerb. Vertical joints shall be close fitting not exceeding 3 mm in width and unjointed. Kerbs laid to curves should be radius kerbs for all radii of 12.000 m or less. All kerbs shall be laid true to line and level; any kerb found to be out of alignment, vertically or horizontally by more than 3 mm, shall be lifted and relaid, at the contractors expense.

5.8.3.7 Expansion joints in kerbs to flexible roads should be at 18.500 m intervals.

5.8.3.8 Where kerbing is associated with concrete roads, expansion joints shall be formed in the kerbing to coincide with the expansion joints in the road. The joint shall extend through the kerbing its bed and backing and shall be filled with filler as specified for the road joint.

5.8.3.9 Kerbing shall be so arranged that the normal close fitting vertical joint between kerbs shall coincide with the contraction joints in the road.

Drawings of typical kerbs and edgings

5.8.3.10 See drawings 6.5.8.1-7 in Chapter 6 for a range of typical kerbs and edgings in a variety of materials which are priced in Chapter 7.

Drawings of typical path edgings

5.8.3.11   See drawings 6.5.8.8-14 in Chapter 6 for a range of typical path edgings, in a variety of alternative materials, which are priced in Chapter 7.

Drawings of typical channels

5.8.3.12   See drawings 6.5.8.15-22 in Chapter 6 for a range of typical channels to roads, paths and paving, in a variety of materials, which are priced out in Chapter 7.

Drawings of mowing margins

5.8.3.13   See drawings 6.5.8.23-29 in Chapter 6 for a range of typical combinations of materials to form mowing margins to grass areas. These are priced out in Chapter 7.

Drawings of car parks

5.8.3.14   See drawings 6.5.8.30-33 in Chapter 6 for alternative arrangements for setting out car parking. Approximate estimates for the cost of alternatives per car are dealt with in Chapter 7.

The marking of car parks

5.8.3.15   Car parking space division strips shall be in 100 mm wide white thermoplastic strips in accordance with B.S. 3262/1 laid hot at 115°C on bitumen macadam surfacing.

5.8.4   FLEXIBLE SURFACES

Tarmacadam 'Tarpaving' for footpaths, playgrounds and similar works;

5.8.4.1   Tarmacadam for footpaths, playgrounds and similar works shall be in accordance with B.S. 1242:1960 incorporating Amendment No. 1:1967, which includes the following summarised conditions:

Materials

5.8.4.2   Coarse aggregate. This shall be one, or a mixture, of the following and shall be free from material passing a 3 mm B.S. sieve:
(A) Crushed rock. Hard, clean and durable crushed rock of one or more of the following types: granite, basalt, gabbro, porphyry, quartzite, hornfels, gritstone, limestone, approved by the purchaser.
(B) Slag. (a) Blastfurnace slag, approved by the purchaser, and shall comply with the requirements (which are specified in the standard) in respect of; stability, sulphur content, water absorption and bulk density or unit weight.
(b) Alternatively, steel slag or other slag of suitable nature may be used with the approval of the engineer.

5.8.4.3   Fine aggregate. Substantially all of this shall pass a 3 mm B.S. sieve and, apart from any added filler, shall be crushed rock or slag, or

Specification—Hard ground finishes

Materials *continued*

5.8.4.3 (*cont'd*) clean sand. If sand is used the content of silt, loam or clay content shall not exceed 3 per cent by weight of the fine aggregate.

5.8.4.4 Filler. If added filler is used in the tarpaving, it shall consist of crushed rock (of the types listed for coarse aggregate), slag, or other material approved by the purchaser, and at least 75 per cent of it shall pass a No. 200 B.S. sieve.

5.8.4.5 Binder. The binder shall be either tar or a tar-bitumen mixture, as specified by the purchaser, and shall comply with the requirements given below under A or B respectively and C.
(A) Tar. The tar shall comply with B.S. 76, Type A or B.
(B) Tar-bitumen mixture. The binder shall be a mixture of tar and bitumen, the tar to comply with B.S. 76.
The tar-bitumen mixture shall be homogeneous and its viscosity should be similar to that specified in the table (not shown here) for the corresponding tar binder.
(C) Viscosity of binder. The viscosity shall be within the limits given in the table according to the weather conditions, method of laying, length of haul, etc.

5.8.4.6 (In the original British Standard a viscosity range table is then shown).

Manufacture

5.8.4.7 Composition of mixtures: Gradings and binder content for base courses and wearing courses shall comply with tables 3 and 4 of B.S. 1242.

5.8.4.8 Temperature of mixing: The binder shall be heated to the appropriate temperature. The aggregate shall be surface dry and mixed with binder at the temperature in accordance with the table in B.S. 1242. Excess heating adversely affects the quality of the resultant tarpaving.

5.8.4.9 Mixing: The materials, including any added filler, shall be weighed or measured into a mechanical mixer and thoroughly mixed in such a manner that all particles of the aggregate are completely coated.

5.8.4.10 Transport: The tarpaving shall be transported from the manufacturing plant to the site of the work in clean vehicles and shall be protected against adverse weather conditions. The use of dust, coated dust, oil or water on the interior of vehicles to facilitate discharge of the tarpaving is permissible, but the amount shall be kept to a minimum, and any excess removed by tipping or brushing.
Tarpaving which is to be laid warm shall be protected to minimize loss of heat during transit, so that all material is delivered in a condition suitable for spreading and compacting.

Laying

5.8.4.11 General: During the whole of the operations, every precaution shall be taken to avoid segregation and to prevent the tarpaving from becoming contaminated with dust or other foreign matter. It shall not be laid under unsuitable weather conditions.

5.8.4.12 Preparation of base: A new base should be adequately compacted and stable, and should be shaped to falls before surfacing, using a roller at least as heavy as that to be used for rolling the tarpaving. On clay or similar sub-grades, a layer of suitable material approved by the engineer e.g. clinker, should be laid beneath the hardcore or other base material.

The surface should be formed and rolled to the line and levels specified or as directed by the engineer. Careful attention shall be given to the removal of all surface water, loose material and foreign matter.

5.8.4.13 Compacted thickness and contour:
(A) The tarpaving shall be laid in one course or more as specified by the engineer, the compacted thickness being within the limits of the table (shown in the British Standard).

In the case of surfacings comprising more than one course the total thickness after compaction should be at least the sum of the thickness specified for the separate courses.

5.8.4.14 (B) The accuracy of the finish of the surface should be determined by placing a 3.000 m straight edge on the tarpaving: the depth of gap at any place between the points at which the straight edge is in contact with the surface should not exceed 10 mm or other limit specified by the engineer.

5.8.4.15 (C) The average cross fall of the finished surface should be agreed with the engineer and should not normally be flatter than 1 in 48.

5.8.4.16 Compaction: Compaction shall be carried out with a roller not exceeding the smaller of either 4 tonne or the weight of the roller used to consolidate the foundation. The tarpaving shall be compacted and finished to the satisfaction of the engineer. A roller shall not stand on tarpaving if the work might thereby be damaged.

Where there is more than one course, each course shall be compacted separately to the specified level and the surface shall be parallel to the finished surface. Subsequent courses shall be laid as soon as possible after compaction of the previous course or courses.

5.8.4.17 Joints: Care shall be taken to secure good adhesion at joints by cutting back the existing material to the full depth of the new material and to provide a dense regular vertical face which shall be painted with bituminous emulsion or hot tar.

Kerbs, channels, manhole covers, and similar fittings shall be adjusted to the correct level, cleaned and painted with bituminous

Specification—Hard ground finishes

5.8.4.17 *Laying continued*
(cont'd) emulsion or hot tar before the surfacing is laid. The tarpaving shall be tamped around and against these so that after final rolling the finished surface shall be left flush or not more than 6 mm above such projections.

5.8.4.18 Surface treatment: When specified, the surface of the tarpaving shall be lightly dusted immediately after compaction with grit of a grading not exceeding 5 mm to dust. The grit shall either be dry or shall have been coated with 2 to 3 per cent of suitable tar or bitumen. Alternatively, the surface may be treated with fine cold asphalt to B.S. 1690. After either treatment it is usually desirable to roll the surface lightly.

Tarmacadam with crushed rock or slag aggregate
5.8.4.19 The above alternative tarmacadam specification is covered by B.S. 802: 1967 and is not detailed here.

Fine cold asphalt
5.8.4.20 The above type of asphalt is covered in B.S. 1690:1962 and is not detailed here.

Rolled asphalt (hot process)
5.8.4.21 Rolled asphalt (hot process) with rock, gravel or slag aggregate shall be in accordance with B.S. 594:1961 which includes the following summarised conditions:

Materials

5.8.4.22 Asphaltic cement: The asphaltic cement shall comply with the requirements given in the appropriate columns in tables 1, 2 or 3 of B.S. 594 (not reproduced here).

5.8.4.23 Type of coarse aggregate: The coarse aggregate shall be material substantially all retained on a No. 7 B.S. sieve; it shall be of a quality approved by the engineer, angular but not flaky, clean and free from dust, and shall consist of one or more of the following:
Rock
Gravel
Slag

5.8.4.24 Size of coarse aggregate: The coarse aggregate shall be of such size as to conform with the appropriate column of Table 4A or 4B, as applicable (not reproduced here).

5.8.4.25 Fine aggregate: The fine aggregate shall consist of hard, non-absorbent, but not necessarily sharp particles of:
(A) Approved clean natural bank, river, dune or pit sand, or
(B) Fines produced in a crushing plant from material which would be suitable for coarse aggregate under this standard, or
(C) A mixture of the above.

Specification—Hard ground finishes

5.8.4.25 ***Materials*** *continued*
(cont'd) The grading shall comply with the requirements given in Table 5 (not shown here) for base course or wearing course mixtures as applicable.

5.8.4.26 Filler: The filler shall consist of limestone or Portland cement; if it is desired to use any other material, the engineer shall be informed and his approval obtained. In any case, the filler shall comply with the requirements set out in Table 6. (not reproduced here; see original British Standard).

5.8.4.27 Mixing: The coarse and fine aggregate shall be thoroughly dried and shall be fed at a temperature of 150-205°C into a mechanical mixer of approved type. The filler and asphaltic cement shall be added, the latter being pre-heated to a temperature not exceeding 175°C. Mixing shall continue until the aggregate has been uniformly mixed and coated with asphaltic cement.

Base, transportation and laying

5.8.4.28 Preparation of base: The base upon which the asphalt is to be laid shall be of adequate strength and stability to take the type and weight of traffic expected to use the road. Where an existing surface to be used as a base shows an excess of binder this shall be removed by heating and planing.

If necessary the base shall be finished by means of a regulating course, so that the maximum depression under a 3.000 m straight edge placed longitudinally and a suitable template placed transversely does not exceed 13 mm when the asphalt surfacing is to consist of two-course work or 10 mm, when the asphalt is to be single-course.

5.8.4.29 Two bases require special measures:

(A) Concrete. Where asphalt is to be superimposed on existing concrete surfaces with defective joints these joints shall be made good by cleaning out and refilling with a material which will not adversely affect the surfacing.

(B) Sett paving. All loose or weak areas shall be removed and replaced with an appropriate thickness of asphalt base course or cement concrete. Excessive bitumen or pitch used to grout the sett joints shall be heat treated and surplus material removed. To ensure the best possible key all joints, after removal of excess filling, shall be cleared of all foreign matter to a depth of about 13 mm.

If specified by the engineer, the setts shall be dressed with bitumen emulsion or suitable hot binder and blinded with 6.5-3 mm chippings at approximately 6 kg/m^2 to provide an adequate key for the asphalt.

5.8.4.30 Tack coat: When a tack coat is specified it shall be of a suitable grade of bitumen emulsion applied at a uniform rate of spread, 0.55 to 0.34 l/m^2. Any collection of the emulsion in depressions shall be

Specification—Hard ground finishes

Base, transportation and laying *continued*

5.8.4.30 (cont'd) brushed out to avoid subsequent bleeding through the asphalt surfacing.

5.8.4.31 Transportation: The hot asphalt shall be transported to the site in lorries with metal-lined wooden or suitably insulated metal bodies, properly sheeted to prevent an excessive drop in temperature and as a protection against adverse weather conditions. For mechanical laying, the delivery of the material shall be co-ordinated with the rate of progress of the spreading machine in order to avoid, as far as possible, interruption of spreading.

The asphalt shall be kept free from uncoated aggregate and foreign matter. Oiling or dusting of the interior of the vehicle to facilitate discharge is permissible, but the amount of oil or dust used must be the minimum necessary.

5.8.4.32 Temperatures of delivery and rolling: The mixture shall be delivered to the site of work at a temperature of 120-160°C for base courses and 135-175°C for wearing courses, and shall be rolled at a temperature within the applicable range in Table 10 of B.S. 594.

5.8.4.33 Laying: The mixture may be laid by means of a mechanical spreader or by manual methods and work shall not proceed during unsuitable weather conditions.

5.8.4.34 (A) Mechanical laying. After the surface on which the asphalt is to be laid has been swept clean the mixture shall be laid by an approved type of mechanical spreader and finisher capable of laying to the required widths, profile, camber or cross-fall without causing segregation, dragging, burning or other surface defects or irregularities, and of being operated at a speed consistent with the character of the mixture and the thickness of the course being laid, so as to produce a uniform density and surface texture. The spreader shall be operated at a uniform rate and the mixture shall be fed to the spreader at such a rate as to permit continuous laying as far as supply and site conditions permit.

Immediately after any course is placed and before rolling is started, the surface shall be checked and all defects and irregularities in alignment, grade or texture corrected by the addition or removal of mixture. The thickness of the course shall be regulated so that after final rolling the finished thickness is as specified by the engineer within the limits specified in Sub-clause D below.

Any asphalt remaining on hopper, spreading mechanism, tampers and screeds shall be cleaned off at the end of each working day. On no account should cleaning solvents come into contact with the road.

The asphalt course shall be rolled with a roller which weighs not less than 6000 kg and is fitted with a quick and smooth-acting reverse, or

Base, transportation and laying *continued*

5.8.4.34 (cont'd) by other approved and equivalent means. The resultant surface, tested with a straight edge 3.000 m long placed parallel to the centre line of the carriageway, shall have no depression greater than 10 mm in the case of base course and 5 mm for wearing surface, due allowance being made for the projection of chippings in the road surface.

The number of rollers required depends on the tonnage laid hourly and the thickness of the asphalt. Rolling shall be in a longitudinal direction from sides to centre so that the lateral overlap between successive passes is not more than 300 mm, the points at which the roller is reversed being staggered. In the event of a temporary delay in laying operations the rolling shall be completed and it may be necessary where a three-wheel roller is employed to turn it round to ensure that all the work is compacted with the rear rollers. The roller shall never be allowed to stand on newly laid asphalt.

In two-course construction, the wearing-course mixture shall be spread on the base course as soon as practicable after the latter has been properly compacted. The base course at the end (and side when the work is carried out in part widths) of each section of work shall be left uncovered for a sufficient length (or width) to break joint with the wearing course. The adhesion of the two courses shall be as complete as possible and the wearing course shall be pressed into and firmly united with the base course.

5.8.4.35 (B) Manual laying: The mixture shall be spread while hot upon the surface on which the asphalt is to be laid, previously swept clean, to such a thickness that after being thoroughly compacted by rolling its finished thickness will be as specified by the engineer within the limits given in sub-clause D below.

The course shall be compacted with a roller weighing not less than 6000 kg and fitted with a quick and smooth-acting reverse, or by other approved and equivalent means. The resultant surface, tested with a straight edge 3.000 m long placed parallel to the centre line of the carriageway, shall have no depression greater than 10 mm in the case of the base course and 6.5 mm for wearing surface, due allowance being made for the projection of chippings in the road surface.

Rolling shall be in a longitudinal direction from sides to centre so that the lateral overlap between successive passes will not be more than 300 mm, the points at which the roller is reversed being staggered. In the event of a temporary delay in laying operations, the rolling should be completed and it may be necessary, where a three-wheel roller is employed, to turn it round to ensure that all the work is compacted with the rear rollers. The roller shall never be allowed to stand on newly laid asphalt.

5.8.4.36 (C) Crossfall: In the case of roads with a straight crossfall, this fall shall be not more than 1 in 40 and not less than 1 in 48 unless otherwise directed by the engineer. With roads to be cambered the

Base, transportation and laying continued

5.8.4.36 (cont'd) average fall of the finished surface from the crown to the channel shall be not more than 1 in 30 and not less than 1 in 45. These requirements for crossfall do not apply to curves with superelevation.

5.8.4.37 (D) Thickness: The total thickness of the compacted courses shall be that specified by the engineer. (The full British Standard gives the limits within which the specified average compacted thickness of each course shall lie).

5.8.4.38 (E) Application of chippings: In the case of asphalt mixtures containing 45 per cent or less of coarse aggregate a roughened surface shall be obtained by the application of coated chippings of approved quality. If a roughened surface is not required the engineer shall specify the omission of coated chippings. In the case of mixtures containing more than 45 per cent of coarse aggregate the application of coated chippings shall be at the discretion of the engineer. Where a roughened surface is required the asphalt shall, after initial compaction and while it is still warm and in a plastic condition, be covered with a layer of 19 mm or 13 mm approved, clean hard chippings complying with B.S. 63. The chippings shall, prior to application, be coated with 1½ to 2½ per cent of asphaltic cement of medium penetration (e.g. 40-80 penetration at 25°C). To enable the chippings to carry the specified proportion of asphaltic cement 1½ to 2½ per cent of filler shall be added, either before or after the addition of the asphaltic cement. The chippings shall be uniformly and evenly distributed at the rate of 9.4 ± 0.7 kg/m^2 for 13 mm chippings and 12.2 ± 1.2 kg/m^2 for 19 mm chippings. The chippings shall then be rolled or otherwise pressed into the surface of the asphalt.

When the chippings are being spread, the channels against the kerbs shall be covered by battens not less than 150 mm wide, so that a smooth channel is maintained to facilitate the flow of surface water to the gulleys.

5.8.4.39 (F) Joints: Care shall be taken to ensure that all joints are properly and truly made. The transverse joints, and longitudinal joints in the case of wearing surfaces, between the sections of work shall be cut back to a vertical face and painted with a thin coat of asphaltic cement so that a permanent bond is obtained. Such joints shall be accurately levelled so that the surface is uniform and true.

5.8.4.40 (G) Projections: Those surfaces of manholes, kerbs, channels and similar projections against which the mixture is to abut shall be cleaned and painted with a thin uniform coating of asphaltic cement before the mixture is laid. The mixture shall be tamped around and against such projections by means of hot tampers, and the finished surface shall be left flush with the top of, or not more than 3 mm above, such projections.

Specification—Hard ground finishes

Base, transportation and laying *continued*

5.8.4.41 (H) Channels: Channels shall be formed to provide a fall sufficient to avoid retention of surface water.

5.8.4.42 (J) Traffic control: Newly laid sections shall not be opened to traffic until the asphalt has cooled to the prevailing atmospheric temperature.

Pea shingle

Surface dressing

5.8.4.43 Clean surface of tarmacadam or asphalt. Spray bituminous emulsion complying with B.S. 434:1960 at the rate of 2.900 m² per 4.546 litres and blind with sand. After a few days spray bituminous emulsion a second time at the rate of 4.200-5.000 m² per 4.546 litres and blind with 6 mm pea gravel at the rate of 0.76 m³ per 117-142 m² and roll with a 508 kg roller. Brush off surplus material.

Gravel

Preparation

5.8.4.44 Prior to laying sub-base and/or base the surface shall be treated with a non-selective weed killer approved by the landscape architect and applied in accordance with the manufacturer's instructions.

Base

5.8.4.45 The base shall consist of 100 mm hardcore, clinker etc., rolled with an 8.128 tonne-10.160 tonne roller for drives or 508 kg-762 kg roller for paths. Watering will be necessary during rolling in dry weather. (For drives a sub-base or a thicker base, say 150 mm-200 mm will be necessary.)

Material

5.8.4.46 Gravel shall be obtained from an approved source and a sample submitted to the landscape architect for his approval prior to work commencing. It shall consist of hard binding gravel with a preponderance of angular material free from an excessive amount of clay and containing sufficient grit, all to enable successful compaction by rolling.

Spreading

5.8.4.47 Spread gravel to pass a 50 mm screen and rolled (watered if necessary) as above to a finished thickness of 50 mm. The gravel shall be evenly spread to a surface true to level and form.

Fine gravel

5.8.4.48 Spread fine gravel with sufficient hoggin to act as a binder, rolled (watered if necessary) as above to a finished thickness of 25 mm. A finish of 19 mm fine gravel to pass a 19 mm mesh, spread and rolled.

Hoggin (stabilised)

Preparation

5.8.4.49 Treat the base and/or sub-base with non-selective weed killer approved by the landscape architect and in accordance with the manufacturer's instructions. (Note: In the vicinity of trees or other plants whose roots might extend under the area to be treated substitute Simazine (Geigy) weedkiller, in accordance with the manufacturer's instructions.)

Base

5.8.4.50 Provide and lay a bed of good clean furnace clinker, free from waste metal or unburnt refuse of any description, sound broken brick, stone or concrete hardcore with sufficient fine material to fill interstices; spread, level and roll to a compacted thickness of 100 mm with a 508 kg vibrating roller. No builder's waste or material of a limey nature shall be used.

Blind base with fine hoggin and water if necessary and roll to a compacted thickness of 12 mm with a 508 kg vibrating roller.

Material

5.8.4.51 The hoggin is to be of a quality approved by the landscape architect and obtained from a named source.

Laying

5.8.4.52 Provide and lay approved hoggin with particles of 50 mm maximum size; level, water if necessary and roll to a compacted thickness of 100 mm with a 508 kg vibrating roller.

Shale

Material

5.8.4.53 Shale should be selected good, clean, red burnt material, free from all extraneous matter.

Preparation

5.8.4.54 Prior to laying the base the surface shall be treated with a non-selective weed killer approved by the landscape architect and applied in accordance with the manufacturer's instructions.

Base

5.8.4.55 The base shall consist of shale not exceeding 50 mm ring, spread, levelled and compacted with a roller in the range 8.128-10.160 tonne, to a finished thickness of 50 mm. Blind base with fine shale and roll with 508 kg-762 kg roller to finished thickness of 25 mm.

Alternative base

5.8.4.56 The base shall consist of 100 mm hardcore rolled with an 8.128-10.160 tonne roller for drives or 508 kg-762 kg roller for paths.

Laying

5.8.4.57 Blind base with fine shale and roll with 508 kg-762 kg roller to finished thickness of 25 mm.

Loose cobbles

Material

5.8.4.58 Kidney flint cobbles shall be hand-picked, smooth-worn and egg-shaped, shall approximate one another in size and shape within the range 50-75 mm and shall be obtained from an approved source.

Laying

5.8.4.59 Spread loose cobbles directly on to compacted, levelled soil to an average depth of 50-75 mm.

Alternative bases

5.8.4.60 Spread loose cobbles on 150 mm of well consolidated hoggin.

5.8.4.61 Spread loose cobbles on 100 mm of well consolidated hard-core blinded with 50 mm of sand.

5.8.4.62 Spread loose cobbles on asphalt roof finish.

5.8.4.63 Spread loose cobbles on 50 mm 1:2:4 concrete blinding on 100 mm hardcore.

Loose chippings

Walley (Thurrock) Limited

5.8.4.64 'Permwhite' chippings; white calcined flint in various grades, the usual ones on landscape work being 19-12.5 mm, 12.5-9.5 mm, 9.5-6 mm and 6-3 mm. The price per tonne is the same within this range of sizes.

Chippings should be spread, loose, on an appropriate base, asphalt or screed on a roof terrace, 100 mm consolidated hoggin on well drained ground or on 1:2:4 concrete blinding on 100 mm hardcore in most ground conditions.

5.8.5 RIGID PAVING

In-situ concrete

Introduction

5.8.5.1 The following specification clauses are taken from 'Specification for Housing Estate and other Minor Roads in Concrete' and are reproduced by kind permission of the Cement and Concrete Association.

Materials

Approved source of supply

5.8.5.2 Sources of supply for all materials, such as cement, aggregates, water, reinforcement, joint fillers and joint sealers, shall be approved by the engineer before these materials are delivered to the site. All materials shall comply with the requirements of the latest appropriate British Standard except where the engineer permits otherwise.

Cement

5.8.5.3 All Portland cement shall be of British manufacture and shall conform to the latest British Standard, as follows:
B.S. 12:1958—Portland cement (ordinary and rapid-hardening)
B.S. 146:1958—Portland blastfurnace cement

All cement shall be delivered in sound condition and shall be stored, and protected from moisture or other damage, to the satisfaction of the engineer. Any cement which has become caked or otherwise damaged shall at once be removed from the site.

All cement shall be gauged by weight, and a bag of cement shall be assumed to weigh 50.80 kg.

Aggregates

5.8.5.4 All aggregates shall conform to the requirements of B.S. 882: 1201:1965 'Aggregates from natural sources for concrete'. The maximum size of coarse aggregate shall be 18 mm. The contractor shall obtain the engineer's approval of the pit or other source from which he proposes to obtain his aggregates and shall submit samples of the materials for approval prior to their delivery to the site.

Coarse and fine aggregates shall be delivered and stocked separately at the site. Stock-piles of sand shall be allowed to drain for at least 12 hours before being used. Aggregates shall not be stored on muddy ground or where they are likely to become dirty or otherwise contaminated. Frozen aggregates or aggregates containing frozen material shall not be used.

Water

5.8.5.5 Only clean water from mains or from other sources approved by the engineer shall be used. The contractor shall provide sufficient water for all purposes, including mixing the concrete, curing and cleaning plant and tools.

Reinforcement

5.8.5.6 The reinforcement shall be of oblong mesh fabric complying in all respects with B.S. 4483:1969 'Steel fabric for the reinforcement of concrete', and shall weigh not less than that specified. The fabric is to be supplied in the form of mats, not rolls: these mats must be flat and free from any permanent set which will cause them to curl when the fresh concrete is vibrated.

The fabric shall be stored on the site in such a way that it does

Specification—Hard ground finishes

5.8.5.6
(cont'd)

Reinforcement *continued*
not become distorted and when installed in the road it must be free from oil, paint, dirt and loose rust. Odd scraps of reinforcement are not to be used and no mat is to be less than 1.830 m long unless a small area is required for completing the reinforcement in a slab.

Plant

Compacting plant

5.8.5.7 The compactors used shall be capable of compacting the full thickness of the concrete, in one or more layers, at the specified water/cement ratio and workability, and of producing the desired surface finish. They shall have the prior approval of the engineer. Pan vibrators shall not be used.

The following are the types of compactor available:

(A) A beam to which one or two vibrating units are attached. These units may be driven electrically or by an internal combustion engine. When two vibrators are attached, they must be phased to operate in unison.

(B) A pneumatic tamper in which pneumatic hammers operate on a steel plate. It is generally used in conjunction with a pneumatic finisher and requires an air compressor.

Concrete

Proportions

5.8.5.8 (See original C.C.A. publication for tables giving full details of the mix proportions).

Construction

Sub-grade

5.8.5.9 The ground shall be prepared by removing the topsoil and excavating or filling to the required formation level; all surplus material from excavations should be removed. If boggy or vegetable soil or other unsuitable material occurs on the site it shall be excavated and removed and replaced by gravel, hoggin or other sound stable material, thoroughly compacted to the proper formation level, to the satisfaction of the engineer; suitable drainage should be provided. Where filling is necessary all turf shall first be stripped and any vegetable or other unstable material removed to the satisfaction of the engineer. All filling shall be done in layers not exceeding 225 mm loose thickness.

Base

5.8.5.10 Alternative A: The prepared sub-grade shall, where required by the engineer, be evenly covered with a layer of approved granular

Specifaction—Hard ground finishes

5.8.5.10 *Base continued*
(cont'd) material, such as hoggin, gravel, sand or well-burned clinker. This layer shall be thoroughly compacted and blinded by a suitable roller to give a dense, even surface. When compaction is completed, the surface shall be checked, by means of a scratch template working off the side forms, to ensure that the levels and shape of the base are correct; any discrepancies found shall be immediately made good. Immediately before the concrete is placed this base shall at the discretion of the engineer be covered with waterproof underlay which shall lap at least 75 mm over adjoining strips.

5.8.5.11 Alternative B: Where the sub-grade is of a granular nature it shall be rolled with a roller weighing 6.100 to 8.130 tonne (or a vibrating roller of equivalent compacting capacity), until it is fully compacted and a dense, close-knit surface is obtained; finer material may be added if necessary. Immediately before the concrete is placed, this formation shall, at the discretion of the engineer be covered with a layer of waterproof underlay which shall lap at least 75 mm over adjoining strips.

5.8.5.12 Alternative C: Lean concrete composed of one part of cement to sixteen parts of aggregate by weight, and containing at least 35 per cent of sand, shall be spread on the prepared sub-grade and thoroughly compacted to the specified thickness. The surface of this concrete shall be brought to a smooth finish. If required it shall be given a dressing of tar or bitumen, at the rate of 1 litre to 0.920 m^2 before the concrete slab is superimposed on it.

Form setting
5.8.5.13 The forms shall be set true to line and level, on a firm foundation, and supported uniformly throughout their length so that they will not be disturbed by the spreading and compaction of the concrete. They shall be secured in position by suitable stakes. The forms shall be set well in advance of concreting operations and shall be checked for level before concreting starts. Forms shall be cleaned and oiled each time before use.

Alternatively the engineer may permit the laying of kerbs prior to the construction of the road slab, provided the slab is constructed in two halves with a centre joint. Construction of the slab shall not be begun until the line and level of the kerbs have been approved by the engineer. Adequate precautions shall be taken to ensure that the kerbs are not damaged or disturbed during the construction of the slab. A steel sheet or temporary rail shall be laid on the top of the kerbs to ensure that the forward motion of the compactor during the finishing process is not affected by the joints between kerbs.

Spreading concrete
5.8.5.14 The concrete shall be placed as soon as possible after being mixed, and in no case shall the addition of extra water to it be allowed after it leaves the mixer. The concrete shall not be transported over the

5.8.5.14 (cont'd)

Spreading concrete continued

prepared formation without the permission of the engineer. It shall be spread to such a thickness that when compacted it shall have the specified finished thickness. When the concrete is laid in two courses, as when the top course is of coloured concrete, the bottom course shall be struck off at such a level as will permit the specified thickness of the top course to be obtained. The top course shall be added and compacted within 30 minutes of placing the bottom course.

5.8.5.15

Compacting concrete and finishing the surface

The compaction and finishing of the concrete shall be effected by the plant specified. In all cases, the equipment used shall be capable of compacting the concrete to its maximum density and to the specified levels; if necessary the engineer may direct that this shall be done in two or more layers.

If the concrete is compacted in two layers the surface of the lower layer shall be brought to a level, but not a smooth finish, and the top layer shall be added and compacted within 30 minutes of spreading the bottom layer.

Shortly after the slab has been brought to the correct finished level, the surface shall be given a brushed texture by drawing a broom over the compacted concrete, the brush marks forming continuous parallel lines across the slab.

5.8.5.16

Curing

As soon as the surface has been finished, it shall be protected against too-rapid drying out by one of the following methods:

(A) by means of waterproof tents kept clear of the surface; the ends of the tents must be sealed to prevent wind blowing over the road surface.

(B) by spraying the surface with an approved proprietary curing medium, which shall be applied according to the manufacturer's instructions. When the concrete has hardened sufficiently for the surface not to be marked, curing by the method A shall be replaced by one of the following methods, which shall be maintained for 7 days or such period as the engineer may require.

(C) by means of hessian, straw mats, a 50 mm thickness of sand, or a 50 mm thickness of earth, kept continuously damp.

(D) by means of waterproof sheeting, kept in close contact with the surface of the concrete; the sheets shall overlap at adjoining edges by at least 75 mm and shall be securely held in position along the sides and ends of the slab.

Coloured concrete work shall be cured by means of method A followed by method D.

5.8.5.17

Frosty weather

Concreting shall cease when the atmospheric temperature is below 3°C on a falling thermometer and shall not be resumed until a

Frosty weather continued

5.8.5.17 (cont'd) temperature of at least 1°C has been reached on a rising thermometer, unless precautions approved by the engineer have been taken. The contractor will, however, be responsible for making good any damage caused by frost.

Removal of forms

5.8.5.18 Forms shall not be removed from freshly placed concrete until it is at least 12 hours old, and then only with the engineer's approval. Care should be taken that in their removal no damage is done to the concrete; should, however, any such damage occur the contractor will be responsible for making it good to the satisfaction of the engineer.

Joints

Expansion joints

5.8.5.19 Expansion joints shall be formed at the intervals shown on the drawings, at right angles to the longitudinal axis of the road and, where the road is constructed in two or more strips, continuous across the road. The joints shall be the specified width, shall be straight and truly vertical and shall extend to the full depth and width of the slab. They shall form a complete separator between two adjoining slabs, and the contractor shall be responsible for ensuring that no concrete or other incompressible material gets into the joint during construction.

The expansion joint shall be filled with the pre-moulded joint filler, which shall extend from the bottom of the slab to 20 mm below the finished surface of the concrete. During construction, a timber or metal cap shall be fitted temporarily on top of the joint filler; the top of this cap shall be flush with the finished surface. Care shall be taken that the filler and the cap are set accurately in position and are maintained in that position during the placing and compaction of the concrete. Care shall be taken to ensure that the concrete on both sides of the joint is dense and fully compacted. If required by the engineer this concrete shall be given extra compaction by means of a suitable immersion vibrator inserted in the concrete and worked along the full length of the joint on both sides. On completion of compaction the arrises of the joint shall be rounded to 10 mm radius by the use of a suitable arrising tool, care being taken that the concrete is not pushed laterally towards the joint, and that the faces of the joint are kept vertical. On completion of arrising, the surface of the concrete on both sides of the joint shall be tested with a 1.525 m straight edge, and any irregularities disclosed shall be immediately made good. In making up any depressions or making good any raw spots, suitable concrete shall be used; the use of cement mortar will not be allowed.

Not earlier than four days after the concrete has been laid, the cavity on top of the joint filler shall be carefully cleaned of all loose

Expansion joints continued

5.8.5.19
(cont'd)
material and sealed with an approved joint-sealing compound. This sealing shall not be done until the concrete is quite dry. The sealer and any primer required shall be applied strictly in accordance with the manufacturer's instructions. The joint shall be sealed flush with the surface of the concrete, the sealing operation being done in two or more operations in quick succession if required. The contractor shall be responsible for ensuring that, prior to sealing, the joint is kept clear of stones, pebbles or any other incompressible material, which might cause spalling of the concrete.

Contraction joints

5.8.5.20
Transverse contraction joints of the dummy type shall be formed in the top of the slab where directed by the engineer. The joints shall be 6 mm wide and one-third of slab depth. They shall be at right angles to the longitudinal axis of the road, shall be vertical and shall be continuous across the full width of the carriageway. The method of forming the joint shall have the prior approval of the engineer. When the concrete has sufficiently hardened, the arrises of the joint shall be rounded to 10 mm radius with a suitable arrising tool, care being taken in so doing that the faces of the joint are kept vertical. Precautions shall be taken to prevent the entry of incompressible material into the joint. When the concrete has dried out, the joint shall be sealed and the levels checked in the manner specified in Clause 5.8.5.19 for expansion joints.

Alternatively, the contraction joints shall be cut in the hardened concrete, by means of a suitable concrete saw, to a depth of not more than 50 mm. If this method is adopted the requirements in the previous paragraph about 6 mm width of joints and the rounding of the arrises will not apply, but the joints shall be sealed with a suitable sealing compound (which shall be of such viscosity as will permit it to fill the groove), or by a pre-moulded joint sealer.

Concrete (road) with exposed aggregate surface

Method A

5.8.5.21
In the case of concrete which does not contain entrained air, the top 50 mm shall be composed of 50.80 kg cement (coloured cement being used if directed by the engineer) to 36.20 kg of sand and 92.52 kg selected coarse aggregate which shall be graded from 20 mm to 10 mm, all material between 10 mm and 5 mm being eliminated. The corresponding weights of similar materials for air entrained concrete shall be 50.80 kg cement to 30.84 kg of sand and 87.09 kg coarse aggregate. This top course shall be laid and compacted within 30 minutes of laying the bottom corner.

The concrete shall be spread, compacted and brought to a smooth finish as specified in Clauses 5.8.5.14 and 5.8.5.15, except that a scraping straight edge need not be used. The surface shall then be brushed with a soft broom to remove any surface laitance, care being taken not to disturb any particles of coarse aggregate. The

Specification—Hard ground finishes

5.8.5.21 *(cont'd)*
Method A *continued*
surface shall then be covered with waterproof paper to protect it against too-rapid drying out.

A second brushing with a stiff broom, and plenty of water applied by a spray, shall be given to the surface when the concrete has hardened to the extent that all surface laitance can be removed without disturbing the coarse aggregate (see Note A). This brushing and watering shall continue until the coarse aggregate is fully exposed; the mortar should be removed to a depth of not more than half the depth of the stone, so that the surface presents a uniform texture. On completion of the brushing, the surface should be protected and cured as specified.

5.8.5.22
Note A: Coloured cement may be used to enhance the effect of exposed aggregate; cement of a similar colour to that of the aggregate is usually used for example, a buff-coloured cement might be used with a gravel aggregate.

5.8.5.23
Note B: The time of the final brushing will depend on the atmospheric conditions, and, to a lesser extent, on the water content of the concrete; it may be done up to four hours after compaction of the concrete. The work should be planned to avoid having to do this final brushing after dark.

5.8.5.24
Note C: As an alternative to the above (Note B) a retarding agent may be used; it should be applied as a spray after the completion of compaction and surface finishing. The time limit for final brushing and exposure of the aggregate can thus be extended up to 24 hours. Plenty of water should be used to ensure that no trace of the retarding agent is left on the surface.

Great care must be exercised in the use of a retarding agent, if a surface of uniform appearance is to be obtained. The retarding agent must be applied at a uniform rate over the surface, and brushed and washed off quickly during the exposure of the aggregate.

5.8.5.25
Method B
The concrete (road) shall be completed as in Clause 5.8.5.15 except that the scraping straight edge shall not be used, and the finished surface shall be 5 mm below the tops of the forms (see Note A). As soon as a bay has been finished, single-sized aggregate of either 20 mm or larger gauge shall be spread uniformly over the surface, one stone thick and completely covering the concrete underneath. This aggregate shall then be forced into the surface, by means of a pneumatic compactor or vibrating hand-tamper, until the new surface is level with the tops of the forms and sufficient mortar has worked up to hold the stones in position.

The method of exposure of the aggregate shall be the same as in Method A but, at the discretion of the engineer, the final brushing shall continue until the single-sized aggregate is slightly proud of the surrounding concrete—thereby imparting a textured finish to the surface.

Method B continued

5.8.5.26   Note A: The concrete in the top course should be graded from 20 mm to 10 mm or 40 mm to 10 mm. The omission of the 10 mm to 5 mm material assists in providing a more uniform appearance to the final surface.

5.8.6   UNIT PAVING

Precast concrete paving slabs

Slabs to B.S. 368:1956, superseded by 1971 revision since going to press, which includes the following specification items:

5.8.6.1   The aggregate shall be approved by the purchaser and no variations or additions to an agreed aggregate shall be made without the consent of the purchaser. Any additional material required to produce special properties such as special texture, colour or grip shall not have any deleterious effect upon the concrete.

5.8.6.2   The flags are supplied in natural colour unless otherwise specified. The purchaser shall state whether the colour is to be throughout the flag or whether only as a surface layer, when it shall be not less than the specified appropriate thickness. Unless otherwise agreed the colour shall be even and of the same shade throughout.

5.8.6.3   The purchaser may agree upon a special surface finish or may accept the finish offered by the manufacturer. The thickness of each flag shall be uniform. All angles shall be right angles, the edges shall be clean and sharp. The wearing surfaces shall be true and free from winding. On being fractured the interior of the flags shall present a clean and homogenous appearance.

Additional or alternative specifications (other than in B.S.)

5.8.6.4   A current test certificate shall be obtained and produced at the request of the engineer.
Either Precast concrete flags shall be laid on a bed of 1:3 mix lime mortar, 25 mm thick, on 100 mm thick 1:2:4 mix concrete on 100 mm hardcore. Flags shall be jointed in 1:3 mix lime mortar tinted as appropriate to match the colour of the slabs. Brush well in and afterwards clean off.

5.8.6.5   *Or* Precast concrete flags shall be spot bedded with five mortar dots, mix 1:5, at the corners and centre on 100 mm of blinded and rolled hardcore. Jointing as above.

5.8.6.6   *Or* Precast concrete flags shall be set on a bed of sand, 40 mm thick, and jointed and grouted as above.

5.8.6.7   Precast concrete flags may be butt-jointed. The flags shall be laid in parallel courses to break joint and laid to falls.

Specification—Hard ground finishes

5.8.6.8 *Drawings of typical path layouts*
See drawings 6.5.8.34-45 in Chapter 6 for a range of typical path layouts using standard size slabs separately and in combination. These are priced out in Chapter 7. These are a guide to comparative prices but many variations are possible, using differing paving slabs and depending on the thickness and nature of the base and bedding.

Atlas Stone Company Limited

5.8.6.9 'Foothold' slabs; 50 mm thick, red, buff or grey with standard lightly figured surface and in all B.S. sizes.

5.8.6.10 'Indented' slabs; 50 mm thick, red, buff or grey with indentations to make non-slip on steeper gradients.

5.8.6.11 '8-gauge' slabs; 50 mm thick, red, buff or grey with a linen-type texture.

5.8.6.12 'Driveway' slabs; 50 mm thick, red, buff or grey. 450 mm square with chamfered edges.

5.8.6.13 'Hortex' slabs; 37 mm thick, red, buff or grey with brush-textured finish, in various sizes.

5.8.6.14 'Super Hortex' slabs; 37 mm thick, red, buff or grey with reproduction natural stone effect on surface, in various sizes.

John Ellis & Sons Limited

5.8.6.15 'Texitone' slabs; made from Leicestershire granite aggregate with an exposed face giving a textured surface. Slabs are made in four colours and are 50 mm thick. One tonne covers approximately 8.400 m^2.

5.8.6.16 'Yorktone' slabs; made from Leicestershire granite aggregate with a smooth surface and a slightly open texture. Slabs are made in three colours and are 50 mm thick.

Hulland Products Limited

5.8.6.17 Coloured flags; to B.S. 368, hydraulically pressed, 50 mm thick with colour throughout slab in red, buff and dark grey. Also supplied 63 mm thick.

5.8.6.18 'Chevron' flags; as coloured flags but with diagonal raised stripes. 50 mm and 63 mm thick.

5.8.6.19 'Fluted' flags; as coloured flags but with straight, narrow flutes. 50 mm and 63 mm thick.

5.8.6.20 'Squared' flags; as coloured flags but with all over pattern of 133 mm squares with recesses between. 50 mm and 63 mm thick.

5.8.6.21 'Barfaced' flags; as coloured flags but non-slip surface of small raised bars. 50 mm and 63 mm thick.

Specification—Hard ground finishes

Hulland Products Limited *continued*

5.8.6.22 'Hobnail' flags; as coloured flags but non-slip surface of small 19 mm raised squares. 50 mm and 63 mm thick.

Marley Buildings Limited

5.8.6.23 'Cobblestone' slabs; 600 x 600 m slabs in dark grey with raised 100 mm squares 37 mm thick.

5.8.6.24 'Colourstone' slabs; textured sawn stone surface, five colours, rectangular hexagonal and circular slabs available.

5.8.6.25 'Marlstone' slabs; textured hand-tooled stone surface in sandstone colour only.

S. Marshall & Sons Limited

5.8.6.26 'Marshalite' coloured slabs; to B.S. 368 hydraulically pressed 50 mm or 63 mm thick in 8 different colours, with standard pimple surface finish.

5.8.6.27 Non slip paving; to B.S. 368, 50 mm thick with non-slip finishes, punched or tooled.

5.8.6.28 'Perfecta' slabs; to B.S. 368, 50 mm, 63 mm and 75 mm thick in three colours with rubbed surface finish to expose aggregate.

Mono Concrete Limited

5.8.6.29 'Chelmsley' slabs; 600 x 600 mm with eight slightly raised rectangles in smooth black concrete, 50 mm thick.

5.8.6.30 'Lambeth' slabs; 600 x 600 mm slabs 75 mm thick with sixteen raised pyramids on each slab as a deterrent to discourage pedestrians from wandering into restricted areas. Smooth grey concrete.

5.8.6.31 'Metric Four Square' slabs; 500 mm square slabs 50 mm thick, in various exposed aggregates with matching coloured matrix.

5.8.6.32 'Monohex' slabs; 50 mm thick hexagonal slabs on a 760 mm grid, with half and quarter slabs available. Variety of colours, textures finishes available.

5.8.6.33 'Pentahex' slabs; pentagonal slabs 750 x 500 mm and 50 mm thick which build up so that four make an elongated hexagon 1.500 m in length. Half slabs available. Same range of colours, textures and finishes as with Monohex slabs.

5.8.6.34 'Stretford' paving; pedestrian deterrent paving slabs with a surface of embedded flint cobbles 40-50 mm in size in a grey matrix. 900 x 600 x 65 mm size of slabs.

5.8.6.35 'Wandsworth' slabs; these are similar to 'Lambeth' slabs but are a vehicular deterrent with only two pyramids to each slab. Sizes are 600 x 300 x 180 mm high to apex of pyramid.

Noelite Limited

5.8.6.36 'Noelite' slabs; 38 or 50 mm thick available in six colours with a slightly corrugated surface texture. Hexagonal and circular slabs are also manufactured.

Redland Tiles Limited

5.8.6.37 'Kentstone' paving; 40 mm thick slabs available in five colours.

5.8.6.38 'Polygon' paving; as Kentstone but polygonal shape.

Precast paving blocks for vehicular use

Mono Concrete Limited

5.8.6.39 'S.F.' Interlocking paving stones; these are 50 mm, 80 mm and 100 mm thick interlocking blocks for heavier duty situations.

They should be laid on 50 mm coarse sand which compacts to approximately 38 mm after vibration of the stones. They must be laid at right angles to the road axis, and this should be checked at regular intervals during laying. The 'S.F.' blocks must be laid close jointed by placing the peaks of the units well into the corresponding angular recesses. The joints between the adjoining units in line should not exceed 2-3 mm. A vibrating plate should be used to finally compact the 'S.F.' paving to the required profile. It is important that the plate used is adequate for this purpose. The joints of the paving should be filled with sand.

Fire-paths in precast units

Mono Concrete Limited

5.8.6.40 'B.G.' slabs; for fire paths, car parks, steep banks, sides of water courses. 600 x 400 x 120 mm thick in concrete with a grid of alternating holes and raised studs, so that soil and grass can be placed between studs, to produce stabilized or reinforced grass to take vehicular traffic. Provide and lay a sub-grade of ballast 150 mm thick which should be well tamped. Slabs should be bedded on 20 mm firm, well-tamped sharp sand. Topsoil should be to B.S. 3882, levelled off 30 mm below the top. Sow grass seed and fill with a further 6 mm of fine soil and level with a hard broom. Final soil level should settle to more than 30 mm below upper surface of the slabs. Seed should always be sown immediately after laying while soil is still loose. Where slabs are used on a sloping surface, every second slab should be staked for extra stability

5.8.6.41 'Hexpot' slabs; hexagonal 292 x 292 mm and 100 mm thick with a central hole 190 mm diameter at the top. Use slabs for fire paths in grass. Lay on 19 mm ash blinding on 150 mm hardcore bedded and jointed in cement mortar. Holes to be filled with topsoil to B.S. 3882, rammed and seeded. They can also be filled with gravel, hoggin or rejects where used as porous areas around trees.

Specification—Hard ground finishes
Flags in natural stone, slate or granite

General specification

5.8.6.42 Provide paving slabs of the specified thickness in random sizes but not less than 25 slabs per 10.000 m² of surface area, to be laid in parallel courses with joints alternately broken, and laid to falls.

Either

5.8.6.43 Natural stone flags shall be laid on a bed of 1:3 mix lime mortar, 25 mm thick, on 100 mm thick 1:2:4 mix concrete on 100 mm hardcore. Flags shall be jointed in 1:3 mix lime mortar tinted as appropriate to match the colour of the flags, to finish with true and even surface.

Or

5.8.6.44 Natural stone flags shall be spot bedded with five mortar dots, mix 1:5, at the corners and centre on 100 mm of blinded and rolled hardcore. Jointing as above.

Or

5.8.6.45 Natural stone flags shall be laid on a bed of sand, 40 mm thick, and jointed and grouted as above.

Yorkstone

5.8.6.46 new flagstones, 50 mm thick.

5.8.6.47 second-hand random rectangular.

5.8.6.48 second-hand crazy paving

Portland stone

5.8.6.49 new slabs, 50 mm thick.

Slate

5.8.6.50 random rectangular slabs 31 mm thick.

Granite

5.8.6.51 new slabs 50 mm thick.

Brick paving

Bricks for paving to B.S. 3921, which includes the following specification item:

5.8.6.52 Bricks shall be hard, well-burnt, non-dusting resistent to frost and Sulphate attack and true to shape, size and sample.

Specification items (other than British Standards)

5.8.6.53 Brick paviors shall be of the type specified and should be laid to the specified bond on either sand or sand/lime (1:4) or on semi-dry 1:3 sand/cement mortar bed 25 mm thick on 100 mm thick 1:2:4 concrete with a 20 mm maximum aggregate and 100 mm hardcore. Joints may

Specification items (other than British Standards) continued

5.8.6.53 be 3-10 mm grouted with cement grout, tinted to match colour of
(cont'd) bricks and afterwards cleaned off, or may be butt jointed if engineering bricks are used.

Drawings of typical brick paved paths
5.8.6.54 See drawings 6.5.8.46-51 in Chapter 6 for a range of typical patterns in which brick paths can be laid. These are priced out in Chapter 7.

Patterned paving bricks by Haunchwood-Lewis Brick & Tile Limited
5.8.6.55 Staffordshire blue diamond chequered in various sizes; typical paving brick is 225 x 112.5 x 50 mm thick.

5.8.6.56 Staffordshire blue two raised panel type, in various sizes; typical paving brick is 225 x 112.5 x 50 mm thick.

5.8.6.57 Staffordshire blue four raised panel type, in various sizes; typical paving brick is 225 x 112.5 x 50 mm thick.

5.8.6.58 Staffordshire blue six raised panel type, in various sizes; typical paving brick is 225 x 112.5 x 50 mm thick.

5.8.6.59 Staffordshire blue eight raised panel type in various sizes; typical paving brick is 225 x 112.5 x 50 mm thick.

Clay tiles

Typical specification
5.8.6.60 Clay tiles should be to B.S. 1286:1945 and shall be reasonably true to shape, flat, free from flaws and frost resistent and true to sample approved by the landscape architect prior to laying. Quarry tiles (or semi-vitrified tiles) shall be of external quality either heather-brown or blue, to size specified; laid on 1:2:4 concrete with 20 mm maximum aggregate 100 mm thick on 100 mm hardcore. The hardened concrete should be well wetted and the surplus water taken off. Tiles shall be thoroughly wetted immediately before laying and then drained and shall be bedded on 19 mm thick 1:3 cement/sand screed.

Joints should be approximately 4 mm (or 3 mm for vitrified tiles) grouted in 1:2 cement/sand mortar and cleaned off immediately.

Granite setts

Setts to B.S. 435:1931, which includes the following specification items:
5.8.6.61 Setts are required to be squarely hammer-dressed and shall not be crooked, feather edged, or tapering, nor shall they show drill holes.

Specification—Hard ground finishes

5.8.61 (cont'd)

Setts to B.S: 435:1931 continued
They are worked to the following sizes: (converted to metric)

Section	Length
mm mm 102 x 102	102 mm
76 x 127 76 x 152 102 x 102 102 x 127	Not less than 127 mm nor more than 254 mm
102 x 152 127 x 102 127 x 152	Not less than 152 mm nor more than 254 mm

5.8.6.62 If granite setts are second-hand the contractor shall allow for cleaning off as may be required as no extras will be considered.

5.8.6.63 Granite setts shall be trimmed to cubical or rectangular shape to confirm to the above conditions. Setts should be laid to the specified bond or pattern, tight butted on a bed of 1:3 cement/sand mortar, 25 mm thick on 100 mm thick 1:2:4 concrete on 100 mm hardcore. Joint by thoroughly brushing in dry 1:6 cement/sand mortar and sweeping off surplus to leave grout humble of top of setts and then watering from a can fitted with a fine rose.

Granite setts to mounds and banks

5.8.6.64 Where granite setts are required to surface mounds and banks, they shall be laid to courses running horizontally. Finished surface must be free from any sharp projections, edges, or corners.

Drawings of typical granite sett paving patterns

5.8.6.65 See drawings 6.5.8.52-55 in Chapter 6 for a range of typical patterns to which granite setts can be laid. These are priced out in Chapter 7.

Cobble paving

Materials and laying

5.8.6.66 Kidney flint cobbles shall be hand-picked, smooth-worn and egg-shaped, shall approximate one another in size and shape within the range 50-75 mm and shall be obtained from an approved source.

5.8.6.67 Excavate for and supply and lay hard coarse clinker, consolidated to a thickness of 75 mm. Lay a 50 mm bed of concrete, 1:2:4 mix with small aggregate. Cobbles should be embedded by hand, tight butted, endwise to a depth of 60% of their length.

Specification—Hard ground finishes

Materials and laying continued

5.8.6.68 The tops of cobbles generally shall be about 25 mm above the level of the adjoining paving; but where cobbled areas abut flag paving, the last three rows of cobbles shall be graded down so that the tops of the cobbles shall be level with the flags. Each stint shall be consolidated, using a wooden mallet.

5.8.6.69 Upon completion of each area, a dry grout of rapid hardening cement and sand (1:2) shall be brushed over the cobbles until the interstices are filled to the level of the adjoining paving.
Surplus grout shall then be brushed off and a light, fine spray of water applied over the area. The area shall again be brushed after 24 hours to remove any free grout adhering to exposed faces of cobbles. Cement for grouting shall be rapid hardening portland cement conforming to B.S. 12:1958, and shall be stored on site in a proper manner to avoid deterioration. (The manufacturer's instructions for using it must be carefully followed).
Either
Cobbles shall present a uniform colour in panels when laid.
Or
Cobbles shall be varied in colour as required.

Tree grids

Drawings of typical grids around trees

5.8.6.70 See drawings 6.5.8.56-61 in Chapter 6 for a variety of grids in different materials for putting around trees situated in hard paved areas. These are priced out in Chapter 7.

5.8.7 DRIVEWAYS

Insitu concrete plus other materials

Drawings of typical layout of drives to domestic garages

5.8.7.1 See drawings 6.5.8.62-69 in Chapter 6 for a range of typical garage drive layouts either of insitu concrete or of concrete with insets of contrasting materials. These alternatives are priced out in Chapter 7.

5.8.8 STEPS

Various materials

Drawings of typical step details

5.8.8.1 See drawings 6.5.8.70-81 in Chapter 6 for a range of typical step details in a variety of different materials or a combination of several. These are priced out in Chapter 7.

5.9 RECREATION AND SPORTS FACILITIES

5.9.1 LAYOUTS

Drawings showing typical layouts and sizes for various sports and games

5.9.1.1 See Chapter 6 for drawings 6.5.9.1-19 showing basic dimensions for use in outline planning. Additional detailed information is available from the National Playing Fields Association or the governing body of the relevant sport.

5.9.2 ARTIFICIAL SURFACES AND FINISHES

Introduction

5.9.2.1 The range of surfaces and finishes on the market changes from month to month and entry into the Common Market will add further to those already in use and being imported from the U.S.A. or made under licence. Many of the surfaces have not yet been fully tested in use, so that final opinions on durability, value for money or permanence cannot always be formed. It should be noted that most of the finishes which are inexpensive to lay are often expensive in time and labour to maintain. As a result, some of the surfaces which appear very expensive in capital costs will, over the years, 'pay their way' by low maintenance requirements.

5.9.2.2 The random sample of typical finishes, surfaces and specialist products below was reasonably representative at the time of going to press but up-dated information should be obtained from the manufacturers concerned, the Technical Unit for Sport, the appropriate regional office of the Sports Council or the National Playing Fields Association.

'Asphumas' by En-Tout-Cas Limited

5.9.2.3 for tennis courts or all-weather pitches for general ball games; red or black bituminous limestone surface on tarred stone or ash on 150 mm broken stone bed.

'Astroturf' by Monsanto

5.9.2.4 impervious artificial grass for all-weather football pitches; 13 mm green nylon blades on 13 mm rubberised pad; to be laid on asphalt base.

'Dri-pla' by En-Tout-Cas Limited

5.9.2.5 waterbound hard porous surface for athletics, tennis and ball games; limited use after rain or frost; laid on 25 mm ash blinding on 150 mm clinker or hardcore.

'Hartco' by Maxwell M. Hart Limited

5.9.2.6 waterbound hard porous surface for athletics, tennis and ball games; limited use after rain or frost, laid on 25 mm ash blinding on 150 mm clinker or hardcore.

Specification—Recreation and sports facilities

5.9.2.7
'K' Surface by En-Tout-Cas Limited
porous surface, mainly for running tracks; requires maintenance between uses; 5 mm thickness of 3 mm rubber crumb and red plastic resin binder on 50 mm two coarse coated macadam on 150 mm clinker or broken stone.

5.9.2.8
'Redgra' by Amalgamated Roadstone Construction Limited
waterbound hard porous surface for athletics, ball games, tennis and jump runways; limited use after rain or frost; usually laid on 25 mm ash blinding on 150 mm clinker or hardcore.

5.9.2.9
'Regupol' by 'S.I.P.A.'
patent porous 10 mm thick surfacing for running tracks and all weather pitches; to be laid on prepared base.

5.9.2.10
'Rub-Kor' by Rub-Kor U.K. Limited
impervious surface for athletics, playgrounds and all-weather pitches; 25 mm thickness of graded granulated rubber and cork particles mixed with graded hot mix bituminous aggregates; coloured seal coat advised for friction sports; to be on base 50 mm hot rolled asphalt on 150 mm clinker or hardcore.

5.9.2.11
'Snowslope' by Dendix Brushes Limited
for artificial ski slopes; white plastic crimped filaments of Vibac P.V.C. in zig-zag diamond mesh pattern to form mats 1.830 m x 914 mm or 1.830 m x 1.200 m; to be fixed to square pig mesh on existing turf slopes.

5.9.2.12
'Springsno' by Glenlivet Sporting Estates Limited
for artificial ski slopes; Utramid 6-nylond on stainless steel stringers; made to order into mats or slopes of any size; to be fixed to prepared ground.

5.9.2.13
'Tartan' Surfacing by 3M U.K. Limited
impervious finish for high class running tracks and all-weather pitches; synthetic Polymer 9 mm or 13 mm red, green or grey sheeting in rolls up to 1.500 mm wide, 27.400 m long or can be wet-pour installation in large areas; should normally be laid on 25 mm fine bitumen macadam on 38 mm bitumen macadam binder course on 100 mm crushed rock on compacted subgrade.

5.9.2.14
'Tartan' Turf by 3M U.K. Limited
impervious artificial grass for all-weather football pitches; 13 mm green nylon strands bonded 13 mm Polymer backing; should normally be laid on 25 mm fine bitumen macadam on 38 mm bitumen macadam binder course on 100 mm crushed rock on compacted sub-base.

Specification—Recreation and sports facilities

'Tennisquick' by En-Tout-Cas Limited
5.9.2.15 for maintenance-free tennis courts and all-weather pitches; 25 mm patent no fines concrete with green or red colouring on 63 mm no fines concrete on 150 mm broken stone base.

'Trintrack' by Limmer & Trinidad Company Limited
5.9.2.16 impervious surface for running tracks and all-weather pitches; 25 mm thickness of mixture of rubber crumb, asbestos and hot rolled asphalt; on 50 mm hot rolled asphalt on 150 mm hardcore or clinker.

5.10 PLAYGROUND EQUIPMENT

5.10.1 INTRODUCTION

5.10.1.1 The range of equipment manufactured or available in Britain is so great that comprehensive coverage would be impossible, especially as designs, specifications and prices vary and also change fairly frequently. Consequently only a limited selection of available items has been included in this section of the book, sufficient to give guidance to anyone designing or equipping a playground, in arriving at a sensible cost plan for a number of pieces of equipment.

5.10.1.2 As in the case of the section on street furniture most of the equipment listed here is included in the C.o.I.D. (now Design Council) Street Furniture Design Index for 1972/73 although this is not always the case.

5.10.1.3 As the number of pieces of equipment included here is fairly small they have been listed under the headings of their manufacturers rather than being divided into various groups such as 'swings' and 'climbing frames'. Nevertheless these divisions are annotated within each manufacturer's group for quick reference. The fact that a particular item does not appear under one manufacturer's name does not necessarily imply that he does not make it. The aim has been to provide a reasonable selection of manufacturers and equipment without undue duplication.

5.10.1.4 In comparing prices, particular note should be taken of the fact that only outline specification details are given here and that other refinements, which are not mentioned, may be the reason for some difference in price between two apparently identical elements.

5.10.2 SELECTED TYPICAL EQUIPMENT

Child's World Agency

Play cubes
5.10.2.1 hollowed cuboctahedron units in moulded high-stress glass fibre; for grouping in clusters, interlocked into various arrangements; 864 mm size in red, blue, yellow, or green. Slides and tunnels as integral part of system also available.

G.L.T. Products and Engineering Limited

Climbing equipment
5.10.2.2 maypole tower; 2.000 m diameter with centre sliding pole and side ladders; in galvanised steel.

5.10.2.3 dome; 2.745 m diameter with three ladders; in galvanised steel.

Slides

5.10.2.4 landslides, especially for building into embankments and sides of mounds; galvanised steel with stainless steel for sliding contact surface; price varies according to length.

Neptune Concrete Limited

Play sculpture

5.10.2.5 P.G.7; saddle shape structure in smooth precast concrete; height 1.580 m x 1.980 m long.

5.10.2.6 P.G.9; concrete tree with nine branches; height 1.829 m with branches projecting 914 mm.

5.10.2.7 P.G.1; tunnel bridge shapes, making semi-circular tunnels by use of units in two parts; length of pair of units 2.130 m with a height of 460 mm.

S.M.P. (Landscapes) Limited

Climbing structures

5.10.2.8 galleon, in welded tubular steel, 4.570 m high, 9.140 m long and 3.050 m wide; complex structure for older children.

5.10.2.9 totem pole; rubber tyres mounted on central tubular steel pole; 2.290 m high.

5.10.2.10 climbing ladders; in welded tubular steel; 1.524 m high; EA31 is a single ladder 381 mm wide and EA32 is a double ladder 726 mm wide.

Play sculpture

5.10.2.11 tapiola; wooden horse with body of peeled larch log; 1.524 m high, with saddle height of 914 mm and overall length of 1.370 m.

5.10.2.12 log cabin shelter; steel framed with roof of half-section larch logs; interior bench planks provided and structure designed to support standard slide over roof; 1.829 m high, 3.660 m long and 1.829 m wide.

Slides

5.10.2.13 safety slides; in stainless steel; can be made up of standard sections; entry section 2.440 m long, straight sections 610 mm, 1.220 m, 1.830 m, 2.440 m long and exit sections 2.440 m long. Convex, concave and run-out sections also available.

Swings

5.10.2.14 arch swings; tubular steel with safety rubber tyre seats on steel chains; seat height 508 mm, width of arch structure 1.829 m with frame heights of 2.440 m, 3.050 m and 3.660 m. Multiple units for multi-seat swings also available in various sizes.

Sportsmark (Equipment) Limited

Climbing frames

5.10.2.15 Playdome; aluminium tubes slotted into aluminium hubs to form a triodetic climbing frame. They are available in three sizes: 'Minidome'; diameter 2.438 m, overall height 1.219 m: 'Playdome Mark 1'; diameter 3.657 m, overall height 1.828 m: 'Playdome Mark II'; diameter 4.876 m, overall height 2.438 m.

The Sutcliffe Moulded Rubber Company Limited

Moving equipment

5.10.2.16 Carousel: with seats for 12 children; diameter of 3.410 m with seats at 550 mm from ground; steel with timber seats.

5.10.2.17 flat rotary disc; for standing while rotating; diameter 2.000 m.

5.10.2.18 fixed see-saw; with four seats at 580 mm from ground and total length of 5.200 m.

Climbing equipment

5.10.2.19 tumbling bar; tubular steel bar at three levels at height of 750 mm, 900 mm and 1.100 m with a total length of 4.550 m.

5.10.2.20 climbing arch; tubular steel with a length of 5.200 m.

Charles Wicksteed & Company Limited

Moving equipment

5.10.2.21 rocking horse; all metal except for plastic seat insert; finished standard mid-green.

5.10.2.22 rota stride; rotating steel cone of 2.135 m diameter with steel handrails on steel column; height to handrails 1.650 m; finished standard mid-green.

5.10.2.23 travelling ring frame; 6 steel hand rings on chains suspended from tubular steel frame, 3.660 m high and 9.760 m long; finished standard mid-green.

Climbing equipment

5.10.2.24 climbing net frame; waterproof rope in 225 mm square mesh on tubular steel 'A' frame 3.355 m x 3.342 m and 2.365 m high; galvanised metalwork.

5.10.2.25 Junglegym; square grid of galvanised steel tubes in three sizes:
Size no. 1; 5.080 m x 2.540 m x 3.175 m high
Size no. 2; 3.175 m x 3.175 m x 3.175 m high
Size no. 3; 2.285 m x 1.725 m x 2.540 m high

Swings

5.10.2.26 traditional set; plastic seat on chains fixed to galvanised tube frame; many sizes available in combinations up to 6 seats; cradle infant swing seats also available. The three frame heights available are 2.440 m, 3.050 m and 3.660 m.

5.11 WATER FEATURES

5.11.1 LAKES AND PONDS

Typical linings
5.11.1.1 In addition to the traditional methods of forming the linings of lakes and ponds in puddled clay or concrete there are now a number of lining materials available. They are mainly used for reservoirs but can also help to form comparatively economical water features especially in soil which is not naturally water-retentive. Three typical examples are given below.

Polythene
5.11.1.2 Black polythene as manufactured by British Visqueen Limited, normal thickness is 250 micrometres, 1000 gauge.

P.V.C.
5.11.1.3 Welded p.v.c., black (14 thou thickness) as welded by Gordon Low Limited and manufactured by B X Plastics Limited.

Rubber Butyl
5.11.1.4 Black butyl sheeting as manufactured by Butyl Products Limited, in thicknesses from 0.5 mm − 2 mm.

5.11.2 ORNAMENTAL POOLS

Concrete linings
5.11.2.1 Small pools may be lined with one of the materials mentioned under lakes and ponds, or may be in brick, rendered, puddled clay or, for the smallest sizes, fibre glass. Most of these tend to be cheaper than waterproof concrete. For approximate estimating purposes basic prices for various sizes of concrete pools are given in 7.11.

5.11.3 SWIMMING POOLS

Standard concrete construction
5.11.3.1 Concrete lining with standard precase concrete edge and waterproof painted surface, including appropriate necessary filtration plant. For approximate estimate purposes various typical sizes are given and priced in 7.11.

5.11.4 FOUNTAINS

Precast concrete units

Mono Concrete Limited

5.11.4.1 'Falkirk'; precast concrete fountain bowl, diameter 1.525 m in white or grey; on pedestal giving total height of 485 m.

5.11.4.2 'Millstone'; cylindrical precast concrete for low fountain jet through centre of top which is smooth and slightly dished; exposed aggregate side surfaces; in various diameters and heights.

Fountain nozzles

G. Allsebrook & Company Limited

5.11.4.3 straight plume; single jet from unit of diameters 19, 38 and 50 mm.

5.11.4.4 multiple plumes; header box to take number of nozzles as 5.11.4.3.

5.11.4.5 rosebowl fountain; unit giving spray in circular arching formation; central plume could also be added.

5.11.4.6 swirl turbulence nozzle; rotating unit.

5.11.4.7 mushroom nozzle; mushroom shape fine spray from central unit; diameters of pipe 19, 25, 32, 38 and 50 mm.

5.11.4.8 adjustable fountain nozzle; enabling combination of upright and sideways jets; pipe diameter 38 and 50 mm.

5.12 STREET FURNITURE

5.12.1 INTRODUCTION

5.12.1.1 The term 'street furniture' means different things to different people and cannot be defined in a completely authoritative way. For the purposes of this publication the term refers mainly to those items included in 'Street Furniture from the Design Index 1972/3' published by the Council of Industrial Design (now Design Council).

5.12.1.2 Some elements included in the CoID publication, such as street and high mast lighting, are omitted from this book as they are somewhat peripheral to main landscape work.

5.12.1.3 Certain items included in the CoID publications are not covered in this section but appear in the appropriate portions of other sections where they are more relevant. For instance fences, pedestrians barriers, concrete and moveable bollards and related items are covered in 5.7 and 7.7; tree grids are covered in 5.8 and 7.8.

5.12.1.4 Most items in this section also appear in the CoID publication; others are additional and some products mentioned by the CoID are not covered here. In making their choice the editors have attempted to present a fair range of manufacturers' products with an emphasis on those which are well designed and are particularly useful in, or sympathetic to, landscape work. Obviously the selection is neither exhaustive nor totally representative but it is intended that in future editions, with the feed-back available from users of this first edition, the range should be more comprehensive.

5.12.2 AMENITY LIGHTING

Columns

Abacus Municipal Limited
5.12.2.1 tubular steel B(2); 4.000 m high column with post top for Atlas 'Gamma five' lantern.

C.M. Churchouse Limited
5.12.2.2 'Litex' tubular steel; 4.267 m high column with extruded aluminium fitting on fluorescent lantern; single bracket or two-way double bracket fittings; also vertical back-to-back and single application with 1.220 m fluorescent fittings.

5.12.2.3 A61339 external globe light; in clear Cabulite material; as single stem 2.584 m high for 100 W tungsten lamp, also in multi-arm version (5 globes) on 4.000 m steel tube.

Specification—Street furniture

G.E.C. (Street Lighting) Limited

5.12.2.4 Aluminium B(2); 4.000 m high eight-sided column with tungsten or mercury post top lantern.

5.12.2.5 reinforced plastics B(2); 4.000 m high circular column with tungsten or mercury post top lantern.

Thorn Lighting Limited

5.12.2.6 tubular steel B(2); 4.000 m high column with integral 'Gamma-7' post top lantern, same diameter as tube shaft; opal acryllic diffuser for tungsten or mercury discharge lamp. Can be combined with bracketed 'Gamma-7' lamps to form a multi-arm column.

5.12.2.7 tubular steel B(2); 4.000 m high steel column with integral 'Gamma-9' post top acryllic diffuser of larger diameter than column; for tungsten, mercury, sodium or fluorescent lighting.

Floodlighting

Thorn Lighting Limited

5.12.2.8 'Sunflood'; for post or wall mounting, general purpose open floodlight for outdoor area lighting; tungsten halogen.

5.12.2.9 'Area Floodlighting'; for post or wall mounting, totally enclosed flood with glass or vandal-resistant polycarbonate.

Lighted bollards

C.M. Churchouse Limited

5.12.2.10 BOL/1050; 850 mm height above ground 140 mm diameter; for low level pedestrian lighting; steel tube post, die cast aluminium body and glass annular fresnal lens for mercury discharge lamp.

Concrete Utilities Limited

5.12.2.11 'Birmingham University' bollard; 838 mm height above ground, diameter 381 mm at top; circular reinforced concrete with exposed aggregate finish, with vertical opal perspex lighting panel on one side only; for tungsten lamp.

5.12.2.12 'Decagon' bollard; 864 mm height above ground, diameter 420 mm; ten-sided reinforced concrete with exposed aggregate finish; opal light cover behind tapered vertical slits in concrete to reduce vandalism; for fluorescent tubes.

5.12.2.13 'Essex University'; 991 mm height above ground, diameter 368 mm at top; circular reinforced concrete with exposed aggregate finish; opal perspex vertical light units to both sides with fluorescent lamps.

Wall brackets

C. M. Churchouse Limited

5.12.2.14 'Litex'; extruded aluminium rectangular fitting in wall bracketed version; overall projection 1.500 m; fluorescent lantern.

5.12.2.15 A.91340 wall mounted external globe; with steel bracket arm extending at right angles to vertical fitting; overall height 533 mm, overall projection 318 mm with 254 mm diameter globe.

G.E.C. (Street Lighting) Limited

5.12.2.16 ZD.10890 bracket and ZD.10877 lantern; overall height 305 mm, width 673 mm, diameter of lantern 508 mm; tungsten or mercury lamp in circular opal bowl on aluminium bracket.

Merchant Adventurers Limited

5.12.2.17 'Square Sphere' series; aluminium wall plates and rectangular section aluminium horizontal arm; glass for tungsten lamp can be transparent smoke or clear glass; diameters 230 mm and 305 mm and overall projections 290 mm to 405 mm.

Thorn Lighting Limited

5.12.2.18 steel wall bracket; with 'Gamma-7' integral lantern in opal acrylic for tungsten or mercury; overall height 349 mm, projection 457 mm.

5.12.2.19 aluminium wall mounted 'Escort EKF 1100 and 1200'; for domestic use, well glass of white opal in two sizes for 60/100 W lamps or 150/200 W lamps.

Low level lighting

C. M. Churchouse Limited

5.12.2.20 A.62360 mushroom landscape light; height above ground 940 mm with dome diameter of 622 mm; steel tube welded to spun aluminium dome over 2 tungsten lamps.

Bulkhead fittings

C. M. Churchouse Limited

5.12.2.21 887 lighting brick; for wall mounting; 216 mm wide and 107.4 mm deep; die-cast aluminium base plate with opal glassware rectangular fitting.

5.12.2.22 907 lighting brick; as 887 but 276 mm wide and 121 mm deep.

Thorn Lighting Limited

5.12.2.23 Escort OB 2008; surface mounted fluorescent bulkhead fitting with aluminium alloy body and high impact acrylic diffuser; 368 mm long, 102 mm wide and 92 mm deep; can be obtained also in recessed version.

5.12.3 LITTER BINS

Concrete

Abacus Municipal Limited

5.12.3.1 Model 631; height 762 mm, diameter at top 1,067 m; exposed aggregate large capacity container with galvanised inner wire basket. Free standing.

5.12.3.2 Model 607; height 762 mm, diameter 508 mm at top; exposed aggregate container with galvanised inner wire basket. Free standing.

Mono Concrete (Northern) Limited

5.12.3.3 'Newstead'; precast concrete, aggregate faced; height 735 mm, diameter 480 mm, with removable wire basket and perforated bottom for drainage. Free standing.

Metal

Abacus Municipal Limited

5.12.3.4 Model 621; height 330 mm, depth 406 mm, width 241 mm; stove enamelled steel for pole or wall mounting.

5.12.3.5 Model 611; height 864 mm, diameter 305 mm; stainless steel cylindrical bin with hard rubber top rim; on short tube with flange for floor mounting.

Braby Group Limited

5.12.3.6 Model A or B; truncated conical aluminium alloy bin with polythene protecting rim; anodised finish; for pole or wall mounting. Model A: height 375 mm with diameter 229–178 mm. Model B: height 450 mm with diameter 229–178 mm.

Burnham & Company (Onyx) Limited

5.12.3.7 'Yorke'; 381 mm x 229 mm stove enamelled steel box with removable galvanised basket; for wall or pole mounting but could be freestanding on short upright.

White and Carter (Councils) Limited

5.12.3.8 'Hykleen'; overall height 513 mm, depth 254 mm, width 257 mm, stove enamelled steel with metal hinged lid; perspex spring load flap in lid and galvanised steel inner container.

5.12.3.9 'Streamline'; height 483 mm, depth 229 mm, width 305 mm; stove enamelled steel with metal hinged lid; perspex spring load flap in lid mounting.

Plastics

Abacus Municipal Limited
5.12.3.10 Model 622; height 762 mm, diameter 267 mm; circular glass fibre with swing lid.

Timber faced

Metaliform Limited
5.12.3.11 'London Parks'; height 1.016 m or 762 mm, top diameter 521 mm or 457 mm; freestanding with tubular ground fixing, oiled teakwood slats and wire inner basket.

White and Carter (Councils) Limited
5.12.3.12 'Diploma 2'; height 375 mm, depth 254 mm, width 305 mm; nearly cylindrical for pole or wall mounting with galvanised steel inner container and vertical Burma teak slats.

5.12.4   OUTDOOR SEATS

Concrete framed

Holton Builders Limited
5.12.4.1 'Reepham'; length 1.52 m, 1.800 m and 2.400 m; concrete frames and mild steel supports to slats of Malayan Kapur.

Neptune Concrete Limited
5.12.4.2 'Southampton Mark 3'; concrete supports with exposed aggregate finish and hardwood slats; length 2.130 m.

Metal framed

Abacus Municipal Limited
5.12.4.3 Outdoor seat with square section steel frames; in various sizes with painted softwood timbers or varnished hardwood iroko, with or without arms.

Geometric furniture
5.12.4.4 'Delta'; narrow iroko slats on black nylon finished square section steel frame; in various sizes.

Orchard seating
5.12.4.5 'Pointer' series; nylon coated steel frame with oiled iroko planks; various sizes from 2.440 m − 1.219 m.

Orchard seating *continued*

5.12.4.6 'Setter'; nylon finished steel frame and narrow oiled iroko slats; length 1.200 m, 1,800 m or 2.400 m.

All timber

Battenhurst Developments

5.12.4.7 Combined bench and picnic table; length 1.800 m or 2.440 m; preservative treated softwood.

5.12.5 PLANT CONTAINERS

Concrete, asbestos cement and fibre glass

Esplana Limited

5.12.5.1 'Architectural range'; made of a patent cement material in several sizes, circular or square; available in white with black plinth or natural rough textured surface.

Glasdon Limited

5.12.5.2 'Glasfibre architectural planters'; fibre glass in various simple shapes and sizes.

Mono Concrete Limited

5.12.5.3 Plant bowls; various shapes and sizes in white precast concrete.

5.12.6 CYCLE STANDS

Metal holders

Le Bas Tube Company Limited

5.12.5.1 'VelopA' bicycle holder; galvanised steel tubing and bar with serrated arms to grip tyre of front wheel; depth 203 mm, width 89 mm, height 464 mm for type for ground fixing and 337 mm for version for wall fixing.

Concrete parking blocks

Mono Concrete Limited

5.12.6.2 'Monohex'; hexagonal cycle stand slabs to fit in paving of hexagonal slabs; 760 mm x 75 mm thick with plain or textured face.

5.12.6.3 'Metric Four Square'; 500 mm square x 50 mm thick exposed aggregate slab to fit within 'Metric Four Square' paving arrangement.

Stelcon Limited

5.12.6.4 'Stelcon' bicycle parking block; robust precast concrete; 600 mm x 300 mm x 100 mm thick.

5.13 MAINTENANCE

5.13.1 INTRODUCTION

5.13.1.1 There is a British Standard for tree work, B.S. 3998 and the standard covering grounds maintenance is in course of preparation. For this reason the only comprehensive specification information given in this section is on tree work. Tree surgery is almost impossible to cover in a price book of this nature and consequently 7.13 does not contain prices for tree work. Each case must be assessed and priced on its merits but the standard of procedure should conform with B.S. 3998. Tree felling and associated works are covered in 5.1 and 7.1.

5.13.2 B.S. 3998:1966 RECOMMENDATIONS FOR TREE WORK (This is summarized below)

Section One: General Clauses

Scope
5.13.2.1 This British Standard gives general recommendations for tree work. All the operations which are described in Section Two will not always be necessary. Each tree should be considered individually, and the work to be done determined in relation to its age, shape, size, character, condition and situation. All operations, whether done for reasons of safety, health of the tree, space requirements or aesthetics, should be carried out so as to leave a well-balanced tree of normal growth and pleasing appearance.

Safety
5.13.2.2 If work on a tree necessitates climbing, it should never be undertaken by one man on his own. It is essential that adequate safety precautions be taken and appropriate insurance arrangements made.
Appendix A lists some safety precautions.

Season
5.13.2.3 Most tree work may be carried out at any time of the year.

Equipment
5.13.2.4 All plant and equipment should be appropriate for the task. All cutting tools should be sharp. Tools should be surface sterilized (with methylated spirit) after use on trees which are known or suspected to be diseased.

Workmanship
5.13.2.5 Adequate skilled supervision is essential throughout tree work both because it may be dangerous and it is irreversible.

Workmanship *continued*

5.13.2.5 (cont'd) All operations should be carefully carried out avoid damage to the trees being treated or to neighbouring trees, either by equipment or by falling branches. Neither heavy mechanical equipment nor building materials should be allowed within the spread of the branches. Trees being retained should not be used as an anchor for winching operations, unless adequately protected.

All diseased wood, fungi, prunings and rubbish should be burned during the course of the work or on completion and the site left clean and tidy. Any holes should be backfilled with suitable material.

Fires should not be lit in such a position that they are able to damage any surrounding trees or shrubs. Before lighting a fire on peat soil, a trench should be dug around the area on which the fire is to be situated. This trench should be at least 380 mm wide and be of sufficient depth to cut right through the peat and into the soil beneath.

Upon completion of the work the fire must be extinguished. When the ashes are cold, the ground covered by the fire should be dug over and the trench around the fire filled in. On peat areas a period of 7 days should elapse before doing this.

Inspection

5.13.2.6 The estimate of work needed will normally have been based on judgement made from ground level. Foreknowledge of hidden defects cannot be expected, but during the course of the work a complete inspection of each tree should be made, to reveal any additional defects or weaknesses.

Section Two: Operations

Cuts

5.13.2.7 All final cuts should be made into living wood to make possible occlusion by the growth of callus tissue. All final cuts should be made flush to either stem or branch. All cuts should be made in such a manner as to prevent the formation of moisture-holding pockets.

All cut surfaces or exposed wounds over 50 mm in diameter should be treated with a fungicidal sealant, preferably within 20 minues, and in any case within 24 hours. Creosote or coal tar should not be used. The surface should be dry when the sealant is applied; artificial methods of drying by heating should not be used. In the case of large wounds, they should, when necessary, be fortified by the addition of a rot-proof flexible reinforcement, such as glass scrim.

Pruning

5.13.2.8 Heavy branches should be removed in sections and undercut to avoid tearing the bark and lowered by slings to avoid damage to the tree and its surroundings. Final cuts should be made as close to the stem or main branch as possible; no branch stumps should be left.

Lifting of crown
5.13.2.9 Lifting of the crown consists of the removal of the lower branches from the main stem or branch system up to a specified height or line indicated. All branches so removed should be cut flush to main stem or parent branch.

Cleaning out
5.13.2.10 Cleaning out consists of the removal of all dead, dying or diseased wood, fungi and rubbish accumulating in forks. It also includes the removal of objects such as wires, clamps or boards, where this can be done without inflicting further damage on the tree. An inspection for defects not visible from the ground should be made.

Crown thinning
5.13.2.11 Crown thinning, the reduction in density of foilage, is carried out to achieve any or all of the following objects:—
 (A) safety
 (B) to preserve balance or improve shape
 (C) to admit more light and air to or through the crown
 (D) to reduce weight
 (E) to lessen wind resistance
 (F) to produce more flower or fruit
 (G) to train and encourage good branch development in young trees
Crown thinning includes the removal of weak, thin, crossing and dangerous branches.

Reducing and Shaping
5.13.2.12 The crown of a tree may be reduced in height and/or spread by shortening the main branches at suitable points to promote the growth of new shoots and to redevelop as far as possible the natural form of the species. This operation is a matter of judicious pruning and should not be construed as lopping or topping (beheading).

All vertical or near-vertical branches should be cut off neatly just above the nearest suitably-placed live growth and the branch should be cut off at an angle no greater than is necessary to ensure rapid run-off of rain water. Trees in restricted spaces may need to be shaped to a suitable natural form where normal development is not possible. Trees so treated will require subsequent attention in order to maintain this form.

Restoration
5.13.2.13 Restoration consists of the careful treatment of otherwise healthy trees which contain dead or diseased wood, or have been mutilated by lopping, or damaged by gales or vandalism. It should include the removal of dead and diseased wood, the thinning of new shoots on sound wood, and the encouragement of new leading shoots where desired.

Repair Work

5.13.2.14 (A) *Bark wounds.* Trees which have lost a portion of bark should have the ragged edge of the wound cut back to healthy tissue.

The whole of the exposed surface should be heavily coated with a fungicidal sealant.

5.13.2.15 (B) *Deep wounds.* All splintered wood should be removed and the interior of the wound trimmed to a smooth surface. The bark should be carefully pared back to live cambium and the wound heavily coated with a fungicidal sealant.

5.13.2.16 (C) *Split branch.* Where it is possible for split branches to be retained they may be supported by cable braces. The interior of the split portion should first be cleaned and if necessary pared and then treated with fungicidal sealant. The end of the branch should then be raised, if necessary by means of pulley blocks, and the split closed as far as is possible.

One or more holes should then be drilled through the split portion, bolts inserted and the split drawn together as the nuts are tightened.

Where old splits in branches have started to form callus it will not be possible to close the split completely without reduction of the callus. In these cases the wound should be thoroughly cleaned, any decayed wood removed, and the interior treated with a fungicidal sealant.

5.13.2.17 (D) *Root wounds.* Damaged roots should be cut to a smooth surface and treated with a fungicidal sealant. They should then be re-covered with soil to their natural depth.

5.13.2.18 (E) *Small cavities.* Small cavities, those with no dimension greater than 150 mm should be cleaned out and filled with a suitable non-rigid filler. This filler should be sloped behind the bark so that it may be covered by callus more rapidly.

5.13.2.19 (F) *Large dry cavities.* A large cavity which is dry should normally be left open. The walls of such a cavity should be thoroughly scraped and brushed to remove any decayed wood and then treated with fungicidal sealant.

5.13.2.20 (G) *Large accessible cavities containing water.* Where a large cavity contains water and is accessible, the water, leaves and debris accumulated in the bottom should be removed, all decayed wood scraped away and the cavity thoroughly dried out and disinfected with a fungicidal sealant. It should then be filled, to the lower edge of the cavity, with a suitable non-rigid filler, the top of the filling being steeply sloped to give a rapid run-off for moisture.

5.13.2.21 (H) *Large inaccessible cavities containing water.* Where a lage cavity contains water and is inaccessible, the depth of the cavity should be measured with a thin probe and the measurement marked against the outside of the tree. A large hole should then be bored upwards at a

Repair Work continued

5.13.2.21 (cont'd) steep angle to strike the bottom of the cavity and drain away the water. A thin gauged copper pipe should be driven into this hole and left protruding to form a short spout. This will prevent callus from forming and closing the hole. The holes should be left open and periodically cleaned out with rods.

5.13.2.22 (J) *Water pockets in forks.* Water pockets in forks should be thoroughly cleaned, dried and filled with a non-rigid filler, the top of the filling being sloped to give a rapid run-off for moisture. Where it is impossible to reach the bottom of narrow water pockets they may be tapped with an auger, the water drained away and the auger hole plugged with a hardwood dowel dipped in wound dressing.

5.13.2.23 (K) *Concrete fillings.* Concrete should only be used as a filling in the lower part of the trunks of large trees. After cleaning the interior and coating it with a fungicidal sealant, the perimeter of the cavity entrance should first be lined with a suitable non-rigid filler, 3 mm to 6 mm in thickness, to form a seal between the concrete and the wood. A strong and almost dry concrete mixture should be carefully tamped in, and when completely dry its surface should be covered with a fungicidal sealant.

Bracing

5.13.2.24 (A) *Bracing with cables.* Any necessary bracing should be carried out with cables of galvanised steel wire, rope, of appropriate lengths and diameter.

Each cable should be secured, by not less than two U clips at each end or by splicing, to eyebolts passing through the branches. Thimbles should be inserted in all eyes formed in the cable. It is essential that all cables should be tightened sufficiently to prevent independent movement of branches.

Cables should be so placed as not to rub against branches. It will frequently be necessary to support a branch by use of more than one cable.

Bolts and cables should form a straight line at the point of attachment.

The point of attachment is usually about two-thirds of the distance from the crotch to the end of the branch.

Clamps, bands and unprotected wire wrapping should never be used.

All cracks, rubbed areas and cut surfaces should be cleaned out and treated with fungicidal sealant.

5.13.2.25 (B) *Touching limbs.* Where two limbs grow in such a manner as to rub against each other it is usually best to remove one of them. If this cannot be done without spoiling the shape of the tree the branches may be braced apart or held tightly together and encouraged to form a graft. This may be done by cutting back the rubbed portion to live cambium, applying a fungicidal sealant to all exposed surfaces and drilling directly through both branches and inserting a bolt.

Bracing continued

5.13.2.26 (C) *Rod bracing.* Weak forks or forks which have split, should be braced by the use of solid bolts with screwed ends, washers and nuts.

Where a fork is split it would be further strengthened by the insertion of a cable brace well above the fork bolts; this should be so tightened as to be always under tension. If water collects in the narrow cavity formed by a split fork, a drain spout should be inserted, as for inaccessible cavities.

Feeding

5.13.2.27 Under certain circumstances trees in poor health, or of low vigour, may need fertilizing. This may or may not be in addition to cultural or soil amelioration operations such as soil aeration, irrigation or incorporation of bulky organic material.

Three examples of the application of fertilizer in straight-forward conditions are given in Appendix D. Feeding may be carried out by use of appropriate liquid pressure feeding or foliar feeding techniques.

Tree Removal

5.13.2.28 (A) *General.* Where it is known that the death of a tree has been caused by the honey fungus, Armillaria mellea, it is essential that the stump and roots should be removed and burned.

5.13.2.29 (B) *Felling.* Trees to be felled should be cut as near to the ground as practicable. Large trees in confined spaces, or near to other trees and shrubs which are to be retained, should be carefully taken down in sections. After felling, the stump should be cleaned off horizontally to present a neat and workmanlike finish.

5.13.2.30 (C) *Killing of Roots and Stumps.* Roots and stumps may be killed by chemical treatment. It should be borne in mind that where there are closely-planted avenues or groups of trees of the same species there are likely to be root grafts. If stumps in these areas are poisoned the adjoining trees may be affected by the poison being conducted through the grafts to their root systems. Roots in these areas may be killed by the continuous removal of all new growth as soon as it appears.

5.13.2.31 (D) *Stump and Root Removal.* The area and depth within which stump and roots are to be removed should be clearly determined. The work may be carried out by grubbing out by hand or by suitable mechanical means, or by destruction with a stump chipper.

Appendix A. General Safety Precautions

5.13.2.32 *General:* At least two men should be employed on tree work so that in the event of an accident there will be someone present to render assistance.

5.13.2.33 *Training:* Before any man attempts to work in trees, he should be trained in the use of ropes, knots, safety belts and saddles, and have the opportunity for enough practice climbing to become proficient in their use. Only men who are physically fit should be allowed in trees.

Specification—Maintenance

5.13.2.34 *Clothing:* Clothing should be sound, strong and of a type not easily caught or torn. Any form of outer garment, such as overcoats, oilskins or scarves, is impractical and highly dangerous. Boots are preferable to shoes for the extra protection they afford. The soles should be of rubber or rubber substitute; on no account should leather or hobnails be used. Any man working in and beneath trees should be protected by wearing a safety helmet.

5.13.2.35 *Conditions:* Trees should not be worked in when wet or during storms, high winds or extreme cold, except in emergencies. Normally only one person should be in any one tree at one time.

5.13.2.36 *Equipment:* Equipment should be of the highest quality, with suitable protection provided to maintain it both in transit and on the site.
 The working load of ropes should not exceed one-fifth of the breaking load. Personal safety equipment, including ropes, should never be used for any other purpose; it should have a breaking load of not less than 1814 kg. Nylon ropes should comply with the requirements of B.S. 3104.

5.13.2.37 *Warning notices:* Danger signals with red flags should be displayed with particular reference to the danger overhead.

5.13.2.38 *Roping-off:* Where pedestrian traffic is heavy, the area surrounding the tree should be roped off. At least one person should remain on the ground to supervise these precautions.

5.13.2.39 *Proximity to highway:* Where work is being carried out adjacent to the highway, the local authority and police should be informed.

5.13.2.40 *Power and Telephone Lines:* Before working near underground or overhead power or telephone lines, the appropriate area engineer should be contacted and the necessary safety precautions and clearances agreed. Work in such areas should never be undertaken by fewer than two persons and it should not be carried on in wet conditions.
 When working near high voltage overhead power lines, no person or equipment or part of a tree should be allowed to come within 3.000 m of the nearest point on any conductor or live equipment. If necessary, ropes should be used to ensure that parts of a tree being removed fall AWAY from the lines.

5.13.2.41 *First aid:* An adequate first aid kit should be carried at all times, including both large wound dressings and an instruction booklet. Preferably more than one person trained in elementary first aid should be included in each crew.

Appendix B. Season
5.13.2.42 (In the original British Standard a table is given here to indicate the appropriate season for each category of tree work).

Appendix C. A method for protecting a large tree to be used as an anchor

5.13.2.43 Pack well-filled sacks of straw around the base of the tree. Then tie against these straw-sacks pieces of cordwood split to a semi-circular section, the cordwood being shorter than the individual sacks and about 100–125 mm in radius. Space these around the tree with one piece of cordwood to each sack of straw.

Place the cable in a loop around the tree with both ends made fast to the winch so that pressure is applied to only one side of the tree and there is no tendency for the cable to slip and destroy the packing.

In no circumstances should the cable be passed around the tree and hooked back onto its own part as, in these conditions, the cable will move when pressure is applied and will displace the packing.

Keep a constant watch on the packing. Make adjustments as necessary as the strain is taken by the cable.

Appendix D. Three methods for feeding trees after tree work

5.13.2.44 *Method 1:* for ease of insertion, and to prevent excessive concentration, bulk the selected fertilizer, with suitable materials, and evenly allocate it to holes at about 460 mm centres, made in a band extending from about 1.500 m inside the spread of the tree to 1.500 m outside the spread. Open the holes to a depth of 300–460 mm for softwood trees and 460–760 mm for hardwood trees. Insert the fertilizer; make good the disturbed surface.

5.13.2.45 *Method 2:* Mark out a band extending from about 1.500 m inside the spread of the tree to 1.500 m outside the spread. With a heavy fork prick over this area as deeply as possible, the lines of the holes being 150 mm apart. Scatter the selected fertilizer over the treated area at the rate of 250 g/m^2. Brush the area so as to work the fertilizer into the holes. Then water at the rate of 10 l/m^2.

5.13.2.46 *Method 3:* Mark out a band extending from about 1.500 m inside the spread of the tree to 1.500 m outside the spread. From this area, remove the top soil or turf to a depth of 150 mm. Dig over the exposed soil to loosen it and then cover it to a depth of 100 mm with well-rotted cow manure. Water at the rate of 10 l/m^2 and replace the top soil and turf.

Appendix E. Examples of methods for treatment of roots with ammonium sulphamate or sodium chlorate

5.13.2.47 *Chemicals:* Both ammonium sulphamate and sodium chlorate are highly soluble crystalline solids and they can be applied dry, or in a water solution, to cut stumps, stems or frill girdles.

Solution strengths

5.13.2.48 Ammonium sulphamate: 400 g per litre of water.
Sodium chlorate: 40 g per litre of water.

Methods of application

5.13.2.49 (A) *Freshly-cut stumps*

(a) Make incisions in the sapwood around the perimeter of stump. These incisions may take the form of slots cut with a power saw, or holes drilled with an auger. They should be from 100 to 150 mm deep.

Fill the slots or holes with solution or dry crystals:

or

(b) Prise away the bark from wood around the circumference of the stump and insert dry crystals or pour in solution until near the point of run off; the solution should not be allowed to overflow:

or

(c) Employ combinations of the above methods.

5.13.2.50 (B) *Stumps cut more than 48 hours previously*

(a) As in 5.13.2.49A above, but in solution for rapid assimilation.

or

(b) cut notches into the base of the stumps not more than 100 mm apart edge to edge; apply dry crystals into the notches at approximately 14 g per notch.

or

(c) Cut a continuous 'frill' girdle around the base of the stump and pour in solution until near the point of run off; the solution should not be allowed to overflow.

5.13.2.51 *Precautions:* Extreme care should be taken, in applying either of these chemicals, to avoid actual contact with nearby plants or spilling on to the ground where it can reach the root system of other plants.

Ammonium sulphamate is corrosive to metal and should be applied only from plastic or stainless steel containers. It is not toxic to animals and does not irritate the skin or have any systemic effects in moderate doses. It is non-volatile and non-flammable.

Sodium chlorate tends to make flammable materials more flammable, especially on drying. It is of particular importance to prevent any of the solution coming into contact with operatives' clothing.

5.13.2.52 *Cleaning of Equipment:* Care should be taken to clean equipment before it is used for any other purpose.

Footnote

5.13.2.53 (See the original British Standard for illustrations showing correct methods of: pruning large branches, removal of complete branches. removal of smaller branches, reducing head, treatment of bark wounds, construction of a retaining wall against roots, treatment of cavities, bracing with cables, rod bracing and cabling, protection of a large tree to be used as an anchor, and feeding after tree work).

5.13.3 GRASS MAINTENANCE

Types of grass cutting

5.13.3.1 Depending on the topography of the grass areas, the slope of the land and the degree of use to be made of the grass, the appropriate method of maintenance should be chosen, the principal types being summarized below:

Tractor gang mowing

5.13.3.2 This is used for large, reasonably flat, obstruction free grass areas such as playing fields, school grounds and public parks. Gang mowing is difficult around closely spaced trees and on slopes so that it may, within a park for instance, have to be used in conjunction with cylinder and rotary mowers.

Cylinder mowing

5.13.3.3 This may be with or without a box for cuttings and is usual among closely spaced trees and in areas such as closely built housing estates, where grass areas will often be in small sections between paths and shrub beds.

Rotary or flail mowing

5.13.3.4 This can be used for flat grass in small areas or around trees, but is particularly suited to steep grassed banks on which other mowers would be uncontrollable and dangerous.

Stone picking

5.13.3.5 Even on reasonably established grass areas, especially on flint soil, stones can work their way to the surface and therefore stone picking can be a regular maintenance item on new grass areas. It can be particularly important on playing fields where sharp surface stones can be dangerous to players.

Spiking

5.13.3.6 In addition to mole and other drainage covered elsewhere in this book, it may be necessary to aerate the soil, especially on heavy clay where there is considerable compaction from use. This is usually done by means of a tractor-drawn spiker.

5.13.4 SHRUB BED MAINTENANCE

Permanent planting

5.13.4.1 The exact cost of such work may vary considerably depending on the plants, and weeding amongst small ground cover plants in their early stages can be more difficult than between larger, wide-spaced shrubs.

Bedding-out planting
5.13.4.2 This, like shrubs, can vary considerably. Nevertheless for approximate costing purposes certain averages can be taken and in this case it is assumed that a continuous seasonal (March—November) display will be achieved and that it will be kept weeded and watered as and when necessary.

Mulch
5.13.4.3 Except in certain alkaline circumstances an annual peat mulch can be an advantage to many plants and should usually be included in maintenance budgeting.

6 Drawings

6.3.1 INSTITUTE OF LANDSCAPE ARCHITECTS FEES

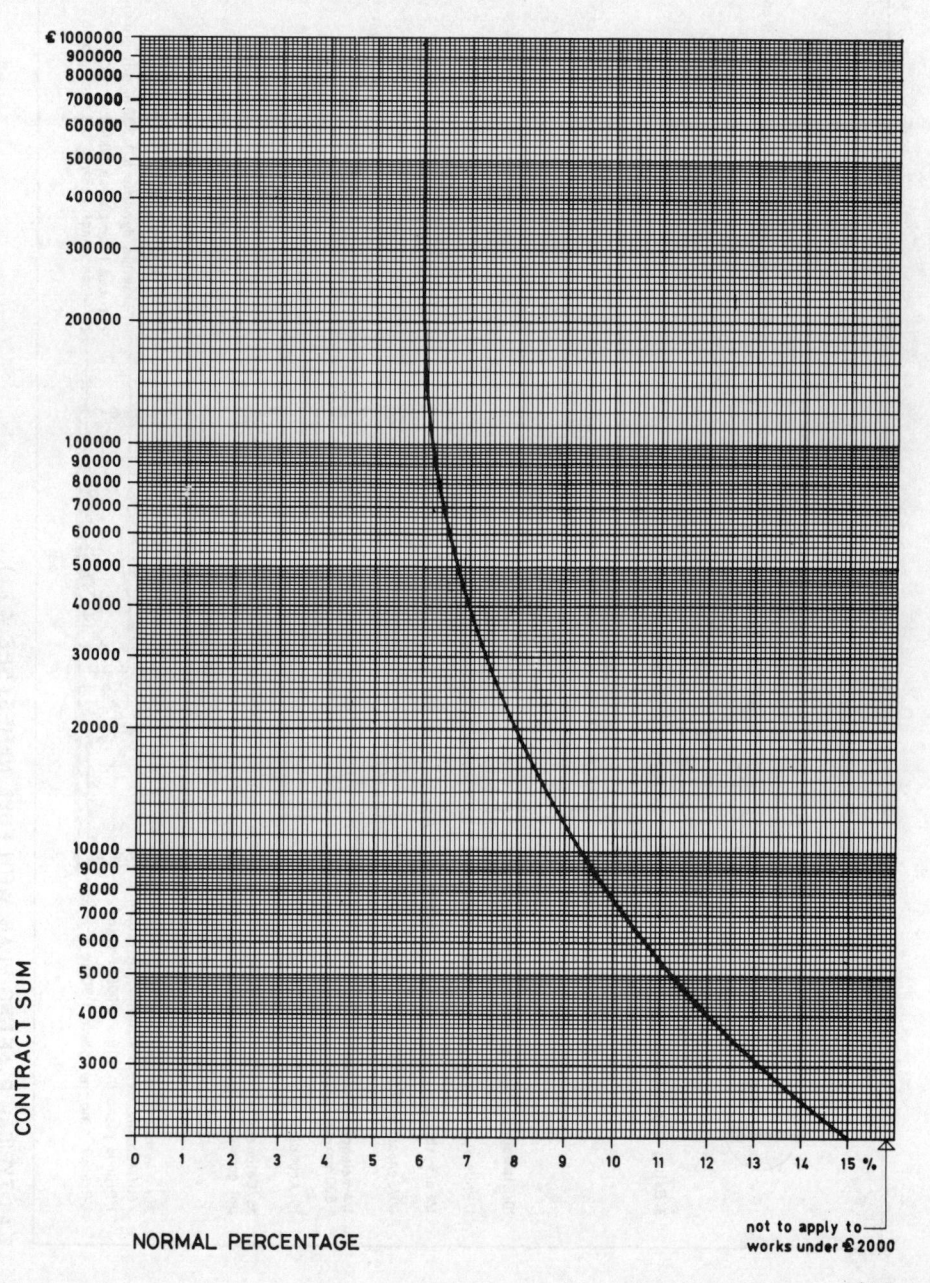

CONTRACT SUM

NORMAL PERCENTAGE

not to apply to works under £2000

225

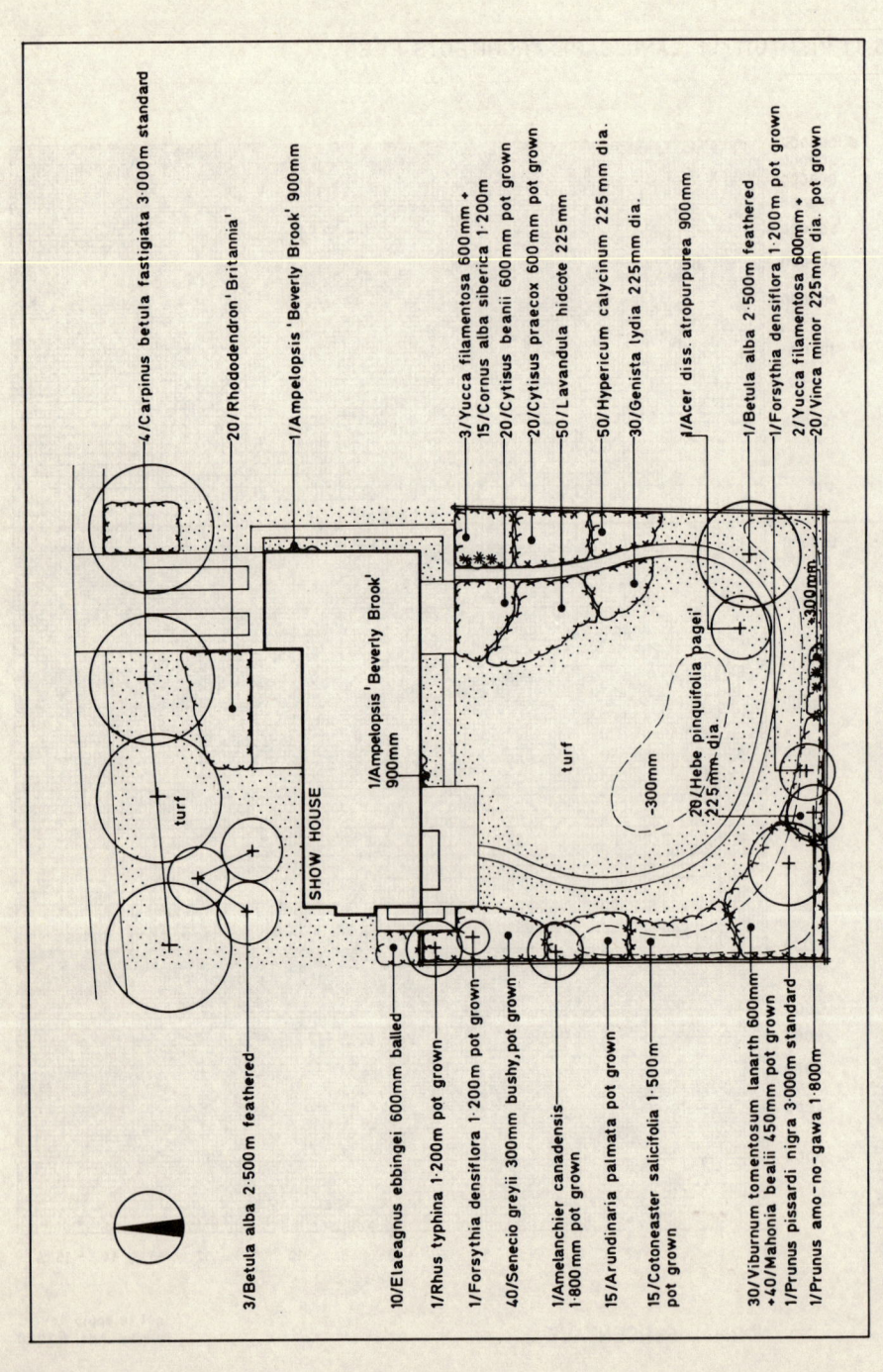

6.4.1 TYPICAL PLANTING PLAN WITH FULL NAMES (SEE 4.2.1)

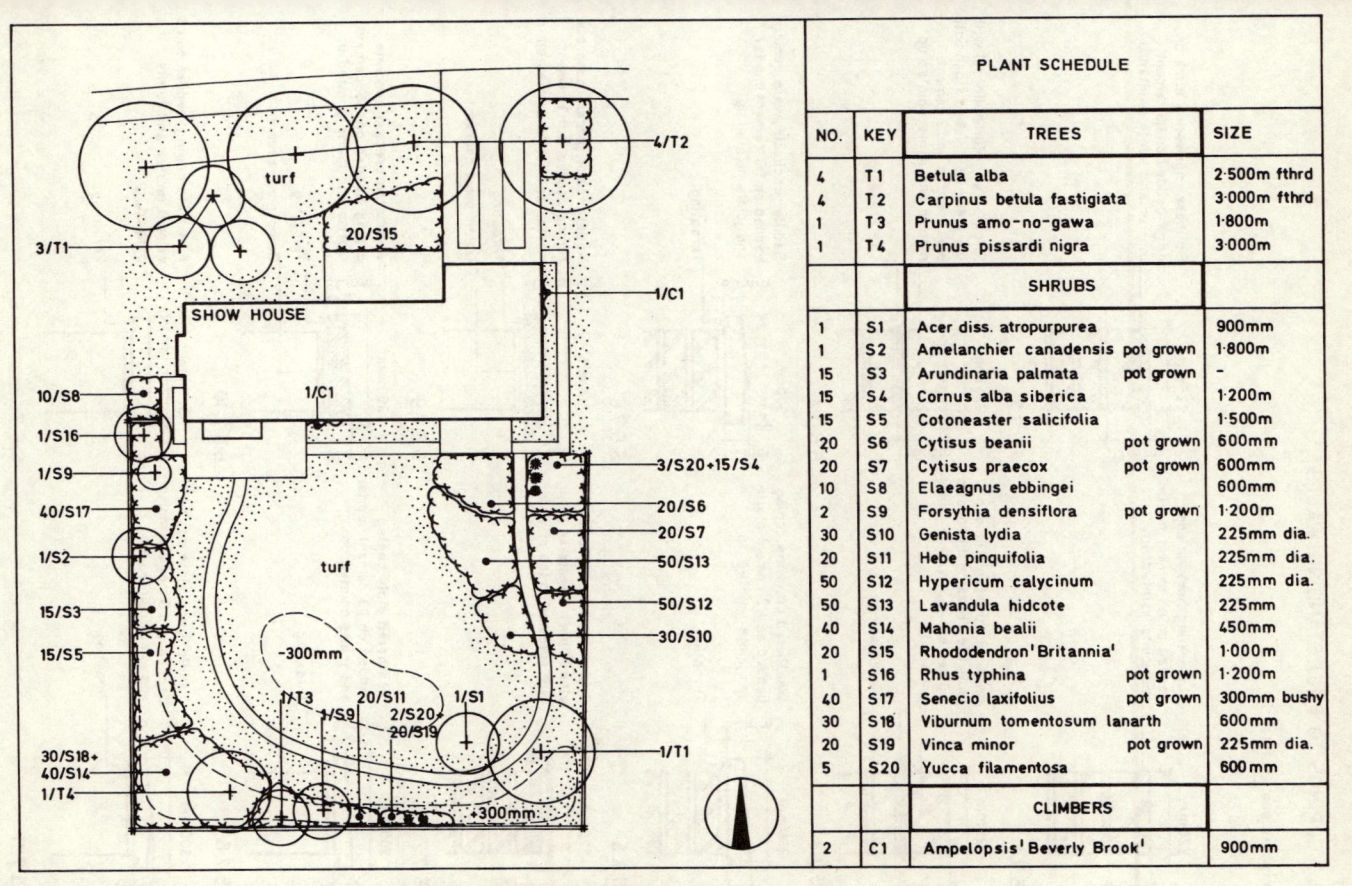

PLANT SCHEDULE

NO.	KEY	TREES	SIZE
4	T1	Betula alba	2·500m fthrd
4	T2	Carpinus betula fastigiata	3·000m fthrd
1	T3	Prunus amo-no-gawa	1·800m
1	T4	Prunus pissardi nigra	3·000m

NO.	KEY	SHRUBS	SIZE
1	S1	Acer diss. atropurpurea	900mm
1	S2	Amelanchier canadensis pot grown	1·800m
15	S3	Arundinaria palmata pot grown	–
15	S4	Cornus alba siberica	1·200m
15	S5	Cotoneaster salicifolia	1·500m
20	S6	Cytisus beanii pot grown	600mm
20	S7	Cytisus praecox pot grown	600mm
10	S8	Elaeagnus ebbingei	600mm
2	S9	Forsythia densiflora pot grown	1·200m
30	S10	Genista lydia	225mm dia.
20	S11	Hebe pinquifolia	225mm dia.
50	S12	Hypericum calycinum	225mm dia.
50	S13	Lavandula hidcote	225mm
40	S14	Mahonia bealii	450mm
20	S15	Rhododendron 'Britannia'	1·000m
1	S16	Rhus typhina pot grown	1·200m
40	S17	Senecio laxifolius pot grown	300mm bushy
30	S18	Viburnum tomentosum lanarth	600mm
20	S19	Vinca minor pot grown	225mm dia.
5	S20	Yucca filamentosa	600mm

NO.	KEY	CLIMBERS	SIZE
2	C1	Ampelopsis 'Beverly Brook'	900mm

6.4.2 TYPICAL PLANTING PLAN WITH KEY SCHEDULE (SEE 4.2.1)

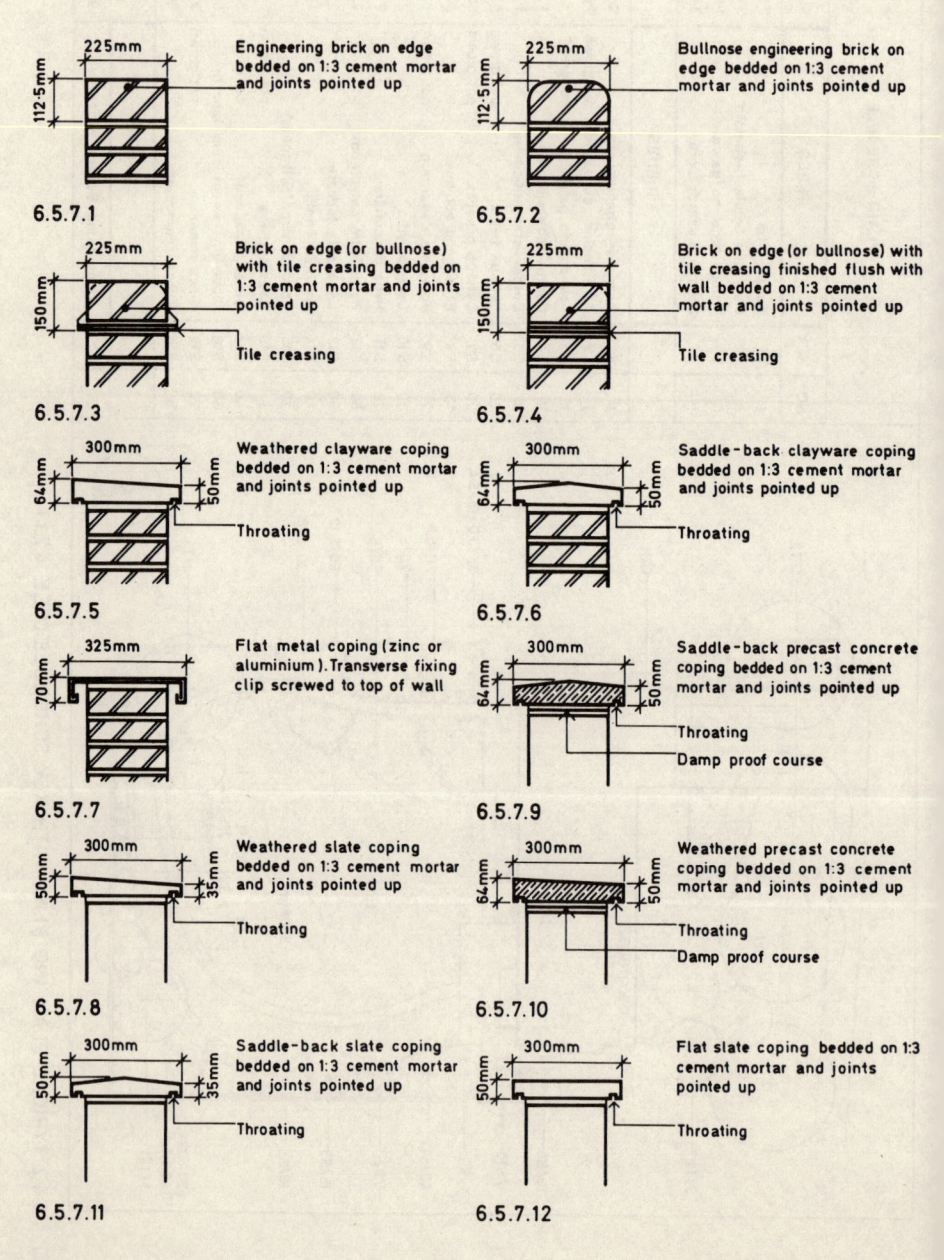

6.5.7 COPINGS TO FREESTANDING WALLS

For prices see Chapter 7

6.5.7.1 Engineering brick on edge bedded on 1:3 cement mortar and joints pointed up (225mm × 112·5mm)

6.5.7.2 Bullnose engineering brick on edge bedded on 1:3 cement mortar and joints pointed up (225mm × 112·5mm)

6.5.7.3 Brick on edge (or bullnose) with tile creasing bedded on 1:3 cement mortar and joints pointed up (225mm × 150mm). Tile creasing.

6.5.7.4 Brick on edge (or bullnose) with tile creasing finished flush with wall bedded on 1:3 cement mortar and joints pointed up (225mm × 150mm). Tile creasing.

6.5.7.5 Weathered clayware coping bedded on 1:3 cement mortar and joints pointed up (300mm × 64mm, 50mm). Throating.

6.5.7.6 Saddle-back clayware coping bedded on 1:3 cement mortar and joints pointed up (300mm × 64mm, 50mm). Throating.

6.5.7.7 Flat metal coping (zinc or aluminium). Transverse fixing clip screwed to top of wall (325mm × 70mm).

6.5.7.9 Saddle-back precast concrete coping bedded on 1:3 cement mortar and joints pointed up (300mm × 64mm, 50mm). Throating. Damp proof course.

6.5.7.8 Weathered slate coping bedded on 1:3 cement mortar and joints pointed up (300mm × 50mm, 35mm). Throating.

6.5.7.10 Weathered precast concrete coping bedded on 1:3 cement mortar and joints pointed up (300mm × 64mm, 50mm). Throating. Damp proof course.

6.5.7.11 Saddle-back slate coping bedded on 1:3 cement mortar and joints pointed up (300mm × 50mm, 35mm). Throating.

6.5.7.12 Flat slate coping bedded on 1:3 cement mortar and joints pointed up (300mm × 50mm). Throating.

6.5.7 COPINGS: TO RETAINING WALLS

For prices see Chapter 7

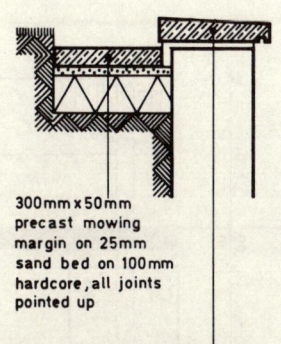

300mm x 50mm precast mowing margin on 25mm sand bed on 100mm hardcore, all joints pointed up

300mm x 50mm weathered and throated precast concrete coping bedded on 1:3 cement mortar, all joints pointed up

6.5.7.13

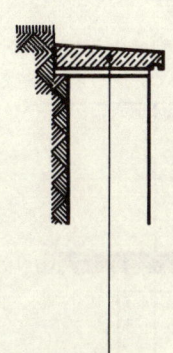

300mm x 50mm weathered and throated concrete coping bedded on bedded on 1:3 cement mortar all joints pointed up

6.5.7.14

225mm x 150mm precast concrete or reconstructed stone coping bedded on 1:3 cement mortar all joints pointed up

6.5.7.15

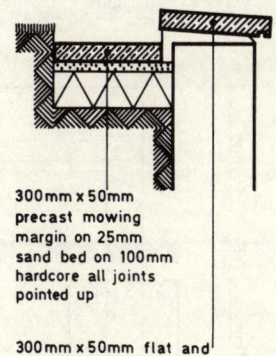

300mm x 50mm precast mowing margin on 25mm sand bed on 100mm hardcore all joints pointed up

300mm x 50mm flat and throated precast concrete coping laid to 20mm fall, bedded on 1:3 cement mortar, all joints pointed up

6.5.7.16

300mm x 50mm flat and throated concrete coping laid to 20mm fall bedded on 1:3 cement mortar, all joints pointed up

6.5.7.17

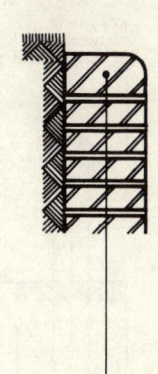

225mm x 112.5mm bullnosed brick laid on edge bedded on 1:3 cement mortar all joints pointed up

6.5.7.18

6.5.7 LOW RAILS: TIMBER, SOFTWOOD

For detailed specification of materials used on these drawings see Chapter 5, Section 7
For prices see Chapter 7

200mm x 38mm nominal size softwood rail, painted, butt jointed and screwed to uprights

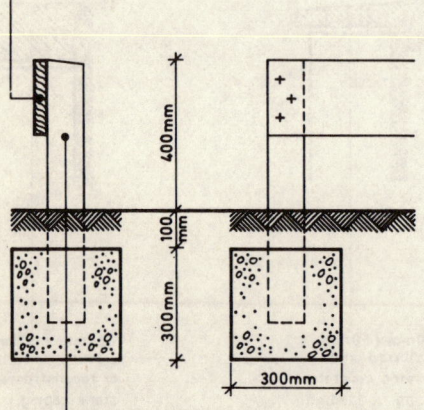

200mm x 38mm nominal size softwood rail, painted, and bolted to plates on uprights

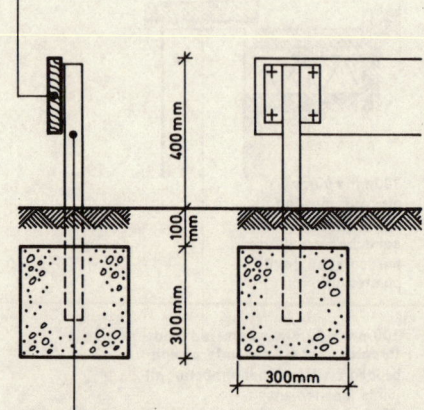

100mm x 100mm nominal size softwood uprights set in concrete, spaced at 1·000 m centres and painted

50mm x 50mm square section mild steel uprights with mild steel plugs to tops. 150mm x 150mm x 6mm plates welded to uprights and drilled to take bolts for rail. Uprights set in concrete and painted, spaced at 1·500m centres

6.5.7.19

6.5.7.20

100mm x 100mm nominal size softwood rail butt jointed to uprights and painted

Mild steel strap fixing with galvanised screws

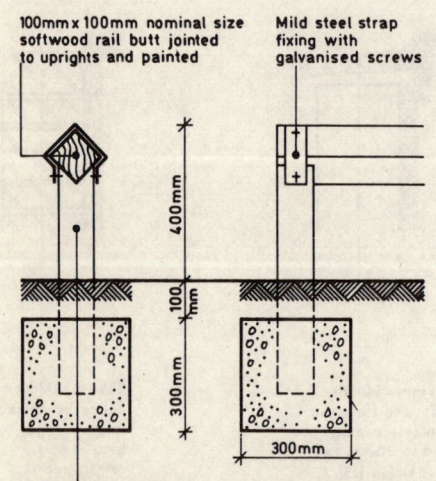

200mm x 38mm nominal size softwood rail, painted, recessed into and screwed to uprights
Waterproof mastic

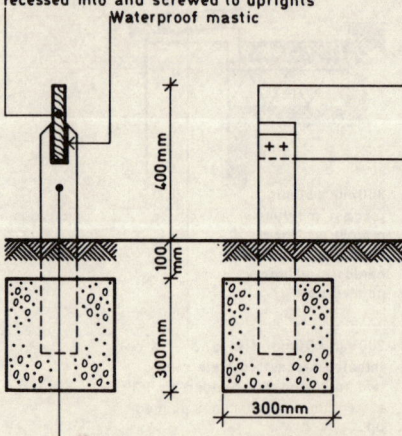

100mm x 100mm nominal size softwood uprights set in concrete, spaced at 1·000m centres and painted

100mm x 100mm nominal size softwood uprights set in concrete, spaced at 1·000m centres and painted

6.5.7.21

6.5.7.22

6.5.7 LOW RAILS: TIMBER, HARDWOOD

For detailed specification of materials used on these drawings see Chapter 5, Section 7
For prices see Chapter 7

150mm x 50mm nominal size western red cedar rail with half checked joints screwed (galvanised or non-ferrous) to upright with 25mm rebate and oiled

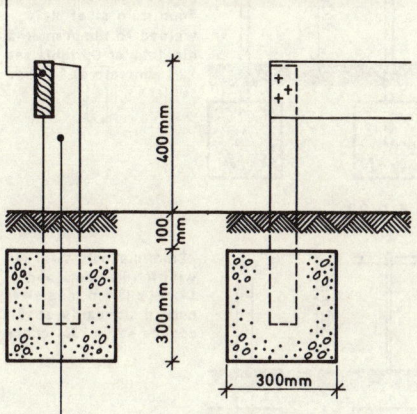

150mm x 75mm nominal size oak rail rebated 15mm to receive uprights. Rails to have half checked joints and to be unpainted

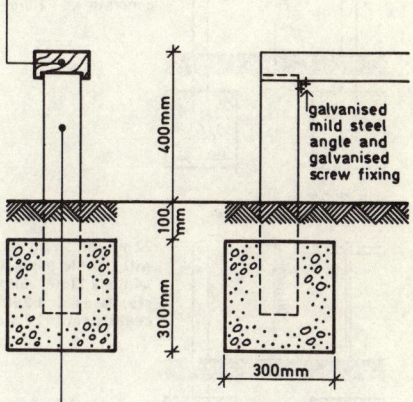

galvanised mild steel angle and galvanised screw fixing

100mm x 75mm nominal size western red cedar uprights, oiled and set in concrete, spaced at 1·000m centres

100mm x 100mm nominal size oak uprights, unpainted and set in concrete, spaced at 1·000m centres

6.5.7.23

6.5.7.24

125mm x 38mm nominal size western red cedar rails, oiled and screwed to uprights with 13mm rebates, joints in rails to be staggered on alternate uprights
125mm x 38mm nominal size western red cedar capping, oiled and screwed to uprights

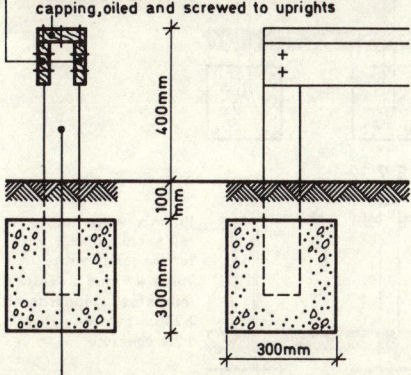

150mm x 100mm nominal size oak rail, unpainted and bolted to upright with 225mm x 15mm coach bolt in 18mm hole
Waterproof mastic

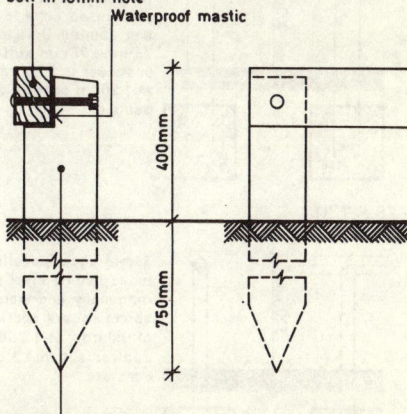

100mm x 100mm nominal size western red cedar uprights, oiled and set in concrete, spaced at 1·000m centres

200mm x 150mm nominal size oak uprights, unpainted and driven into firm ground, spaced at 1·000m centres

6.5.7.25

6.5.7.26

231

6.5.7 LOW RAILS: METAL

For detailed specification of materials used on these drawings see Chapter 5, Section 7
For prices see Chapter 7

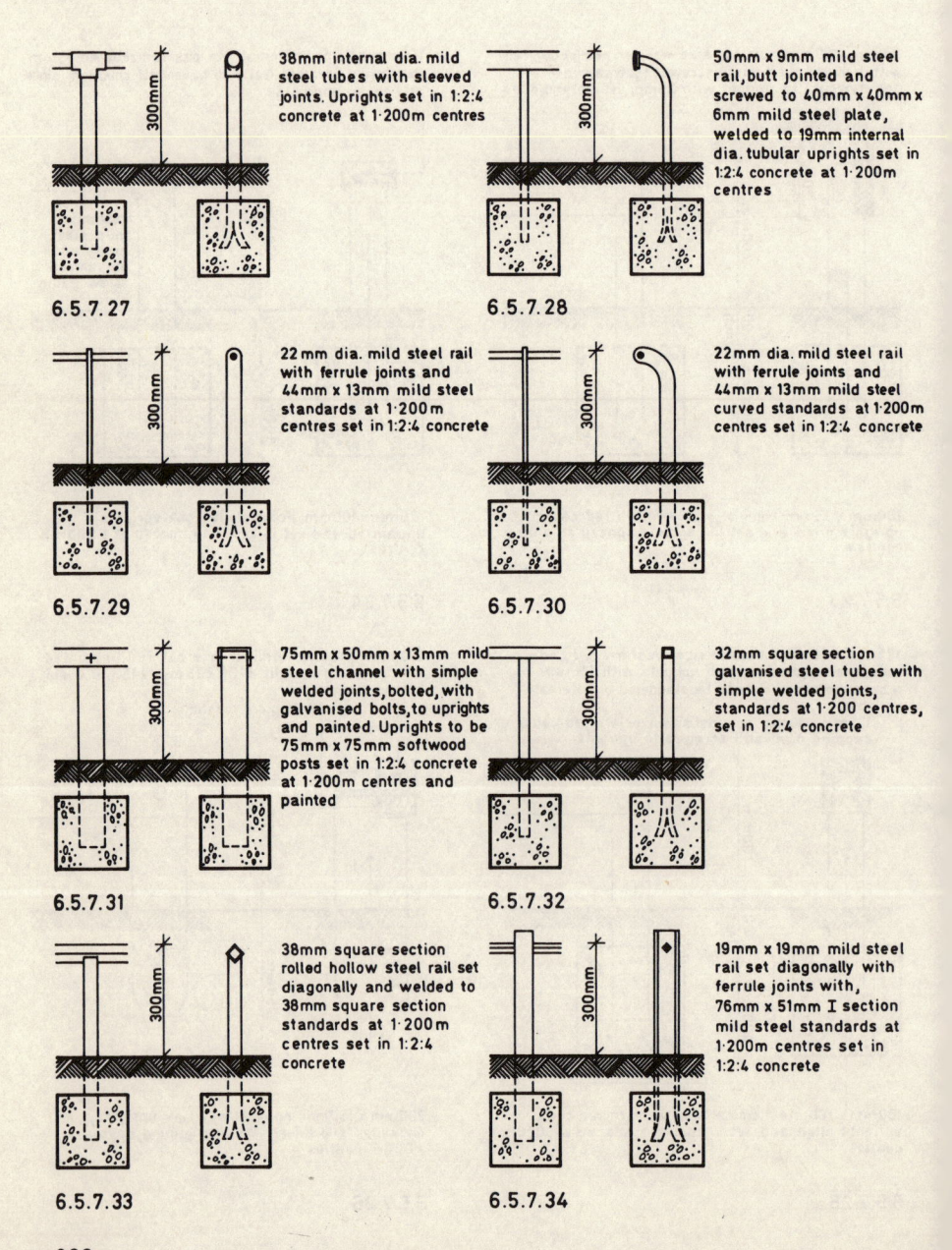

6.5.7.27 38mm internal dia. mild steel tubes with sleeved joints. Uprights set in 1:2:4 concrete at 1·200m centres

6.5.7.28 50mm x 9mm mild steel rail, butt jointed and screwed to 40mm x 40mm x 6mm mild steel plate, welded to 19mm internal dia. tubular uprights set in 1:2:4 concrete at 1·200m centres

6.5.7.29 22mm dia. mild steel rail with ferrule joints and 44mm x 13mm mild steel standards at 1·200m centres set in 1:2:4 concrete

6.5.7.30 22mm dia. mild steel rail with ferrule joints and 44mm x 13mm mild steel curved standards at 1·200m centres set in 1:2:4 concrete

6.5.7.31 75mm x 50mm x 13mm mild steel channel with simple welded joints, bolted, with galvanised bolts, to uprights and painted. Uprights to be 75mm x 75mm softwood posts set in 1:2:4 concrete at 1·200m centres and painted

6.5.7.32 32mm square section galvanised steel tubes with simple welded joints, standards at 1·200 centres, set in 1:2:4 concrete

6.5.7.33 38mm square section rolled hollow steel rail set diagonally and welded to 38mm square section standards at 1·200m centres set in 1:2:4 concrete

6.5.7.34 19mm x 19mm mild steel rail set diagonally with ferrule joints with, 76mm x 51mm I section mild steel standards at 1·200m centres set in 1:2:4 concrete

6.5.7 FENCES (TIMBER)

For prices see Chapter 7
Fences on this drawing are hardwood, 6.5.7.36 can be softwood also

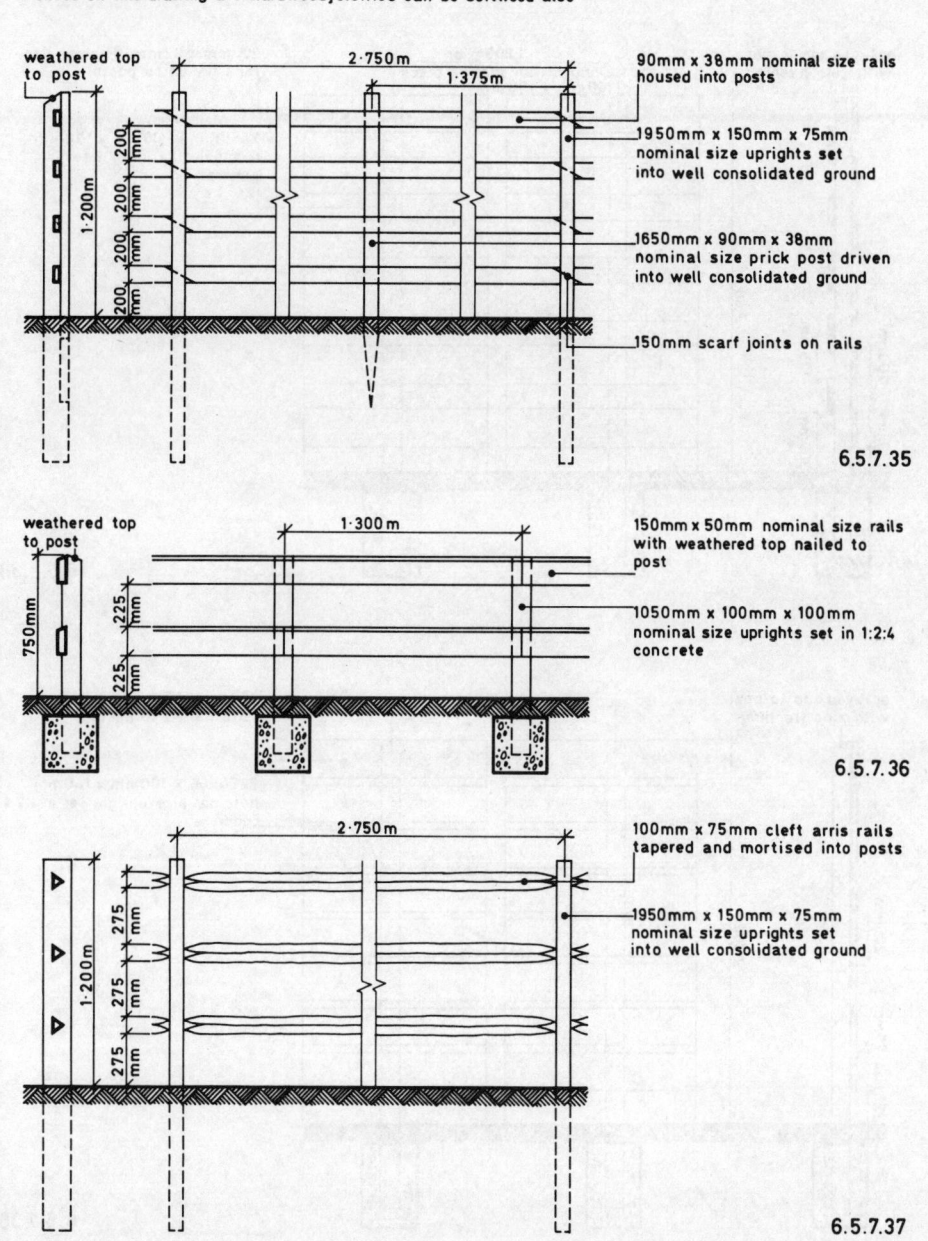

weathered top to post
2·750 m
1·375 m
90mm x 38mm nominal size rails housed into posts
1950mm x 150mm x 75mm nominal size uprights set into well consolidated ground
1·200m
200
200
200
200
1650mm x 90mm x 38mm nominal size prick post driven into well consolidated ground
150mm scarf joints on rails

6.5.7.35

weathered top to post
1·300 m
150mm x 50mm nominal size rails with weathered top nailed to post
750mm
225mm
225mm
1050mm x 100mm x 100mm nominal size uprights set in 1:2:4 concrete

6.5.7.36

2·750 m
100mm x 75mm cleft arris rails tapered and mortised into posts
1·200m
275mm
275mm
275mm
1950mm x 150mm x 75mm nominal size uprights set into well consolidated ground

6.5.7.37

233

6.5.7 FENCES (TIMBER)

For prices see Chapter 7
Fences on this drawing can be either hardwood or softwood

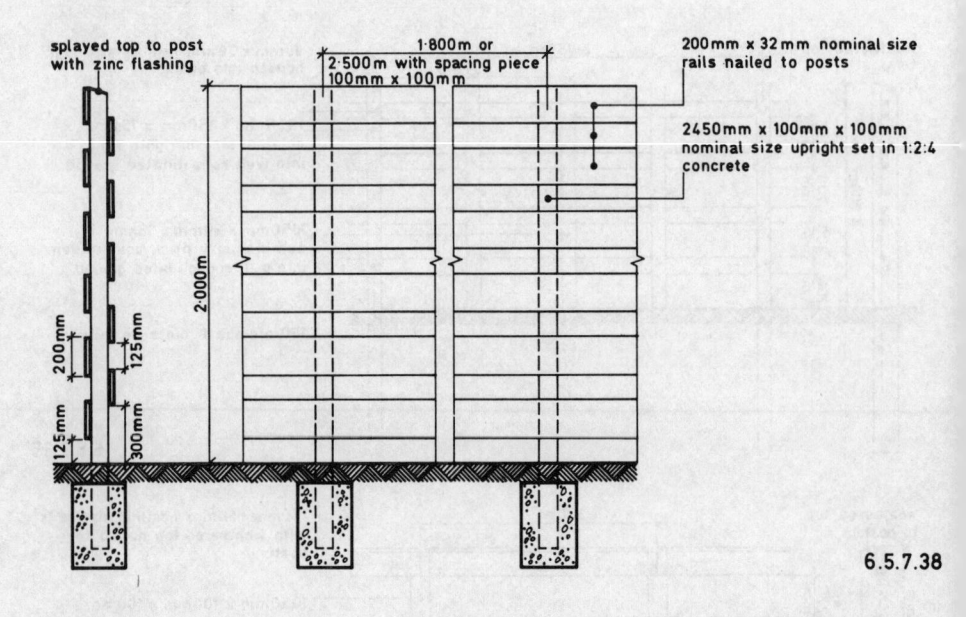

6.5.7.38

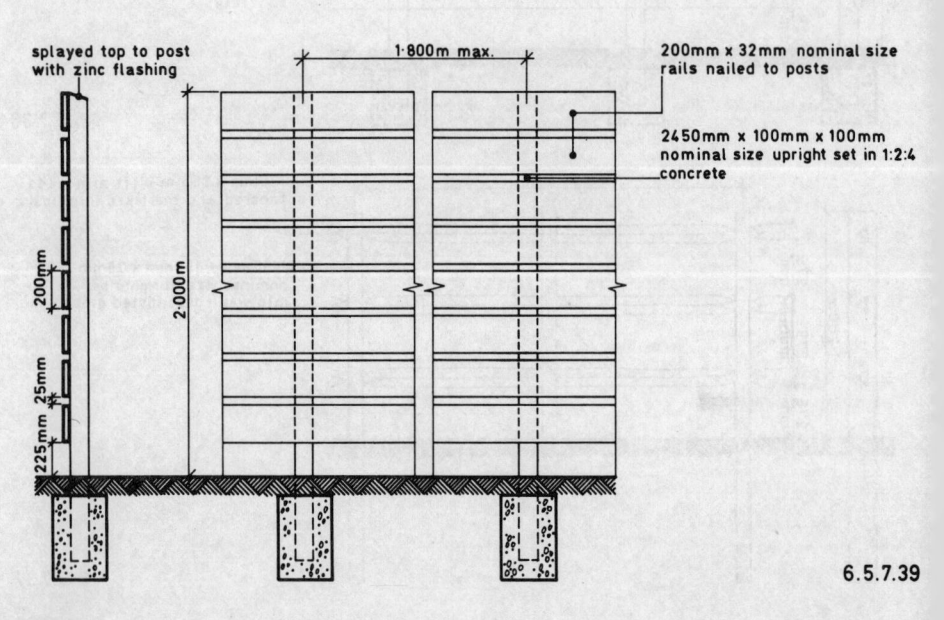

6.5.7.39

234

6.5.7 FENCES (TIMBER)

For prices see Chapter 7
Fences on this drawing are hardwood only

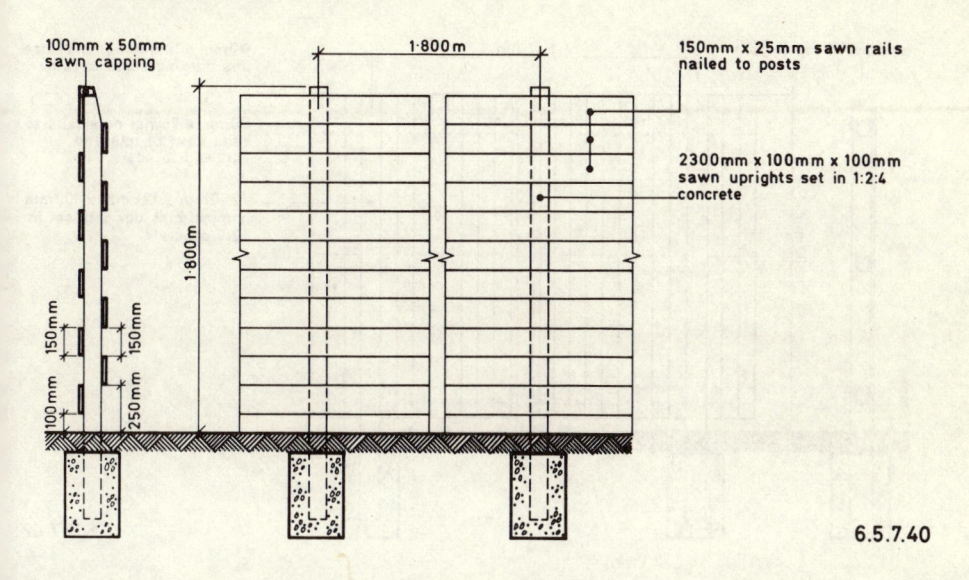

100mm x 50mm sawn capping

1·800m

150mm x 25mm sawn rails nailed to posts

2300mm x 100mm x 100mm sawn uprights set in 1:2:4 concrete

1·800m

150mm
100mm
150mm
250mm

6.5.7.40

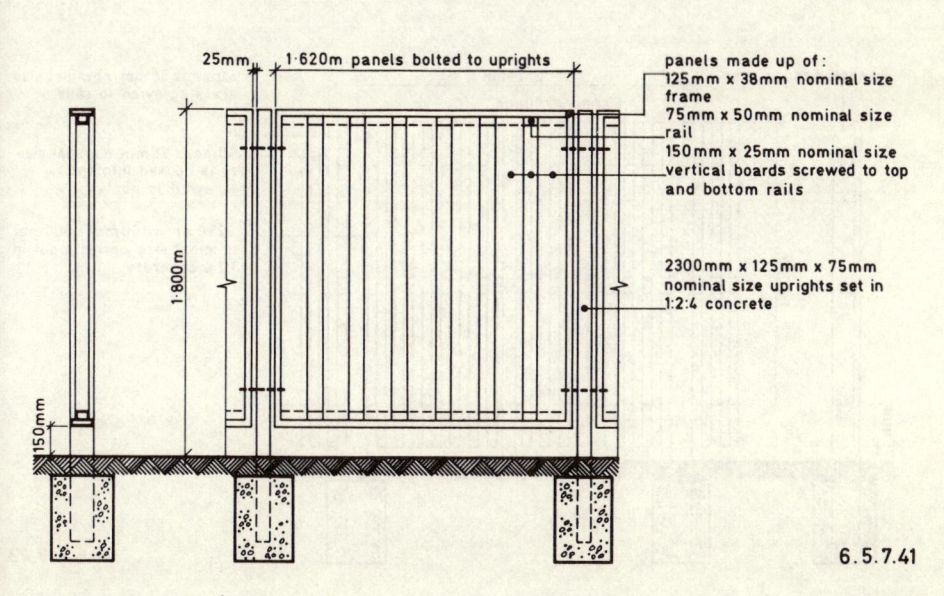

25mm
1·620m panels bolted to uprights

panels made up of:
125mm x 38mm nominal size frame
75mm x 50mm nominal size rail
150mm x 25mm nominal size vertical boards screwed to top and bottom rails

2300mm x 125mm x 75mm nominal size uprights set in 1:2:4 concrete

1·800m
150mm

6.5.7.41

235

6.5.7 FENCES (TIMBER)

For prices see Chapter 7
Fences on this drawing are hardwood only

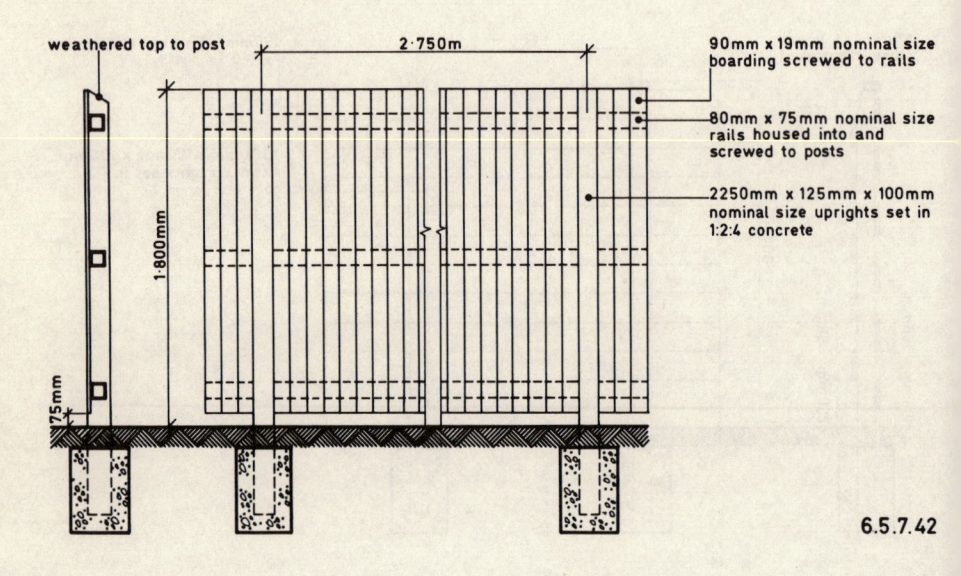

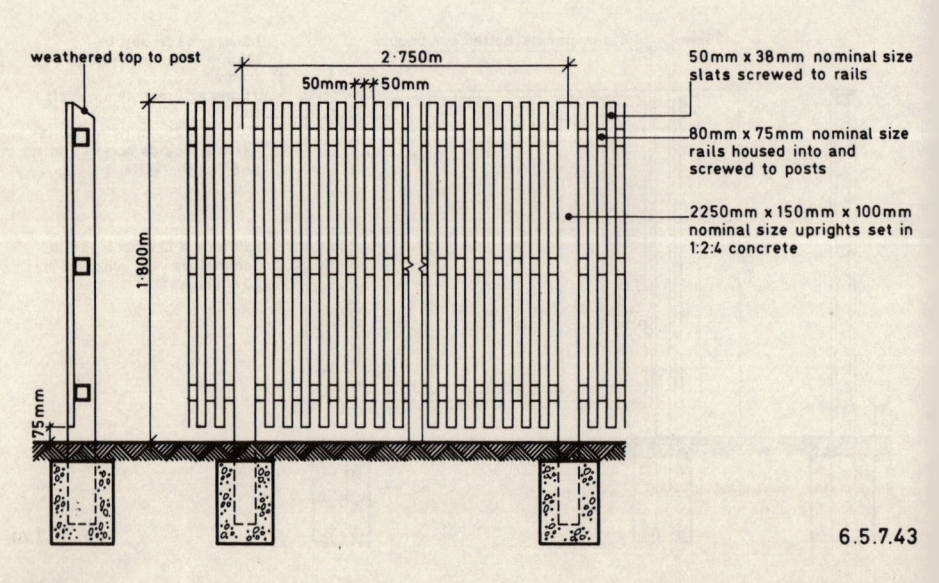

weathered top to post

2·750m

90mm x 19mm nominal size boarding screwed to rails

80mm x 75mm nominal size rails housed into and screwed to posts

2250mm x 125mm x 100mm nominal size uprights set in 1:2:4 concrete

1·800mm

75mm

6.5.7.42

weathered top to post

2·750m

50mm ⟵⟶ 50mm

50mm x 38mm nominal size slats screwed to rails

80mm x 75mm nominal size rails housed into and screwed to posts

2250mm x 150mm x 100mm nominal size uprights set in 1:2:4 concrete

1·800m

75mm

6.5.7.43

236

6.5.7 FENCES (METAL)

For prices see Chapter 7

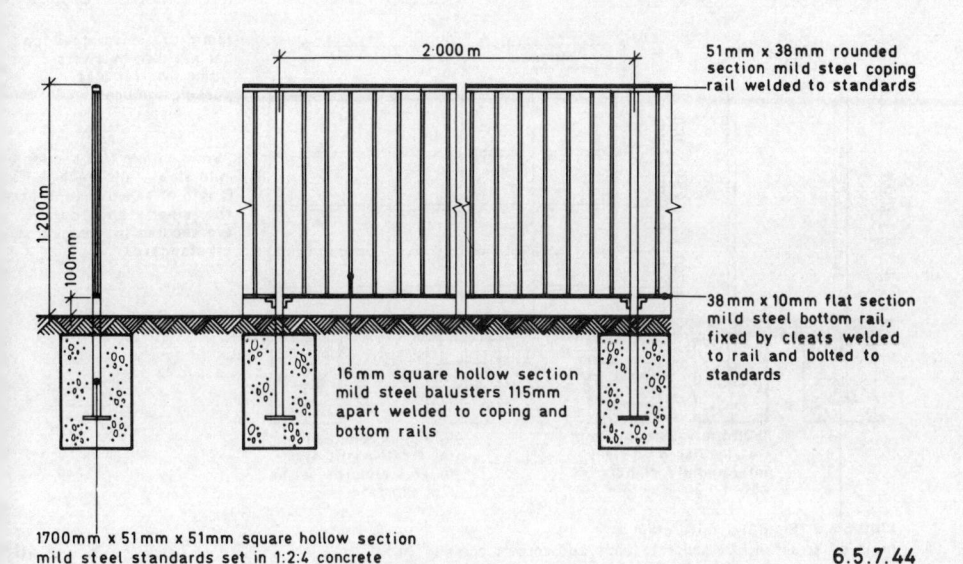

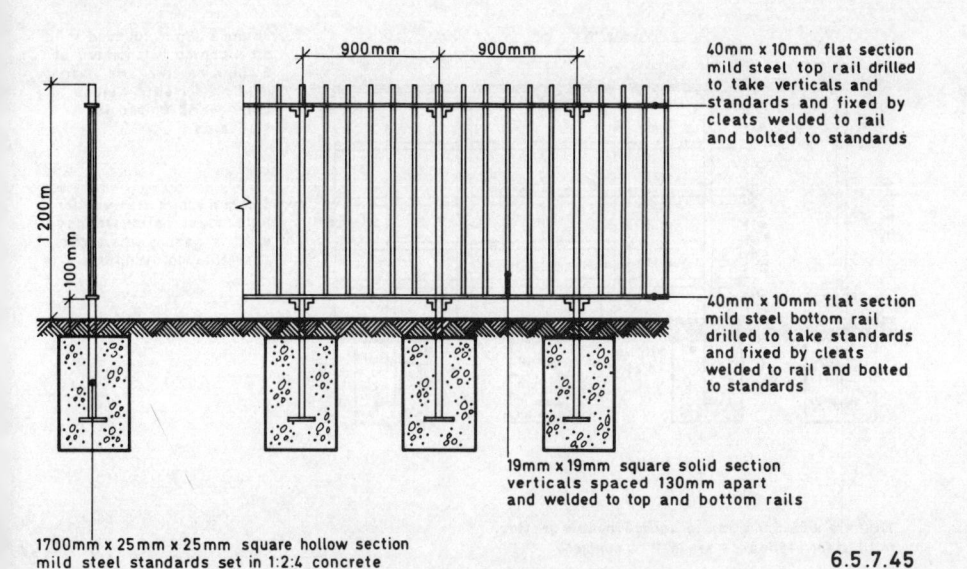

51mm x 38mm rounded section mild steel coping rail welded to standards

38mm x 10mm flat section mild steel bottom rail, fixed by cleats welded to rail and bolted to standards

16mm square hollow section mild steel balusters 115mm apart welded to coping and bottom rails

1700mm x 51mm x 51mm square hollow section mild steel standards set in 1:2:4 concrete

6.5.7.44

40mm x 10mm flat section mild steel top rail drilled to take verticals and standards and fixed by cleats welded to rail and bolted to standards

40mm x 10mm flat section mild steel bottom rail drilled to take standards and fixed by cleats welded to rail and bolted to standards

19mm x 19mm square solid section verticals spaced 130mm apart and welded to top and bottom rails

1700mm x 25mm x 25mm square hollow section mild steel standards set in 1:2:4 concrete

6.5.7.45

6.5.7 FENCES (METAL)

For prices see Chapter 7

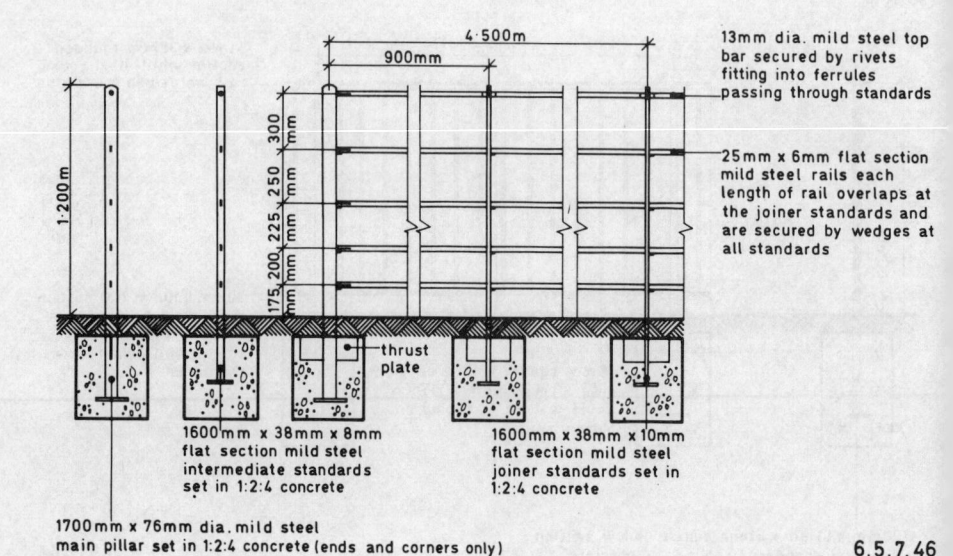

6.5.7.46

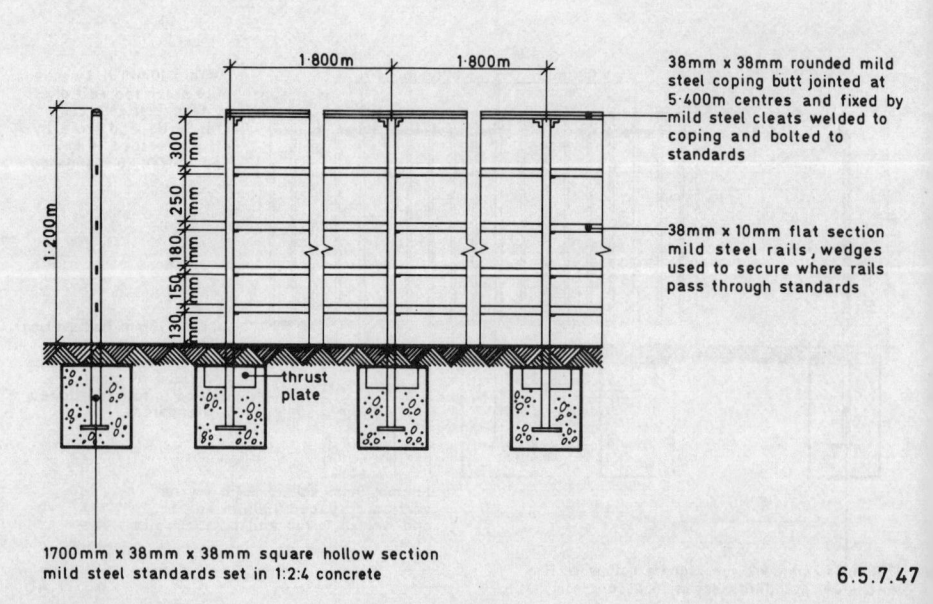

- 13mm dia. mild steel top bar secured by rivets fitting into ferrules passing through standards
- 25mm x 6mm flat section mild steel rails each length of rail overlaps at the joiner standards and are secured by wedges at all standards
- 1600mm x 38mm x 8mm flat section mild steel intermediate standards set in 1:2:4 concrete
- 1600mm x 38mm x 10mm flat section mild steel joiner standards set in 1:2:4 concrete
- 1700mm x 76mm dia. mild steel main pillar set in 1:2:4 concrete (ends and corners only)
- thrust plate
- 1·200m
- 4·500m, 900mm
- 300, 250, 225, 200, 175 mm

6.5.7.47

- 38mm x 38mm rounded mild steel coping butt jointed at 5·400m centres and fixed by mild steel cleats welded to coping and bolted to standards
- 38mm x 10mm flat section mild steel rails, wedges used to secure where rails pass through standards
- 1700mm x 38mm x 38mm square hollow section mild steel standards set in 1:2:4 concrete
- thrust plate
- 1·200m
- 1·800m, 1·800m
- 300, 250, 180, 150, 130 mm

6.5.7 GATES

For prices see Chapter 7

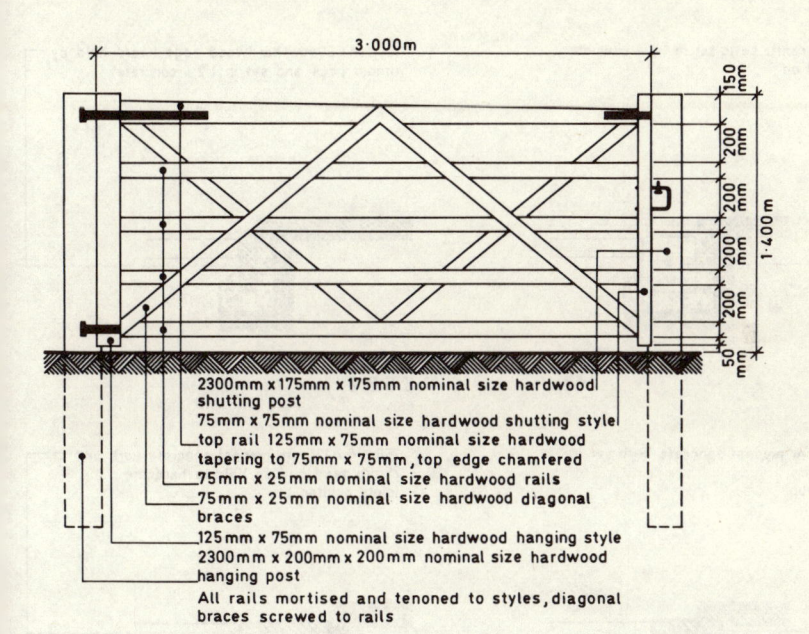

2300mm x 175mm x 175mm nominal size hardwood shutting post
75mm x 75mm nominal size hardwood shutting style
top rail 125mm x 75mm nominal size hardwood tapering to 75mm x 75mm, top edge chamfered
75mm x 25mm nominal size hardwood rails
75mm x 25mm nominal size hardwood diagonal braces
125mm x 75mm nominal size hardwood hanging style
2300mm x 200mm x 200mm nominal size hardwood hanging post
All rails mortised and tenoned to styles, diagonal braces screwed to rails

6.5.7.48

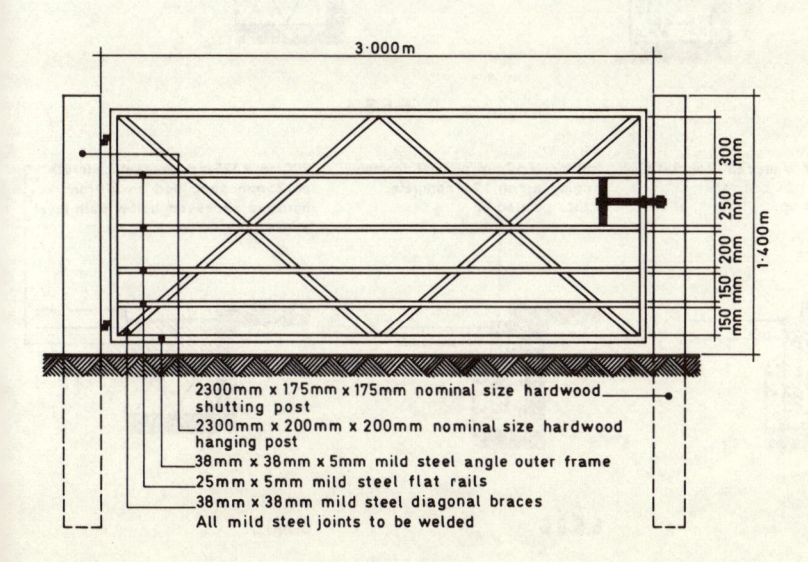

2300mm x 175mm x 175mm nominal size hardwood shutting post
2300mm x 200mm x 200mm nominal size hardwood hanging post
38mm x 38mm x 5mm mild steel angle outer frame
25mm x 5mm mild steel flat rails
38mm x 38mm mild steel diagonal braces
All mild steel joints to be welded

6.5.7.49

6.5.8 PATH EDGINGS
For detailed specification of materials used on these drawings see Chapter 5, Section 8
For prices see Chapter 7

Random size granite setts set in 1:2:4 concrete joints pointed up

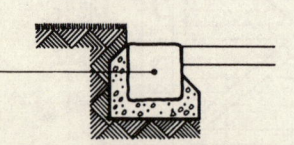

6.5.8.1

150mm x 50mm hardwood edge board held by timber pegs and set in 1:2:4 concrete

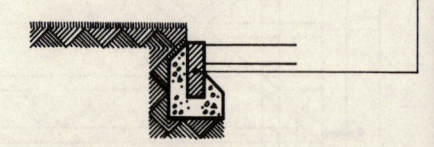

6.5.8.2

250mm x 125mm precast concrete kerb set in 1:2:4 concrete joints pointed up

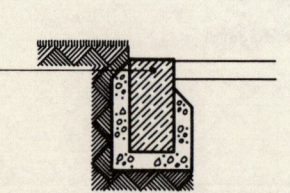

6.5.8.3

250mm x 125mm precast concrete kerb on 25mm sand bed on 100mm hardcore joints pointed up

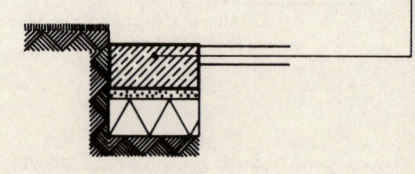

6.5.8.4

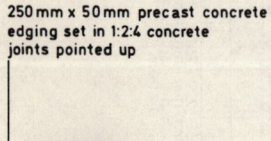

250mm x 50mm precast concrete edging set in 1:2:4 concrete joints pointed up

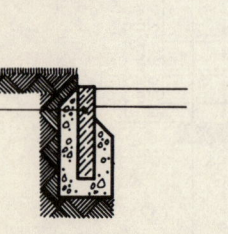

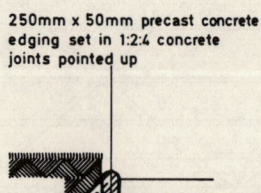

6.5.8.5

250mm x 50mm precast concrete edging set in 1:2:4 concrete joints pointed up

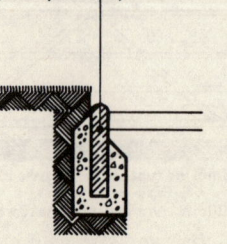

6.5.8.6

250mm x 125mm precast concrete on 25mm sand bed on 100mm hardcore; recessed below path level joints pointed up

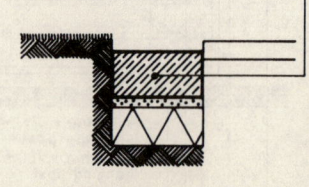

6.5.8.7

240

6.5.8 PATH EDGINGS

For detailed specification of materials used on these drawings see Chapter 5, Section 8
For prices see Chapter 7

50mm-75mm kidney flint cobbles bedded in 1:2:4 concrete on 50mm sand bed on 75mm hardcore
150mm x 50mm precast concrete edging set in 1:2:4 concrete

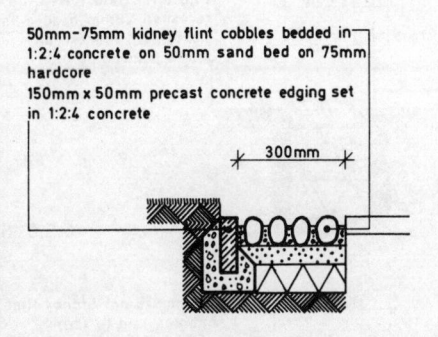

6.5.8.8

50mm fine gravel on 50mm coarse hoggin on 100mm hardcore
150mm x 50mm hardwood gravel board held by timber pegs set in 1:2:4 concrete

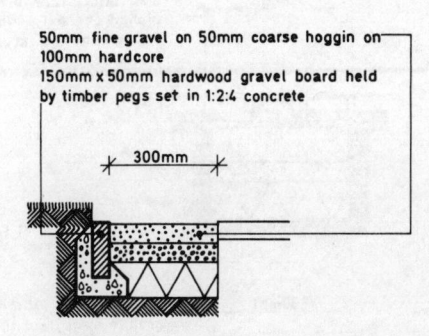

6.5.8.9

3no. paving bricks laid flat bedded on 25mm sand on 75mm hardcore and all joints pointed up
paving brick on edge set in 1:2:4 concrete

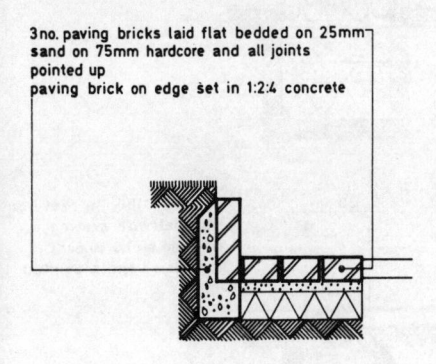

6.5.8.10

1no. paving brick laid flat bedded on 25mm sand on 75mm hardcore and all joints pointed up
paving brick on edge set in 1:2:4 concrete

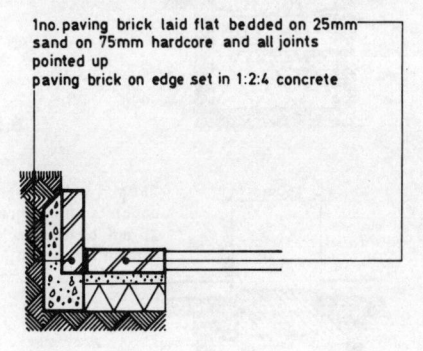

6.5.8.11

paving brick on end set in 1:2:4 concrete and all joints pointed up

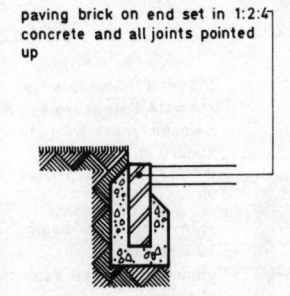

6.5.8.12

paving brick laid flat on 25mm sand on 75mm hardcore and all joints pointed up

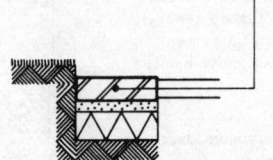

6.5.8.13

paving brick laid flat on 25mm sand on 75mm hardcore and all joints pointed up; recessed below path level

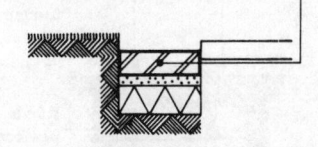

6.5.8.14

6.5.8 CHANNELS

For detailed specification of materials used on these drawings see Chapter 5 Section 8
For prices see Chapter 7

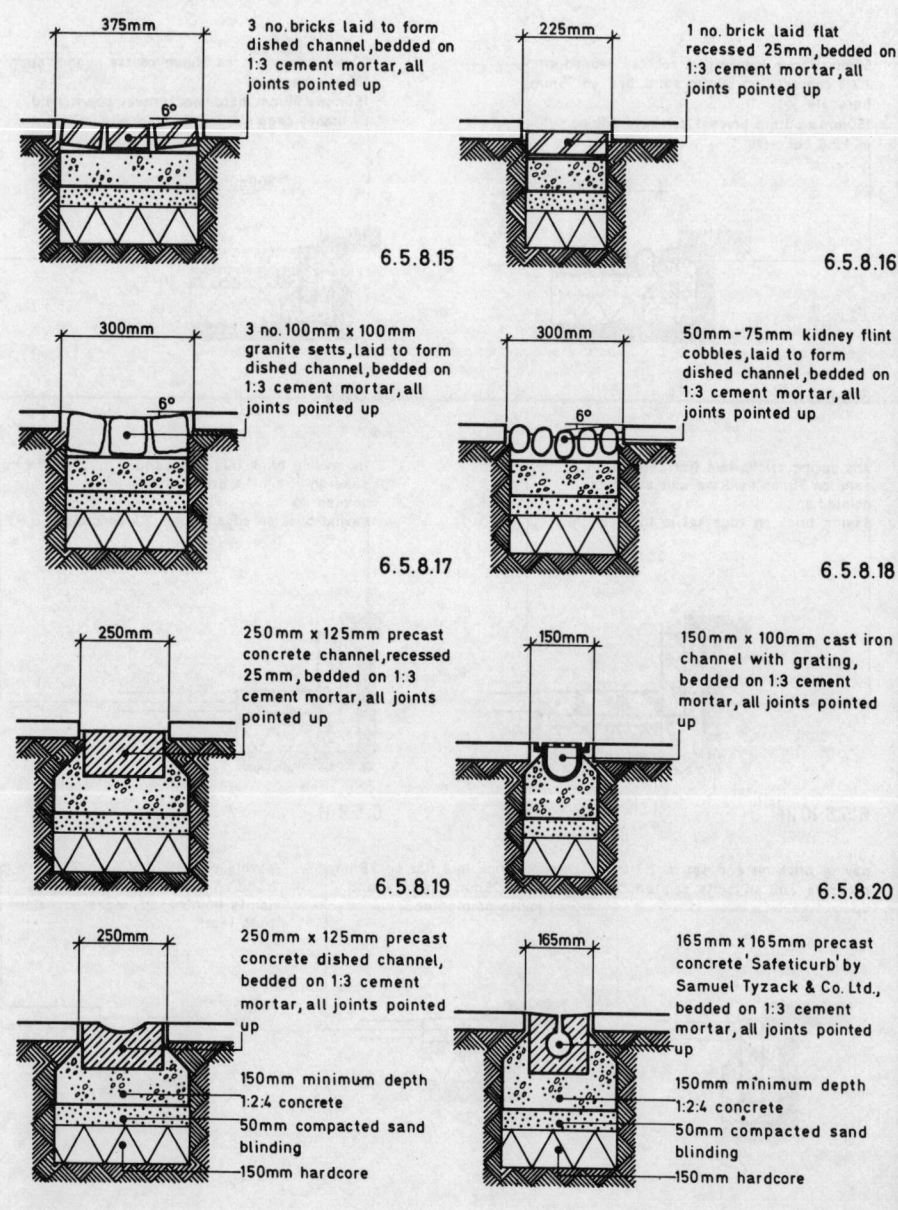

6.5.8.15 — 375mm — 3 no. bricks laid to form dished channel, bedded on 1:3 cement mortar, all joints pointed up

6.5.8.16 — 225mm — 1 no. brick laid flat recessed 25mm, bedded on 1:3 cement mortar, all joints pointed up

6.5.8.17 — 300mm — 3 no. 100mm x 100mm granite setts, laid to form dished channel, bedded on 1:3 cement mortar, all joints pointed up

6.5.8.18 — 300mm — 50mm-75mm kidney flint cobbles, laid to form dished channel, bedded on 1:3 cement mortar, all joints pointed up

6.5.8.19 — 250mm — 250mm x 125mm precast concrete channel, recessed 25mm, bedded on 1:3 cement mortar, all joints pointed up

6.5.8.20 — 150mm — 150mm x 100mm cast iron channel with grating, bedded on 1:3 cement mortar, all joints pointed up

6.5.8.21 — 250mm — 250mm x 125mm precast concrete dished channel, bedded on 1:3 cement mortar, all joints pointed up
- 150mm minimum depth 1:2:4 concrete
- 50mm compacted sand blinding
- 150mm hardcore

6.5.8.22 — 165mm — 165mm x 165mm precast concrete 'Safeticurb' by Samuel Tyzack & Co. Ltd., bedded on 1:3 cement mortar, all joints pointed up
- 150mm minimum depth 1:2:4 concrete
- 50mm compacted sand blinding
- 150mm hardcore

6.5.8 MOWING MARGINS
For detailed specification of materials used on these drawings see Chapter 5, Section 8
For prices see Chapter 7

250mm x 50mm precast slab on 25mm sand bed on 100mm hardcore.
joints pointed between slabs and against wall.

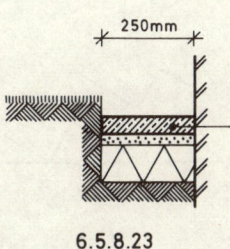

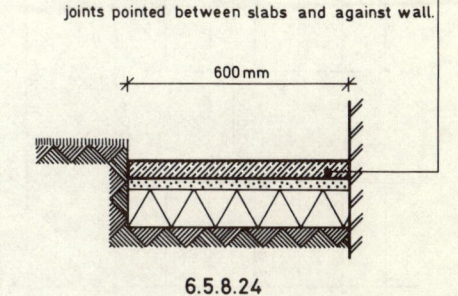

250mm

6.5.8.23

600mm x 50mm precast slab on 25mm sand bed on 100mm hardcore.
joints pointed between slabs and against wall.

600mm

6.5.8.24

75mm in situ concrete strip on 25mm sand bed on 100mm hardcore.

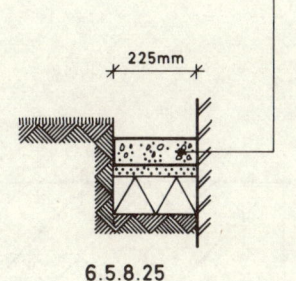

225mm

6.5.8.25

paving brick bedded on 25mm sand on 75mm hardcore and all joints pointed.

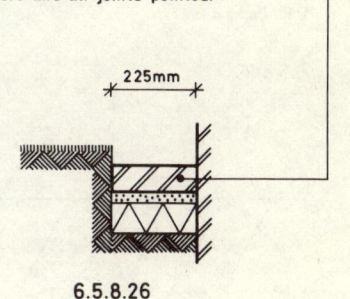

225mm

6.5.8.26

50-75mm kidney flint cobbles bedded in consolidated hoggin on 150mm hardcore.
150mm x 50mm hardwood edge board held by timber pegs.

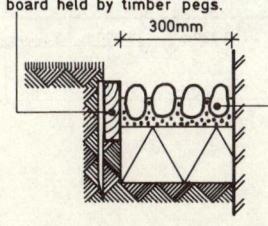

300mm

6.5.8.27

50-75mm kidney flint cobbles bedded in 1:2:4 concrete on 50mm sand bed on 75mm hardcore.

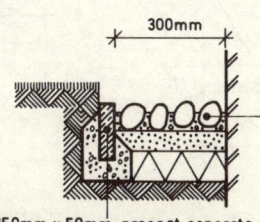

300mm

150mm x 50mm precast concrete edging set in 1:2:4 concrete

6.5.8.28

50mm fine gravel on 50mm coarse hoggin on 100mm hardcore.
150mm x 50mm hardwood gravel board held by timber pegs.

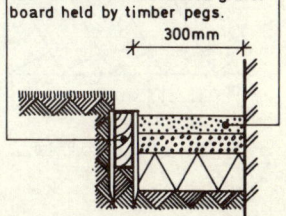

300mm

6.5.8.29

243

6.5.8. TYPICAL PARKING LAYOUTS

For detailed specification of materials used on these drawings see Chapter 5, Section 8
For prices see Chapter 7
All car parking spaces shown are 5·500m x 2·400m

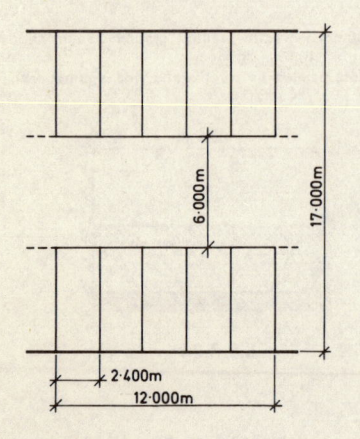

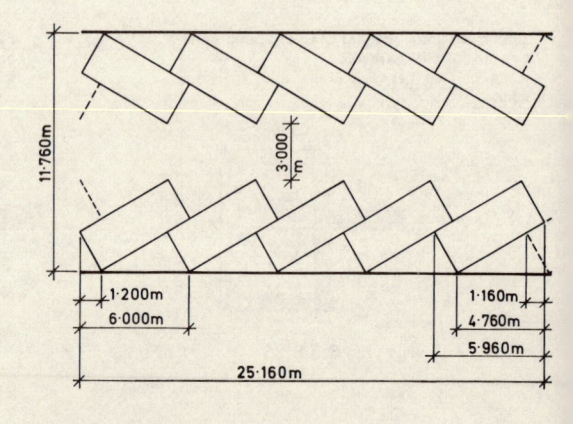

L 90° Parking

6.5.8.30

30° Parking

6.5.8.31

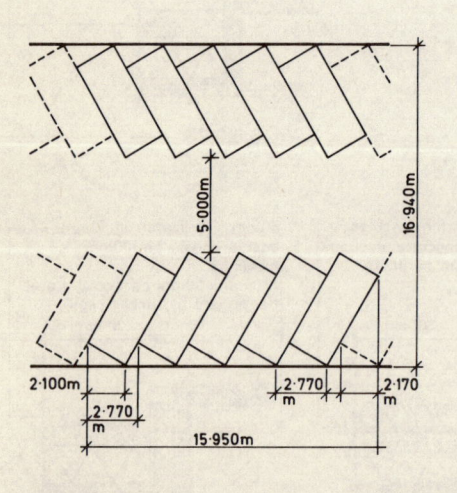

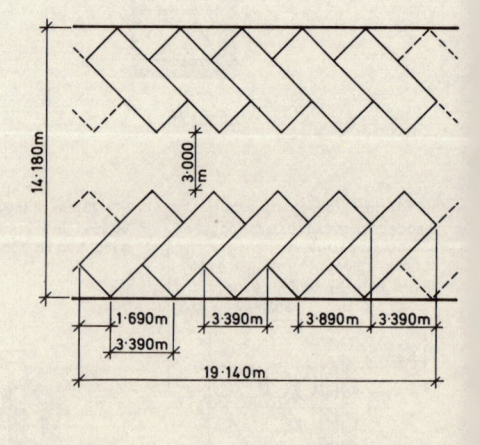

60° Parking

6.5.8.32

45° Parking

6.5.8.33

244

6.5.8 PATHS: PRECAST PAVING SLABS

For detailed specification of materials used on these drawings see Chapter 5, Section 8
For prices see Chapter 7

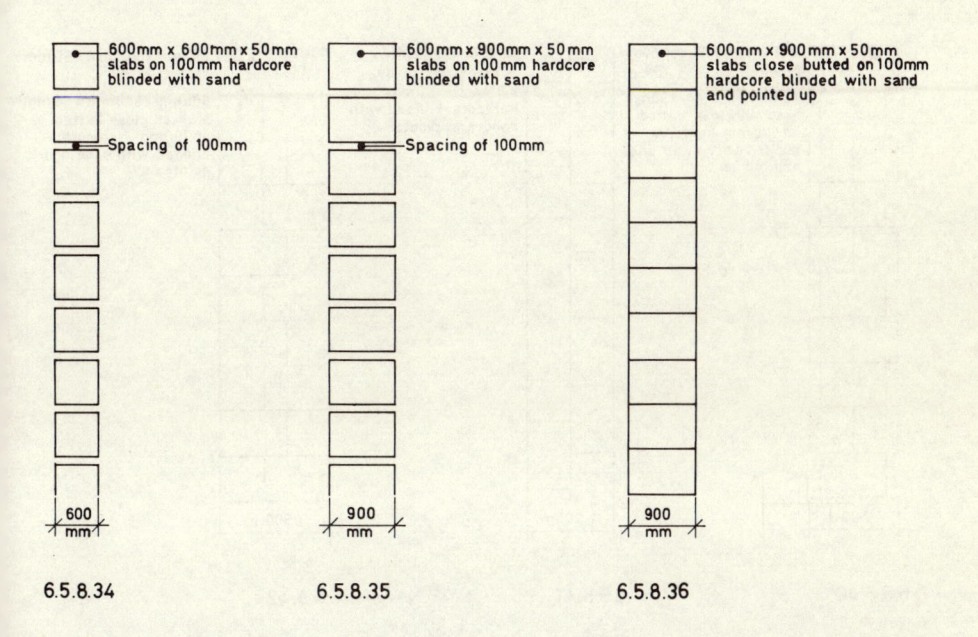

6.5.8.34 — 600mm x 600mm x 50mm slabs on 100mm hardcore blinded with sand. Spacing of 100mm. 600mm.

6.5.8.35 — 600mm x 900mm x 50mm slabs on 100mm hardcore blinded with sand. Spacing of 100mm. 900mm.

6.5.8.36 — 600mm x 900mm x 50mm slabs close butted on 100mm hardcore blinded with sand and pointed up. 900mm.

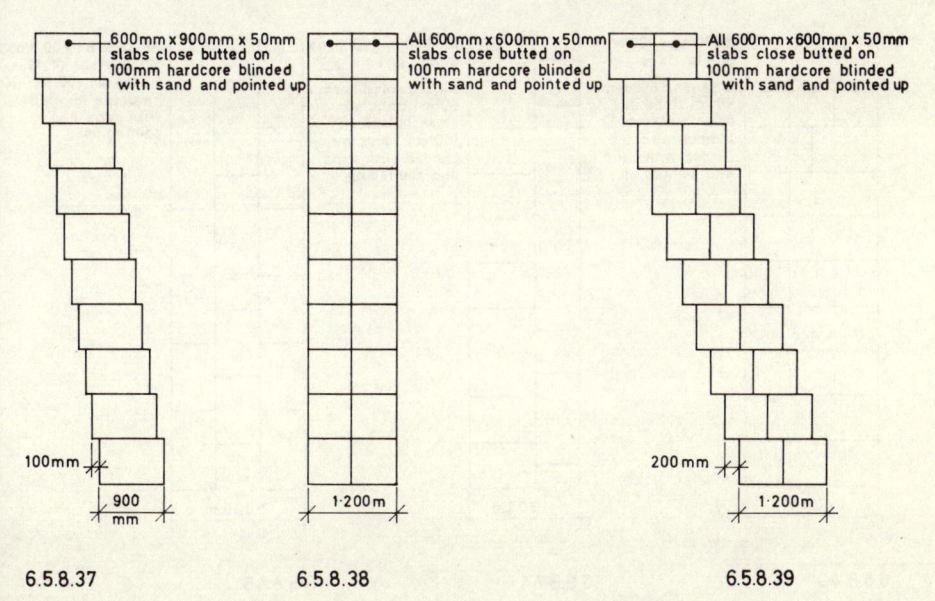

6.5.8.37 — 600mm x 900mm x 50mm slabs close butted on 100mm hardcore blinded with sand and pointed up. 100mm. 900mm.

6.5.8.38 — All 600mm x 600mm x 50mm slabs close butted on 100mm hardcore blinded with sand and pointed up. 1·200m.

6.5.8.39 — All 600mm x 600mm x 50mm slabs close butted on 100mm hardcore blinded with sand and pointed up. 200mm. 1·200m.

245

6.5.8 PATHS: PRECAST PAVING SLABS

For detailed specification of materials used on these drawings see Chapter 5, Section 8
For prices see Chapter 7

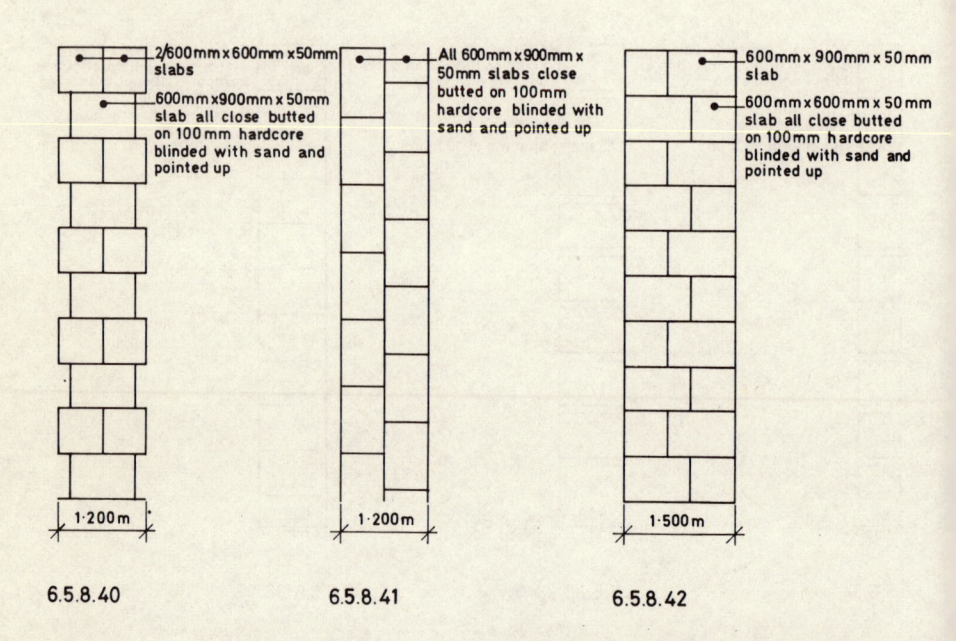

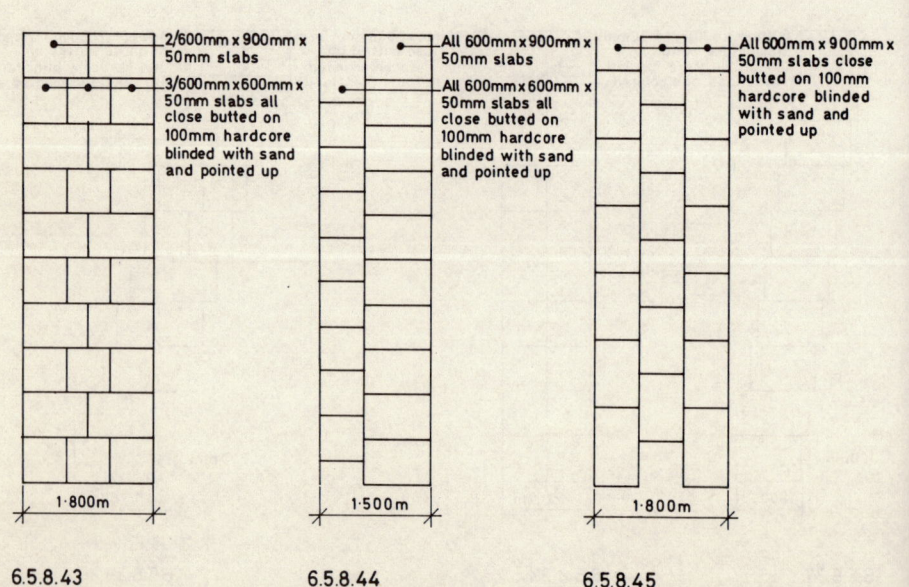

6.5.8.40 — 2/600mm x 600mm x 50mm slabs. 600mm x 900mm x 50mm slab all close butted on 100mm hardcore blinded with sand and pointed up. 1·200m

6.5.8.41 — All 600mm x 900mm x 50mm slabs close butted on 100mm hardcore blinded with sand and pointed up. 1·200m

6.5.8.42 — 600mm x 900mm x 50mm slab. 600mm x 600mm x 50mm slab all close butted on 100mm hardcore blinded with sand and pointed up. 1·500m

6.5.8.43 — 2/600mm x 900mm x 50mm slabs. 3/600mm x 600mm x 50mm slabs all close butted on 100mm hardcore blinded with sand and pointed up. 1·800m

6.5.8.44 — All 600mm x 900mm x 50mm slabs. All 600mm x 600mm x 50mm slabs all close butted on 100mm hardcore blinded with sand and pointed up. 1·500m

6.5.8.45 — All 600mm x 900mm x 50mm slabs close butted on 100mm hardcore blinded with sand and pointed up. 1·800m

6.5.8 PATHS: BRICK PAVING

For detailed specification of materials used on these drawings see Chapter 5, Section 8
For prices see Chapter 7

Stretcher bond along path
bedded on 1:2:4 concrete
blinding on 100mm hardcore
and pointed up

6.5.8.46

Stretcher bond across path
bedded on 1:2:4 concrete
blinding on 100mm hardcore
and pointed up

6.5.8.47

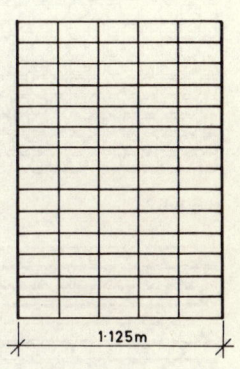

Stack bond
bedded on 1:2:4 concrete
blinding on 100mm hardcore
and pointed up

6.5.8.48

Basket weave pattern
bedded on 1:2:4 concrete
blinding on 100mm hardcore
and pointed up

6.5.8.49

Herringbone pattern (flat)
bedded on 1:2:4 concrete
blinding on 100mm hardcore
and pointed up

6.5.8.50

Herringbone (brick on edge)
bedded on 1:2:4 concrete
blinding on 100mm hardcore
and pointed up

6.5.8.51

247

6.5.8 PAVING: GRANITE SETTS

For detailed specification of materials used on these drawings see Chapter 5, Section 8
For prices see Chapter 7

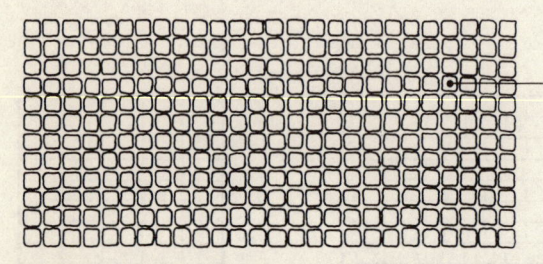

6.5.8.52 — 100mm x 100mm x 100mm granite setts laid stack bond in mortar on 100mm 1:2:4 concrete on 100mm hardcore, joints pointed up

6.5.8.53 — 100mm x 100mm x 200mm granite setts laid stretcher bond in mortar on 100mm 1:2:4 concrete on 100mm hardcore, joints pointed up

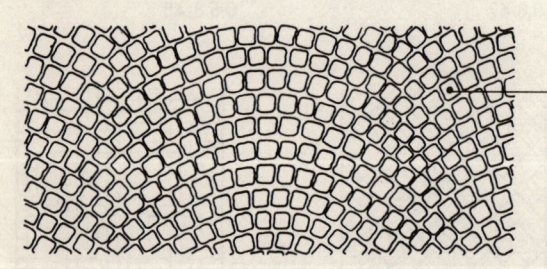

6.5.8.54 — 100mm x 100mm x 100mm granite setts laid in curved pattern in mortar on 100mm 1:2:4 concrete on 100mm hardcore, joints pointed up

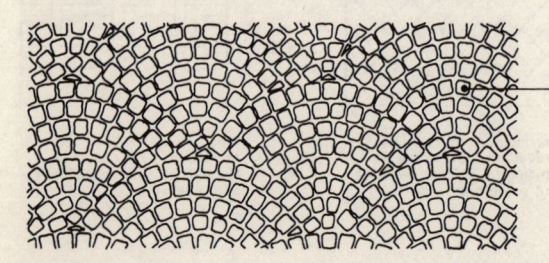

6.5.8.55 — 100mm x 100mm x 100mm granite setts laid in fan pattern in mortar on 100mm 1:2:4 concrete on 100mm hardcore, joints pointed up

6 5 8 TREE GRIDS

For prices see Chapter 7

6.5.8.56 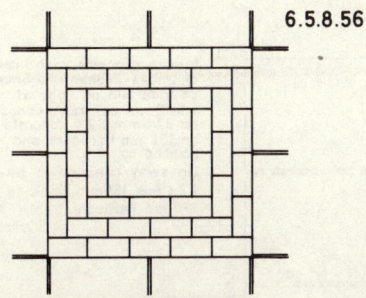
1·125m square of brick paving bedded on 50mm sand, with 450mm square hole left for tree

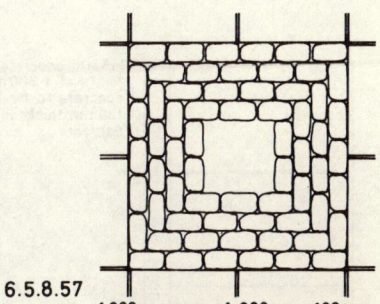

6.5.8.57
1·200m square of 200mm x 100mm x 100mm granite setts bedded on 50mm sand, with 400mm square hole left for tree

6.5.8.58 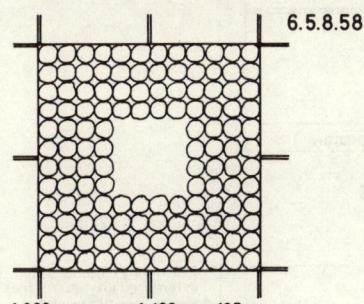
1·200m square of 100mm–125mm kidney flint cobbles bedded on 50mm sand, with 400mm square hole left for tree

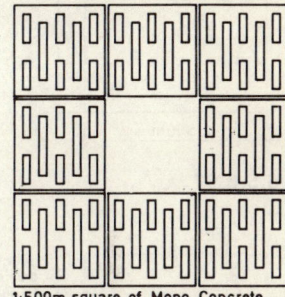

6.5.8.59
1·500m square of Mono Concrete Metric 4 square tree grilles bedded on 50mm sand, with 500mm square hole left for tree

6.5.8.60 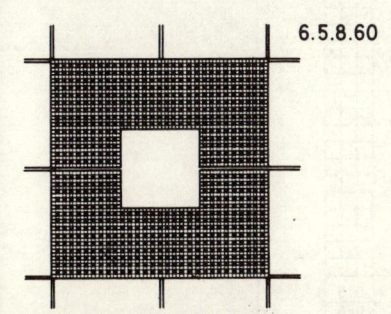
1·200m square cast iron tree grid made in two sections, bedded on 50mm sand, with 400mm square hole left for tree

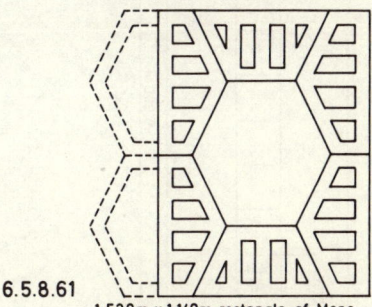

6.5.8.61
1·520m x 1·140m rectangle of Mono Concrete Monohex tree grilles bedded on 50mm sand

249

6.5.8 CONCRETE DRIVEWAYS

For detailed specification of materials used on these drawings see Chapter 5, Section 8
For prices see Chapter 7

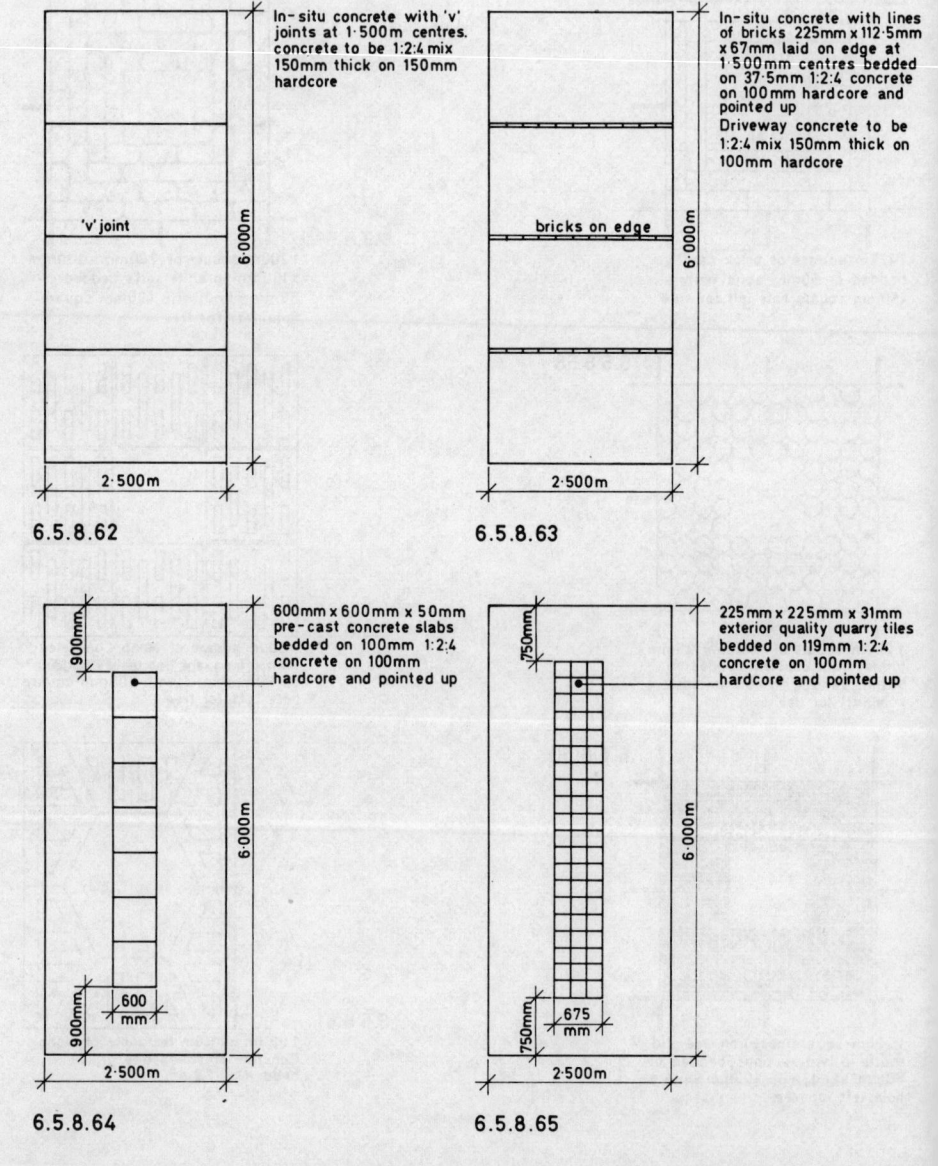

6.5.8.62

'v' joint
2·500m
6·000m

In-situ concrete with 'v' joints at 1·500m centres. concrete to be 1:2:4 mix 150mm thick on 150mm hardcore

6.5.8.63

bricks on edge
2·500m
6·000m

In-situ concrete with lines of bricks 225mm x 112·5mm x 67mm laid on edge at 1·500mm centres bedded on 37·5mm 1:2:4 concrete on 100mm hardcore and pointed up
Driveway concrete to be 1:2:4 mix 150mm thick on 100mm hardcore

6.5.8.64

900mm
900mm
600 mm
2·500m
6·000m

600mm x 600mm x 50mm pre-cast concrete slabs bedded on 100mm 1:2:4 concrete on 100mm hardcore and pointed up

6.5.8.65

750mm
750mm
675 mm
2·500m
6·000m

225mm x 225mm x 31mm exterior quality quarry tiles bedded on 119mm 1:2:4 concrete on 100mm hardcore and pointed up

6.5.8 CONCRETE DRIVEWAYS

For detailed specification of materials used on these drawings see Chapter 5, Section 8
For prices see Chapter 7

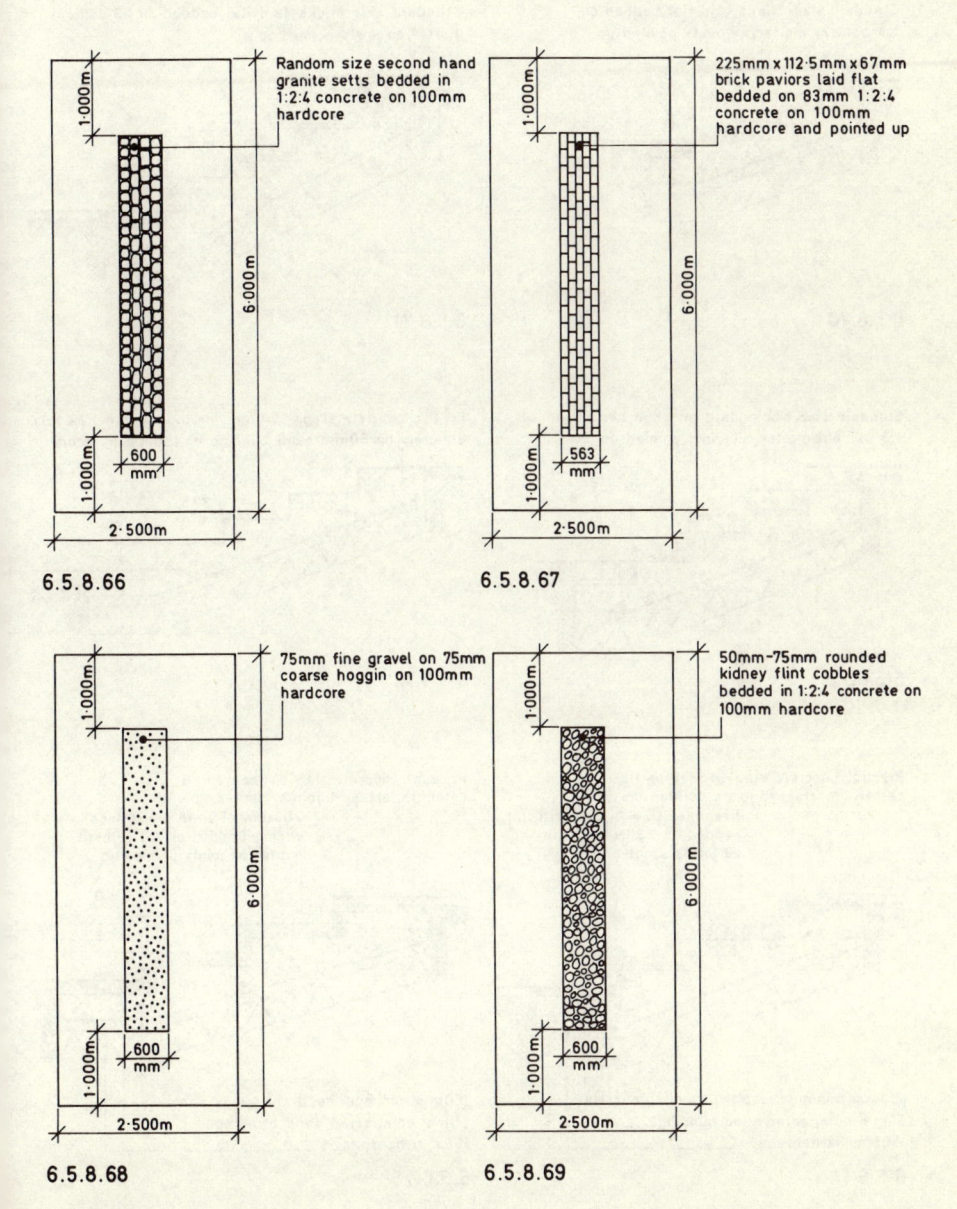

Random size second hand granite setts bedded in 1:2:4 concrete on 100mm hardcore

6.5.8.66

225mm x 112·5mm x 67mm brick paviors laid flat bedded on 83mm 1:2:4 concrete on 100mm hardcore and pointed up

6.5.8.67

75mm fine gravel on 75mm coarse hoggin on 100mm hardcore

6.5.8.68

50mm–75mm rounded kidney flint cobbles bedded in 1:2:4 concrete on 100mm hardcore

6.5.8.69

251

6.5.8 STEPS

For detailed specification of materials used on these drawings see Chapter 5, Section 8
For prices see Chapter 7

Standard size bricks, laid flat, bedded on 1:3 cement mortar, all joints pointed up

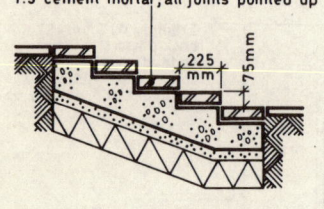

225 mm / 75 mm

6.5.8.70

Standard size bricks, laid flat, bedded on 1:3 cement mortar, all joints pointed up

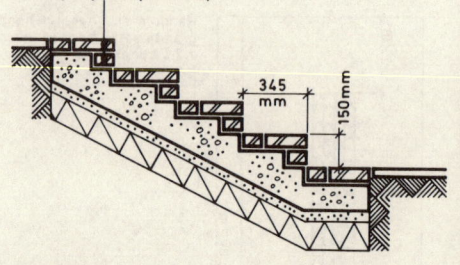

345 mm / 150 mm

6.5.8.71

Standard size bricks, laid on edge, bedded on 1:3 cement mortar, all joints pointed up

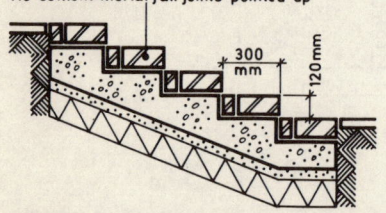

300 mm / 120 mm

6.5.8.72

In-situ concrete steps. 150mm minimum depth 1:2:4 mix concrete on 50mm sand blinding on 150mm hardcore

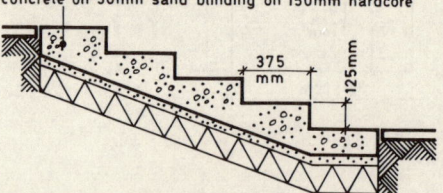

375 mm / 125 mm

6.5.8.73

Precast concrete slab bedded on 1:3 cement mortar, all joints pointed up
Standard size bricks, laid flat, bedded on 1:3 cement mortar, all joints pointed up

450 mm / 125 mm

150mm minimum depth 1:2:4 mix concrete
50mm compacted sand blinding
150mm hardcore

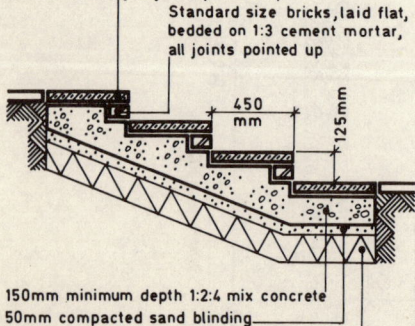

6.5.8.74

Precast concrete slab bedded on 1:3 cement mortar, all joints pointed up
200mm x 50mm precast concrete edging bedded on 1:3 cement mortar, all joints pointed up

510 mm / 150 mm

150mm minimum depth 1:2:4 mix concrete
50mm compacted sand blinding
150mm hardcore

6.5.8.75

6.5.8 STEPS

For detailed specification of materials used on these drawings see Chapter 5, Section 8
For prices see Chapter 7

Precast concrete or reconstructed stone blocks, bedded on 1:3 cement mortar, all joints pointed up

325 mm
150 mm

6.5.8.76

Precast concrete or reconstructed stone blocks, bedded on 1:3 cement mortar, all joints pointed up

325 mm
125 mm

6.5.8.77

Second hand granite setts, bedded on 1:3 cement mortar, all joints pointed up
250mm x 125mm precast concrete kerb, bedded on 1:3 cement mortar, all joints pointed up
450 mm
150 mm

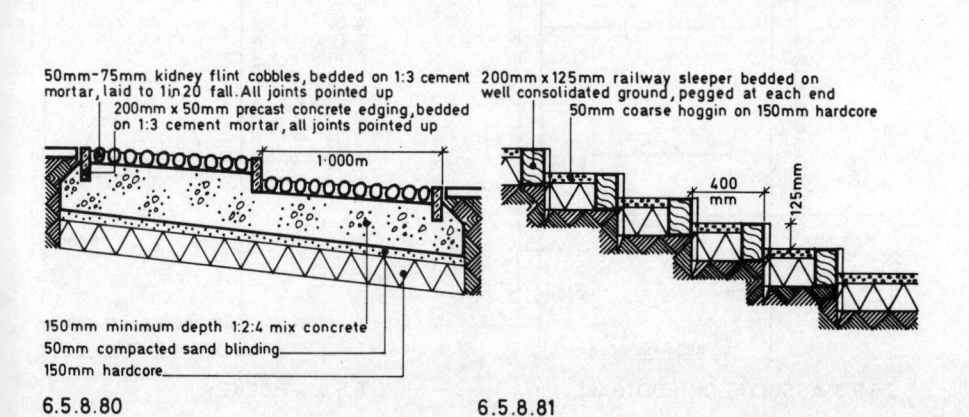

6.5.8.78

Second hand granite setts, bedded on 1:3 cement mortar, all joints pointed up

400 mm
100 mm

6.5.8.79

50mm-75mm kidney flint cobbles, bedded on 1:3 cement mortar, laid to 1 in 20 fall. All joints pointed up
200mm x 50mm precast concrete edging, bedded on 1:3 cement mortar, all joints pointed up
1·000m

150mm minimum depth 1:2:4 mix concrete
50mm compacted sand blinding
150mm hardcore

6.5.8.80

200mm x 125mm railway sleeper bedded on well consolidated ground, pegged at each end
50mm coarse hoggin on 150mm hardcore

400 mm
125 mm

6.5.8.81

253

6.5.9 RECREATION AND SPORTS FACILITIES

For prices see Chapter 7

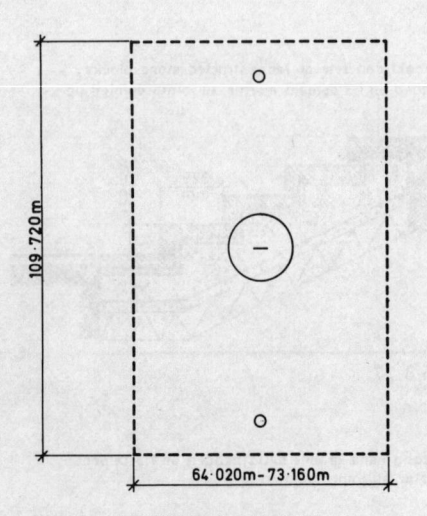

6.5.9.1 LACROSSE (WOMENS)
109.720 m
64.020 m – 73.160 m

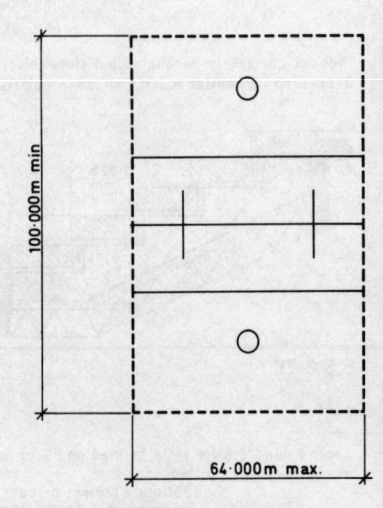

6.5.9.2 LACROSSE (MENS)
100.000 m min
64.000 m max.

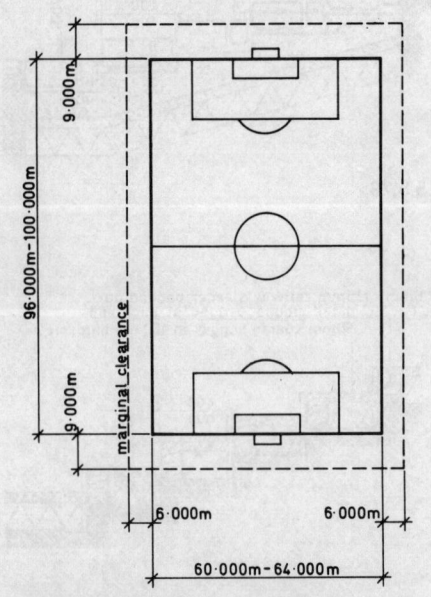

6.5.9.3 ASSOCIATION FOOTBALL
96.000 m – 100.000 m
9.000 m
9.000 m
marginal clearance
6.000 m
6.000 m
60.000 m – 64.000 m

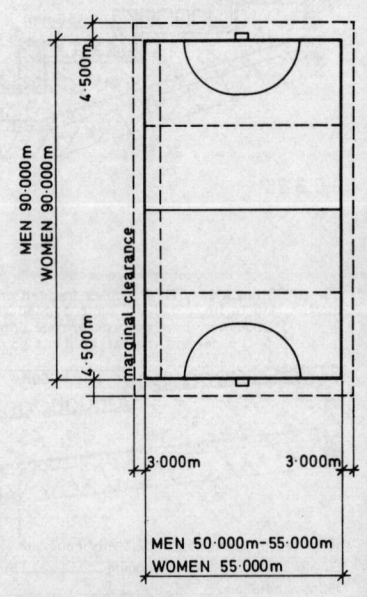

6.5.9.4 HOCKEY
MEN 90.000 m
WOMEN 90.000 m
4.500 m
4.500 m
marginal clearance
3.000 m
3.000 m
MEN 50.000 m – 55.000 m
WOMEN 55.000 m

254

6.5.9 RECREATION AND SPORTS FACILITIES

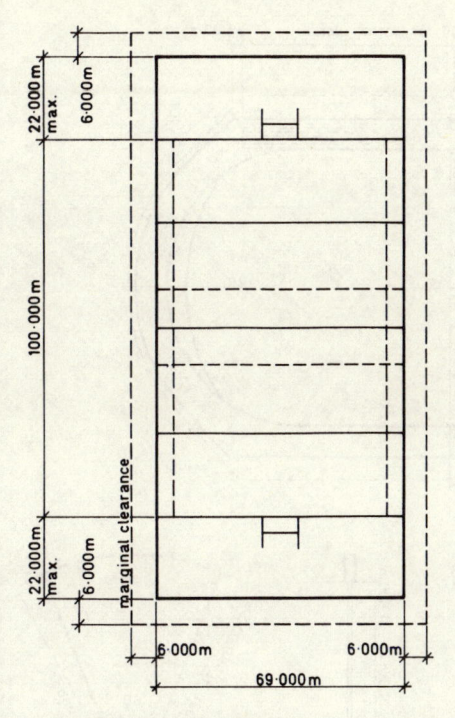

For prices see Chapter 7

6.5.9.5 RUGBY UNION

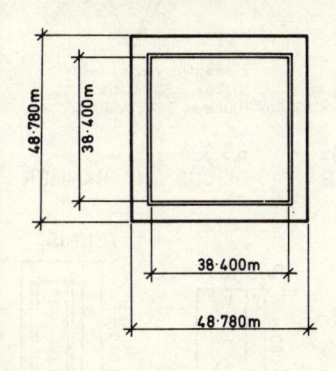

6.5.9.6 RUGBY LEAGUE

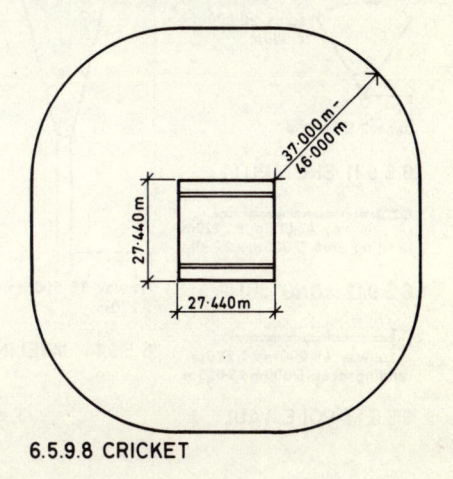

6.5.9.7 6 RINK BOWLING GREEN

6.5.9.8 CRICKET

6.5.9 RECREATION AND SPORTS FACILITIES

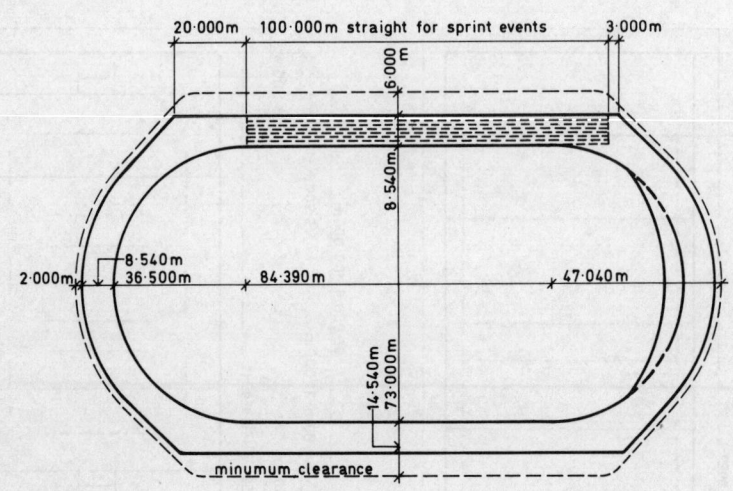

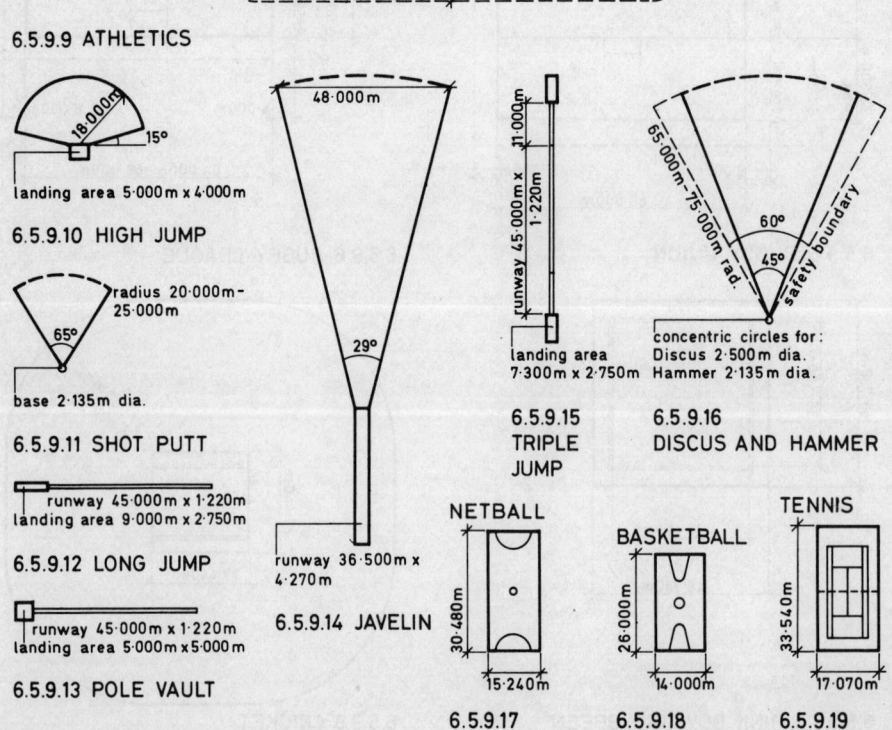

For prices see Chapter 7

6.5.9.9 ATHLETICS

6.5.9.10 HIGH JUMP
landing area 5·000m x 4·000m

6.5.9.11 SHOT PUTT
base 2·135m dia.

6.5.9.12 LONG JUMP
runway 45·000m x 1·220m
landing area 9·000m x 2·750m

6.5.9.13 POLE VAULT
runway 45·000m x 1·220m
landing area 5·000m x 5·000m

6.5.9.14 JAVELIN
runway 36·500m x 4·270m

6.5.9.15 TRIPLE JUMP
runway 45·000m x 1·220m
landing area 7·300m x 2·750m

6.5.9.16 DISCUS AND HAMMER
concentric circles for:
Discus 2·500m dia.
Hammer 2·135m dia.

6.5.9.17 NETBALL
30·480m x 15·240m

6.5.9.18 BASKETBALL
26·000m x 14·000m

6.5.9.19 TENNIS
33·540m x 17·070m

7 Pricing

7.0 INTRODUCTION

7.0.1　It has been assumed in the pricing of the items in this chapter that the landscape work is undertaken as a main contract. Where landscape work is a sub-contract an addition should be made to these figures for the main contractor's discount and profit.

7.0.2　The prices are intended as average for medium size contracts (except bowling greens); of between 5000 m^2 and 10 000 m^2 for soft landscaping which includes between 500 m^2 and 1000 m^2 of planting.

7.0.3　Prices in large cities will normally be higher than those stated here and may also be higher in remote areas of the country. Preliminaries are priced separately in the appropriate section of *Spon's Architects' and Builders' Price Book*.

7.0.4　The prices include for 10% profit and overheads.

7.0.5　For basic prices of labour and for materials for hard landscaping, see *Spon's Architects' and Builders' Price Book*.

7.0.6　The figures for earth works are as for 'medium soil' as defined in B.S. 3882. The prices for cutting down and disposal of trees assume that satisfactory access is available. Tree felling is exclusive of any possible credit from the sale of resulting timber.

7.0.7　The units of measurement have been varied to suit the type of work and care should be taken when using any prices to ascertain the unit basis being used.

7.1 PREPARATORY OPERATIONS

FOR LANDSCAPE CONTRACTS

		unit	£

All clause numbers refer to the specification paragraphs in Chapter 5.

Enclosure

Temporary fencing

5.1.2.1 Cleft chestnut fencing complying with
B.S. 1722 part 4:

	unit	£
1.200 m high	m	0.90
1.400 m high	m	1.10
1.600 m high	m	1.23
1.800 m high	m	1.36

Chain link fencing complying with
B.S. 1722 part 1:

	unit	£
1.200 m high	m	1.11
1.500 m high	m	2.16
1.800 m high	m	2.67
2.100 m high	m	3.60

75 mm diameter larch posts @ 1.000 m centres with 3 No. strands of wire:

	unit	£
1.200 m high	m	1.14
1.500 m high	m	1.32

5.4.4.2 Tempory protection to work (and clear away) . m . 0.71

Existing artifacts

Turf removal

5.1.2.5 lift existing turf and stack for transporting . 100 m² . 6.82

Site clearance

5.1.2.6 cutting down and raking rough grass and weeds and burning on site . 100 m² . 0.79
clearing average density scrub, grubbing up roots and burning on site . 100 m² . 3.73
cutting down hedges not exceeding 2.000 m high, grubbing up roots and burning on site . 100 m . 47.50

Tree felling; up to 1.500 m girth
(N.B. trees of similar girth can differ considerably in height or spread depending on the species; the prices below are for average shape trees)
cutting down tree to ground level and burning on site:
girth up to 500 mm . No. . 2.75

See Stop Press page vii; % additions to rates; September 1972 wage settlement

Pricing–Preparatory Operations

5.1.2.6.
(cont'd)

Tree felling; up to 1.500 m girth continued

	unit	£
extra for grubbing up roots	No.	2.25
extra for carting tree and roots to tip from site n.e. 15 km	No.	3.75
girth 500 mm to 750 mm	No.	3.25
extra for grubbing up roots	No.	2.75
extra for carting tree and roots to tip from site n.e. 15 km	No.	7.25
girth 750 mm to 1.000 m	No.	3.75
extra for grubbing up roots	No.	3.75
extra for carting tree and roots to tip from site n.e. 15 km	No.	8.75
girth 1.000 m to 1.250 m	No.	4.50
extra for grubbing up roots	No.	4.75
extra for carting tree and roots to tip from site n.e. 15 km	No.	10.00
girth 1.250 m to 1.500 m	No.	5.75
extra for grubbing up roots	No.	6.25
extra for carting tree and roots to tip from site me. 15 km	No.	11.50

Tree felling over 1.500 m girth
cutting down tree to ground level, stacking saleable timber and burning remainder on site (no credit allowed for saleable timber)

	unit	£
girth 1.500 m to 1.750 m	No.	7.60
extra for grubbing up roots	No.	7.50
extra for carting unsaleable timber and roots to tip from site n.e. 15 km	No.	9.50
girth 1.750 m to 2.000 m	No.	13.00
extra for grubbing up roots	No.	13.25
extra for carting unsaleable timber and roots to tip from site n.e. 15 km	No.	10.50
girth 2.000 m to 2.250 m	No.	17.50
extra for grubbing up roots	No.	17.50
extra for carting unsaleable timber and roots to tip from site n.e. 15 km	No.	15.50
girth 2.250 m to 2.500 m	No.	22.25
extra for grubbing up roots	No.	19.50
extra for carting unsaleable timber and roots to tip from site n.e. 15 km	No.	17.00
girth 2.500 m to 2.750 m	No.	30.50
extra for grubbing up roots	No.	29.00
extra for carting unsaleable timber and roots to tip from site n.e. 15 km	No.	22.00
girth 2.750 m to 3.000 m	No.	43.50
extra for grubbing up roots	No.	40.00
extra for carting unsaleable timber and roots		

See Stop Press page vii; % additions to rates; September 1972 wage settlement

5.1.2.6 (cont'd)	*Tree felling over 1.500 m girth continued* to tip from site n.e. 15 km (N.B. above this size trees become so large that average pricing could be misleading; each one needs special individual pricing)		unit No.	£ 26.50

Removal of materials for re-use

5.1.2.9   Take up:

	unit	£
stone slab paving	m²	0.99
granite sett paving	m²	1.73
brick paving	m²	1.43
extra for carting a distance not exceeding 15 km;		
stone slab paving	m³	4.29
granite sett paving	m³	3.93
brick paving	m³	3.51

See Stop Press page vii; % additions to rates; September 1972 wage settlement

7.2 GROUNDWORKS

All clause numbers refer to the specification paragraphs in Chapter 5.

5.2.3 DEMOLITION

break up old concrete bases and stack for re-use as hardcore not more than 100 m away:

average 100 mm thick	m^2	0.54
„ 150 mm thick	m^2	0.80
„ 200 mm thick	m^2	1.01
„ 250 mm thick	m^2	1.34
„ 300 mm thick	m^2	1.60
extra for carting from site to tip not more than 15 km from site	m^3	1.28

HAND EXCAVATION

Preserving topsoil
excavate vegetable topsoil and deposit in spoil heaps ready for re-spreading not exceeding 100 m from excavation:

average 100 mm deep	m^2	0.24
„ 150 mm deep	m^2	0.32
„ 200 mm deep	m^2	0.38
„ 250 mm deep	m^2	0.44
„ 300 mm deep	m^2	0.50
extra for turning topsoil if stacked over 12 months	m^3	0.65

Excavating
reduce levels, over 300 mm deep, depositing on site in spoil heaps not exceeding 100 m from excavation . . . . m^3 2.70

Preparation for shrubs   unit   £
hand dig ground to depth of 225 mm m^2 0.28

Disposal
removing surplus excavated material from site to tip not exceeding 15 km from site . . . m^3 1.82

MECHANICAL EXCAVATION

Preserving topsoil
excavate vegetable topsoil and deposit in spoil heaps ready for re-spreading not exceeding

See Stop Press page vii; % additions to rates; September 1972 wage settlement

5.2.3 (cont'd)	Preserving topsoil continued	unit	£
	100 m from excavation:		
	average 100 mm deep	m²	0.06
	average 150 mm deep	m²	0.09
	average 200 mm deep	m²	0.14
	average 250 mm deep	m²	0.19
	average 300 mm deep	m²	0.25
	extra for turning topsoil if stacked over 12 months	m³	0.23

Excavating

reduce levels, over 300 mm deep, depositing on site in spoil heaps not exceeding 100 m from excavation . . . . m³   0.45
(using excavator with skimmer attachment and loading into dumpers)
surfaces to reduce levels over 300 mm deep, depositing and filling in, making up levels in maximum 150 mm layers not exceeding 100 m from excavation (using scraper 5.000 m³) . m³   0.18

Preparation for planting; hedges

excavate trench 450 mm wide and 300 mm deep and deposit on site in spoil heaps not exceeding 100 m from excavation . . . . m   0.46

Preparation for planting; tree pits

excavate pits:

900 mm × 900 mm × 600 mm deep . . No.	0.88
1.000 m × 1.000 m × 600 mm deep . . No.	1.32
1.250 m × 1.250 m × 600 mm deep . . No.	1.76
1.500 m × 1.500 m × 750 mm deep . . No.	2.20
1.750 m × 1.750 m × 750 mm deep . .. No.	2.63
2.000 m × 2.000 m × 900 mm deep . . No.	3.29

Disposal

removing surplus excavated material from site to tip not exceeding 15 km from site . . . m³   1.05

TOPSOIL

Importation of topsoil

(including transport not exceeding 15 km to site of works)

5.2.2   medium texture, pH, in accordance with B.S.3882:
quantity below 100 m³ . . . . m³   2.20

See Stop Press page vii; % additions to rates; September 1972 wage settlement

5.2.2 (cont'd) **Importation of topsoil** continued

	unit	£
quantity 100–1000 m³	m³	2.15
quantity 1000–5000 m³	m³	2.05
quantity over 5000 m³	m³	2.00

Handwork

Soiling for seeding, turfing and planting
topsoil selected from spoil heaps (of imported or stripped soil), removing not exceeding 100 m and lightly consolidating:

	unit	£
100 mm thick	m²	0.30
150 mm thick	m²	0.38
300 mm thick	m²	0.55
450 mm thick	m²	0.68
600 mm thick	m²	0.81
on banks 15°–30°:		
100 mm thick	m²	0.33
150 mm thick	m²	0.42
on banks over 30°:		
100 mm thick	m²	0.36
150 mm thick	m²	0.46

5.2.3 **CULTIVATION**

Handwork

	unit	£
cultivation by pedestrian-operated machine to general surfaces	100 m²	3.40
evenly grading to general surfaces to finished levels	100 m²	6.07
evenly grading of banks 15°–30°:	100 m²	6.83
over 30°:	100 m²	7.58

Stone picking

	unit	£
clear stones 50 mm and over from surfaces and remove from site	ha	22.05
clear stones 38 mm and over from surfaces and remove from site	ha	29.50
clear stones 25 mm and over from surfaces and remove from site	ha	39.35

See Stop Press page vii; % additions to rates; September 1972 wage settlement

5.2.2 TOPSOIL

	unit	£

Machine work

Soiling for seeding, turfing and planting
topsoil selected from spoil heap (of imported or stripped soil), removing not exceeding 100 m and lightly consolidating:

	unit	£
100 mm thick	m²	0.13
150 mm thick	m²	0.20
300 mm thick	m²	0.32
450 mm thick	m²	0.41
600 mm thick	m²	0.47
on banks 15°–30°:		
100 mm thick	m²	0.15
150 mm thick	m²	0.22
on banks over 30°:		
100 mm thick	m²	0.16
150 mm thick	m²	0.24

5.2.3 CULTIVATION

Machine work
plough, break up furrows, cultivate to fine tilth; depth of ploughing:

	unit	£
75 mm	ha	102.25
100 mm	ha	113.25
125 mm	ha	127.64
150 mm	ha	145.54
subsoiling at 1.000 m centres evenly grading to		85.10
general surfaces to finished levels	ha	99.85
evenly grading of banks:		
15°–30°	ha	109.80
over 30°	ha	124.81

See Stop Press page vii; % additions to rates; September 1972 wage settlement

7.3 DRAINAGE *unit £*

All clause numbers refer to specification paragraphs in Chapter 5.

APPROXIMATE ESTIMATES

'Tile' Drains: Introduction

5.3.4.1–5 For calculation of drainage per hectare, the following table can be used:

Lateral drains

4.000 m centres	2500 m per hectare
6.000 m centres	1670 m per hectare
8.000 m centres	1250 m per hectare
10.000 m centres	1000 m per hectare
15.000 m centres	670 m per hectare
25.000 m centres	400 m per hectare
30.000 m centres	330 m per hectare

Main drains (per hectare)

1 No.	(at 100.000 m centres)	100 m per ha
2 No.	(at 50.000 m centres)	200 m per ha
3 No.	(at 33.333 m centres)	300 m per ha
4 No.	(at 25.000 m centres)	400 m per ha

Prices include for excavating by mechanical means and laying pipes and backfilling by hand and re-laying vegetable soil:

Clayware

5.3.4.3 over one hectare, in herringbone pattern, 75 mm diameter, 600 mm deep; with 100 mm diameter main drain:

	unit	£
laterals at 4.000 m centres	ha	2158.00
laterals at 6.000 m centres	ha	1644.00
laterals at 8.000 m centres	ha	1138.00
laterals at 10.000 m centres	ha	934.00
laterals at 15.000 m centres	ha	665.00
laterals at 25.000 m centres	ha	445.00
laterals at 30.000 m centres	ha	387.00

Rigid plastic perforated

5.3.4.4 over one hectare, in herringbone pattern, 50 mm diameter, 600 mm deep:

	unit	£
laterals at 4.000 m centres	ha	2071.00
laterals at 6.000 m centres	ha	1579.00
laterals at 8.000 m centres	ha	1095.00
laterals at 10.000 m centres	ha	900.00
laterals at 15.000 m centres	ha	643.00

See Stop Press page vii; % additions to rates; September 1972 wage settlement

Pricing–Drainage

5.3.4.4 (cont'd)	**Rigid Plastic Perforated** continued	unit	£
	laterals at 25.000 m centres	ha	432.00
	laterals at 30.000 m centres	ha	377.00

5.3.4.3	*Clayware main drains*		
	100 mm diameter, 600 mm deep:		
	100.000 m centres	ha	118.00
	50.000 m centres	ha	236.00
	33.333 m centres	ha	354.00
	25.000 m centres	ha	472.00
	150 mm diameter, 600 mm deep:		
	100.000 m centres	ha	137.00
	50.000 m centres	ha	273.50
	33.333 m centres	ha	410.00
	25.000 m centres	ha	547.00

Prices include for laying pipes by mole plough:

5.3.4.5	*Flexible plastic perforated* over one hectare, in herringbone pattern 70 mm diameter, 450 mm deep:		
	laterals at 4.000 m centres	ha	1660.00
	laterals at 6.000 m centres	ha	1241.50
	laterals at 8.000 m centres	ha	830.00
	laterals at 10.000 m centres	ha	664.00
	laterals at 15.000 m centres	ha	445.00
	laterals at 25.000 m centres	ha	265.00
	laterals at 30.000 m centres	ha	219.00

UNIT PRICES

'Tile' drainage operations

Excavation

5.3.4.12	remove 150 mm depth of topsoil 300 mm wide and deposit beside trench	100 m	2.97
	remove 150 mm depth of topsoil 300 mm wide and cart to spoil heap not more than 100.000 m	100 m	3.17
5.3.4.13–14	excavate trenches (with minimum run of 500.000 m) by trenching machine, including carting sub-soil to spoil heap not exceeding 100.000 m:		
	width 150 mm:		
	depth 450 mm	100 m	24.64
	depth 600 mm	100 m	26.89
	depth 750 mm	100 m	29.66

See Stop Press page vii; % additions to rates; September 1972 wage settlement

Pricing–Drainage

5.3.4.13–14 (cont'd)

Excavation *continued*

	unit	£
width 225 mm:		
depth 450 mm	100 m	25.50
depth 600 mm	100 m	28.28
depth 750 mm	100 m	34.64
width 300 mm:		
depth 450 mm	100 m	26.89
depth 600 mm	100 m	29.60
depth 750 mm	100 m	32.43
depth 900 mm	100 m	35.20
depth 1.000 m	100 m	36.59
width 375 mm:		
depth 600 mm	100 m	32.43
depth 750 mm	100 m	35.20
depth 900 mm	100 m	37.97
depth 1.000 m	100 m	39.36

excavate trenches (with minimum run of 500.000 m) by back-acter excavator including carting sub-soil to spoil heaps not exceeding 100.000 m.

	unit	£
width 300 mm:		
depth 450 mm	100 m	27.98
depth 600 mm	100 m	30.87
depth 750 mm	100 m	33.75
depth 900 mm	100 m	36.63
width 375 mm:		
depth 600 mm:	100 m	33.75
depth 750 mm	100 m	36.63
depth 900 mm	100 m	39.51
depth 1.000 m	100 m	40.95
width 450 mm:		
depth 600 mm	100 m	35.19
depth 750 mm	100 m	38.07
depth 900 mm	100 m	40.95
depth 1.000 m	100 m	42.39

Laying

5.3.4.15–19 provide and lay clayware pipes by hand with butted joints in trench in 300 mm lengths:

	unit	£
75 mm diameter	100 m	19.64
100 mm diameter	100 m	29.09
150 mm diameter	100 m	47.87
225 mm diameter	100 m	89.31

extra over for clayware junction connections between laterals and mains:

	unit	£
75 mm × 75 mm	No.	0.64
75 mm × 100 mm	No.	0.64
75 mm × 150 mm	No.	0.94
100 mm × 100 mm	No.	0.64

See Stop Press page vii; % additions to rates; September 1972 wage settlement

Pricing–Drainage

5.3.4.15–19 (cont'd)

Laying continued

	unit	£
100 mm × 150 mm	No.	0.94
100 mm × 225 mm	No.	1.94

provide and lay porous concrete pipes by hand with butted joints in trench in 300 mm lengths:

100 mm diameter	100 m	29.16
150 mm diameter	100 m	43.28
225 mm diameter	100 m	68.92

provide an lay rigid plastic pipes 50 mm in diameter, by pipe chute attached to trencher, on bed of trench, in 6.000 m lengths, slotted together:

	100 m	16.09
as above but 90 mm diameter	100 m	30.77

extra over for plastic junction connections:

50 mm × 50 mm	No.	0.57
50 mm × 90 mm	No.	0.68
90 mm × 90 mm	No.	0.68

provide and lay flexible plastic perforated pipes by mole plough with pipe laying attachment to a minimum depth of 450 mm:

52 mm diameter	100 m	36.58
70 mm diameter	100 m	56.39
110 mm diameter	100 m	91.78

Filling

5.3.4.20–24 fill trench, after pipe laying with gravel rejects and cover of fine ash to within 150 mm of surface level of trench; including replacement of topsoil:

width 150 mm:

depth 450 mm	100 m	25.83
depth 600 mm	100 m	32.08
depth 750 mm	100 m	38.32

width 225 mm:

depth 450 mm	100 m	35.43
depth 600 mm	100 m	43.28
depth 750 mm	100 m	53.12

width 300 mm:

depth 450 mm	100 m	44.88
depth 600 mm	100 m	56.32
depth 750 mm	100 m	67.77
depth 900 mm	100 m	79.21

width 375 mm:

depth 600 mm	100 m	68.66
depth 750 mm	100 m	83.40
depth 900 mm	100 m	97.80
depth 1.000 m	100 m	107.51

width 450 mm:

depth 600 mm	100 m	80.86

See Stop Press page vii; % additions to rates; September 1972 wage settlement

			unit	£
5.3.4.20–24 (cont'd)	**Filling** continued			
	depth 750 mm	. . . . .	100 m	91.94
	depth 900 mm	. . . . .	100 m	116.24
	depth 1.000 m	. . . . .	100 m	127.91

fill cut, formed by drain laying mole plough, with gravel rejects to within 150 mm of surface:

width 50 mm:				
depth 450 mm	. . . . .	100 m	6.41
depth 600 mm	. . . . .	100 m	9.54
depth 750 mm	. . . . .	100 m	12.67
depth 900 mm	. . . . .	100 m	14.75
depth 1.000 m	. . . . .	100 m	16.61
width 70 mm:				
depth 600 mm	. . . . .	100 m	13.05
depth 750 mm	. . . . .	100 m	16.53
depth 900 mm	. . . . .	100 m	20.00
depth 1.000 m	. . . . .	100 m	23.13
width 110 mm:				
depth 600 mm	. . . . .	100 m	19.44
depth 750 mm	. . . . .	100 m	24.31
depth 900 mm	. . . . .	100 m	29.17
depth 1.000 m	. . . . .	100 m	32.89

Catchwater or french drains

5.3.4.25 fill trench, after pipe laying, with gravel rejects and 40 mm of fine ash to within 10 mm of surface:

width 150 mm:			
depth 450 mm	. . . . .	100 m	24.00
depth 600 mm	. . . . .	100 m	29.89
depth 750 mm	. . . . .	100 m	35.79
width 225 mm:			
depth 450 mm	. . . . .	100 m	32.32
depth 600 mm	. . . . .	100 m	40.81
depth 750 mm	. . . . .	100 m	49.66
depth 900 mm	. . . . .	100 m	58.51
width 300 mm:			
depth 600 mm	. . . . .	100 m	52.09
depth 750 mm	. . . . .	100 m	63.53
depth 900 mm	. . . . .	100 m	74.98
width 375 mm:			
depth 600 mm	. . . . .	100 m	63.02
depth 750 mm	. . . . .	100 m	72.44
depth 900 mm	. . . . .	100 m	92.15
depth 1.000 m	. . . . .	100 m	102.56
width 450 mm:			
depth 600 mm	. . . . .	100 m	73.94
depth 750 mm	. . . . .	100 m	91.63
depth 900 mm	. . . . .	100 m	109.32

See Stop Press page vii; % additions to rates; September 1972 wage settlement

5.3.4.25 (cont'd)	Catchwater or french drains continued	unit	£
	depth 1.000 m	100 m	121.82

Silt pits and inspection chambers

5.3.4.26–28	silt pit 900 mm × 600 mm with 225 mm brick wall and 100 mm thick concrete cover:		
	Class 'B' engineering brick:		
	1.050 m deep	No.	27.00
	1.375 m deep	No.	34.00
	common brick, rendered:		
	1.050 m deep	No.	21.00
	1.375 m deep	No.	26.00
	inspection chamber 600 mm × 600 mm in 225 mm brick with 100 mm thick concrete cover:		
	Class 'B' engineering brick:		
	750 mm deep	No.	38.00
	1.050 m deep	No.	48.00
	common brick, rendered:		
	750 mm deep	No.	31.00
	1.050 m deep	No.	38.00
	extra for providing and fixing C.I. cover and frame 600 mm × 475 mm clear opening (B.S.497 Grade 'C'), coated, single seal; frame bedded in 1:3 cement mortar; cover in grease and sand	No.	5.40
	as above but Grade 'B' solid top	No.	17.40
	inspection chamber 400 mm × 450 mm in half brick walls and 75 mm thick concrete cover:		
	class 'B' engineering brick:		
	750 mm deep	No.	16.00
	1.050 m deep	No.	20.00
	common brick, rendered:		
	750 mm deep	No.	14.00
	1.050 m deep	No.	17.00
5.3.4.30	reinforced concrete outfall to watercourse, with flank walls, for 150 mm diameter tile drain outlet; overall dimension 900 mm × 1.050 m × 900 mm high	No.	40.00 –100.00

Soakaways

5.3.4.31–32	soakaway constructed with perforated concrete pipes (B.S.1194) and light duty concrete chamber cover (B.S.556) with tile drain inlet set at 600 mm depth		
	900 mm diameter × 1.500 m deep	No.	35.00
	900 mm diameter × 1.800 m deep	No.	40.50
	1.200 m diameter × 1.800 m deep	No.	64.50

See Stop Press page vii; % additions to rates; September 1972 wage settlement

Pricing—Drainage

			unit	£
5.3.4.31–32 (cont'd)	**Soakaways** continued			
	1.200 m diameter × 2.100 m deep		No.	73.00
5.3.4.33–34	soakaway constructed in 225 mm common brickwork, dry jointed, with 100 mm thick concrete cover and tile drain inlet set at 600 mm depth:			
	900 mm × 900 mm × 1.500 m deep		No.	45.00
	900 mm × 900 mm × 1.800 m deep		No.	52.00
	1.200 m × 1.200 m × 1.800 m deep		No.	61.50
	1.200 m × 1.200 m × 2.100 m deep		No.	79.00
	extra for circular coated C.I. cover and frame, clear opening 510 mm diameter (to B.S.497 Grade 'B') finished flush with ground level; frame bedded in 1:3 cement mortar; cover in grease and sand		No.	13.40
	Mole drainage			
5.3.4.36	drain by mole plough with 50 mm diameter mole set at depth of 450 mm in parallel runs:			
	1.200 m centres		ha	54.35
	1.500 m centres		ha	49.73
	2.000 m centres		ha	45.11
	2.500 m centres		ha	40.50
	3.000 m centres		ha	35.87
	drain by mole plough with 75 mm diameter mole set at depth of 450 mm in parallel runs:			
	1.200 m centres		ha	74.04
	1.500 m centres		ha	67.67
	2.000 m centres		ha	61.30
	2.500 m centres		ha	54.93
	3.000 m centres		ha	48.57
	Ditching			
	Excavation			
5.3.4.39–40	clean and trim existing ditch with average bed width of 600 mm and average depth of 600 mm (price depending on state)		100 m	7.50 –15.00
5.3.4.41	excavate ditch with 45° side slopes:			
	width at bottom of ditch 300 mm:			
	600 mm deep		100 m	22.52
	900 mm deep		100 m	37.13
	1.200 m deep		100 m	58.47
	1.500 m deep		100 m	84.02
	width at bottom of ditch 600 mm:			
	600 mm deep		100 m	25.98
	900 mm deep		100 m	43.96

See Stop Press page vii; % additions to rates; September 1972 wage settlement

Pricing–Drainage

5.3.4.41 (cont'd)

Excavation continued	unit	£
1.200 m deep	100 m	68.86
1.500 m deep	100 m	97.88
width at bottom of ditch 900 mm:		
600 mm deep	100 m	31.19
900 mm deep	100 m	52.62
1.200 m deep	100 m	79.26
1.500 m deep	100 m	111.74
width at bottom of ditch 1.200 m:		
600 mm deep	100 m	36.48
900 mm deep	100 m	61.28
1.200 m deep	100 m	89.65
1.500 m deep	100 m	129.06
width at bottom of ditch 1.500 m:		
600 mm deep	100 m	41.58
900 mm deep	100 m	68.21
1.200 m deep	100 m	100.05
1.500 m deep	100 m	136.00

Piped ditches

5.3.4.42–45

excavate ditch, lay concrete pipes (to B.S.4101) with open joints and backfill, as described:		
ditch 600 mm deep:		
pipe 300 mm diameter	m	3.47
pipe 450 mm diameter	m	4.97
ditch 900 mm deep:		
pipe 300 mm diameter	m	5.08
pipe 450 mm diameter	m	6.61
pipe 600 mm diameter	m	8.77
ditch 1.200 m deep:		
pipe 300 mm diameter	m	7.34
pipe 450 mm diameter	m	8.87
pipe 600 mm diameter	m	11.05
pipe 900 mm diameter	m	15.87
ditch 1.500 m deep:		
pipe 300 mm diameter	m	10.20
pipe 450 mm diameter	m	11.75
pipe 600 mm diameter	m	13.95
pipe 900 mm diameter	m	18.85
pipe 1.200 m diameter	m	26.79

Culverts

5.3.4.46

excavate for, joint and surround with 150 mm concrete; concrete pipes (to B.S.4101) and backfill:		
excavation 600 mm deep:		
pipe 300 mm diameter	m	5.78
pipe 450 mm diameter	m	7.93

See Stop Press page vii; % additions to rates; September 1972 wage settlement

Pricing—Drainage

5.3.4.46
(cont'd)

Culverts continued

	unit	£
excavation 900 mm deep:		
pipe 300 mm diameter	m	6.06
pipe 450 mm diameter	m	8.44
pipe 600 mm diameter	m	11.68
excavation 1.200 m deep:		
pipe 300 mm diameter	m	6.70
pipe 450 mm diameter	m	9.08
pipe 600 mm diameter	m	12.34
pipe 900 mm diameter	m	19.04
excavation 1.500 m deep:		
pipe 300 mm diameter	m	7.50
pipe 450 mm diameter	m	9.89
pipe 600 mm diameter	m	13.17
pipe 900 mm diameter	m	20.20
pipe 1.200 m diameter	m	30.88

See Stop Press page vii; % additions to rates; September 1972 wage settlement

7.4 SEEDING OF GRASS AREAS

All clause numbers refer to the specification paragraphs in Chapter 5.

PREPARATION FOR SEEDING

clause	description	unit	£
5.4.2.1	pre-seed granular fertiliser @ 55 g/m^2	100 m^2	0.36
5.4.2.2	preparation of seed bed 25 mm deep	100 m^2	0.16
	preparation of seed bed 100 mm deep	100 m^2	0.24
5.4.2.4	supply and lay turf (B.S. quality) margin 300 mm wide (p.c. of £12.00 per 100 m^2)	100 m	9.75
5.4.2.7	pre-emergent weedkiller, 'Weedol' by Plant Protection in accordance with manufacturer's instructions	m^2	0.03

SEEDING

Seeding of grass in accordance with B.S.3969: 1965 as detailed in paragraphs 5.4.2.3–8, for all the following typical grass mixtures, with prices given for the seeding rates mentioned in each case.

Maxwell Hart Mixtures

Non-Ryegrass

clause	description	unit	£
5.4.3.1	Hart Sea Marsh Mixture; 45 g/m^2:		
	on normal levels	100 m^2	3.87
	on slopes over 30°	100 m^2	3.92
5.4.3.2	Hart No. 1; 45 g/m^2:		
	on normal levels	100 m^2	3.08
	on slopes over 30°	100 m^2	3.38
5.4.3.3	Hart No. 2; 45 g/m^2:		
	on normal levels	100 m^2	2.68
	on slopes over 30°	100 m^2	2.95
5.4.3.4	Hart Economy; 45 g/m^2:		
	on normal levels	100 m^2	2.21
	on slopes over 30°	100 m^2	2.44
5.4.3.5	Hart 3X; 45 g/m^2:		
	on normal levels	100 m^2	2.29
	on slopes over 30°	100 m^2	2.51
5.4.3.6	Hart No. 7; 45 g/m^2:		
	on normal levels	100 m^2	3.23
	on slopes over 30°	100 m^2	3.56
5.4.3.7	D.C. 'Arista'; 45 g/m^2		
	on normal levels	100 m^2	3.43
	on slopes over 30°	100 m^2	3.76

See Stop Press page vii; % additions to rates; September 1972 wage settlement

For MAJOR LANDSCAPE and SPORTSGROUND CONSTRUCTION

Hard Areas   Drainage   Earth Moving
Paving   Fencing   Golf Courses
Bowling Greens   Tennis Courts   Running Tracks

CHARLES LAMBERT (Lawns) LTD

Dudley Court, Cramlington, Northumberland
Telephone: Cramlington 4121/2

The quality of living

The significance of a well-planned landscape does not escape Maxwell Hart of Berkshire. From social amenity to sports complex Hart expertise produces something more than value for money. Municipal authorities look to Maxwell Hart for integrity and real understanding in constructing the amenities of tomorrow.

Maxwell M. Hart
Winnersh, Wokingham

WEST FOREST 5655

Amenity Grass and the Environment

After considerable research – much of it in collaboration with experimental centres and plant breeders throughout the world – Mommersteeg have bred a series of grass strains for amenity and environmental application. Mixtures are now available for a number of problem areas such as road verges, sand dunes, colliery and industrial waste reclaimation, as well as for sports turf and agricultural use.

Mommersteeg have established a Landscape Management Division to deal with the specific problems of local authorities, property developers, architects and public utilities. They have also set up International Environmental Consultants to advise on overseas developments.

A new booklet, Amenity Grass and the Environment, is available on request from the Mommersteeg Seed Company Ltd, Station Road, Finedon, Wellingborough, Northamptonshire, England. Telephone Finedon 674. Telex 341314.

Mommersteeg

Maxwell Hart Mixtures unit £

Ryegrass

5.4.3.8	Hart No. 4; 200 kg/hectare:		
	on normal levels	ha	97.57
	on slopes over 30°	ha	106.88
5.4.3.9	Hart No. 5; 200 kg/hectare:		
	on normal levels	ha	87.45
	on slopes over 30°	ha	95.74
5.4.3.10	Hart No. 6; 200 kg/hectare:		
	on normal levels	ha	76.89
	on slopes over 30°	ha	84.24
5.4.3.11	Hart No. 8; 200 kg/hectare:		
	on normal levels	ha	62.59
	on slopes over 30°	ha	68.40
5.4.3.12	Hart No. 9; 200 kg/hectare:		
	on normal levels	ha	54.89
	on slopes over 30°	ha	60.37
5.4.3.13	Hart No. 12; 200 kg/hectare:		
	on normal levels	ha	78.00
	on slopes over 30°	ha	85.34
5.4.3.14	D.F. 'Pelo'; 150 kg/hectare:		
	on normal levels	ha	82.67
	on slopes over 30°	ha	92.27
5.4.3.15	R.G. 1 Aberystwyth; 150 kg/hectare:		
	on normal levels	ha	59.73
	on slopes over 30°	ha	66.47
5.4.3.16	D.E. 'Compas'; 150 kg/hectare:		
	on normal levels	ha	74.91
	on slopes over 30°	ha	83.66

En-Tout-Cas Co. Ltd. (Johnsons) Mixtures

5.4.3.17	Super A (without Ryegrass); 45 g/m^2		
	on normal levels	100 m^2	2.68
	on slopes over 30°	100 m^2	2.95
5.4.3.18	B; (without Ryegrass); 45 g/m^2		
	on normal levels	100 m^2	2.29
	on slopes over 30°	100 m^2	2.51
5.4.3.19	C; 200 kg/hectare:		
	on normal levels	ha	83.49
	on slopes over 30°	ha	91.73
5.4.3.20	D; 200 kg/hectare:		
	on normal levels	ha	61.49
	on slopes over 30°	ha	67.17
5.4.3.21	'Dawson' (without Ryegrass); 45 g/m^2		
	on normal levels	100 m^2	2.88
	on slopes over 30°	100 m^2	3.16

See Stop Press page vii; % additions to rates; September 1972 wage settlement

Pricing–Seeding of Grass Areas

En-Tout-Cas Co. Ltd (Johnsons) Mixtures continued

		unit	£
5.4.3.22	'Prato' (without Ryegrass); 200 kg/hectare:		
	on normal levels	ha	116.49
	on slopes over 30°	ha	127.69
5.4.3.23	'Pelo' (with Ryegrass); 200 kg/hectare:		
	on normal levels	ha	94.49
	on slopes over 30°	ha	103.49
5.4.3.24	'King' (with Ryegrass); 200 kg/hectare:		
	on normal levels	ha	100.00
	on slopes over 30°	ha	109.54
5.4.3.25	'C/W' (Cricket Wicket); 45 g/m^2:		
	on normal levels	100 m^2	2.68
5.4.3.26	'F'; 200 kg/hectare:		
	on normal levels	100 m^2	1.25
	on slopes over 30°	100 m^2	1.47
5.4.4.1	apply mixture of two fertilisers		
	on normal levels	ha	68.69
	on slopes over 30°	ha	98.49

OTHER ITEMS AFTER SEEDING

5.4.4.2	protective fencing (and clear away)	m	0.71
5.4.4.3	top dress with fishmeal fertiliser		
	on normal levels	ha	45.89
	on slopes over 30°	ha	61.95
5.4.4.4 and 5.4.2.8	1st cut to new grass by gang mower during period of maintenance	ha	23.56
	cut grass ten times by gang mower during period of maintenance	ha	226.60
	cut grass ten times by box mower, 914 mm (36 in) stacking mowings on site, during period of maintenance	ha	303.16
	cut grass ten times with auto-scythe to slopes over 30°, leaving cuttings on site	100 m^2	2.32
	extra over for raking up cuttings and stacking on site	100 m^2	1.20
	stone picking: clear stones 25 mm and over from surfaces and remove from site	ha	19.42
5.4.4.5	apply selective weed killer:		
	May & Baker 'Actrilawn'	100 m^2	0.34
	ICI 'Weedkiller for new grass' (small areas only)	m^2	0.05

See Stop Press page vii; % additions to rates; September 1972 wage settlement

7.5 TURF AND TURFING

All clause numbers refer to the specification paragraphs in Chapter 5.

Clause	Description	unit	£
5.5.2.1–7	B.S.3969:1965 for the supply and delivery of turf (p.c. of £12.00 per 100 m^2)	100 m^2	13.20
5.5.3.1	treatment, prior to lifting, with selective weedkiller	100 m^2	0.34
5.5.3.2	supply and delivery of extra quality meadow turf (p.c. of £15.00 per 100 m^2)	100 m^2	16.50
5.5.3.3	supply and delivery of Cumberland turf (p.c. of £20.00 per 100 m^2)	100 m^2	22.00
5.5.4.1	cultivation to fine tilth, 25 mm deep	100 m^2	0.16
5.5.4.2–4 & 12	laying only to B.S.4428:1969 of B.S. quality or meadow turf:		
	on normal levels	100 m^2	14.31
5.5.4.5–10 & 12	on slopes over 30°	100 m^2	25.74
5.5.4.11–12	alternative method on slopes over 30° (N.B. The cost of supply only of turf on this item to be doubled)	100 m^2	50.27
5.5.4.10 or 11	extra over for laying turf to slopes for covering with wire netting	100 m^2	17.10
5.5.4.2–4 & 12	laying only to B.S.4428:1969, of Cumberland turf:		
	on normal levels	100 m^2	0.27
5.5.5.1	cultivation to fine tilth 100 mm deep	100 m^2	0.24
5.5.5.2	apply Fisons P.S.5. pre-turfing fertiliser at 55 g per m^2	100 m^2	0.36
	ditto to slopes over 30° by hand	100 m^2	0.51
5.5.5.3	apply I.C.I. 'Garden Plus' pre-turfing fertiliser at 55 g per m^2	100 m^2	0.95
	ditto to slopes over 30° by hand	100 m^2	1.15
5.5.5.4	apply mixture of two fertilizers at 70 g per m^2 each	100 m^2	0.69
	ditto to slopes over 30° by hand	100 m^2	0.99
5.5.5.5	apply I.C.I Sydol (B.H.C.) insecticide	100 m^2	0.36
	ditto to slopes over 30° by hand	100 m^2	0.53
5.5.5.6	top dress with fine soil	100 m^2	5.93
5.5.5.7	cut grass ten times by gang mower during period of maintenance	ha	226.60
	cut grass ten times by box mower, 914 mm (36 in) stacking mowings on site, during period of maintenance	100 m^2	3.03
	cut grass ten times with auto-scythe to slopes over 30°, leaving cuttings on site	100 m^2	2.32
	extra over for raking up cuttings and stacking on site	100 m^2	1.20
5.5.5.8	top dress with fish meal fertilizer at 70 g per m^2	100 m^2	0.46
	ditto to slopes over 30° by hand	100 m^2	0.62

See Stop Press page vii; % additions to rates; September 1972 wage settlement

			unit	£
5.5.5.9	apply Fisons 'Mecodex'	. . . .	100 m²	0.19
	ditto to slopes over 30° by hand	. .	100 m²	0.34
5.5.5.10	apply Fisons 'Cambadex'	. . . .	100 m²	0.18
	ditto to slopes over 30° by hand	. .	100 m²	0.32
5.5.5.11	apply I.C.I 'Weedkiller for New Grass' (small areas only)		m²	0.05

See Stop Press page vii; % additions to rates; September 1972 wage settlement

Pricing–Plants and Planting

| 7.6 | PLANTS AND PLANTING INCLUDING SEMI-MATURE TREES | unit | £ |

All clause numbers refer to specification paragraphs in Chapter 5.

5.6.2 NURSERY STOCK, TREES AND SHRUBS IN ACCORDANCE WITH B.S.3936 Part 1: 1965

5.6.4 Planted in accordance with the appropriate clauses of B.S.4428:1969.

Extra large nursery stock trees:
6.000 m tall, balled; planted price includes planting in excavated pit, measured elsewhere, re-filling with soil from spoil heap, incorporating manure, provision of single stake and 2 ties. Supply only price is ex-nursery. Transporting assumed to be not exceeding 75 km.

Acer platanoides:
| supply only | . | . | . | . | . | . | No. | 27.50 |
| supply and plant | . | . | . | . | . | No. | 32.32 |

Acer pseudo-platanus:
| supply only | . | . | . | . | . | . | No. | 27.50 |
| supply and plant | . | . | . | . | . | No. | 32.32 |

Aesculus hippocastanum:
| supply only | . | . | . | . | . | . | No. | 30.80 |
| supply and plant | . | . | . | . | . | No. | 35.62 |

Betula alba:
| supply only | . | . | . | . | . | . | No. | 25.30 |
| supply and plant | . | . | . | . | . | No. | 30.12 |

Carpinus betulus:
| supply only | . | . | . | . | . | . | No. | 29.70 |
| supply and plant | . | . | . | . | . | No. | 34.52 |

Fraxinus excelsior:
| supply only | . | . | . | . | . | . | No. | 27.50 |
| supply and plant | . | . | . | . | . | No. | 32.32 |

Platanus acerifolia:
| supply only | . | . | . | . | . | . | No. | 30.80 |

FOREST AND ORNAMENTAL
TREE DISEASE CONSULTANT
R. G. PAWSEY, M.Sc, Ph.D, F.S.F, M.I.Biol.
Registered consultant (specialist technologist) Society of Foresters of Great Britain
YEW COTTAGE, GREAT MILTON, OXON. Tel. Gr. Milton 416

See Stop Press page vii; % additions to rates; September 1972 wage settlement

5.6.4 (cont'd) **Extra Large Nursery Stock Trees** continued

	unit	£
supply and plant	No.	35.62
Prunus avium:		
supply only	No.	27.50
supply and plant	No.	32.32
Robinia pseudoacacia:		
supply only	No.	30.80
supply and plant	No.	35.62
Salix vitellina pendula:		
supply only	No.	30.80
supply and plant	No.	35.62
Sorbus aria:		
supply only	No.	29.70
supply and plant	No.	34.52
Tilia euchlora:		
supply only	No.	30.80
supply and plant	No.	35.62
extra per tree for double staking	No.	1.00

Extra large nursery stock trees:
4.500 m tall, bare rooted; planted price includes planting in excavated pit, measured elsewhere, refilling with soil from spoil heap, incorporating manure, provision of single stake and 2 ties. Supply price is ex-nursery. Transporting assumed to be not exceeding 75 km.

	unit	£
Acer platanoides:		
supply only	No.	8.80
supply and plant	No.	12.80
Acer pseudo-platanus:		
supply only	No.	8.80
supply and plant	No.	12.80
Aesculus hippocastanum:		
supply only	No.	9.90
supply and plant	No.	13.90
Betula alba:		
supply only	No.	8.80
supply and plant	No.	12.80
Carpinus betulus:		
supply only	No.	9.90
supply and plant	No.	13.90
Fraxinus excelsior:		
supply only	No.	8.80
supply and plant	No.	12.80
Platanus acerifolia:		
supply only	No.	9.90
supply and plant	No.	13.90

See Stop Press page vii; % additions to rates; September 1972 wage settlement

B.A.L.I.

THE BRITISH ASSOCIATION OF LANDSCAPE INDUSTRIES

Representing Reliable

Landscape Contractors

throughout the country

FULL MEMBERSHIP LIST AND DETAILS OF
FIELD OFFICER SERVICES
AVAILABLE FROM:—

B.A.L.I., 44 BEDFORD ROW, LONDON W.C.1

OUR LANDSCAPE SERVICE...

✱ A staff experienced in every aspect of hard and soft Landscaping for Commerce, Ministries and Local Authorities

✱ Modern Equipment, Up-to-date Methods and Complete Mobility

✱ Top Quality Plant material from our own extensive Nurseries

Bernhard's
LANDSCAPES

RUGBY · WARWICKSHIRE ☎ RUGBY 6464 · 4 lines

THE MEASUREMENT OF ENGINEERING SERVICES
W. F. J. Fussell, Chartered Quantity Surveyor

$9\frac{1}{2} \times 6\frac{1}{4}''$: 252pp: 57 illus: £4.50

Since engineering services form such a large part of the total cost of construction, it is essential that reliable cost data should be collated in a form that can be digested not only by the engineering designer, but also by the quantity surveyor responsible for the preparation of the cost plan for the whole project. The author, therefore, provides in this volume a logical analytical approach to the preparation of bills of quantities for engineering services, thereby encouraging sound tendering procedure and contract arrangements which in turn, will generate a feedback of cost information essential to those responsible for the design of engineering services within defined financial limits.

'It has been accepted by the RICS as one of the books recommended for those taking Final Part II (in Quantity Surveying) and should also be considerable value to those practising quantity surveyors who are cost planning and billing both mechanical and electrical services.' *The Chartered Surveyor*

E & F N Spon
11 New Fetter Lane, London EC4P 4EE

5.6.4 (cont'd) **Extra Large Nursery Stock Trees** continued

	unit	£
Prunus avium:		
supply only	No.	9.90
supply and plant	No.	13.90
Robinia pseudoacacia:		
supply only	No.	9.90
supply and plant	No.	13.90
Salix vitellina pendula:		
supply only	No.	9.90
supply and plant	No.	13.90
Sorbus aria:		
supply only	No.	9.90
supply and plant	No.	13.90
Tilia euchlora:		
supply only	No.	9.90
supply and plant	No.	13.90
extra per tree for double staking	No.	1.00

Standard trees:
3.000 m tall, bare rooted; planted price includes planting in excavated pit, measured elsewhere, re-filling with soil from spoil heap, incorporating manure, provision of single stake and 2 ties. Supply only price is ex-nursery. Transporting assumed to be not exceeding 75 km.

	unit	£
Acer platanoides:		
supply only	No.	1.27
supply and plant	No.	4.33
Acer pseudo-platanus:		
supply only	No.	1.27
supply and plant	No.	4.33
Aesculus hippocastanum:		
supply only	No.	1.65
supply and plant	No.	4.71
Alnus glutinosa:		
supply only	No.	1.27
supply and plant	No.	4.33
Betula alba:		
supply only	No.	1.21
supply and plant	No.	4.27
Carpinus betulus:		
supply only	No.	1.65
supply and plant	No.	4.71
Fraxinus excelsior:		
supply only	No.	1.16
supply and plant	No.	4.22
Malus floribunda:		
supply only	No.	1.38
supply and plant	No.	4.44

See Stop Press page vii; % additions to rates; September 1972 wage settlement

Pricing—Plants and Planting

5.6.4 (cont'd)

Standard trees continued   unit   £

Platanus acerifolia:
- supply only . . . . . . No. 1.43
- supply and plant . . . . . No. 4.49

Populus alba:
- supply only . . . . . . No. 1.00
- supply and plant . . . . . No. 4.06

Prunus avium:
- supply only . . . . . . No. 1.16
- supply and plant . . . . . No. 4.22

Prunus yedoensis:
- supply only . . . . . . No. 1.65
- supply and plant . . . . . No. 4.71

Robinia pseudoacacia:
- supply only . . . . . . No. 1.21
- supply and plant . . . . . No. 4.27

Salix vitellina pendula:
- supply only . . . . . . No. 1.05
- supply and plant . . . . . No. 4.11

Sorbus aria:
- supply only . . . . . . No. 1.54
- supply and plant . . . . . No. 4.60

Sorbus aucuparia:
- supply only . . . . . . No. 1.21
- supply and plant . . . . . No. 4.27

Tilia euchlora:
- supply only . . . . . . No. 1.98
- supply and plant . . . . . No. 5.04

Tilia platyphyllos:
- supply only . . . . . . No. 1.65
- supply and plant . . . . . No. 4.71

Half standard trees:
2.000 m tall, bare rooted; planted price includes planting in excavated pit, measured elsewhere, re-filling with soil from spoil heap, incorporating manure, provision of single stake and one tie. Supply only price is ex-nursery. Transporting assumed to be not exceeding 75 km.

Crataegus crus-galli:
- supply only . . . . . . No. 0.94
- supply and plant . . . . . No. 3.38

Malus floribunda:
- supply only . . . . . . No. 0.83
- supply and plant . . . . . No. 3.27

Prunus yedoensis:
- supply only . . . . . . No. 1.27
- supply and plant . . . . . No. 3.71

See Stop Press page vii; % additions to rates; September 1972 wage settlement

5.6.4 (cont'd)

Bush trees: unit   £

1.000 m tall, bare rooted (unless otherwise stated); planted price includes planting in excavated pit, measured elsewhere, re-filling with soil from spoil heap, incorporating manure, provision of single stake and one tie. Supply only price is ex-nursery. Transporting assumed to be not exceeding 75 km.

	unit	£
Amelanchier canadensis:		
supply only	No.	0.42
supply and plant	No.	2.43
Crataegus crus-galli:		
supply only	No.	0.47
supply and plant	No.	2.48
Malus floribunda:		
supply only	No.	0.51
supply and plant	No.	2.52
Magnolia soulangeana (root balled)		
supply only	No.	1.60
supply and plant	No.	3.81
Prunus yedoensis:		
supply only	No.	0.61
supply and plant	No.	2.62
Salix caprea:		
supply only	No.	0.22
supply and plant	No.	2.23

Conifers:

750 mm tall, balled; planted price includes planting in excavated pit, measured elsewhere, re-filling with soil from spoil heap, incorporating manure, provision of single stake and one tie. Supply only price is ex-nursery. Transporting assumed to be not exceeding 75 km.

	unit	£
Cedrus libani (limited supply):		
supply only	No.	3.03
supply and plant	No.	4.80
Chamaecyparis lawsoniana:		
supply only	No.	0.55
supply and plant	No.	2.32
Larix leptolepsis:		
supply only	No.	0.33
supply and plant	No.	2.10
Picea omorika:		
supply only	No.	0.73
supply and plant	No.	2.50
Pinus sylvestris:		
supply only	No.	0.36
supply and plant	No.	2.13

See Stop Press page vii; % additions to rates; September 1972 wage settlement

Pricing—Plants and Planting

5.6.4
(cont'd)

Conifers continued

	unit	£
Taxus baccata:		
supply only	No.	0.80
supply and plant	No.	2.57
Thuya plicata:		
supply only	No.	0.60
supply and plant	No.	2.37
Tsuga canadensis:		
supply only	No.	0.69
supply and plant	No.	2.46

Tree guards

	unit	£
provide and fix 1.830 m high galvanised tree guard to tree stake (p.c of £2.00)	No.	2.60
provide and fix tree guard as above but using two guards combined for double staked tree (p.c. of £4.00)	No.	5.40

Wrapping to trees

	unit	£
provide and fix hessian wrapping to bottom 2.000 m of tree trunk price per tree	No.	1.55
ditto; plastic wrapping to bottom 1.000 m	No.	0.40

Mulch to tree circles

mulch of peat only to circle in grass around tree:

	unit	£
300 mm diameter:		
50 mm thick	No.	0.10
75 mm thick	No.	0.12
600 mm diameter:		
50 mm thick	No.	0.23
75 mm thick	No.	0.30
900 mm diameter		
50 mm thick	No.	0.45
75 mm thick	No.	0.58

mulch of peat mixed with 10% by bulk of bonemeal to circle in grass around tree:

	unit	£
300 mm diameter:		
50 mm thick	No.	0.12
75 mm thick	No.	0.15
600 mm diameter:		
50 mm thick	No.	0.32
75 mm thick	No.	0.41
900 mm diameter:		
50 mm thick	No.	0.65
75 mm thick	No.	0.83

Weeding and maintenance

keeping soil circle around tree clear of weeds

See Stop Press page vii; % additions to rates; September 1972 wage settlement

5.6.4 (cont'd)	**Weeding and Maintenance** continued for one growing season and giving attention to tree stake and ties as necessary (average 6 visits a year):	unit	£
	diameter of circle 300 mm	No.	0.30
	diameter of circle 600 mm	No.	0.43
	diameter of circle 900 mm	No.	0.73

Shrubs: open ground

600 mm tall (unless otherwise stated). Supply only price is ex-nursery. Transporting is assumed to be not exceeding 75 km.

Acer palmatum 'Atropurpureum':
supply only	No.	1.32
supply and plant	No.	1.59

Amelanchier canadenis:
supply only	No.	0.24
supply and plant	No.	0.51

Berberis thunbergii:
supply only	No.	0.31
supply and plant	No.	0.58

Berberis thunbergii 'Atropurpurea':
supply only	No.	0.31
supply and plant	No.	0.58

Cornus alba:
supply only	No.	0.28
supply and plant	No.	0.55

Cornus stolonifera flaviramea:
supply only	No.	0.25
supply and plant	No.	0.52

Euonymus europaea:
supply only	No.	0.22
supply and plant	No.	0.49

Forsythia intermedia:
supply only	No.	0.20
supply and plant	No.	0.47

Hypericum patulum 'Hidcote' (450 mm):
supply only	No.	0.19
supply and plant	No.	0.46

Kerria japonica:
supply only	No.	0.26
supply and plant	No.	0.53

Philadelphus coronarius:
supply only	No.	0.28
supply and plant	No.	0.55

Rhus typhina (750 mm):
supply only	No.	0.39
supply and plant	No.	0.66

See Stop Press page vii; % additions to rates; September 1972 wage settlement

5.6.4 (cont'd)

Shrubs: open ground continued

	unit	£
Rosa rubrifolia:		
supply only	No.	0.22
supply and plant	No.	0.49
Rosa rugosa:		
supply only	No.	0.17
supply and plant	No.	0.44
Sambucus nigra:		
supply only	No.	0.20
supply and plant	No.	0.47
Spirea bumalda 'A. Waterer' (450 mm):		
supply only	No.	0.25
supply and plant	No.	0.52
Spirea vanhouttei:		
supply only	No.	0.28
supply and plant	No.	0.55
Viburnum opulus:		
supply only	No.	0.22
supply and plant	No.	0.49
Weigelia florida:		
supply only	No.	0.28
supply and plant	No.	0.55

Shrubs: root-balled

600 mm tall (unless otherwise stated). Supply only price is ex-nursery. Transporting is assumed to be not exceeding 75 km.

	unit	£
Berberis darwinii (450 mm):		
supply only	No.	0.44
supply and plant	No.	0.73
Berberis julianae (450 mm):		
supply only	No.	0.44
supply and plant	No.	0.73
Berberis stenophylla:		
supply only	No.	0.47
supply and plant	No.	0.76
Cotoneaster franchetii (900 mm):		
supply only	No.	0.45
supply and plant	No.	0.74
Cotoneaster salicifolius:		
supply only	No.	0.46
supply and plant	No.	0.75
Elaeagnus ebbingei (750 mm):		
supply only	No.	0.79
supply and plant	No.	1.08
Ilex aquifolium:		
supply only	No.	0.83
supply and plant	No.	1.12
Prunus laurocerasus (900 mm):		
supply only	No.	0.55

See Stop Press page vii: % additions to rates: September 1972 wage settlement

Notcutts 5 Star Landscape service.

Notcutts, East Anglia's leading landscape contractors and nurserymen, serve all Southern and Eastern England.

✳ Landscape and construction work of all types is carried out by our own skilled and experienced staff to the highest standards. Estimates promptly given.

✳ More than 2,000 varieties of plants are available in quantity from our own nurseries of over 240 acres. Book Catalogue considered as standard reference free on request.

✳ Deliveries are made by our own transport anywhere on the UK mainland.

✳ Our skilled landscape staff are particularly experienced in carrying out preparation and planting in all soil types and conditions.

✳ Our Advisers and Designers are always available to give technical advice on plant selection for all sites.

By appointment
to HM The Queen
Nurserymen

Notcutts Nurseries Ltd

Woodbridge, Suffolk.
Telephone Woodbridge 3344

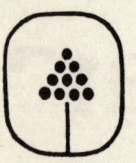

coblands nurseries limited

(incorporating arthur charlton & sons ltd.)

specialist shrub growers, landscape contractors and florists

amenity tree and shrub planting on any scale for private, public and industrial sites, and all facets of ornamental garden design and construction.

eridge road garden centre, tunbridge wells, kent.

tel: tunbridge wells 26326

ivy hatch, sevenoaks, kent. tel: plaxtol 284

TACCHI'S NURSERIES

Suppliers to Landscape trade
of low maintenance shrubs,
ground-covers, conifers,
roses and trees

Catalogue available on request

TACCHI'S NURSERIES
SHYTON, HUNTINGDON

Huntingdon (0480) 5338

Pricing—Plants and Planting

5.6.4 (cont'd)	Shrubs: root-balled continued	unit	£
	supply and plant	No.	0.84
	Prunus lusitanica:		
	supply only	No.	0.83
	supply and plant	No.	1.12
	Rhododendron – hybrids (750 mm):		
	supply only	No.	2.31
	supply and plant	No.	2.60
	Rhododendron –Ghent azalea:		
	supply only	No.	1.71
	supply and plant	No.	2.00
	Rhododendron – Japanese azalea (450 mm):		
	supply only	No.	1.21
	supply and plant	No.	1.50
	Viburnum rhytidophyllum:		
	supply only	No.	0.77
	supply and plant	No.	1.06
	Shrubs:pot grown		
	450 mm tall (unless otherwise shown). Supply only price is ex-nursery. Transporting assumed to be not exceeding 75 km		
	Arbutus unedo:		
	supply only	No.	0.77
	supply and plant	No.	0.95
	Buddleia davidii (750 mm):		
	supply only	No.	0.36
	supply and plant	No.	0.54
	Camelia japonica:		
	supply only	No.	1.10
	supply and plant	No.	1.28
	Chaenomeles japonica:		
	supply only	No.	0.36
	supply and plant	No.	0.54
	Cytisus praecox:		
	supply only	No.	0.41
	supply and plant	No.	0.59
	Escallonia 'Donard Seedling' (600 mm):		
	supply only	No.	0.33
	supply and plant	No.	0.51
	Genista hispanica (250 mm):		
	supply only	No.	0.33
	supply and plant	No.	0.51
	Hebe traversii:		
	supply only	No.	0.28
	supply and plant	No.	0.46
	Olearia haastii:		
	supply only	No.	0.39
	supply and plant	No.	0.57

See Stop Press page vii; % additions to rates; September 1972 wage settlement

Pricing–Plants and Planting

5.6.4
(cont'd)

Shrubs: pot grown continued

Viburnum tinus:

	unit	£
supply only	No.	0.61
supply and plant	No.	0.79

Shrubs: container-grown

600 mm tall (unless shown otherwise). Supply only price is ex-nursery. Transporting assumed to be not exceeding 75 km.

Acer palmatum 'Atropurpureum':

supply only	No.	1.47
supply and plant	No.	1.76

Amelanchier canadensis (900 mm):

supply only	No.	0.55
supply and plant	No.	0.84

Berberis thunbergii 'Atropurpurea':

supply only	No.	0.44
supply and plant	No.	0.73

Ilex aquifolium 'J. C. Van Thol':

supply only	No.	1.10
supply and plant	No.	1.39

Prunus lusitanica:

supply only	No.	1.00
supply and plant	No.	1.29

Rhus typhina 'Laciniata' (750 mm):

supply only	No.	0.50
supply and plant	No.	0.79

Spirea bumalda 'A. Waterer':

supply only	No.	0.36
supply and plant	No.	0.65

Viburnum burkwoodii:

supply only	No.	0.77
supply and plant	No.	1.06

Mulch to shrub beds:

peat:

50 mm thick	m^2	0.48
75 mm thick	m^2	0.71

peat mixed with 10% by bulk of bonemeal:

50 mm thick	m^2	0.68
75 mm thick	m^2	1.04

Weeding and maintenance of shrub beds

keeping shrub beds clear of weeds for one growing season and attention to shrubs as and when necessary (average 6 visits a year) . . m^2 0.52

Hedging plants

600 mm tall. Supply only price is ex-nursery.

See Stop Press page vii; % additions to rates; September 1972 wage settlement

5.6.4 (cont'd) **Hedging Plants** continued
Transporting assumed to be not exceeding 75 km.

	unit	£
Acer campestre:		
supply only	100 No.	11.00
supply and plant	100 No.	24.50
Carpinus betulus:		
supply only	100 No.	8.80
supply and plant	100 No.	22.30
Cotoneaster simonsii:		
supply only	100 No.	12.10
supply and plant	100 No.	25.60
Crataegus monogyna:		
supply only	100 No.	5.50
supply and plant	100 No.	19.00
Fagus sylvatica:		
supply only	100 No.	9.90
supply and plant	100 No.	23.40
Ligustrum ovalifolium:		
supply only	100 No.	9.35
supply and plant	100 No.	22.45
Lonicera nitida:		
supply only	100 No.	9.90
supply and plant	100 No.	23.40
Prunus laurocerasus 'Rotundifolia':		
supply only	100 No.	33.00
supply and plant	100 No.	46.50
Prunus spinosa:		
supply only	100 No.	9.90
supply and plant	100 No.	23.40

Shrubs – ground cover plants
2-year growth (pot grown where shown). Supply only price is ex-nursery. Transporting assumed to be not exceeding 75 km.

	unit	£
Berberis candidula (pot grown):		
supply only	No.	0.36
supply and plant	No.	0.42
Cotoneaster horizontalis (pot grown):		
supply only	No.	0.36
supply and plant	No.	0.42
Erica carnea (pot grown):		
supply only	No.	0.19
supply and plant	No.	0.35
Erica vagans (pot grown):		
supply only	No.	0.19
supply and plant	No.	0.35
Erica vulgaris (pot grown)		
supply only	No.	0.19

See Stop Press page vii; % additions to rates; September 1972 wage settlement

5.6.4 (cont'd)

Shrubs – ground cover plants continued		unit	£
supply and plant	. . . . .	No.	0.35
Euonymus radicans (pot grown):		
supply only	. . . . .	No.	0.19
supply and plant	. . . . .	No.	0.35
Hedera helix (pot grown):		
supply only	. . . . .	No.	0.22
supply and plant	. . . . .	No.	0.38
Hypericum calycinum (pot grown)		
supply only	. . . . .	No.	0.16
supply and plant	. . . . .	No.	0.32
Juniperus sabina tamariscifolia:		
supply only	. . . . .	No.	0.47
supply and plant	. . . . .	No.	0.63
Lavandula spica 'Hidcote':		
supply only	. . . . .	No.	0.11
supply and plant	. . . . .	No.	0.27
Mahonia aquifolium:		
supply only	. . . . .	No.	0.20
supply and plant	. . . . .	No.	0.36
Pachysandra terminalis:		
supply only	. . . . .	No.	0.17
supply and plant	. . . . .	No.	0.33
Prunus laurocerasus Zabelliana (balled):		
supply only	. . . . .	No.	0.33
supply and plant	. . . . .	No.	0.49
Santolina chamaecyparissus:		
supply only	. . . . .	No.	0.10
supply and plant	. . . . .	No.	0.26
Viburnum davidii (pot grown)		
supply only	. . . . .	No.	0.77
supply and plant	. . . . .	No.	0.93
Vinca major (pot grown):		
supply only	. . . . .	No.	0.17
supply and plant	. . . . .	No.	0.33
Vinca minor (pot grown):		
supply only	. . . . .	No.	0.17
supply and plant	. . . . .	No.	0.33

Climbing plants

750 mm tall, pot grown. Supply only price is ex-nursery. Transporting assumed to be not exceeding 75 km.

Campsis radicans: | | |
---|---|---|---
supply only | . . . . . | No. | 0.53
supply and plant | . . . . . | No. | 0.85
Clematis – Jackmanii group: | | |
supply only | . . . . . | No. | 0.44

See Stop Press page vii; % additions to rates; September 1972 wage settlement

Pricing—Plants and Planting

5.6.4 (cont'd)	Climbing plants continued		unit	£
	supply and plant		No.	0.76
	Clematis – Montana group:			
	supply only		No.	0.44
	supply and plant		No.	0.76
	Hedera hibernica:			
	supply only		No.	0.36
	supply and plant		No.	0.68
	Hydrangea petiolaris:			
	supply only		No.	0.88
	supply and plant		No.	1.20
	Lonicera japonica:			
	supply only		No.	0.39
	supply and plant		No.	0.71
	Polygonum baldschuanicum:			
	supply only		No.	0.33
	supply and plant		No.	0.65
	Vitis quinquefolia:			
	supply only		No.	0.41
	supply and plant		No.	0.73
	Wistaria sinensis:			
	supply only		No.	0.74
	supply and plant		No.	1.06
	Bulbs			
	Mixed crocus for naturalising:			
	supply only; per 100		No.	2.00
	supply only; per 1000		No.	17.00
	supply and plant; per 100		No.	2.78
	supply and plant; per 1000		No.	24.80
	Daffodils for naturalising:			
	supply only; per 100		No.	2.90
	supply only; per 1000		No.	21.90
	supply and plant; per 100		No.	4.07
	supply and plant; per 1000		No.	33.40

5.6.3	NURSERY STOCK, FOREST TREES IN ACCORDANCE WITH B.S.3936 Part 4:1966			
5.6.6	Planted in accordance with the appropriate clauses of B.S.4428:1969. Supply only price is ex-nursery. Transporting assumed as not exceeding 75 km.			
	Conifers: 200 mm tall			
	Larix decidua:			
	supply only		100 No.	1.20

See Stop Press page vii; % additions to rates; September 1972 wage settlement

5.6.6 (cont'd)	Conifers: 200 mm tall continued	unit	£
	supply and plant	100 No.	5.35
	Picea abies:		
	supply only	100 No.	1.27
	supply and plant	100 No.	5.42
	Pinus sylvestris:		
	supply only	100 No.	1.43
	supply and plant	100 No.	5.59
	Pinus nigra calabrica (corsicana)		
	supply only	100 No.	1.76
	supply and plant	100 No.	5.96
	Pseudotsuga taxifolia:		
	supply only	100 No.	1.87
	supply and plant	100 No.	6.08
	Tsuga heterophylla:		
	supply only	100 No.	1.65
	supply and plant	100 No.	5.84
	Deciduous; 300 mm tall		
	Acer platanoides:		
	supply only	100 No.	1.98
	supply and plant	100 No.	6.20
	Alnus incana:		
	supply only	100 No.	1.32
	supply and plant	100 No.	5.47
	Fagus sylvatica:		
	supply only	100 No.	2.20
	supply and plant	100 No.	6.44
	Quercus petraea:		
	supply only	100 No.	1.98
	supply and plant	100 No.	6.20
	Sorbus aucuparia:		
	supply only	100 No.	1.65
	supply and plant	100 No.	5.84

5.6.7   SEMI-MATURE TREES SUPPLIED AND PLANTED IN ACCORDANCE WITH B.S.4043:1966

5.6.7.37–44   **Guying and securing**
Methods of guying are specified in Chapter 5; 5.6.7.37–40 for overhead guying, 5.6.7.41–44 for underground securing. Planted price includes planting in excavated pit, measured elsewhere, refilling with soil from spoil heap incorporating manure. Supply only price is ex-nursery. Transporting assumed as not exceeding 75 km.

See Stop Press page vii; % additions to rates; September 1972 wage settlement

TREES STANDARD & SEMI-MATURE
12 feet to 20 feet

**MOUNTAIN ASH - WHITEBEAM - MAPLE
ELM - CHESTNUT - ROBINIA - PLANE
HORNBEAM - ASH - PRUNUS - LIME
BIRCH - ELDER etc.**

1. All trees have been pruned to make good specimens.
2. All trees are grown in compost to produce fibrous roots.
3. All trees are grown 10 to 15 feet apart to allow free development.
4. All the larger trees have been root pruned to facilitate transplanting.
5. All trees are lifted with a balled root and wrapped in canvas.

GERALD WILLIAMS
Crockham House, Westerham, Kent.
Telephone: Crockham Hill 215

LORD'S TREE SERVICES LTD

TREE SURGERY & FELLING

TREE PLANTING & MAINTENANCE

LANDSCAPING

FENCING

HEAD OFFICE
75 HARPUR STREET, BEDFORD
TEL. BEDFORD 59303 (3 LINES)

AREA OFFICE
55 LONDON ROAD HORSHAM
HORSHAM 32265

SEMI-MATURE TREES
and EXTRA LARGE NURSERY TREES —

STOCKS IN
TWENTY
COUNTIES

—

BRANCHES IN
BUCKINGHAMSHIRE
DERBYSHIRE
YORKSHIRE
GLOUCESTERSHIRE

—

WE SUPPLY,
DELIVER,
PLANT and
MAINTAIN

The courtyard separating the P&O and Commercial Union buildings in the City of London was landscaped by Civic Trees with 10 m high semi-mature Limes.

STOCK and PRICE LIST available from

CIVIC TREES
(TREE MOVERS) LIMITED

91 HIGH STREET, GREAT MISSENDEN, BUCKS.
Tel (03206) 3661

BRANCHES: Derby 42667, Barton (Yorks) 459

Semi-mature trees 7.500 m tall

	unit	£
Acer platanoides:		
supply only	No.	60.50
supply, plant and overhead guy	No.	80.00
supply, plant and underground secure	No.	83.00
Aesculus hippocastanum:		
supply only	No.	66.00
supply, plant and overhead guy	No.	85.50
supply, plant and underground secure	No.	88.50
Betula alba:		
supply only	No.	55.00
supply, plant and overhead guy	No.	74.50
supply, plant and underground secure	No.	77.50
Fagus sylvatica:		
supply only	No.	66.00
supply, plant and overhead guy	No.	85.50
supply, plant and underground secure	No.	88.50
Fraxinus excelsior:		
supply only	No.	60.50
supply, plant and overhead guy	No.	80.00
supply, plant and underground secure	No.	83.00
Platanus acerifolia:		
supply only	No.	66.00
supply, plant and overhead guy	No.	85.50
supply, plant and underground secure	No.	88.50
Prunus avium:		
supply only	No.	60.50
supply, plant and overhead guy	No.	80.00
supply, plant and underground secure	No.	83.00
Quercus robur:		
supply only	No.	66.00
supply, plant and overhead guy	No.	85.50
supply, plant and underground secure	No.	88.50
supply, plant and underground secure		
Salix vitellina pendula:		
supply only	No.	66.00
supply, plant and overhead guy	No.	85.50
supply, plant and underground secure	No.	88.50
Tilia euchlora:		
supply only	No.	66.00
supply, plant and overhead guy	No.	85.50
supply, plant and underground secure	No.	88.50

Semi-mature trees. 10.000 m tall

Acer platanoides:		
supply only	No.	110.00
supply, plant and overhead guy	No.	132.00
supply, plant and underground secure	No.	137.50

See Stop Press page vii; % additions to rates; September 1972 wage settlement

5.6.7.37–44 (cont'd)	**Semi-mature trees 10.000 m tall** *continued*	unit	£
	Betula alba:		
	supply only	No.	110.00
	supply, plant and overhead guy	No.	132.00
	supply, plant and underground secure	No.	137.50
	Fagus sylvatica:		
	supply only	No.	132.00
	supply, plant and overhead guy	No.	154.00
	supply, plant and underground secure	No.	159.50
	Fraxinus excelsior:		
	supply only	No.	110.00
	supply, plant and overhead guy	No.	132.00
	supply, plant and underground secure	No.	137.50
	Platanus acerifolia:		
	supply only	No.	132.00
	supply, plant and overhead guy	No.	154.00
	supply, plant and underground secure	No.	159.50
	Quercus robur:		
	supply only	No.	132.00
	supply, plant and overhead guy	No.	154.00
	supply, plant and underground secure	No.	159.50
	Tilia euchlora:		
	supply only	No.	132.00
	supply, plant and overhead guy	No.	154.00
	supply, plant and underground secure	No.	159.50
	Mulch		
5.6.7.24	peat mulch 50 mm thick to circle of 90 mm around tree	No.	0.45
	Wrapping		
5.6.7.27	wrapping of trunk with hessian up to height of 3.000 m	No.	6.50
	Anti-desiccant spray		
5.6.7.16	spray tree with spray in accordance with manufacturers instructions:		
	to tree of 7.500 m	No.	0.50–1.00
	to tree of 10.000 m	No.	1.00–2.00
	(price varies according to species and season)		

See Stop Press page vii; % additions to rates; September 1972 wage settlement

Many heads are better than one

Mathematically. BASAL is the sum of experience, professionalism and know-how that is yours when you call on any member.

Effectively. BASAL is a group of the leading contractors throughout the country, admitted on merit and bound together by a professional association which in turn is affiliated internationally.

Practically. BASAL is the pooling of ideas, techniques and developments for the mutual benefit of our clients and ourselves. Sports grounds, parks, landscaping, afforestation, from concept through realisation to upkeep. However large or small your project, at whatever stage, BASAL is available to channel your enquiry to the right source.

For further information on our work or members contact the secretary, W.F.P. Bishop

British Association of Sportsground and Landscape Contractors

87 London Road, Croydon, CR0 2RF
Telephone: 01-688 3681

BASAL

TILHILL
Landscaping Services

Specialists in landscaping developments in the public and private sectors of the construction industry.

Tree and Shrub Planting
Turfing and Seeding
Fencing
Contract Maintenance
Sports Grounds
Tree Surgery
Site Clearance
Rock Gardens
Paving and Walling

Our own extensive Nurseries carry a wide range of planting stocks up to semi-mature size and ensure availability and quality control.

TILHILL LANDSCAPING SERVICES
(Member of the Tilhill Group)
'Greenhills', Tilford, Farnham, Surrey. Tel: Frensham 3265

Gavin Jones Nurseries Limited

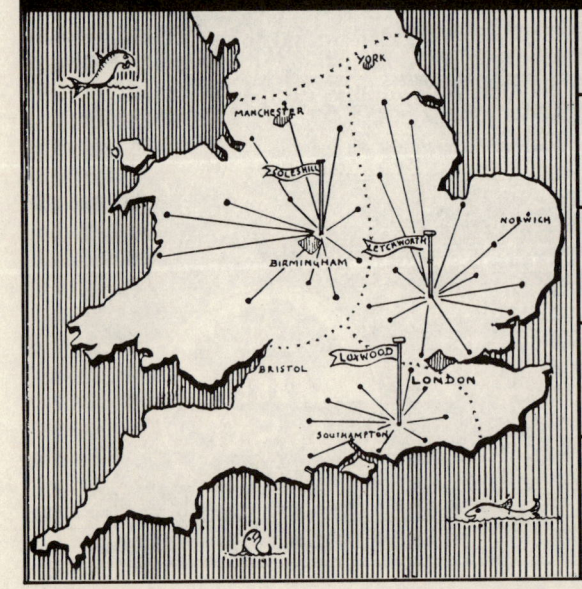

LANDSCAPE CONTRACTORS AND NURSERYMEN ORGANISED TO COVER A WIDE FIELD

HEAD OFFICE AND NURSERIES
BALDOCK ROAD
LETCHWORTH, HERTS
Phone: LETCHWORTH 3663

MIDLAND DIVISION
GRIMSTOCK HILL
COLESHILL, BIRMINGHAM
Phone: COLESHILL 63525

SOUTHERN DIVISION
4 BURLEY CLOSE, LOXWOOD
BILLINGSHURST, SUSSEX
Phone: LOXWOOD 629

We offer a service of the highest standard, backed by practical experience and sound organisation. We invite enquiries at any of the above addresses

Pricing—Enclosure

			unit	£
7.7	**ENCLOSURE**			
	All clause numbers refer to the specification paragraphs in Chapter 5, except where reference is made to Chapter 6.			
5.7.2	**SCREEN WALLS**			
	Copings to freestanding walls			
	Drawings of copings			
5.7.2.1	Key numbers refer to illustrations in Chapter 6 and prices are inclusive of bedding and pointing as shown on each drawing:			
6.5.7.1	blue-black engineering brick laid on edge		m	2.07
6.5.7.2	blue-black bullnose engineering brick, on edge		m	2.25
6.5.7.3	brick on edge with projecting tile creasing:			
	engineering brick — rectangular		m	3.68
	engineering brick — bullnose		m	3.87
	hard stock brick		m	3.33
6.5.7.4	brick on edge with flush tile creasing:			
	engineering brick — rectangular		m	3.79
	engineering brick — bullnose		m	3.96
	hard stock brick		m	3.37
6.5.7.5	300 mm wide weathered clayware		m	3.64
6.5.7.6	300 mm wide saddle-back clayware		m	5.03
6.5.7.7	325 mm wide flat metal coping (16 g):			
	zinc		m	2.09
	aluminium		m	1.95
6.5.7.8	300 mm wide weathered slate		m	9.85
	alternative for 38 mm thick slate		m	7.81
6.5.7.9	300 mm wide saddle-back precast concrete		m	3.17
6.5.7.10	300 mm wide weathered precast concrete		m	3.13
6.5.7.11	300 mm wide saddle-back slate		m	10.01
	alternative for 38 mm thick slate		m	7.97
6.5.7.12	300 mm wide flat slate		m	9.67
	alternative for 38 mm thick slate		m	7.63
5.7.3	**RETAINING WALLS**			
	Copings to retaining walls			
	Drawings of copings			
5.7.3.1	Key numbers refer to illustrations in Chapter 6 and prices are inclusive of bedding and pointing as shown on each drawing:			
6.5.7.13	300 mm wide weathered precast concrete coping with 300 mm wide precast concrete mowing			

See Stop Press page vii; % additions to rates; September 1972 wage settlement

Pricing–Enclosure

		unit	£
6.5.7.13 (cont'd)	*Drawings of copings* continued margin to B.S.368:1971	m	3.83
6.5.7.14	300 mm wide weathered precast concrete coping	m	2.57
6.5.7.15	225 mm × 150mm precast conrete coping; in standard natural grey conrete	m	4.10
	in reconstructed stone	m	4.47
6.5.7.16	300 mm wide flat precast concrete coping with 300 mm wide precast concrete mowing margin to B.S.368:1971	m	3.86
6.5.7.17	300 mm wide flat precast concrete coping	m	2.60
6.5.7.18	225 mm wide brick on edge coping:		
	engineering brick – bullnose	m	1.88
	engineering brick – rectangular	m	2.10
	hard stock brick	m	1.72

5.7.4 TRAFFIC BARRIERS

Moveable bollards

Borer Engineering Company

5.7.4.1	'Borer' telescopic lockable steel post; supplied and fixed:		
	in quantity up to 9 no.	No.	12.54
	in quantity from 10–49 no.	No.	11.66
	in quantity over 50 no.	No.	10.73

Le Bas Tube Company Limited

5.7.4.2	'AutopA' collapsible hinged steel post: supplied and fixed:		
	in quantity up to 4 no.	No.	12.65
	in quantity from 5–20 no.	No.	11.55
	in quantity from 21–100 no.	No.	10.45

Fixed bollards

Atlas Stone Company Limited

5.7.4.3	concrete bollard: 330 mm high, supplied and set in concrete in ground:		
	grey finish	No.	7.15
	white finish	No.	8.03

Bloc Products

5.7.4.4	'Gamma' concrete bollard, triangular, white, supplied and set in concrete in ground	No.	8.25
	Ditto; grey	No.	7.43

See Stop Press page vii; % additions to rates; September 1972 wage settlement

		unit	£
	Concrete Utilities Limited		
5.7.4.5	'Enfield' concrete bollard, 838 mm high, supplied and set in concrete in ground:		
	natural finish	No.	7.70
	Mather & Smith Limited		
5.7.4.6	cast iron; traditional bollard, supplied and set in concrete in ground	No.	20.90
	Mono Concrete Limited		
5.7.4.7	concrete bollards; various types of which ones below are typical, supplied and set in concrete in ground:		
	'Bridgford'; smooth grey	No.	10.76
	'Bridgford'; mineralite finish	No.	20.06
	'Truro'; smooth grey	No.	14.63
	'Truro'; mineralite finish	No.	35.55
	'Wexham'; exposed aggregate	No.	14.11
	'Wexham major'; exposed aggregate	No.	22.55

Crash barriers

	Standard safety barrier		
5.7.4.8	600 mm high corrugated sheet steel fender, on softwood posts, fixed	m	4.50
	British Aluminium Company Limitied		
5.7.4.9	'Baco Parapet 1'; alluminium alloy, three horizontal rails, fixed	m	18.70
5.7.4.10	'Baco Parapet 2'; aluminium alloy, three horizontal rails and mesh, fixed	m	22.06
	British Steel Corporation		
5.7.4.11	'Group P.1'; steel barrier of rectangular hollow sections with three horizontal rails, fixed (galvanised)	m	16.18

Pedestrian guard rails

	Abacus Municipal Limited		
5.7.4.12	pedestrian barrier; steel to B.S.3049; galvanised finish, fixed	m	6.49
	Highfield Engineering (Telford) Co. Ltd.		
5.7.14.13	pedestrian barrier; steel, galvanised finish, fixed	m	9.93

See Stop Press page vii; % additions to rates; September 1972 wage settlement

Pricing–Enclosure

Pedestrian guard rails continued

		unit	£

Norman & Sons (Marketing) Limited

5.7.4.14 pedestrian barrier; steel to B.S.3049; galvanised finish, fixed . . . . m 8.21

Street Furniture Limited

5.7.4.15 'Dura-Rail X'; aluminium pedestrian guard rail;
- natural finish . . . . . . m 13.75
- bronze . . . . m 26.40

Low rails

Drawings of typical softwood timber low rails:
as drawings 6.5.7.19–22 in Chapter 6

5.7.4.16 Specification details as on drawings, with all rails supplied and fixed in ground; key numbers refer to illustrations in Chapter 6.

6.5.7.19 200 mm × 38 mm softwood rail, painted, including screwing to uprights . . . m 0.93
100 mm × 100 mm softwood post, painted, including excavation and concrete base . No. 1.08
complete post and rail as on drawing for runs of 10.000 m – 100.000 m . . . m 2.01

6.5.7.20 200 mm × 38 mm softwood rail, painted, including bolting to fixing plates . . m 1.16
50 mm × 50 mm square m.s. upright, including welded plate drilled to take bolts and including excavation and concrete base . No. 2.10
complete post and rail as on drawing for runs of 10.000 m – 100.000 m . . . m 2.56

6.5.7.21 100 mm × 100 mm softwood rail, painted, including m.s. strap fixing to posts . . m 1.37
100 mm × 100 mm softwood upright, painted, including excavation and concrete base . No. 1.08
complete post and rail as on drawing for runs of 10.000 m – 100.000 m . . . m 2.45

6.5.7.22 200 mm × 38 mm softwood rail, painted including mastic jointing and screwing to posts . . m 1.52
100 mm × 100 mm softwood upright, painted, including excavation and concrete base . No. 1.08
complete post and rail, as on drawing for runs of 10.000 m – 100.000 m . . . m 2.60

Drawings of typical hardwood timber low rails;
as drawings 6.5.7.23–26 in Chapter 6

5.7.4.17 Specification details as on drawings, with all rails supplied and fixed in ground; key numbers refer to illustrations in Chapter 6.

See Stop Press page vii; % additions to rates; September 1972 wage settlement

Pricing—Enclosure

		unit	£
6.5.7.23	150 mm × 50 mm western red cedar rail, oiled, including screwing to posts	m	1.10
	100 mm × 75 mm western red cedar, oiled, upright, including rebate for rail, excavation and concrete base	No.	1.50
	complete post and rail, as on drawing, for runs of 10.000 m – 100.000 m	m	2.60
6.5.7.24	150 mm × 75 mm oak rail, rebated to receive uprights, including m.s. angle and screw fixing	m	2.20
	100 mm × 100 mm oak upright including excavation and concrete base	No.	1.36
	complete post and rail, as on drawing, for runs of 10.000 m – 100.000 m	m	3.56
6.5.7.25	composite rail of 3 No. 125 mm × 38 mm western red cedar members, oiled, screwed to uprights	m	2.75
	100 mm × 100 mm western red cedar upright, oiled, including rebates for rails, excavation and concrete base	No.	1.61
	complete post and rail, as on drawing for runs of 10.000 m – 100.000 m	m	4.36
6.5.7.26	150 mm × 100 mm oak rail including mastic jointing and bolting to posts	m	2.24
	200 mm × 150 mm oak upright driven into firm ground	No.	3.80
	complete post and rail, as on drawing for runs of 10.000 m – 100.000 m	m	6.04

Drawings of typical metal low rails;

5.7.4.18	as drawings 6.5.7.27–34 in Chapter 6 Specification details as on drawings, with all rails supplied and fixed in ground; key numbers refer to illustrations in Chapter 6.		
6.5.7.27	38 mm internal diam. m.s. tube rail with sleeved joint, galvanised, including fixing to uprights	m	0.82
	38 mm internal diam. m.s. tube post, galvanised, including excavation and concrete base	No.	2.00
	complete post and rail as on drawing for runs of 10.000 m – 100.000 m	m	2.63
6.5.7.28	50 mm × 9 mm m.s. rail screwed to 40 mm × 40 mm × 6 mm m.s plate, galvanised including welding to uprights	m	0.33
	19 mm internal diam. m.s tubular upright, galvanised, including excavation and concrete base	No.	1.53
	complete post and rail as on drawing for runs of 10.000 m – 100.000 m	m	1.66
6.5.7.29	22 mm diam. m.s. rail, galvanised, with ferrule joints fixed to standards	m	0.86

See Stop Press page vii; % additions to rates; September 1972 wage settlement

Pricing—Enclosure

		unit	£
6.5.7.29 (cont'd)	**Drawings of typical metal low rails** continued 44 mm × 13 mm m.s. standard, galvanised, including excavation and concrete base	No.	1.68
	complete post and rail as on drawings for runs of 10.000 – 100.000 m	m	2.22
6.5.7.30	22 mm diam. m.s. rail, galvanised, with ferrule joints fixed to standards	m	0.86
	44 mm × 13 mm m.s. curved standard, galvanised, including excavation and concrete base	No.	2.09
	complete post and rail as on drawing for runs of 10.000 m – 100.000 m	m	2.55
6.5.7.31	75 mm × 50 mm × 13 mm m.s channel, galvanised, bolted to timber uprights	m	6.53
	75 mm × 75 mm softwood post, including excavation and concrete base	No.	1.61
	complete post and rail as on drawing for runs of 10.000 m – 100.000 m	m	8.25
6.5.7.32	32 mm square section m.s. tube, galvanised, welded to standard	m	0.81
	32 mm square section m.s. tube standard, galvanised, including excavation and concrete base	No.	2.15
	complete post and rail as on drawing for runs of 10.000 m – 100.000 m	m	2.68
	38 mm square section hollow m.s tube, galvanised, set diagonally and welded to standards	m	1.10
	38 mm square section hollow m.s. tube, galvanised, including excavation and concrete base	No.	2.58
	complete post and rail as on drawing for runs of 10.000 m – 100.000 m	m	3.24
6.5.7.34	19 mm square m.s. rail, galvanised, set diagonally with ferrule joints and fixed to standards	m	0.88
	76 mm × 51 mm 'I' section m.s. standards, galvanised, including excavation and concrete base	No.	3.71
	complete post and rail as on drawing for runs of 10.000 m – 100.000 m	m	3.93

Drawings of timber fences;
as drawings 6.5.7.35–43 in Chapter 6

5.7.5.2	Specification details as on drawings, with all fences supplied and fixed in ground; key numbers refer to illustrations in Chapter 6.
6.5.7.35	four rail fence 1.200 m high, with 150 mm × 75 mm posts at 2.750 m centres driven into ground and intermediate prick posts; complete fence as drawing for runs 25.000 m – 200.000 m:

See Stop Press page vii; % additions to rates; September 1972 wage settlement

Pricing–Enclosure

			unit	£
6.5.7.35 (cont'd)	*Drawings of timber fences continued*			
	in oak		m	2.08
	in western red cedar		m	3.82
6.5.7.36	two rail fence, 750 mm high, with 100 mm × 100 mm posts at 1.300 m centres, including excavation and concrete base; complete fence as drawing for runs 25.000 m – 200.000 m:			
	in oak		m	3.42
	in western red cedar		m	4.95
	in softwood, primed for painting		m	3.92
	in softwood, pressure treated		m	3.20
6.5.7.37	three rail fence, 1.200 m high, with 100 mm × 75 mm cleft arris rails mortised into 150 mm × 75 mm posts at 2.750 m centres, driven into the ground; complete fence as drawing for runs 25.000 m – 200.000 m:			
	in oak		m	2.10
6.5.7.38	'hit and miss' horizontal rail fence, 2.000 m high, with 100 × 100 mm posts at 1.800 m centres or at 2.500 m centres with spacing piece 100 × 100 mm between each post; including excavation and concrete base; complete fence as drawing, for runs 25.000 m – 200.000 m:			
	posts at 1.800 m centres:			
	in western red cedar		m	13.57
	in softwood primed for painting		m	9.24
	in softwood, pressure treated		m	8.79
	posts at 2.500 m centres;			
	in western red cedar		m	14.69
	in softwood, primed for painting		m	9.75
	in softwood, pressure treated		m	9.25
6.5.7.39	horizontal rail fence, 2.000 m high, with 100 mm × 100 mm posts at 1.800 m centres; including excavation and concrete base; complete fence as drawing for runs 25.000 m – 200.000 m:			
	in western red cedar		m	11.00
	in softwood, primed for painting		m	7.12
	in softwood, pressure treated		m	6.78
6.5.7.40	'hit and miss' horizontal rail fence, 1.800 m high, with 100 mm × 100 mm posts at 1.800 m centres; including excavation and concrete base; complete fence as drawing, for runs 25.000 m – 200.000 m			
	in oak		m	5.01
	in western red cedar		m	9.05
6.5.7.41	'hit and miss' vertical rail fence, 1.800 m high, in frames bolted to 125 mm × 75 mm posts at 1.745 m centres; including excavation and concrete base; complete fence as drawing, for runs 25.000 m – 200.000 m:			

See Stop Press page vii; % additions to rates; September 1972 wage settlement

Pricing—Enclosure

		unit	£
6.5.7.41 (cont'd)	**Drawings of timber fences** *continued*		
	in oak	m	12.09
	in western red cedar	m	18.85
6.5.7.42	vertical close-boarded fence, 1.800 m high, with 125 mm × 100 mm posts at 2.750 m centres; including excavation and concrete base; complete fence, as drawing, for runs 25.000 m – 200.00 m:		
	in oak	m	6.50
	in western red cedar	m	11.50
6.5.7.43	narrow vertical slatted fence, 1.800 m high, with 150 mm × 100 mm posts at 2.750 m centres; including excavation and concrete base; complete fence, as drawing, for runs 25.000 m – 200.000 m:		
	in oak	m	6.50
	in western red cedar	m	11.50
	Drawings of metal fences; as drawings 6.5.7.44–47 in Chapter 6		
5.7.5.3	Specification details as on drawings with all fences supplied and fixed in ground; key numbers refer to illustrations in Chapter 6.		
6.5.7.44	1.200 m high steel fence with m.s balusters at 115 mm centres and 51 mm square hollow section m.s. standards at 2.000 m centres; including excavation and concrete base; complete fence, as drawing, for runs 25.000 m – 200.000 m;		
	galvanised finish	m	13.82
	primed for painting	m	10.63
6.5.7.45	1.200 m high steel fence with railing verticals at 130 mm centres and 25 mm square hollow section m.s standards at 900 mm centres; including excavation and concrete base; complete fence, as drawing, for runs 25.000 m – 200.000 m:		
	galvanised finish	m	15.00
	primed for painting	m	12.50
6.5.7.46	1.200 m high 5 bar horizontal steel fence 38 mm × 10 mm joiner standards at 4.500 m centres and 38 mm × 8 mm intermediate standards at 900 mm centres; including excavation and concrete base; complete fence system, as drawing, for runs 25.000 m – 200.000 m:		
	galvanised finish	m	6.83
	primed for painting	m	5.72
	extra over for 76 mm diameter m.s. end and corner posts:		
	galvanised finish	No.	8.62

See Stop Press page vii; % additions to rates; September 1972 wage settlement

CAMLAND

ADVISORY — Land Surveys for — Development, Reclamation, Evaluation, Planning, Irrigation.
Land Drainage — Surveys, Preparation of Plans, Bills of Quantities and Supervision to Completion. Product Development, Soil and Plant Programming.

AND

ANALYSIS — Soil, Topsoil (B.S.I.) Plants, Water Supply, Waste Water, Organic Manures, Fertilisers: Eelworm.

SERVICE — Details from
Camland, Fowlmere, Royston, Herts. SG8 7TD
Telephone: Fowlmere 286, STD 076-382 286

For all types of Steel Fencing, Pedestrian Guardrail and Bridge Railings
consult
THE BAYLISS FENCING & GATE DIVISION
of

Highfield Engineering (Telford) Co. Ltd.,
Haldane, Halesfield, TELFORD, Salop, TF7 4LR
Telephone; Telford 586477 (STD Code 0952)

Successors to Bayliss Jones & Bayliss Fencing Division of G.K.N. Machinery Ltd.
(Fencing manufacturers for over 140 Years)

Griffin and Legg

LANDSCAPE CONTRACTORS TO THE CONSTRUCTION INDUSTRY

Willaston Wirral Cheshire L64 1SP
051-327 4241/2

Pricing—Enclosure

			unit	£
6.5.7.46 (cont'd)	**Drawings of metal fences** continued primed for painting		No.	6.67
6.5.7.47	1.200 m high 5 bar horizontal steel fence with m.s. coping and 38 mm square hollow section m.s. standards at 1.800 m centres; including excavation and concrete base; complete fence system, as drawing, for runs 25.000 m – 200.000 m:			
	galvanised finish		m	17.24
	primed for painting		m	13.34
	Drawings of gates: as drawings 6.5.7.48–49 in Chapter 6.			
5.7.5.4	Specification details as on drawings, with all gates supplied and fixed complete with posts and ironmongery.			
6.5.7.48	1.400 m high five bar horizontal gate with opening width between posts at 3.000 m; gate posts 200 mm square set in ground, including excavation:			
	in oak		No.	28.00
6.5.7.49	1.400 m high six bar horizontal steel gate with opening width between oak posts at 3.000 m; gate posts 200 mm square set in ground, including excavation:			
	galvanised finish		No.	43.00
	primed for painting		No.	33.00

Temporary protective fencing

5.7.5.5   See 'Preparatory Operations' section 7.1 for prices of various types.

Standard fencing (not shown in drawings)

Concrete slab fencing

		unit	Height of fence		
			1.220 m £	1.520 m £	1.830 m £
5.7.5.6	slab panels between concrete twice grooved posts, set in ground, including base and excavation; for runs 25.000 m–200.000 m .	m	4.95	5.85	7.15

Timber picket fence

5.7.5.7   vertical softwood picket fence in softwood, primed for painting including posts and their

See Stop Press page vii; % additions to rates; September 1972 wage settlement

5.7.5.7 (cont'd)	**Timber Picket fence** continued bases and excavation, for runs 25.000 m – 200.000 m	unit m	£ 2.58		

Timber close boarded with concrete posts

		unit	\multicolumn{4}{c}{Height of fence}
			915 mm £	1.070 m £	1.220 m £	1.373 m £
5.7.5.8	oak pales, lapped, on two rails with conrete posts, including bases and excavation; for runs 25.000 m – 200.000 m	m	4.10	4.20	4.50	4.68

		unit	\multicolumn{2}{c}{Height of fence}	
			1.675 m £	1.830 m £
5.7.5.9	as above, with three rails and concrete posts	m	6.00	6.15

Timber close boarded with timber posts

		unit	\multicolumn{3}{c}{Height of fence}		
			1.070 m £	1.375 m £	1.830 m £
5.7.5.10	oak pales, lapped on two rails with oak posts, including bases and excavation; for runs 25.000 m – 200.000 m	m	2.75	3.10	–
5.7.5.11	as above with three rails and oak posts	m	–	–	4.55

Interwoven timber panels; overlap

		unit	\multicolumn{3}{c}{Height of fence}		
			610 mm £	1.220 m £	1.830 m £
5.7.5.12	standard panels in creosoted softwood with creosoted softwood posts; for runs 25.000 m – 200.000 m	m	1.68	2.25	2.75
	standard panels in western red cedar with sawn oak posts; for runs 25.000 m – 200.000 m	m	2.05	2.50	3.50

Interwoven timber panels; interlace:

		unit	\multicolumn{3}{c}{Height of fence}		
			610 m £	1.220 m £	1.830 m £
5.7.5.13	standard panels in creosoted softwood with creosoted posts; for runs 25.000 m–200.000 m	m	1.80	2.40	2.95
	standard panels in western red cedar with sawn oak posts; for runs 25.000 m–200.000 m	m	2.17	2.65	3.70

See Stop Press page vii; % additions to rates; September 1972 wage settlement

Pricing—Enclosure

Wrought iron railings

		unit	Height of fence		
			1.220 m	1.830 m	2.140 m
			£	£	£
5.7.5.14	traditional pattern; spiked tops; including excavation and concrete bases; for runs 25.000 m–200.000 m	m	9.00	12.50	14.50

		unit	Height of fence		
			1.220 m	1.375 m	1.525 m
			£	£	£
5.7.5.15	traditional park type; hooped tops; including excavation and concrete bases; for runs 25.000 m – 200.000 m	m	10.00	13.50	15.50

Strained wire; three lines and concrete posts

		unit	Height of fence			
			915 mm	1.070 m	1.220 m	1.375 m
			£	£	£	£
5.7.5.16	three lines of plain wire and concrete posts; including excavation and back-filling for runs 25.000 m–200.000 m	m	0.67	0.68	0.80	0.89
	extra for galvanised barbed wire in place of plain wire	m	0.13	0.13	0.13	0.13
			£	£	£	£
5.7.5.17	extra for concrete straining corner post with one strut; including excavation and back filling	No.	3.98	4.10	4.45	4.80
5.7.5.18	extra for concrete straining corner post with two struts; including excavation and back filling	No.	5.90	6.15	6.50	6.80

Strained wire; five lines and concrete posts

5.7.5.19	as 5.7.5.4 but with five horizontal wires; for runs 25.000 m–200.000 m	m	0.82	0.83	0.95	1.04
	extra for galvanised barbed wire in place of plain wire	m	0.21	0.21	0.21	0.21

Chain link fencing on concrete posts

5.7.5.20 51 mm mesh galvanised m.s. chain link and concrete setting posts; including excava-

See Stop Press page vii; % additions to rates; September 1972 wage settlement

Pricing—Enclosure

5.7.5.20 (cont'd) Chain link fencing on concrete posts continued

Ref	Description	unit	915 mm	1.220 m	1.830 m
	tion and back filling; for runs 25.000 m–200.000 m	m	1.30	1.50	2.25
5.7.5.21	extra for aluminium alloy line and tying wires	m	0.30	0.50	1.00
5.7.5.22	extra for concrete straining corner post with one strut including excavation and back filling	No.	4.02	4.45	6.30
5.7.5.23	extra for concrete straining post with two struts; including excavation and back filling	No.	6.25	6.90	9.35

Height of fence applies to the three right-hand columns.

Chain link fencing on steel angle posts

Ref	Description	unit	915 mm	1.220 m	1.830 m
5.7.5.24	51 mm mesh galvanised m.s. chain link and galvanised m.s. angle posts: including excavation and back filling; for runs 25.000 m–200.000 m	m	1.40	1.70	2.30
5.7.5.25	extra for aluminium alloy line and tying wires	m	0.44	0.76	1.12
5.7.5.26	extra for m.s. angle corner straining post with one angle strut; including excavation and back filling	No.	4.50	5.20	6.50
5.7.5.27	extra for m.s angle corner straining post with two angle struts; including excavation and back filling	No.	7.45	7.70	9.50

Tennis court surround

5.7.5.28 standard assembly of galvanised chain link or m.s. angle framework for tennis court, size 36.000 m × 18.000 m, with one gate:

Description	unit	£
fencing 2.745 m high with standards at 3.660 centres	No.	335.00
fencing 3.660 m high with standards at 2.745 m centres	No.	455.00

Some typical fencing systems

Concrete

Bell & Webster Limited

5.7.5.29 'Belcon' solid panel fence in natural grey finish including concrete base and excavation

See Stop Press page vii; % additions to rates; September 1972 wage settlement

Pricing–Enclosure

Bell & Webster Limited *continued*

	unit	\multicolumn{3}{c}{Height of fence}	
		915 mm £	1.830 m £	2.520 m £
for runs up to 25.000 m	m	5.20	8.23	10.02
for runs up to 25.000 m–50.000 m . . .	m	4.48	7.34	9.47
for runs over 100.000 m	m	4.10	6.68	8.92

5.7.5.30 **Ebor Fencing Limited**
Type PLI solid concrete panel fence with weather-board profile on one side; for runs 25.000 m–200.000 m; including concrete base for posts and excavation:

	unit	915 mm £	1.830 m £	2.750 m £
sandfaced texture . .	m	14.05	26.00	36.63
exposed aggregate . .	m	17.68	33.25	48.85

5.7.5.31 **Marley Buildings Ltd.**
ranch walling; reinforced concrete with exposed aggregate concrete finish on one side only; for runs 25.000 m–200.000 m; including concrete base and excavation . . . .

unit	\multicolumn{3}{c}{Height of fence}		
	915 mm £	1.375 m £	1.830 m £
m	5.74	7.23	8.78

P.V.C. Fencing

5.7.5.32 **P. J. P. Trading Limited**
'Intrad' horizontal P.V.C. rails on P.V.C. covered steel posts set 500 mm into ground; for runs 25.000 m–200.000 m; including concrete base and excavations to posts . .
as above on concrete posts .

unit	\multicolumn{3}{c}{Height of fence}		
	800 mm £	1.200 m £	1.900 m £
m	5.20	8.50	13.10
m	5.15	8.38	13.35

Plastic coated chain link

5.7.5.33 **Colorguard Limited**
vinyl-coated chain link and rectangular hollow section posts; typical examples with

See Stop Press page vii; % additions to rates; September 1972 wage settlement

5.7.5.33 (cont'd) **Colorguard Limited** continued posts set in ground including excavation and concrete base for runs 25.000 m–200.000 m and average number of corner (square) posts:

	unit	Height of fence		
		900 mm £	1.800 m £	2.800 m £
anti-intruder type; 50 mm mesh and 3.55 mm gauge core, with posts at 3.000 m centres	m	3.95	5.75	8.00
multi-purpose type; 50 mm mesh and 3.55 mm gauge core, with posts at 3.000 m centres	m	3.95	5.75	8.00

tennis court type:	unit	Height of fence		
		2.800 m £	3.250 m £	3.600 m £
45 mm mesh and 3.15 mm gauge core, with posts at 3.000 m centres	m	7.35	7.88	9.00

See Stop Press page vii; % additions to rates; September 1972 wage settlement

7.8 HARD GROUND FINISHES   unit   £

All clause numbers refer to the specification paragraphs in Chapter 5, except where reference is made to Chapter 6.

5.8.2 PREPARATORY ITEMS

For paving, paths and roads

Excavation by hand
excavate, depositing in spoil heaps not exceeding 100 m from excavation works:

	unit	£
average 100 mm deep	m^2	0.29
average 125 mm deep	m^2	0.36
average 150 mm deep	m^2	0.43
average 175 mm deep	m^2	0.50
average 200 mm deep	m^2	0.58
average 250 mm deep	m^2	0.72
average 300 mm deep	m^2	0.86
excavate to reduce levels over 300 mm deep, depositing in spoil heaps not exceeding 100 m from excavation works	m^3	2.60
disposal of surplus excavated material, removing from site to tip not exceeding 15 km from site	m^3	2.14

Excavation by machine
excavate, depositing in spoil heaps not more than 100 m from excavation works:

	unit	£
average 100 mm deep	m^2	0.09
average 150 mm deep	m^2	0.14
average 200 mm deep	m^2	0.18
average 250 mm deep	m^2	0.23
average 300 mm deep	m^2	0.28
excavate to reduce levels over 300 mm deep depositing in spoil heaps not more than 100 m from excavation works	m^3	0.76
disposal of surplus excavated material, removing from site to tip not exceeding 15 km from site	m^3	2.03

5.8.2.15 *Hardcore*

provide, fill and make up levels:

	unit	£
average 75 mm thick	m^2	0.37
average 100 mm thick	m^2	0.43
average 150 mm thick	m^2	0.57
average 200 mm thick	m^2	0.72
average 250 mm thick	m^2	0.90
average 300 mm thick	m^2	1.02

See Stop Press page vii; % additions to rates; September 1972 wage settlement

5.8.2.15 (cont'd)	**Hardcore** *continued* provide, fill and make up levels over 300 mm thick; depositing and compacting in layers by 5 tonne rollers	*unit* m^3	£ 3.00
	surface of hardcore; levelling, blinding, compacting by 5 tonne roller	m^2	0.12
	Coarse ashes provide, fill and make up levels:		
	average 75 mm thick	m^2	0.30
	average 100 mm thick	m^2	0.39
	average 150 mm thick	m^2	0.53
	average 200 mm thick	m^2	0.72
	average 250 mm thick	m^2	0.85
	average 300 mm thick	m^2	1.00
	provide, fill and make up levels over 300 mm thick; depositing and compacting in layers by 5 tonne rollers	m^3	3.24
	surface of coarse ashes; levelling, grading to cambers, compacting by 5 tonne roller . .	m^2	0.13
5.8.2.16	***Blinding*** blind hardcore with 50 mm of sharp sand . .	m^2	0.18
	blind hardcore with 50 mm of 1:2:4 mix concrete	m^2	0.64
	blind hardcore with 50 mm fine ashes . .	m^2	0.16

5.8.3	**KERBS AND EDGINGS**		
	Precast concrete		
5.8.3.1	***To B.S.340*** kerb; 250 × 125 mm rectangular (figure 2 in B.S.) haunched with in-situ concrete on one side	m	1.04
	kerb; as above but curved to mean radius 5.000 m	m	1.44
	edging; 150 × 50 mm (fingure 11 in B.S.) haunched with in-situ concrete on both sides .	m	0.75
	channel; 250 × 125 mm (figure 8 in B.S.) bedding and jointing in 1:3 cement mortar		1.06
	channel; as above but curved to mean radius 5.000 m	m	1.46

See Stop Press page vii; % additions to rates; September 1972 wage settlement

Granite and whinstone unit £

5.8.3.2 **To B.S.435**
kerb; 250 × 125 mm haunched with in-situ
concrete on one side . . . . . m 5.28
kerb; as above but curved to mean radius
5.000 m . . . . m 5.83

Sandstone

5.8.3.3 **To B.S.706**
kerb; yorkstone 250 mm × 150 mm haunched
with in-situ concrete on one side . . . m 9.13
kerb; yorkstone as above but curved to mean
radius 5.000 m . . . . . . m 15.17

Drawings of typical kerbs and edgings

As drawings 6.5.8.1–7
5.8.3.10 For detailed specification of materials used
see Chapter 5 section 8. Key numbers refer to
illustrations in Chapter 6 and prices are
inclusive of all excavation, base and bedding
as shown on each drawing. Path materials are
priced separately.

6.5.8.1 second hand granite setts . . . . m 1.34
 alternative; new granite setts . . . m 1.48
6.5.8.2 150 mm × 50 mm hardwood edge board . . m 1.31
 alternative; fixed with pegs only, no concrete
 bed and haunching . . . . . m 0.97
6.5.8.3 250 mm × 125 mm precast concrete upright
 kerbs to B.S.340 . . . . . . m 1.92
6.5.8.4 250 mm × 125 mm precast concrete flat kerb to
 B.S.340 . . . . m 1.50
6.5.8.5 250 mm × 50 mm precast concrete square
 ended edging to B.S.340 . . . . m 1.52
6.5.8.6 250 mm × 50 mm precast concrete rounded
 edging to B.S.340 . . . . . m 1.56
6.5.8.7 250 mm × 125 mm precast concrete kerb to
 B.S.340 recessed below path level . . m 1.52

Drawings of typical path edgings

As drawings 6.5.8.8–14
5.8.3.11 For detailed specification of materials used
see Chapter 5, section 8. Key numbers refer to
illustrations in Chapter 6 and prices are inclusive

See Stop Press page vii; % additions to rates; September 1972 wage settlement

Pricing—Hard Ground Finishes

		unit	£
5.8.3.11 (cont'd)	*As drawings 6.5.8.8–14 continued* of all excavation, base and bedding as shown on each drawing. Path materials are priced separately.		
6.5.8.8	300 mm strip of cobbles held in place by 150 mm × 50 mm precast concrete edging to B.S.340	m	4.40
6.5.8.9	300 mm strip of gravel held in place by hardwood gravel board	m	1.89
	alternative; fixed with pegs only. no bed and haunching	m	1.61
6.5.8.10	wide brick edging detail:		
	stock bricks (p.c. of £26.50 per 1000)	m	3.30
	engineering bricks (p.c. of £50 per 1000)	m	3.83
6.5.8.11	narrow brick edging detail:		
	stock bricks (p.c. of £26.50 per 1000)	m	2.65
	engineering bricks (p.c. of £50 per 1000) 1	m	3.11
6.5.8.12	brick trim on end:		
	stock bricks (p.c. of £26.50 per 1000)	m	1.48
	engineering bricks (p.c. of £50 per 1000)	m	1.71
6.5.8.13	brick trim laid flat:		
	stock bricks (p.c. of £26.50 per 1000)	m	1.19
	engineering bricks (p.c. of £50 per 1000)	m	1.42
6.5.8.14	brick trim laid flat and recessed below path level:		
	stock bricks (p.c of £26.50 per 1000)	m	1.24
	engineering bricks (p.c. £50 per 1000)	m	1.47

Drawings of typical channels

5.8.3.12	*As drawings 6.5.8.15–22* For detailed specification of materials used see Chapter 5, section 8. Key numbers refer to illustrations in Chapter 6 and prices are inclusive of all excavation, base and bedding as shown on each drawing. Path and road materials are priced separately.		
6.5.8.15	375 mm wide dished brick channel	m	3.46
6.5.8.16	225 mm wide brick recessed channel	m	2.09
6.5.8.17	300 mm wide granite setts (second hand)	m	4.62
	alternative; in new setts	m	5.07
6.5.8.18	300 mm wide channel of kidney flint cobbles	m	4.20
6.5.8.19	250 mm wide, flat precast concrete channel to B.S.340	m	3.39
6.5.8.20	150 mm wide cast iron channel and cover grating	m	17.86
6.5.8.21	250 mm wide precast concrete dished channel to B.S.340	m	3.67
6.5.8.22	165 mm wide 'Safeticurb' channel	m	4.07

See Stop Press page vii; % additions to rates; September 1972 wage settlement

Pricing—Hard Ground Finishes

Drawings of typical mowing margins   *unit*   £

As drawings 6.5.8.23–29

5.8.3.13   For detailed specification of materials used see Chapter 5, section 8. Key numbers refer to illustrations in Chapter 6 and prices are inclusive of all excavation, base and bedding as shown on each drawing.

6.5.8.23	precast concrete edging laid flat to B.S.340; 250 mm wide	m	0.90
6.5.8.24	precast concrete paving slabs to B.S.368; 600 mm wide	m	1.67
6.5.8.25	in-situ concrete, mix 1:2:4, 225 mm wide	m	0.84
6.5.8.26	paving bricks 225 mm wide:		
	hard stock bricks (p.c. of £26.50 per 1000)	m	1.22
	blue engineering bricks (p.c. of £50.00 per 1000)	m	1.48
	add or deduct for every £1.00 per 1000 on cost of bricks	m	0.01
	extra over for bedding in lime/sand composition	m	0.04
6.5.8.27	cobbles set in hoggin, 300 mm wide	m	3.62
	alternative with edging in pressure-treated softwood (125 × 30 mm)	m	3.27
6.5.8.28	cobbles set in concrete, 300 mm wide	m	4.02
6.5.8.29	gravel, 300 mm wide	m	1.28
	alternative with edging in pressure-treated softwood (125 × 30 mm)	m	0.95

Drawings of typical parking layouts

Drawings 6.5.8.30–33

5.8.3.14   These drawings show areas of hardstanding required for various typical car parking layouts. These are for approximate cost estimating purposes. By using these drawings the areas of excavation, hardcore and surfacing and the lengths of kerbs and edging can be calculated for various layouts and multiplied by the appropriate prices. The specification for these constituent items can be found in Chapter 5, the drawings in Chapter 6 and the prices of the relevant elements in this chapter. It should be noted that the angled parking layouts could have the areas of hard surfacing reduced by the kerbs following a serrated profile instead of the straight one shown on the drawings. In such cases any saving in hardstanding will be

See Stop Press page vii; % additions to rates; September 1972 wage settlement

			unit	£
5.8.3.14 (cont'd)	*Drawings 6.5.8.30–33 continued* offset by the extra length of kerb for a serrated profile. The most economical answer will therefore depend on the materials chosen."			
	Marking of car parks apply 100 mm wide thermoplastic white strips in accordance with B.S.3262/1 . . .		m	0.11
5.8.4	**FLEXIBLE SURFACES**			
5.8.4.1–18	**Tarmacadam**			
	B.S.1242 38 mm base coat Table 3; 13 mm wearing coat Table 4; rolled:			
	50 mm work to pavements to falls not exceeding 15° to hardcore base measured separately		m^2	1.11
	ditto to areas exceeding 5000 m^2 . .		m^2	0.97
5.8.4.19	**Tarmacadam with crushed rock or slag aggregate**			
	B.S.802 Table 1b; rolled with an 8.128 tonne roller:			
	75 mm one-coat work to pavements; to falls or slopes not exceeding 15° to hardcore base measured separately		m^2	1.09
	ditto to areas exceeding 5000 m^2 . .		m^2	1.03
	B.S.802 51 mm base coat of 38 mm graded material, Table 1a; 25 mm wearing coat of 13 mm graded material Table 3; rolled with 8.128 tonne roller:			
	75 mm work to pavements; to falls or slopes not exceeding 15°, to hardcore base measured separately		m^2	1.19
	ditto to areas exceeding 5000 m^2 . .		m^2	0.95
5.8.4.20	**Fine cold asphalt**			
	B.S.1690 covering with bitumen coated 13 mm limestone chippings rolled in:			
	19 mm work to pavements; to falls or slopes not exceeding 15° to tarmacadam base			

See Stop Press page vii; % additions to rates; September 1972 wage settlement

Pricing—Hard Ground Finishes

		unit	£
5.8.4.20 (cont'd)	**B.S.1690** continued		
	measured separately	m²	0.55
	ditto to areas exceeding 5000 m² . .	m²	0.40

5.8.4.21–42 **Rolled asphalt (hot process)**

B.S.594

	Tack coat of bitumen emulsion on base course .	m²	0.05
	38 mm work to roads, to falls or slopes not exceeding 15° to base measured separately .	m²	0.89
	ditto to areas exceeding 5000 m² . .	m²	0.81
5.8.4.38	surface dressing of 19 mm coated chippings to B.S.63	m²	0.12
	surface dressing of 13 mm coated chippings to B.S.63	m²	0.10

Pea shingle

Surface dressing

5.8.4.43	6 mm pea gravel surface dressing on bituminous emulsion complying with B.S.434 . . .	m²	0.28

Gravel

For drives and paths

5.8.4.44–48	50 mm coarse gravel, single layer to hardcore base measured separately, to falls and slopes not exceeding 15°.	m²	0.27
	50 mm coarse gravel with 13 mm fine gravel surface dressing to produce 63 mm thickness on hardcore, to falls and slopes not exceeding 15° .	m²	0.45
5.8.4.48	25 mm fine gravel and hoggin with surface dressing of 19 mm fine gravel to produce 44 mm thickness on hardcore, to falls and slopes not exceeding 15°	m²	0.39

Hoggin (stabilised)

for paths

5.8.4.49–52   provide, lay and roll 100 mm thickness of

See Stop Press page vii; % additions to rates; September 1972 wage settlement

		unit	£
5.8.4.49–52 (cont'd)	**For paths** continued hoggin on hardcore, measured separately, to falls and slopes not exceeding 15°	m²	0.38

Shale

for paths

| 5.8.4.53–55 | provide, lay and roll coarse base of shale 50 mm thick finished with 25 mm fine shale | m² | 0.49 |
| 5.8.4.57 | provide, lay and roll fine shale blinding 25 mm thick to hardcore base measured separately | m² | 0.26 |

Loose cobbles

| 5.8.4.58–63 | provide and spread 50–75 km kidney flint cobbles on prepared base | m² | 2.83 |

Loose chippings

Walley (Thurrock) Limited

| 5.8.4.64 | provide and spread 'Permwhite' calcined flint, grade 12.5 – 9.5 mm in layer 25 mm thick on prepared base | m² | 0.75 |

5.8.5 RIGID PAVING

In-situ concrete

5.8.5.1–26	**For roads and paths** in-situ concrete unreinforced with brushed or tamped surface, including contraction joints as specified;		
	100 mm thick	m²	1.27
	150 mm thick	m²	1.85
	200 mm thick	m²	2.43
	extra over for exposed aggregate brushed finish	m²	0.60
	in-situ concrete reinforced with brushed or tamped surface;		
	100 mm thick	m²	1.49
	150 mm thick	m²	1.96
	200 mm thick	m²	2.59
	extra over for exposed aggregate brushed finish	m²	0.60

See Stop Press page vii; % additions to rates; September 1972 wage settlement

Pricing—Hard Ground Finishes

5.8.5.1–26 (cont'd)

Reinforcement   unit   £
Fabric; B.S.4483; 150 mm side laps, 300 mm end laps
    mesh 200 × 200 mm × 2.22 kg/m^2 . . m^2 0.40
    mesh 200 × 200 mm × 3.02 kg/m^2 . . m^2 0.54

Formwork
edges, risers or beds; 100 mm wide . . . m   0.30
    extra over for each additional 25 mm width . m   0.08
    extra over for curved radius of 6.000 m . %   33 $^1/_3$%
steel road forms 150 mm wide . . . m   0.46

Expansion joints
for in-situ concrete, formwork for 100 mm thick
slab with one coat bitumen on one edge . . m   0.28
    extra over for each 25 mm . . . m   0.07
for in-situ concrete, formwork 15 × 100 mm,
filling with bitumen-impregnated fibre board
75 mm wide; sealed with 15 × 25 mm
polysulphide-based sealant one side . m   1.32

Building paper
150 mm lapped joints, horizontal on foundations
or similar . . . . m^2 0.05½

UNIT PAVING

Precast paving slabs

5.8.6.1–3

slabs to B.S.368
natural finish bedded in lime mortar and jointing
in cement mortar; standard 900 × 600 mm and
600 × 600 mm slabs, 50 mm thick . . . m^2 1.53
    raking cutting . . . . . . m   0.21
    curved cutting . . . . . . m   0.32

Drawings of typical path layouts

5.8.6.8

As drawings 6.5.8.34–45
For detailed specification of materials used see
Chapter 5 section 8. Key numbers refer to illustrations in Chapter 6 and prices are inclusive of
all excavation, base and bedding as shown on
each drawing. Edgings and kerbs are not included

See Stop Press page vii; % additions to rates; September 1972 wage settlement

Pricing—Hard Ground Finishes

	As drawings 6.5.8.34–45 continued	unit	£
6.5.8.34	stepping stone path 600 mm wide:		
	precast concrete slabs to B.S.368: 1971,		
	natural finish	m	1.56
	coloured precast slabs	m	1.64
	exposed aggregate precast slabs	m	2.22
6.5.8.35	stepping stone path 900 mm wide:		
	precast concrete slabs to B.S.368: 1971,		
	natural finish	m	2.43
	coloured precast slabs	m	2.52
	exposed aggregate precast slabs	m	3.09
6.5.8.36	straight butted path 900 mm wide:		
	precast concrete slabs to B.S.368: 1971,		
	natural finish	m	2.66
	coloured precast slabs	m	2.76
	exposed aggregate precast slabs	m	3.74
6.5.8.37	staggered path 900 mm wide:		
	precast concrete slabs to B.S.368: 1971,		
	natural finish	m	3.05
	coloured precast slabs	m	3.15
	exposed aggregate precast slabs	m	4.24
6.5.8.38	straight butted path 1.200 m wide:		
	precast concrete slabs to B.S.368: 1971,		
	natural finish	m	3.37
	coloured precast slabs	m	3.56
	exposed aggregate precast slabs	m	4.80
6.5.8.39	staggered path 1.200 m wide:		
	precast concrete slabs to B.S.368: 1971,		
	natural finish	m	3.95
	coloured precast slabs	m	4.13
	exposed aggregate precast slabs	m	5.38
6.5.8.40	indented path 1.200 m wide		
	precast concrete slabs to B.S.368: 1971,		
	natural finish	m	3.40
	coloured precast slabs	m	3.54
	exposed aggregate precast slabs	m	4.21
6.5.8.41	straight butted path 1.200 m wide:		
	precast concrete slabs to B.S.368: 1971,		
	natural finish	m	3.56
	coloured precast slabs	m	3.68
	exposed aggregate precast slabs	m	4.99
6.5.8.42	straight butted path 1.500 m wide:		
	precast concrete slabs to B.S.368: 1971,		
	natural finish	m	4.28
	coloured precast slabs	m	4.44
	exposed aggregate precast slabs	m	5.70
6.5.8.43	straight butted path 1.800 m wide:		
	precast concrete slabs to B.S.368: 1971,		
	natural finish	m	4.33

See Stop Press page vii; % additions to rates: September 1972 wage settlement

Planning the new environment?

Consult Blakedown Landscapes, the expert landscape artists; small shopping precincts, schools, industrial developments, golf courses.
Blakedown Landscapes have designed and constructed them all; their expertise at handling these and other types of landscaping is at your service; phone Blakedown 553.

Blakedown Landscapes Ltd

Belbroughton Road Blakedown Kidderminster Worcs

Super Hortex paving.

Atlas Stone materials for the garden

Hortex paving, walling, screen walling and classic balustrades. For full details contact:

The Atlas Stone Company Limited
Artillery House, Artillery Row, London SW1P 1RU Tel: 01-222 2091

Pricing—Hard Ground Finishes

	As drawings 6.5.8.34–45 continued	unit	£
	coloured precast slabs	m	5.52
	exposed aggregate precast slabs	m	7.10
6.5.8.44	straight butted path 1.500 m wide: precast concrete slabs to B.S.368: 1971,		
	natural finish	m	4.44
	coloured precast slabs	m	4.60
	exposed aggregate precast slabs	m	5.05
6.5.8.45	straight butted path 1.800 m wide: precast concrete slabs to B.S.368: 1971,		
	natural finish	m	5.33
	coloured precast slabs	m	5.51
	exposed aggregate precast slabs	m	6.73

Proprietary Products

Atlas Stone Company Limited

5.8.6.9	'Foothold' slabs; in B.S. sizes, bedded and jointed:		
	grey, 50 mm thick	m^2	1.93
	coloured, 50 mm thick	m^2	2.17
5.8.6.10	'Indented' slabs; in B.S. sizes, bedded and jointed:		
	grey, 50 mm thick	m^2	1.98
	coloured, 50 mm thick	m^2	2.33
5.8.6.11	'8 gauge' slabs; in B.S. sizes bedded and jointed:		
	grey, 50 mm thick	m^2	2.11
	coloured 50 mm thick	m^2	2.33
5.8.6.12	'Driveway' slabs; 450 mm square, bedded and jointed:		
	grey, 50 mm thick	m^2	2.08
	coloured 50 mm thick	m^2	2.31
5.8.6.13	'Hortex' slabs; bedded and jointed:		
	coloured 37 mm thick	m^2	2.56
5.8.6.14	'Super Hortex' slabs; in B.S. sizes, bedded and jointed:		
	coloured 37 mm thick	m^2	2.90

John Ellis & Son Limited

5.8.6.15	'Texitone' slabs; in B.S. sizes, bedded and jointed:		
	coloured 50 mm thick	m^2	2.96
5.8.6.16	'Yorkstone' slabs; in B.S. sizes, bedded and jointed:		
	coloured 50 mm thick	m^2	2.52

Hulland Products Limited

5.8.6.17	Coloured flags; to B.S.368, in B.S. sizes, bedded and jointed:		
	coloured, 50 mm thick	m^2	1.82

See Stop Press page vii; % additions to rates; September 1972 wage settlement

Pricing—Hard Ground Finishes

		unit	£
5.8.6.17 (cont'd)	**Hulland Products Limited** continued coloured, 63 mm thick	m²	2.12
5.8.6.18	'Chevron' flags; to B.S.368, in B.S. sizes, bedded and jointed:		
	natural grey 50 mm thick	m²	1.48
	natural grey 63 mm thick	m²	2.23
5.8.6.19	'Fluted' flags; to B.S. 368, in B.S. sizes, bedded and jointed:		
	natural grey 50 mm thick	m²	1.48
	natural grey 63 mm thick	m²	2.23
5.8.6.20	'Squared' flags; to B.S.368, in B.S. sizes, bedded and jointed:		
	natural grey 50 mm thick	m²	1.48
	natural grey 63 mm thick	m²	2.23
5.8.6.21	'Barfaced' flags; to B.S.368 in B.S. sizes, bedded and jointed:		
	natural grey 50 mm thick	m²	1.48
	natural grey 63 mm thick	m²	2.23
5.8.6.22	'Hobnail' flags; to B.S.368 in B.S. sizes, bedded and jointed:		
	natural grey 50 mm thick	m²	1.48
	natural grey 63 mm thick	m²	2.23
	Marley Buildings Limited		
5.8.6.23	'Cobblestone' slabs; 600 mm square, bedded and jointed:		
	dark grey 37 mm thick	m²	2.83
5.8.6.24	'Colourstone' slabs; various sizes, rectangular, bedded and jointed:		
	coloured 37 mm thick	m²	2.61
5.8.6.25	'Marlstone' slabs; various sizes, bedded and jointed:		
	sandstone, coloured 37 mm thick	m²	2.83
	S. Marshall & Sons Limited		
5.8.6.26	'Marshalite' slabs; to B.S.368, B.S. sizes, bedded and jointed		
	natural 50 mm thick	m²	1.98
	natural 63 mm thick	m²	2.22
	red or buff 50 mm thick	m²	2.18
	red or buff 63 mm thick	m²	3.18
5.8.6.27	non-slip paving slabs to B.S.368, 900 × 600 mm and 600 mm square, bedded and jointed:		
	natural grey 50 mm thick	m²	2.58
	buff 50 mm thick	m²	3.39
5.8.6.28	'Perfecta' slabs; to B.S.368, 600 mm square, bedded and jointed:		
	natural, 50 mm thick	m²	2.51

See Stop Press page vii; % additions to rates; September 1972 wage settlement

Pricing—Hard Ground Finishes

5.8.6.28
(cont'd)

	unit	£
natural, 63 mm thick	m²	2.88
natural, 75 mm thick	m²	3.89
red or buff 50 mm thick	m²	2.72
red or buff 63 mm thick	m²	3.29
red or buff 75 mm thick	m²	4.21

Mono Concrete Limited

5.8.6.29 'Chelmsley' slabs; 600 mm square, bedded and jointed:
black 50 mm thick	m²	4.63

5.8.6.30 'Lambeth' slabs; 600 mm square, bedded and jointed:
grey 75 mm thick	m²	4.72

5.8.6.31 'Metric Four Square' slabs; 500 mm square, bedded and jointed:
exposed aggregate 50 mm thick	m²	4.23

5.8.6.32 'Monohex' slabs; hexagonal, bedded and jointed:
plain, 50 mm thick	m²	3.34
textured, 50 mm thick	m²	3.72

5.8.6.33 'Pentahex' slabs; pentagonal, bedded and jointed:
plain, 50 mm thick	m²	5.63
textured, 50 mm thick	m²	6.45

5.8.6.34 'Stretford' paving; 900 × 600 mm size, bedded and jointed . . . m² 7.48

5.8.6.35 'Wandsworth' slabs; 600 × 300 mm, bedded and jointed:
natural grey 180 mm thick	m²	9.98

Noelite Limited

5.8.6.36 'Noelite' slabs; various sizes, rectangular, bedded and jointed:
coloured 38 mm thick	m²	1.80
coloured 50 mm thick	m²	2.20

Redland Tiles Limited

5.8.6.37 'Kentstone' paving; various sizes, rectangular bedded and jointed:
coloured 40 mm thick	m²	2.66

5.8.6.38 'Polygon' paving; polygonal, bedded and jointed:
coloured 40 mm thick	m²	3.30

See Stop Press page vii; % additions to rates; September 1972 wage settlement

Precast paving blocks for vehicular use

Mono Concrete Limited

5.8.6.39 'S.F.' interlocking paving; irregular shaped, bedded and jointed (with sand):

	unit	£
natural grey 50 mm thick	m²	3.52
natural grey 80 mm thick	m²	4.70
natural grey 100 mm thick	m²	5.65
coloured 50 mm thick	m²	3.93
coloured 80 mm thick	m²	5.37
coloured 100 mm thick	m²	6.25

Fire-paths in precast units

Mono Concrete Limited

5.8.6.40 'B.G' slabs; 600 × 400 mm, bedded ready for soiling and seeding:
natural grey, 120 mm thick . . . m² 3.65

5.8.6.41 'Hexpot' slabs; hexagonal, 292 mm, bedded ready for soiling and seeding:
natural grey, 100 mm thick . . . m² 5.36

5.8.6.42–5 **Flags in natural stone, slate or granite**

Yorkstone

5.8.6.46 new flagstones, random rectangular, 50 mm thick, bedded and jointed . . . m² 10.94

5.8.6.47 second-hand flagstones, random rectangular, bedded and jointed . . . m² 6.96

5.8.6.48 second-hand flagstones used as crazy paving, bedded and jointed . . . m² 5.95

Portland stone

5.8.6.49 new slabs 50 mm thick, rectangular . . m² 17.46

Slate

5.8.6.50 new slabs, random rectangular, 31 mm thick . m² 17.71

See Stop Press page vii; % additions to rates; September 1972 wage settlement

Pricing–Hard Ground Finishes

		unit	£
	Granite		
5.8.6.51	new slabs, random rectangular:		
	25 mm thick	m^2	39.00

Brick paving

5.8.6.52–3	*stock bricks*		
	(p.c. of £26.50 per 1000) including bedding and jointing:		
	stretcher or stack bond	m^2	2.85
	raking cutting	m	0.55
	curved cutting	m	0.66
	basket weave bond	m^2	3.02
	raking cutting	m	0.55
	curved cutting	m	0.66
	herringbone, laid flat	m^2	3.27
	raking cutting	m	0.55
	curved cutting	m	0.66
	herringbone, laid on edge	m^2	5.15
	raking cutting	m	0.60
	curved cutting	m	0.75

5.8.6.52–3	*Staffordshire blue bricks*		
	(p.c. of £50.00 per 1000) including bedding and jointing:		
	stretcher or stack bond	m^2	4.03
	raking cutting	m	0.80
	curved cutting	m	0.95
	basket weave bond	m^2	4.28
	raking cutting	m	0.80
	curved cutting	m	0.95
	herringbone, laid flat	m^2	4.45
	raking cutting	m	0.80
	curved cutting	m	0.90
	herringbone, laid on edge	m^2	7.63
	raking cutting	m	1.21
	curved cutting	m	1.72

Drawings of typical brick paved paths

	As drawings 6.5.8.46–51
5.8.6.54	Key numbers refer to illustrations in Chapter 6 and prices are inclusive of all excavation, base and bedding as shown on each drawing. Edgings and kerbs are not included.

See Stop Press page vii; % additions to rates; September 1972 wage settlement

Pricing—Hard Ground Finishes

	As drawings 6.5.8.46–51 continued	unit	£
6.5.8.46	stretcher bond (along length) path 1.125 m wide:		
	stock bricks (p.c. £26.50 per 1000)	m	5.03
	engineering bricks (p.c. £50.00 per 1000)	m	6.34
6.5.8.47	stretcher bond (across width) path 1.125 m wide:		
	stock bricks (p.c. £26.50 per 1000)	m	5.07
	engineering bricks (p.c. £50.00 per 1000)	m	6.40
6.5.8.48	stack bond path 1.125 m wide:		
	stock bricks (p.c. £26.50 per 1000)	m	5.03
	engineering bricks (p.c. £50.00 per 1000)	m	6.34
6.5.8.49	basket weave pattern path 1.125 m wide:		
	stock bricks (p.c. £26.50 per 1000)	m	5.21
	engineering bricks (p.c. £50.00 per 1000)	m	6.63
6.5.8.50	herringbone pattern (flat face) path 1.125 m wide:		
	stock bricks (p.c. £26.50 per 1000)	m	6.39
	engineering bricks (p.c. £50.00 per 1000)	m	8.10
6.5.8.51	herringbone pattern (on edge) path, 1.125 m wide:		
	stock bricks (p.c. £26.50 per 1000)	m	9.13
	engineering bricks (p.c £50.00 per 1000)	m	12.64

Patterned paving bricks by Haunchwood-Lewis Brick & Tile Limited

Staffordshire blue bricks including bedding and jointing:

		unit	£
5.8.6.55	diamond chequered type	m^2	4.47
5.8.6.56	two raised panel type	m^2	4.47
5.8.6.57	four raised panel type	m^2	4.47
5.8.6.58	six raised panel type	m^2	4.47
5.8.6.59	eight raised panel type	m^2	4.47

Clay tiles

External quality quarry tiles

		unit	£
5.8.6.60	including bedding and jointing		
	blue/black 150 mm square 19 mm thick	m^2	3.61
	blue/black 200 mm square 28 mm thick	m^2	5.64
	blue/black 225 mm square 31 mm thick	m^2	4.74
	heather brown 150 mm square 19 mm thick	m^2	2.99
	heather brown 200 mm square 28 mm thick	m^2	3.46
	heather brown 225 mm square 31 mm thick	m^2	3.59

See Stop Press page vii; % additions to rates; September 1972 wage settlement

Pricing–Hard Ground Finishes

		unit	£
5.8.6.61–4	**Granite setts**		

Drawing of typical granite sett paving patterns

5.8.6.65 — Key numbers refer to illustrations in Chapter 6 and prices are inclusive of all excavation, base and bedding as shown on each drawing. Edgings and kerbs are not included

6.5.8.52	100 mm × 100 mm × 100 mm setts laid stack bond:		
	new	m²	7.48
	second-hand	m²	6.23
6.5.8.53	100 mm × 100 mm × 200 mm setts laid stretcher bond:		
	new	m²	7.16
	second-hand	m²	6.12
6.5.8.54	100 mm × 100 mm × 100 mm setts in curved pattern:		
	new	m²	7.69
	second-hand	m²	6.68
6.5.8.55	100 mm × 100 mm × 100 mm setts in fan pattern:		
	new	m²	8.23
	second-hand	m²	7.18

Cobble paving

Cobbles set in concrete

5.8.6.66–9	50–75 mm cobbles set in concrete	m²	8.59

Tree grids

Drawings of typical grids around trees

As drawings 6.5.8.56–61

5.8.6.70 — Key numbers refer to illustrations in Chapter 6. All prices include all materials on drawings as noted and assume excavations to have been done at at time of tree pit excavation and tree planting. No edgings or surrounding paving to grids is included in these prices.

6.5.8.56	brick paving 1.125 m square with 450 mm square hole for tree:		
	hard stock bricks	No.	4.59
	blue engineering bricks	No.	5.91
6.5.8.57	granite setts to 1.200 m square with 400 mm square hole for tree:		
	200 × 100 × 100 mm setts	No.	16.38
	100 × 100 × 100 mm setts	No.	17.75

See Stop Press page vii; % additions to rates; September 1972 wage settlement

Pricing–Hard Ground Finishes

Drawings of typical grids around trees *continued*

		unit	£
6.5.8.58	100–125 mm kidney flint cobbles to 1.200 m square with 400 mm square hole for tree .	No.	14.77
6.5.8.59	'Mono Concrete'; 'Metric Four Square' grilles to 1.500 m square with 500 mm square hole for tree	No.	12.72
6.5.8.60	Cast iron grid to 1.200 m square with 400 mm square hole for tree	No.	33.27
6.5.8.61	'Mono Concrete'; 'Monohex' tree grilles to 1.520 × 1.140 m shape (made up of half slabs) with hexagonal hole for tree . . .	No.	11.44
	As above but with full hexagonal 'Monohex' grille slabs on all sides of hexagonal hole for tree	No.	21.03

5.8.7   **DRIVEWAYS**

Drawings of typical layouts of drives to domestic garages

As drawings 6.5.8.62–69

5.8.7.1	For detailed specification of materials see Chapter 5 section 8. Key numbers refer to illustrations in Chapter 6 and prices are inclusive of all excavation, base and bedding as shown on each drawing. Edgings and kerbs are not included.		
6.5.8.62	6.000 m × 2.500 m in-situ concrete driveway:		
	smooth trowelled finish	No.	50.27
	board tamped finish	No.	47.35
	exposed brushed Thames Valley or similar aggregate finish	No.	54.64
	reduction to each of above if on 100 mm hardcore	No.	3.32
6.5.8.63	6.000 m × 2.500 m in-situ concrete driveway with engineering brick divisions:		
	smooth trowelled finish	No.	51.58
	board tamped finish	No.	48.67
	exposed brushed Thames Valley or similar aggregate finish	No.	55.95
6.5.8.64–9	standard in-situ concrete surround to alternative infill materials. 6.000 m × 2.500 m overall × 150 mm thick on 100 mm hardcore, including excavation and hardcore to infill:		
	smooth trowelled finish	No.	39.70
	board tamped finish	No.	37.34

See Stop Press page vii; % additions to rates; September 1972 wage settlement

Pricing–Hard Ground Finishes

		unit	£
6.5.8.64–9 (cont'd)	As drawings 6.5.8.62–69 continued exposed brushed Thames Valley or similar aggregate finish	No.	43.25
6.5.8.64	600 mm × 600 mm × 50 mm precast concrete slab infill; base, bedding and jointing:		
	standard to B.S.368	No.	7.57
	coloured slabs	No.	7.85
	exposed aggregate slabs . . .	No	10.75
6.5.8.65	225 mm × 225 mm × 31 mm exterior quality quarry tile infill, 675 mm wide; base, bedding and jointing:		
	heather brown	No.	14.73
	blue/black	No.	19.81
6.5.8.66	second-hand granite setts infill, 600 mm wide	No.	22.82
6.5.8.67	225 mm × 112.5 mm brick pavior infill, 563 mm wide	No.	17.20
6.5.8.68	75 mm fine gravel. 600 mm wide . .	No.	1.82
6.5.8.69	kidney flint cobbles. 600 mm wide .; . .	No.	27.53

STEPS

Drawings of typical step details

	As drawings 6.5.8.70–81		
5.8.8.1	For specification details see Chapter 5 section 8. Key numbers refer to illustrations in Chapter 6. All prices are inclusive of excavation, hardcore, blinding and concrete as on drawings; based on a minimum flight of 5 No. steps. Price is for steps only and not for any retaining walls or edging on each side of flight, which should be measured separately.		
6.5.8.70	brick paving laid flat for 900 mm width, steps @ 225 mm × 75 mm, price per step:		
	hard stock brick	No.	2.17
	engineering brick	No.	2.30
6.5.8.71	brick paving, laid flat for 900 mm width, steps @ 345 mm × 150 mm, price per step:		
	hard stock brick	No.	4.15
	engineering brick	No.	4.67
6.5.8.72	brick paving, laid on edge for 900 mm width, steps @ 300 mm × 120 mm, price per step:		
	hard stock brick	No.	2.98
	engineering brick	No.	3.30
6.5.8.73	in-situ concrete, for 900 mm width, steps @ 375 mm × 125 mm, price per step:		
	smooth trowelled finish	No.	2.75

See Stop Press page vii; % additions to rates; September 1972 wage settlement

		unit	£
6.5.8.73 (cont'd)	**As drawings 6.5.8.70–81** continued		
	tamped finish	No.	2.69
	exposed brushed Thames Valley or similar aggregate finish	No.	3.27
6.5.8.74	precast concrete slabs to B.S.368, for 900 mm width steps at 450 mm × 125 mm, price per step:		
	with riser in hard stock brick . . .	No.	4.50
	with riser in engineering brick . . .	No.	4.60
	precast concrete slabs to B.S.368, for 900 mm width, steps at 300 mm × 125 mm, price per step:		
	with riser in hard stock brick . . .	No.	3.39
	with riser in engineering brick . . .	No.	3.49
	precast concrete slabs to B.S.368, for 900 mm width, steps at 600 mm × 125 mm, price per step:		
	with riser in hard stock brick . . .	No.	5.78
	with riser in engineering brick . . .	No.	5.88
	precast concrete slabs to B.S.368, for 900 mm width, steps @ 900 mm × 125 mm, price per step:		
	with riser in hard stock brick . . .	No.	7.97
	with riser in engineering brick . . .	No.	8.08
6.5.8.75	precast concrete slabs to B.S.368 and precast concrete edging to B.S.340 for 900 mm width price per step:		
	steps @ 350 mm × 150 mm . . .	No.	4.58
	steps @ 510 mm × 150 mm . . .	No.	5.29
	steps @ 660 mm × 150 mm . . .	No.	6.16
	steps @ 960 mm × 150 mm . . .	No.	8.92
6.5.8.76	precast blocks for 900 mm width, steps @ 325 mm × 150 mm, price per step:		
	smooth p.c. concrete . . .	No.	6.88
	exposed aggregate p.c. concrete . . .	No.	8.15
	reconstructed stone	No.	15.57
	cast stone (faced on tread and riser) . .	No.	14.00
	precast blocks for 900 mm width, steps @ 325 mm × 125 mm, price per step:		
	smooth p.c. concrete . . .	No.	5.91
	exposed aggregate p.c. concrete . . .	No.	6.92
	reconstructed stone	No.	13.44
	cast stone (faced on tread and riser) . .	No.	12.12
	precast blocks for 900 mm width, steps @ 325 mm × 100 mm, price per step:		
	smooth p.c. concrete . . .	No.	5.02
	exposed aggregate p.c. concrete . . .	No.	5.73
	reconstructed stone	No.	11.54
	cast stone (faced on tread and riser) . .	No.	10.33

See Stop Press page vii; % additions to rates; September 1972 wage settlement

Pricing—Hard Ground Finishes

As drawings 6.5.8.70–81 continued

		units	£
6.5.8.77	precast 'L' shaped blocks for 900 mm width, steps 325 mm × 125 mm, price per step:		
	smooth p.c. concrete	No.	5.41
	exposed aggregate p.c. concrete	No.	6.40
	reconstructed stone	No.	10.62
	cast stone (faced on tread and riser)	No.	9.25
6.5.8.78	second-hand granite setts and precast concrete kerbs to B.S.340, for 900 mm width, steps @ 450 mm × 150 mm, price per step	No.	7.30
6.5.8.79	second-hand granite setts, for 900 mm width, steps @ 400 mm × 100 mm, price per step:	No.	6.15
6.5.8.80	ramped Roman steps in kidney flint cobbles with risers in precast concrete edging to B.S.340, risers @ approx. 100 mm, price per step:		
	tread of 1.000 m	No.	14.20
	tread of 1.250 m	No.	17.25
	tread of 1.500 m	No.	20.82
	tread of 1.750 m	No.	23.15
	tread of 2.000 m	No.	27.10
6.5.8.81	railway sleeper risers used on edge and hoggin treads, steps @ 400 mm × 125 mm, price per step:	No.	2.55
	railway sleeper risers laid flat and hoggin treads, steps @ 400 mm × 100 mm, price per step:	No.	2.28

See Stop Press page vii; % additions to rates; September 1972 wage settlement

7.9 RECREATION AND SPORTS FACILITIES

All clause numbers refer to the specification paragraphs in Chaper 5, except where reference is made to Chapter 6.

5.9.1 LAYOUTS

Drawings of layouts shown in Chapter 6

5.9.1.1 For approximate estimating purposes, a number of guidance price ranges for average facilities are given below. These will vary according to the site conditions, standards required and size of contract:

		unit	£
grass playing fields including cut and fill drainage and seeding for contracts 10–100 hectares		ha	1750–3000
golf courses		ha	1800–2200
golf courses		hole	4000–5000
6.5.9.7 6 rink bowling green		No.	6500
6.5.9.19 tennis court (including 2.750 m high plastic-coated chain link on angle iron frame, not including levelling of ground):			
En-Tout-Cas: 'Tennisquick'		No.	2650–2750
En-Tout-Cas: 'Gragreen'		No.	1350–1450
En-Tout-Cas: 'Red Championship'		No.	1350–1450
En-Tout-Cas: 'Asphumas' – red		No.	1425–1525
En-Tout-Cas: 'Asphumas' – black		No.	1350–1450

(prices for multiples of more than one court will not be in ratio as the amount of space for two courts is less than twice that for one; consequently there is a considerable reduction for quantity)

5.9.2 ARTIFICIAL SURFACES AND FINISHES

Introduction

5.9.2.1 In comparing the prices below it should be noted that some include base work whereas others are for a specialist surface only on to a base prepared and costed separately.

'Asphumus' by En-Tout-Cas Limited

5.9.2.3 surface and base; complete price (including edging foundations and surface drains):

	unit	£
red surface	m^2	1.60–1.70
black surface	m^2	1.40–1.60

See Stop Press page vii; % additions to rates; September 1972 wage settlement

		unit	£
5.9.2.4	*'Astroturf'* by Monsanto surface only	m²	14.75 −15.00
5.9.2.5	*'Dri-pla'* by En-Tout-Cas Limited surface and base; complete price	m²	1.30−1.50
5.9.2.6	*'Hartco'* by Maxwell M. Hart Limited surface and base; complete price	m²	2.00−2.50
5.9.2.7	*'K' Surface* by En-Tous-Cas Limited surface and base; complete price	m²	5.40−5.80
5.9.2.8	*'Redgra'* by Amalgamated Roadstone Construction Limited surface and base; complete price	m²	1.30−1.60
5.9.2.9	*'Regupol'* by *'S.I.P.A.'* surface only	m²	8.00−9.00
5.9.2.10	*'Rub-Kor'* by Rub-Kor U.K. Limited surface and base; complete price	m²	3.50
5.9.2.11	*'Snowslope'* by Dendix Brushes Limited surface only	m²	13.00 −13.50
5.9.2.12	*'Springsno'* by Glenlivet Sporting Estates Ltd. surface only	m²	8.50
5.9.2.13	*'Tartan'* Surfacing by 3M U.K. Limited 9 mm thick, surface only 13 mm thick, surface only	m² m²	10.00 11.00
5.9.2.14	*'Tartan' Turf* by 3M U.K. Limited surface only	m²	subject to negotiation
5.9.2.15	*'Tennisquick'* by En-Tout-Cas Limited surface and base; complete price	m²	4.00−4.50
5.9.2.16	*'Trintrack'* by Limmer & Trinidad Co. Ltd. surface and base; complete price	m²	4.00

See Stop Press page vii; % additions to rates; September 1972 wage settlement

7.10 PLAYGROUND EQUIPMENT   unit   £

All clause numbers refer to the specification paragraphs in Chapter 5.

5.10.2   SELECTED TYPICAL EQUIPMENT

Note that all prices are inclusive of supply and fixing (where necessary) to normal hard surfaced playground and are for approximate estimating purposes.

Child's World Agency

Play cubes

5.10.2.1	standard units 864 mm across	No.	70.00

G.L.T Products & Engineering Limited

Climbing equipment

5.10.2.2	maypole tower; 2.000 m diameter	No.	85.00
5.10.2.3	dome; 2.745 m diameter	No.	80.00

Slides

5.10.2.4	landslides:		
	2.440 m	No.	65.00
	4.880 m	No.	110.00
	6.100 m	No.	130.00
	8.000 m	No.	165.00

Neptune Concrete Limited

Play sculpture

5.10.2.5	P.G.7; saddle shape	No.	63.00
5.10.2.6	P.G.9; concrete tree	No.	90.00
5.10.2.7	P.G.1; tunnel bridge in two parts	No.	15.00

FOR ADVENTURE PLAYGROUND EQUIPMENT or for our 'Southampton outdoor seats' send for our brochure of shapes in concrete to:—	**NEPTUNE CONCRETE LTD** QUAYSIDE ROAD, BITTERNE MANOR, SOUTHAMPTON SO9 4YP Tel: (0703) 25513

See Stop Press page vii; % additions to rates; September 1972 wage settlement

E.T.S. LANDSCAPING SERVICES

Landscape Consultancy Service
Reclamation — Hard & Soft Landscape Contractors
Large & Small Amenity — Play & Adventure Areas
Golf & Sportsground Construction — Aftercare
Earthmoving — Turfing — Seeding
Country wide design & construction service
Equipped and qualified staff

CONSULT

E.T.S. Hydraulic Seeders Ltd.,
Otley,
Leeds, LS21 1DR.
Tel: Otley 3771

E.T.S. Southern Landscapes Ltd.,
3A, South Bar,
Banbury, Oxon.
Tel: Banbury 52985

HAVERING
Group of Companies

Spearman Construction Limited

HAVERING HOUSE, THORNWOOD, EPPING, ESSEX.

Telephone: Epping 2252 (6 lines)

Specialist Contractors for:

*Golf Course Construction

*Hard Play Area Construction

*Sports Ground Construction

* We WELCOME your enquiries NATIONWIDE *

SMP
designed for safety's sake

The SMP range of quality Playground Equipment and Landscape Furniture is simply designed and built stronger to last longer. First choice of Local Authorities, Schools, and Landscape Architects throughout the country.

Please write or phone for a copy of our latest comprehensive catalogue.

SMP

Quality play equipment and landscape furniture manufacturers.
SMP (Landscapes) Limited, Ferry Lane, Hythe End, Staines, Middlesex.
Telephone: Wraysbury 2225

CoID design award 1972

Photographs by permission of the Council of Industrial Design (Copyright) and the Zoological Society of London.

S.M.P. (Landscapes) Limited   unit   £

Climbing structures

5.10.2.8	galleon; in tubular steel	No.	680.00
5.10.2.9	totem pole; steel and rubber	No.	100.00
5.10.2.10	climbing ladders; in steel:		
	EA.31 single	No.	25.00
	EA.32 double	No.	35.00

Play sculpture

5.10.2.11	tapiola; wooden horse	No.	55.00
5.10.2.12	log cabin shelter; wood and steel	No.	300.00

Slides

5.10.2.13	safety slides; in stainless steel: supply only		
	entry section 2.440 m long	No.	61.00
	straight section 610 mm long	No.	15.25
	straight section 1.220 m long	No.	30.50
	straight section 1.830 m long	No.	45.75
	straight section 2.440 m long	No.	61.00
	exit section 2.440 m long	No.	61.00

Swings

5.10.2.14	arch swings; single units:		
	height of arch frame 2.440 m	No.	45.00
	height of arch frame 3.050 m	No.	50.00
	height of arch frame 3.660 m	No.	55.00

Sportsmark (Equipment) Limited

Climbing frames

5.10.2.15	Playdome; all aluminium structure:		
	'Minidome'	No.	70.00
	'Playdome Mark I'	No.	140.00
	'Playdome Mark II'	No.	250.00

The Sutcliffe Moulded Rubber Company Limited

Moving equipment

5.10.2.16	carousel; rotating unit	No.	220.00
5.10.2.17	flat rotary disc	No.	170.00
5.10.2.18	fixed see-saw	No.	80.00

See Stop Press page vii; % additions to rates; September 1972 wage settlement

The Sutcliffe Moulded Rubber Co. Ltd. *continued*

Climbing equipment

		unit	£
5.10.2.19	tumbling bar at three levels	No.	22.00
5.10.2.20	climbing arch	No.	80.00

Charles Wickstead & Company Limited

Moving equipment

5.10.2.21	rocking horse; painted	No.	150.00
5.10.2.22	rota stride; painted	No.	160.00
5.10.2.23	travelling ring frame; painted	No.	160.00

Climbing equipment

5.10.2.24	climbing net frame; waterproof rope and galvanised steel	No.	105.00
5.10.2.25	Junglegym; galvanised steel:		
	size no. 1	No.	240.00
	size no. 2	No.	205.00
	size no. 3	No.	100.00

Swings

5.10.2.26	traditional set; various heights and sizes with middle size range given below:		
	3.050 m high		
	2 seats; 1 bay	No.	60.00
	3 seats; 1 bay	No.	70.00
	4 seats; 2 bays	No.	95.00
	6 seats; 2 bays	No.	120.00

See Stop Press page vii; % additions to rates; September 1972 wage settlement

Pricing—Water Features 335

7.11 WATER FEATURES   unit   £

All clause numbers refer to the specification paragraphs in Chapter 5.

5.11.1 LAKES AND PONDS

Typical linings

5.11.1.1 All prices are for supply, fabrication, welding (or other method of jointing sheets) for lakes or ponds where excavation, drainage, preparatory work or edging construction work have been measured separately. Where lining is to be protected by a layer of sand or covered by gravel or loose cobbles these should be added at the appropriate rates. Prices are approximate for budget calculations only.

Polythene

5.11.1.2 black polythene 1000 gauge:
- for areas below 1 hectare . . . . ha 3300.00
- for areas 1–5 hectares . . . . ha 3000.00
- for areas 5–25 hectares ; ; . . ha 2900.00

P.V.C.

5.11.1.3 black welded P.V.C. (14 thou);
- for areas below 1 hectare . . . . ha 4400.00
- for areas 1-5 hectares . . . . ha 4000.00
- for areas 5-25 hectares . . . . ha 3850.00

Rubber butyl

5.11.1.4 black butyl sheeting;
0.75 mm thick:
- for areas below 1 hectare . . . . ha 11000.00
- for areas 1-5 hectares . . . . ha 10500.00

1 mm thick:
- for areas below 1 hectare . . . . ha 12500.00
- for areas 1-5 hectares . . . . ha 12000.00

1.5 mm thick:
- for areas 1-5 hectares . . . . ha 15000.00

5.11.2 ORNAMENTAL POOLS

5.11.2.1 Prices exclude excavation, drainage, filtration and fountains or pumps. Price is for waterproof concrete lining in prepared excavation;

See Stop Press page vii; % additions to rates; September 1972 wage settlement

Pricing–Water Features

5.11.2.1
(cont'd)

Ornamental Pools continued
concrete finished fair-faced:

	unit	£
2.000 m square; 300 mm deep in 100 mm concrete	No.	25.00 –50.00
5.000 m square; 600 mm deep in 150 mm concrete	No.	50.00 –100.00
7.500 m × 10.000 m; 900 mm deep in 200 mm concrete	No.	400.00 –600.00

5.11.3 **SWIMMING POOLS**

Standard concrete construction

5.11.3.1 Prices exclude excavation, drainage, and surrounds, diving boards, heaters etc. and other items which will vary from pool to pool; normal depth with shallow and deep end to each pool:

	unit	£
10.000 m × 4.000 m	No.	1250.00 –1500.00
10.000 m × 6.000 m	No.	1500.00 –1750.00
12.500 m × 6.000 m	No.	1750.00 –2000.00
15.000 m × 6.000 m	No.	2000.00 –2500.00
15.000 m × 7.500 m	No.	2500.00 –3000.00
15.000 m × 10.000 m	No.	3000.00 –3500.00

(simple curved shapes generally cost the same per m^2 of area as rectangular pools but the more complex shapes are the most expensive)

5.11.4 **FOUNTAINS**

Precast concrete units

Mono Concrete Limited

5.11.4.1 'Falkirk' precast concrete fountain bowl, without pump; supply price . . . . No. 40.50

5.11.4.2 'Millstone' fountains in precast concrete without pump; supply price
600 mm diameter (type 24) 305 mm high . No. 17.00

See Stop Press page vii; % additions to rates; September 1972 wage settlement

Pricing–Water Features

			unit	£
5.11.4.2 (cont'd)	Mono Concrete Limited continued			
	600 mm diameter (type 24) 455 mm high	.	No.	20.50
	750 mm diameter (type 30) 305 mm high	.	No.	21.50
	750 mm diameter (type 30) 455 mm high	.	No.	26.75
	890 mm diameter (type 36) 305 mm high	.	No.	26.50
	890 mm diameter (type 36) 455 mm high	.	No.	33.00

Fountain nozzles

G. Allsebrook & Company Limited

5.11.4.3	straight plume; single jet; supply only price:			
	19 mm diameter	.	No.	4.50
	38 mm diameter	.	No.	7.50
	50 mm diameter	.	No.	10.00
5.11.4.4	multiple plumes; header box for nozzles; supply only price:			
	two unit box	.	No.	10.00
	four unit box	.	No.	15.00
5.11.4.5	rose bowl fountain; supply only price:			
	75 mm diameter	.	No.	10.00
	100 mm diameter	.	No.	20.00
5.11.4.6	swirl turbulence nozzle; supply only price:	.	No.	6.00
5.11.4.7	mushroom nozzle; supply only price:			
	pipe diameter 19 mm . . .	.	No.	8.50
	pipe diameter 25 mm . . .	.	No.	10.00
	pipe diameter 32 mm . . .	.	No.	12.50
	pipe diameter 38 mm . . .	.	No.	15.00
	pipe diameter 50 mm . . .	.	No.	25.00
5.11.4.8.	adjustable fountain nozzle; supply only price:			
	38 mm diameter	.	No.	22.50
	50 mm diameter	.	No.	25.00

See Stop Press page vii; % additions to rates; September 1972 wage settlement

7.12 STREET FURNITURE

All clause numbers refer to the specification paragraphs in Chapter 5.

5.12.2 AMENITY LIGHTING

Columns

All prices are inclusive of supply, fixing in ground, light fitting and priming, but do not include final painting or electric wiring, connections or related fixtures such as switch gear and time-clock mechanisms.

Clause	Description	unit	£
	Abacus Municipal Limited		
5.12.2.1	tubular steel B(2); 4.000 m high column with Atlas 'Gamma five' post top lantern	No.	33.02
	C.M. Churchouse Limited		
5.12.2.2	'Litex' tubular steel; 4.267 m high with fluorescent fittings:		
	LW7185; single bracket (horizontal) 2 × 40 W	No.	55.96
	LW7185D; double bracket (horizontal) 2/1 × 40 W	No.	72.34
	LV7160; vertical single 1 × 40 W	No.	56.44
	LV7160D; vertical back to back 2 × 40 W	No.	78.12
5.12.2.3	A.61339 external globe light; tungsten lamp:		
	on single stem tube 2.584 m high	No.	37.59
	multi-arm (5 globes), 4.000 m high	No.	76.31
	GEC (Street Lighting) Limited		
5.12.2.4	aluminium B(2); 4.000 m high eight-sided column (ZP.2200) with post top lantern (Z.5670 NU)	No.	38.48
5.12.2.5	reinforced plastics B(2); 4.000 m high circular column (ZP. 3000) with post top lantern (Z.5670 NU)	No.	38.48
	Thorn Lighting Limited		
5.12.2.6	tubular steel B(2); 4.000 m high steel column with integral 'Gamma-7' post top lamp	No.	39.88
5.12.2.7	tubular steel B(2); 4.000 m high steel column with integral 'Gamma-9' post top lantern	No.	41.14

Floodlighting

	Thorn Lighting Limited		
5.12.2.8	'Sun flood' 500 W, HA. 46001 wall mounted	No.	10.37

See Stop Press page vii; % additions to rates; September 1972 wage settlement

SPON'S MECHANICAL AND ELECTRICAL SERVICES PRICE BOOK 1973

4th Edition   Edited by Davis, Belfield & Everest, Chartered Quantity Surveyors

25% to 40% of total building costs are attributable to the cost of engineering services alone.

Lack of price data and traditional "lump sum" quoting methods for mechanical and electrical installations have hindered the rigorous cost control generally recognised as vital.

This is the only book to set out in detail data useful to contractors, estimators and quantity surveyors for the preparation of cost plans and bills, and the analysis of tenders, involving engineering services.

This book is now in its fourth completely revised edition and is published annually.

This is a vital tool for cost control and analysis and an essential companion to *Spon's Architects' and Builders' Price Book*.

No engineer involved in services design can afford to be without this unique office reference.

Short table of contents:

Part I: Mechanical Installations: Directions; Rates of wages and working rules; Market prices of materials; Prices for measured work.

Part II: Electrical Installations: Directions; Rates of wages and working rules; Market prices of materials; Prices for measured work.

Part III: Approximate Estimating: Directions; Mechanical installations; Lift and escalator installation; Electrical installations; Cost indices.

Part IV: Day Work: Heating and ventilating industry; Electrical industry.

Part V: Fees for Professional Services: Consulting engineers' fees.

$8\frac{1}{4} \times 5\frac{7}{8}$": 220pp: hardback: £4.00

E & F N SPON
11 New Fetter Lane, London EC4P 4EE
For full details write to the publisher

THE SITTING DUCK
Churchouse Bollards.
Punishment can't ruffle their feathers.

No screws or sharp edges. We designed it safe for children. The C.O.I.D. included it in Design Index.

Lens in impact-resistant Makrolon. We can't smash it with .22 bullets. So a well-placed kick won't matter.

Annular Fresnel lens throws out all light between 6° and 16° below horizontal. Without dazzle.

Access is easy. Undo the lock, remove lighting head, and open the door.

Slightly sprung top shrugs off minor impacts.

Choose from 100W or 150W tungsten, or long-run 50W MBF/U lamps.

Without a key, nobody can get the head off our bollard.

The post stands up to weather and the public. Ready-finished in stove enamel charcoal grey.

Every Churchouse lighting fitting has a lot to say for itself. Just think what a whole brochure could tell you.

Amenity, emergency, decorative and special-purpose lighting for interior and exterior use. Our free advisory service helps you make the most of the wide range.

Churchouse.
Lighting for living with.

C. M. Churchouse Limited, Lichfield Road, Brownhills, Staffs. Tel: Brownhills 3551-6.

	Pricing–Street Furniture		
	Thorn Lighting Limited continued	unit	£
5.12.2.9	'Area Floodlighting' 400 W, OACG 400; wall mounted	No.	66.99

Lighted bollards
All prices are inclusive of supply, fixing in ground, light fitting and priming, but do not include final painting or electric wiring, connections or related fixtures such as switch gear and time-clock mechanisms.

	C. M. Churchouse Limited		
5.12.2.10	BOL/1050; 856 mm high, steel and aluminium .	No.	28.27
	Concrete Utilities Limited		
5.12.2.11	'Birmingham University'; concrete bollard .	No.	34.54
5.12.2.12	'Decagon'; concrete bollard	No.	54.04
5.12.2.13	'Essex University'; concrete bollard . . .	No.	59.95

Wall brackets
All prices are inclusive of supply fixing to wall, light fitting and priming, but do not include final painting or electric wiring, connections or related fixtures such as switch gear and time-clock mechanisms.

	C. M. Churchouse Limited		
5.12.2.14	'Litex'; 1.500 m long rectangular wall bracketed lamp	No.	24.01
5.12.2.15	A.91340 wall bracket globe	No.	9.35
	GEC (Street Lighting) Limited		
5.12.2.16	ZD.10890 metal bracket and ZD.10877 circular opal lantern	No.	31.98
	Merchant Adventurers Limited		
5.12.2.17	'Square Sphere' series used as bracket lights; transparent smoke glass lamps:		
	230 mm diameter	No.	11.50
	305 mm diameter	No.	13.13
	Thorn Lighting Limited		
5.12.2.18	steel wall bracket and 'Gamma-7' lantern . .	No.	21.63
5.12.2.19	aluminium wall mounted, 'Escort EKF 1100 & 1200':		
	'1100'; small for 60/100 Watt lamp . .	No.	5.23
	'1200'; large for 150/200 Watt lamp . .	No.	5.97

See Stop Press page vii; % additions to rates; September 1972 wage settlement

	Low level lighting	unit	£
	C. M. Churchouse Limited		
5.12.2.20	A. 62360 mushroom light with 2 tungsten lamps	No.	17.17
	Bulkhead fittings		
	C. M. Churchouse Limited		
5.12.2.21	887 lighting brick	No.	6.91
5.12.2.22	907 lighting brick	No.	16.79
	Thorn Lighting Limited		
5.12.2.23	Escort OB.2008; fluorescent bulkhead . .	No.	11.11
5.12.3	LITTER BINS		

Concrete
Supplied and fitted and primed for painting where appropriate

Burnham Signs
Kangley Bridge Road, London, S.E.26

Approved by the Design Centre, the Yorke Litter Bin was originally designed by the Design Research Unit. It is available for fixing in earth or concrete, wall mounted, or free standing on a water filled plastic base.

SPECIFICATION
Bin only: Height 18¾ in, Width 15¼ in, Depth 9¼ in,

Fixed in concrete: Height 28¼ in. With base: Height 28¼ in (approx). Plastic base; Material: Low density polythene. Surface area; 240 sq. in (approx)

Weights: (approx). Water filled 28lb. Wet Sand 45lb. Empty 5¼lb. Water Capacity: 18 pints

For information on the Yorke Litter bin and other products from our range contact:

**BURNHAM SIGNS,
KANGLEY BRIDGE ROAD,
LONDON S.E. 26** TEL 01-778 7041

THE YORKE LITTER BIN

See Stop Press page vii; % additions to rates; September 1972 wage settlement

Pricing–Street Furniture 341

		unit	£
	Abacus Municipal LImited		
5.12.3.1	Model 631; large capacity container	No.	41.47
5.12.3.2	Model 607; standard size container	No.	14.08
	Mono Concrete (Northern) Limited		
5.12.3.3	'Newstead'; precast concrete	No.	23.86

Metal

	Abacus Municipal Limited		
5.12.3.4	Model 621; stove enamelled steel	No.	5.63
5.12.3.5	Model 611; stainless steel	No.	12.54
	Braby Group Limited		
5.12.3.6	Model A; aluminium, small	No.	3.30
	Model B; aluminium, large	No.	3.40
	Burnham and Company (Onyx) Limited		
5.12.3.7	'Yorke'; stove enamelled steel, wall mounted	No.	14.14
	White and Carter (Councils) Limited		
5.12.3.8	'Hykleen'; stove enamelled, steel with lid	No.	10.58
5.12.3.9	'Streamline'; stove enamelled steel	No.	5.64

Plastics

	Abacus Municipal Limited		
5.12.3.10	Model 623; glass fibre with lid	No.	13.78

Timber faced

	Metalform Limited		
5.12.3.11	'London Parks'; with teakwood vertical slats		
	large	No.	23.65
	small	No.	20.57
	White and Carter (Councils) Limited		
5.12.3.12	'Diploma 2'; with Burma teak slats	No.	9.43

5.12.4   OUTDOOR SEATS

Concrete framed
prices include supply and fixing by bolting into

See Stop Press page vii; % additions to rates; September 1972 wage settlement

		unit	£
5.12.4 (cont'd)	**Outdoor seats** continued existing paving or concrete bases provided separately		

Holton Builders Limited

5.12.4.1 'Reepham'; concrete with timber slats:

1.500 m long	. . . . .	No.	18.35
1.800 m long	. . . . .	No.	18.97
2.400 m long	. . . . .	No.	20.08

Neptune Concrete Limited

5.12.4.2 'Southampton Mark 3'; concrete with hardwood slats . . . . No. 30.87

Metal framed

Abacus Municipal Limited

5.12.4.3 outdoor seat; steel and timber:

306 S; 1.829 m softwood without arms	No.	27.99
306 SA; 1.829 m softwood with arms	No.	29.01
306 H; 1.829 m hardwood without arms	No.	29.88
306 HA; 1.829 m hardwood with arms	No.	34.13

(other sizes also manufactured)

Theta and Delta outdoor seat benches are designed and produced by Geometric Furniture Limited and have been selected for Design Index by the Council of Industrial Design

Careful selection of Iroko kiln dried hardwoods, plated fastenings and nylon coated standards combine pleasing appearance with ability to withstand weather and hard knocks.

Special designs both in concrete and metal have been produced to requirement for many environmental and landscaping schemes.

GEOMETRIC FURNITURE LIMITED,
19 Bell Street,
OLDHAM, Lancashire.
Telephone 061-633 1119

See Stop Press page vii; % additions to rates; September 1972 wage settlement

Pricing—Street Furniture

		units	£
	Geometric Furniture		
5.12.4.4	'Delta'; narrow iroko slats		
	1.800 m long	No.	21.80
	2.400 m long	No.	27.80
	Orchard Seating		
5.12.4.5	'Pointer' series; iroko broad planks on stout steel frame:		
	P.4; 1.219 m long	No.	15.00
	P.6; 1.829 m long	No.	18.00
	P.8; 2.440 m long	No.	23.00
5.12.4.6	'Setter'; narrow iroko slats:		
	1.200 m long	No.	25.00
	1.800 m long	No.	28.00
	2.400 m long	No.	33.50
	Battenhurst Developments		
5.12.4.7	Combined bench and picnic table:		
	softwood; 1.800 m long	No.	27.50
	softwood; 2.440 m long	No.	37.50

5.12.5 **PLANT CONTAINERS**

Concrete, asbestos cement and fibreglass
Prices are supply only; filling, planting etc. must be calculated separately.

	Esplana Limited		
5.12.5.1	'Architectural range'; patent cement typical sizes:		
	400 mm square × 400 mm high;		
	black and white	No.	9.75
	natural	No.	8.75
	900 mm diameter × 450 mm high;		
	black and white	No.	10.47
	natural	No.	8.70
	600 mm diameter × 393 mm high;		
	black and white	No.	5.84

CANADIAN STYLE COMBINED TABLES AND BENCHES
Specially designed for parks and recreation areas.
6ft or 8ft Models available in treated softwood or hardwoods.
Also litter bins and litter collection tools.
Details from
BATTENHURST DEVELOPMENTS, SANDHURST, KENT.
Tel: SANDHURST 300

See Stop Press page vii; % additions to rates; September 1972 wage settlement

Pricing–Street Furniture

		unit	£
5.12.5.1 (cont'd)	**Esplana Limited** *continued* natural 450 mm diameter × 525 mm high; black and white natural	No. No. No.	4.70 13.35 11.80
5.12.5.2	**Glasdon Limited** 'Glasfibre architectural planters'; fibre glass; typical sizes circular; 450 mm diameter × 300 mm high circular; 610 mm diameter × 530 mm high circular; 910 mm diameter × 400 mm high square; 610 × 610 mm × 400 mm high square; 910 × 910 mm × 400 mm high rectangular; 1.220 m × 610 mm × 400 mm hexagonal; 900 mm × 400 mm high	 No. No. No. No. No. No. No.	 14.47 22.89 36.69 39.29 64.53 57.40 43.57
5.12.5.3	**Mono Concrete Limited** plant bowls; white precast concrete; typical sizes: 'Majorca'; elliptical, 750 × 550 mm × 600 mm high 'Elba'; circular, 970 mm diameter × 470 mm high 'Chelsea'; 1.220 m diameter × 355 mm high 'Norwich'; 915 mm diameter × 285 mm high 'Worthing'; 915 mm diameter × 570 mm high 'Kew'; 710 mm diameter × 300 mm diameter 'Wisley'; 890 mm diameter × 450 mm high	 No. No. No. No. No. No. No.	 17.06 19.53 22.86 12.90 16.92 14.89 19.04
5.12.6	**CYCLE STANDS** **Metal holders**		
5.12.6.1	**Le Bas Tube Company Limited** 'Velopa' bicycle holder; galvanised steel: type SRV; fixed in ground type R, fixed to wall **Concrete parking blocks**	 No. No.	 3.34 3.26
5.12.6.2 5.12.6.3	**Mono Concrete Limited** 'Monohex'; hexagonal slabs: plain finish textured face 'Metric Four Square'; square slabs: exposed aggregate	 No. No. No.	 1.83 1.95 2.22
5.12.6.4	**Stelcon Limited** 'Stelcon' bicycle parking block	No.	1.51

			unit	£
7.13		**MAINTENANCE** All clause numbers refer to the specification paragraphs in Chapter 5.		
5.13.3		**Grass**		
5.13.3.2		tractor gang mowing; leaving cuttings; per cut	ha	25.00
5.13.3.3		mowing with 914 mm wide mower; leaving cuttings; per cut	100 m^2	0.30
		mowing with 914 mm wide mower; with box; stacking mowings on site; per cut	100 m^2	0.34
5.13.3.4		rotary or flail mowing; leaving cuttings; per cut	100 m^2	0.25
		extra for raking up cuttings and stacking on site; per cut	100 m^2	0.13
5.13.3.5		stone picking of all stones on surface over 25 mm and removing from site	100 m^2	0.21
5.13.3.6		aerate ground by using a tractor drawn spiker	ha	22.50
5.13.4		**Shrub beds**		
5.13.4.1		keep shrub beds of mixed permanent planting weed free for one growing season (6 times per season)	m^2	0.57
5.13.4.2		provide seasonal bedding out plants (p.c. of £1.00 per m^2) and plant and maintain for one growing season changing plants twice during period	m^2	3.50
5.13.4.3		spread 50 mm thick mulch of peat over area of shrub bed	m^2	0.50

See Stop Press page vii; % additions to rates; September 1972 wage settlement

8 Machinery and equipment: round-up of recent innovations

8.1 INTRODUCTION

8.1.1 The intention of this chapter is to summarise recent innovations in machinery and equipment used in landscape construction and maintenance work. As this is the first edition of the Landscape Handbook the chapter covers a number of new items of machinery or modifications to existing ones which have occurred over the past few years. In future editions the period under review will be more limited, covering only the time since the previous edition.

8.1.2 As has been mentioned in similar cases in other chapters the range of items which could be considered for inclusion in this chapter is very extensive. Consequently the following list gives only a typical range and does not purport to be a comprehensive list of manufacturers or their products.

8.2 AERATORS AND SCARIFIERS

H. Pattisson & Co. (Stanmore, Middlesex)

8.2.1 *The 'Sportsfield Aerator'* is designed for use on outfields etc., under very wet conditions. There are three different types available: diamond shaped tines for slitting, knife blades for use on very wet surfaces and hook or bayonet shaped tines for maximum sub-surface disturbance, aeration etc. The maximum length of the tines is 127 mm. This machine is driven in work and overground travel by a 4-stroke engine. Manual lifting is eliminated by a built-in lifting mechanism controlled by a small hand lever which raises the spiking assembly. Another device applies extra weight to assist tine penetration without sustained manual effort. The machine has 36 tines and the width of the spiking drum is 990 mm.

8.2.2 *The 'Deep Hole Drill Aerator'* has been developed for use on fine turf. By means of a boring or drill action the tines penetrate at least 150 mm into the ground, but the penetration is limited only to the length of the drills used and the drilled holes have uncompacted walls. The spoil from the operation is brought to the surface for collection. The drill tines are of varying diameter and length up to 228 mm and aeration can be achieved with this machine whenever such really deep tining is considered necessary.

8.2.3 Rental Equipment Manufacturing Co. (Englewood, Colorado, U.S.A.)

The *'Blue Bird' scarifier* is available from Andrew's Lawn Edgers Limited (Sunningdale, Berks), who are the sole distributors in the U.K. Its cutting width is 457 mm and it has either 5 h.p. or 7 h.p. 4-stroke Briggs engine. The propulsion over the surface is given by the forward rotation of the rotor. The latter is of heavy cast steel and carries 52 free swinging, case-hardened, flail type steel blades which turn in a full circle. Each blade measures 3 x 25 x 100 mm. Also available is a knife reel with ten blade carriers spaced at 50 mm centres, each carrier having two blades. This reel allows continuous slits to be made in good turf to a depth of 50 mm. A 6 mm thick rubber deflector extending the full rear width of the machine absorbs any shocks which could arise from stray stones, pebbles etc.

8.2.4 Sisis Equipment (Macclesfield) Ltd. (Macclesfield, Cheshire)

The *'Autocrat'* is a new powered aerator and has been introduced for use on all fine turf areas. The interchangeable standard Sisis 'Auto-Turfman' tines can be fitted to this new machine. The 5 h.p. 4-stroke petrol engine gives an operating speed of 1.2 km/hr and with the eight co-ordinating tines a golf green of approximately 500 m² can be tined in 30 minutes, and an average bowling green in 1½ hours. This machine can be turned in its own length and tining can continue when turning at the end of the swathe. The depth of the tine penetration can be adjusted up to 100 mm.

8.3 GRADERS

8.3.1 Universal Graders Ltd. (Pentre, Deeside, Flintshire)

The *'Universal Grader' D4A and D4B* is for towing by tractor. The wheels of the D4A model can be hydraulically steered up to 25 degrees left or right with the blade at any angle, making the grader very manouverable. The blade can be lowered or raised, angled or tilted and the optional scarifier raised or lowered from the fully adjustable rear control seat. The mechanical differences between the two models are that the D4B is not steerable, the blade does not angle by hydraulic means and the grader is controlled by the tractor operator.

8.4 MOWERS

8.4.1 John Allen & Sons (Oxford) Ltd. (Cowley, Oxford)

'Mayfield' range; three new units consisting of a cylinder mower, a rotary grasscutter and a scythe have been added to this range of equipment. The Mayfield tractor is common to all machines and is available with a 6 h.p. Briggs & Stratton engine or an 9 h.p. Kohler cast iron engine. The gear box is three speed with the option of a reverse gear. There is also a choice of wheel sizes; 508 mm or 533 mm. The

Machinery and equipment: round-up of recent innovations

8.4.1
(cont'd)
cylinder mower of 762 mm cutting width has a fabricated steel frame and an adjustable deflector for front and rear throw. A front bumper guard is fitted as standard equipment.
The cutting cylinder has three blades of 196 mm diameter and produces from 34 cuts per metre to 93 cuts per metre. Height of cut is adjustable from 19 mm to 54 mm. The grassbox is available as an optional extra.
The rotary cutter has twin blades and a cutting width of 812 mm. Individual wheel adjustment determines the height of cut from 25 mm to 100 mm in four different positions. Front wheels can be mounted inside or outside the width of cut and a front safety guard is a standard fitting. The motor scythe is fitted with a 914 mm Allen reciprocating cutterbar which can be offset to the left or right. Heavy duty units 609 mm or 1.219 m are optional extras.

8.4.2
The Allen 5.26 'Ride-on' rotary mower has a Briggs & Stratton 4-stroke 5 h.p. engine and recoil starter. It has a two speed and reverse gear box with forward speeds of 2½ m.p.h. and 4 m.p.h., and reverse 2¾ m.p.h. The cutter unit is a single piece pressed steel deck with 660 mm spring steel cutterbar. Cutting height is adjustable through six positions from 25 mm to 88 mm with additional front adjustment by single pin and locking clip to 114 mm. The seat is a pressed steel seat pan with detachable foam padded upholstery. Steering is centre-link with tiller control giving a turning circle of 3.700 m. Rate of cut is up to 0.303 ha per hour.

8.4.3
The Allen 'Champion' is suitable for heavy duty work on large areas, along highways, on sports grounds etc. The engine is Briggs & Stratton 6 h.p. with rewind starter. The cutter is a fully balanced aluminium disc fitted with four replaceable cutting sections giving 660 mm width of cut. Four cutting heights can be selected from a minimum 19 mm.

R. K. Allett (Stamford, Lincs.)

8.4.4
The Allett 'Mk 4' (914 mm) and 'Mk 14' (762 mm) are both heavy duty mowers and are the same except for the width of cut. The engine is four cylinder with electric starting. The twist grip throttle control will give speeds from 1½ m.p.h. to 8 m.p.h. and the travelling and cutter clutches are operated independently. No reverse gear is fitted. The grassbox is glassfibre and a parking brake is a standard fitting for both machines.

Charles H. Pugh Ltd. (Birmingham)

8.4.5
The 'Atco Groundsman' Models 28 and 34 are two new additions to the professional range of fully powered cylinder mowers. They have cutting widths of 711 mm and 863 mm respectively. Other than the difference in the cutting width, both models are of the same design and are powered by a 256 cc. 4-stroke engine with fan and cowl cooling. Electric self-starter, battery and automatic system are fitted as standard equipment. The six bladed heavy duty cutting cylinder gives 89 cuts per metre and power drive with the cutters stationary can be obtained by hand operation of a cutter clutch lever. The grassbox is of reinforced

Water
What the hell for!

If the penny hasn't dropped we're simply suggesting that all landscaping (concrete jungles apart) needs to be considered in relation to existing water supplies. (Rainfall's not enough, ask any gardener). And the best and most economical time is when you're planning. Turf, shrubs, flower-beds all benefit from controlled, regular watering and that's where **we** come in! We even design and produce fully automated watering systems for golf courses — like St Andrews, Parkstone, Wentworth and many more.... We have equipment for watering all types of sports pitches too. Get the benefit of our international know-how, clip and mail the coupon now or write detailing your problems . . .

Wright Rain

WRIGHT RAIN LIMITED
RINGWOOD, HAMPSHIRE TEL: 2251

BIRMID QUALCAST

NAME..................................
ADDRESS...............................
....
....

SLH 72

Make sure you always use the <u>current</u> editions of Spon . . . Inflation has made last year's editions obsolete

SPON'S ARCHITECTS' AND BUILDERS' PRICE BOOK 1973

98th edition   Edited by Davis, Belfield & Everest, Chartered Quantity Surveyors

At a time of continuing inflation and labour unrest within the building industry, the A & B continues to provide vital and reliably up-dated pricing guidance. Perhaps more than ever before — with a rise of 10%–15% on measured work prices, and some $8\frac{1}{2}$% on overall costs since the 1972 edition — the need to use the current edition is of paramount importance.

The 1973 A & B takes into account the latest materials prices, and the latest rates for social insurances and similar on-costs, current at the time of going to press.

As regards wages, for lack of a wage settlement on press date, the editors have assumed a wage rate of £25.20 p.w. for craftsmen and £21.20 for labourers. However the 'Stop Press' section provides the necessary factors to apply if the wage settlement eventually negotiated differs from these assumptions.

In this edition the 'Constants' section has been re-introduced in metric form. As a further contribution to the change to metric — which the B.S.I. recommend be completed by end 1972 — the sections have been rearranged to give priority to metric information. Where materials continue to be available in imperial sizes, the imperial size is given together with a metric conversion.

The 'European Section' — an innovation in the 1972 edition — was well received and is now up-dated and revised, as well as expanded to provide similar data for Denmark, Italy and Norway.

Make sure you reserve your copy of this essential reference work today.

$8\frac{1}{4} \times 5\frac{7}{8}$": 500pp: hardback: £3.30

E & F N SPON
11 New Fetter Lane, London EC4P 4EE
For full details write to the publisher

Machinery and equipment: round-up of recent innovations

8.4.5 (cont'd) glassfibre and is of the 'swing over' type. The lower section of the box has been recessed to allow for use with swivel front rollers when required. The standard Atco trailer seat can be used with both machines but is an optional extra.

8.4.6 The 'Atco' 508 mm heavy duty sidewheel powered motor is designed for use in difficult conditions such as grass verges and semi-rough conditions. The machine has heavy duty side plates and rigid cross sections. The engine is a 119 cc. 4-stroke Norton Villiers with recoil starter. The five bladed cutting cylinder produces 34 cuts per metre and the height of the cut is adjustable from 6 mm to 41 mm. The risk of cutter end damage is minimised by steel guards at each end of the cutting cylinder. The full width back roller is a one piece tubular steel construction and runs on sealed heavy duty ball races.

8.4.7 The 'Atco Vari-gang' is a design which permits easy build up from one unit to three, five and higher multiples as well as conversion of the triple set to hydraulic lift. There is a choice of a five bladed or eight bladed cutting cylinder giving 29 cuts per metre of 44 cuts per metre respectively. The cylinder can be easily removed and replaced without any disturbance of the main structure or gear case. For relatively close mowing the full width back roller is adjusted to provide heights from 13 mm to 38 mm in increments of 6 mm. For rougher cutting and for mowing at higher levels the drawbar quadrant can be adjusted to any one of five positions giving heights of cut from 13 mm to 25 mm and then by increments of 25 mm to a maximum 100 mm.

8.4.8 The 'Atco Mini Gang' has recently been introduced for use as a triple set or as twin outriggers to a conventional large area power mower. The overall cutting width of the triple set is 1.422 m. The units have a heavy duty bottom blade and a five bladed cutting cylinder of 152 mm diameter which gives 34 cuts per metre. Height of cut is adjustable from 6 mm to 50 mm.

Dennis Bros. Ltd. (Guildford, Surrey)
8.4.9 The 'Rotorider' is a ride-on rotary mower with a cutting width of 508 mm. Frame and deck are of steel construction and the body is of pressed steel on which stainless steel screen-grids are provided. The engine is a 4 h.p. Aspera 4-stroke with a recoil starter and a float type carburettor. Variable forward and reverse speeds are obtainable on throttle.

8.4.10 The 'Rotomatic' is a self-propelled pedestrian operated rotary mower with a cutting width of 508 mm. The 3.5 h.p. Aspera 4-stroke engine has a recoil starter. Other features of this machine include the side ejection of cuttings, automatic height adjustment of the wheels and the fitting of a mulcher plate.

8.4.11 The 'Supreme' is a sidewheel self-propelled cylinder mower with a 406 mm cutting width. The machine is powered by a recoil started

8.4.11 (cont'd) 2.3 h.p. Aspera 4-stroke engine which is fitted with a special silencer. The cutting cylinder is five bladed. A grass catcher is available as an optional extra.

Hayter Ltd. (Bishop's Stortford, Herts)

8.4.12 *The 'Condor'* is a roller propelled cylinder mower and has a 258 cc. MAG 4-stroke engine developing 6.2 h.p. with a recoil starter and three forward gears and one reverse. There are three alternative mowing attachments. The 762 mm five bladed cutting cylinder is for fine lawn areas giving up to 122 cuts per metre depending on gear selection. Cutting height ranges from 9 mm to 38 mm. The three bladed cutting cylinder is for use on road verges etc., giving up to 50 cuts per metre again depending on gear selection; cutting heights vary from 12 mm to 44 mm. The main frame of the 762 mm rotary cutting attachment is fitted with twin, cutterhead assemblies which contra-rotate to provide a single swathe. A single cutting height adjustment lever gives a cutting height range of 19 mm to 50 mm. Either wheeled or trailer type seats are available as optional extras.

8.4.13 *The 482 mm 'Hawk Major'* is a larger and more powerful version of the 304 mm Hawk. This new machine is powered by a 5 h.p. Briggs & Stratton 206 cc. 4-stroke engine with a recoil starter. The 482 mm cutterbar is steel and austempered to give toughness and durability. The height of the cut is adjustable from 22 mm to 45 mm. The grass deflector is fitted with a nylon rubbing pad and ensures a clean cut against walls and kerbs. As an alternative a 406 mm cutterbar can be supplied as an extra for heavy duty reclamation work and the machine can have a combination of wheels only or wheel and rollers to suit varying conditions.

8.4.14 *The 1.828 m 'Haytermower'* is a fully trailed machine and is coupled to the tractor by a drawbar which is hinged on the machine to allow ease of travel over rough ground. The cutterhead assembly is fitted with a circular bottom plate with fixed blades, which are suitable for topping and maintenance mowing, while the other assembly is fitted with a cutterbar. The cutterbars, which are optional, are suitable for reclamation, scrub clearance and rough grass areas. The changing from bottom plates to cutterbars involves the removal of 4 fixing bolts. The cutting range height is from 25 mm to 127 mm. The rate of cut is 1.215 ha per hour. Hinged guarding is fitted to the front of the machine as standard, and a special stone guarding at the rear of the machine for use on sports grounds, golf courses and public areas can be supplied as an extra. To assist transportation from one site to another a transport lift attachment is available as an optional extra.

G. D. Mountfield Ltd. (Maidenhead, Berks)

8.4.15 *The 'Mk 2' version of the Mountfield Mk 4 Minor 457 mm rotary mower* has a 3 h.p. Aspera 4-stroke engine. Height of cut has been altered from unit and bolt adjustment to independent finger tip control

8.4.15 (cont'd) levers. By means of the levers, the height of cut produced by the hardened manganese steel blade will vary between 13 mm and 64 mm. The machine frame is of tough pressure die cast aluminium alloy and the large capacity polythene grassbox is available as an optional extra.

Portec (U.K.) Ltd. (Ruabon, Wrexham)

8.4.16 *The Portec Brott 'Cropet' 800 mm flail grasscutter* has been designed for use where grass collection is not required. It can be used either as a pedestrian controlled machine or with a towed sulky seat. There are two alternative 7 h.p. 4-stroke engines available, namely the Honda G.65 or MAG 1026 SRL and variable forward speeds are given by hydrostatic drive, and range from zero to 11.3 km per hour and a reverse speed of 1.6 km per hour. Height of cut is adjustable by means of a direct acting lever from 13 mm to 102 mm and flails and revolving parts are fully guarded.

Ransomes, Sims & Jefferies Ltd. (Ipswich)

8.4.17 *The 609 mm 'Matador'* is a heavy duty lawn mower which in its standard form is recommended for the cutting of tennis courts, public gardens and large lawns. This machine also forms the power unit for the mini-gang outfit which with its two outrigger trailing units, cuts a width of 1.524 m, doubling its cutting capacity. Power is provided by a 4-stroke air-cooled petrol engine, with automatic lubrication to all moving parts. The 146 mm all-welded cutting reel has five blades and runs on ball bearings. The height of cut is variable from 6 mm to 28 mm and is controled by a handscrew. Two types of landrolls are available, cast iron or rubber treaded. The grassbox is of the large capacity steel 'tip over' type. The landroll brake operated by Bowden cable, transport carriage with pneumatic tyres and a trailing seat are optional extras. The cutting performance when pedestrian operated is 1600 m^2 per hour, and with trailing seat and operator 2150 m^2 per hour.

8.4.18 *The 'Mastiff' mower* is available in two sizes, either 762 mm or 914 mm. Both sizes are powered by a 4-stroke engine with a recoil starter. An electric starter is available as an optional extra on the 914 mm model only. Power is transmitted from the engine through a centrifugal clutch to the gearbox. Separate dog clutches are provided for the reel drives enabling the machine to be used for rolling only. In addition the landroll drive is provided with a half speed reverse gear. The cutting reel is 6-bladed and of 196 mm diameter, running in self-aligning ball bearings. The grass-box is of the all-metal, tip-over type, fitted with side-lifting handles. A self emptying grassbox is available as an optional extra. Height of cut ranges from 5 mm to 35 mm with a cutting ratio of 65 cuts per metre. The cutting performance of the 762 mm model is 2070 m^2 per hour, and with the 914 mm machine 2500 m^2 per hour. A trailing seat, outrigger units and drawbars are available as extras.

8.4.19 *The 'Pedestrian Flail Mower'* has a cutting width of 762 mm. Chassis and flail housing are of fabricated sheet steel construction—the flail housing incorporates a hinged flap at the front and hinged flaps are also provided at the rear to protect the operator's feet. The 4-stroke MAG 1045 SRL engine is recoil started and has a continuous output of 9.5 h.p. at maximum governed engine speed. The gearbox gives a selection of three forward speeds and reverse and has a built-in differential. At maximum governed engine speed, forward speeds are as follows:— first gear 2.3 km per hour, second gear 4.1 km per hour, third gear 6.0 km per hour. Reverse speed is 3.3 km per hour. Each rear wheel has an independently operated drum brake for power steering. The toughened steel flails are mounted in pairs along a balanced shaft and revolve at high speed. According to site and surface conditions this machine will operate on slopes of up to 1 in 3.

8.4.20 *The Mounted 3-unit Gang Mower* has had its transporting width slimmed down while retaining the full cutting width of 2.134 m. The 'folded in' width of 2.464 m is well within the permissible road transporting width. The adjustment of two locking pins and stabilising chains allows the mower to be converted from transport to working position within a very short time. These mounted gangs can be lifted immediately by the tractor's hydraulic power. Each cutting unit is flexibly hitched to the tubular steel frame and is free to follow any undulations in the ground. While working, the mower has complete freedom of trail from a single-point universal hitch so that cutting close to trees and other such obstacles is easily carried out. Either the 'Sportcutter' or 'Magna' cutting units can be used according to the class of work required. The reel is driven at both ends from the road wheels through hardened steel machine cut gears, totally enclosed in an oil bath. Performance is as follows: 1.21 ha per hour at 8.05 km per hour, 1.62 ha per hour at 11.27 km per hour, and 2.43 ha per hour at 16.09 km per hour.

Stemport Marketing Co. Ltd. (Aylesbury, Bucks)

8.4.21 *The Masport 'Commander'* is a new 609 mm power driven rotary mower which has the 5 h.p. Briggs & Stratton engine with vee belt transmission. When adjusting the height of cut the blade housing moves up and down with the blade thereby ensuring that optimum cutting efficiency and safety are maintained whether cutting high or low. The cutter-blade and stiffener have been specially hardened. Height of cut adjustment from 10 mm to 102 mm is made independently, front and rear. There is a side discharge chute which throws the mowings away from the operator and is fitted with a safety deflector flap, ensuring that no build-up or re-circulation of clippings can take place under the housing. Further protection is given from flying stones and any other debris by a fixed rear safety skirt.

8.4.22 *The 'Monarch'* is another new product and is a ride-on rotary grasscutter of 660 mm cutting width with positive front wheel steering. Power is provided by a 7 h.p. Briggs & Stratton 4-stroke engine from

Machinery and equipment: round-up of recent innovations

8.4.22 which the belt drive incorporates an exclusive power transfer drive
(*cont'd*) system. There are four forward gears and a reverse giving a range of speed from crawling pace to 8 km per hour. The clutch and brake pedal are combined and work simultaneously and a blade clutch control allows for machine drive without blade rotation. The high carbon steel cutterblade is specially toughened and the heavy gauge steel housing is quickly replaceable. A front safety skirt is an integral part of this machine. Again height of cut is adjustable independently front and rear from 10 mm to 102 mm. The seat, which is contoured and padded, is covered with heavy duty vinyl.

Toro Manufacturing Corporation (Minneapolis, Minnesota U.S.A.)

8.4.23 The *'new-look' Trojan II* is available from Flymo Ltd. (Watford, Herts). It is designed to power the 1.270 m 'Wirlwind' rotary mower but several new optional extras such as 1.219 m leaf/snow sweeper, or snow blade etc., gives this machine all-the-year-round maintenance ability. The engine is 12.5 h.p. with a 12-volt electric starter. A battery is not provided. The four speed gear transmission and differential are enclosed in a single gear case. At 3400 r.p.m. speeds of up to 8 km per hour can be achieved. The mowing capacity is approximately 4.86 ha a day at a speed of 4.83 km per hour. Height of cut ranges from 25 mm to 203 mm and is adjustable front and rear.

8.4.24 The *'Toro Super Pro'* also available from Flymo Ltd. is a more powerful version of the 'Professional'. Available as a three-unit mower the Super Pro has a 12 h.p. engine with a four speed transaxle and reverse gear. An electric starter, parking brake and foam cushion seat are standard equipment. There is a choice of the five or six bladed cutting reels which are adjustable from 9 mm to 69 mm, and width of cut of the three units is 2.057 m. Mowing capacity is 11.33 ha per day.

8.4.25 The *'Spartan VII' gang unit* is designed to improve the performance and cutting capacity of the Toro Parkmaster and is now available from Flymo Ltd. These units, in conjunction with the Parkmaster, can be used in outfits of three, five or seven giving a cutting width of 4.6 m. Each unit has a seven bladed cutting cylinder and is available with either 355 mm or 406 mm pneumatic tyred wheels. The former type gives 46 cuts per metre and the latter 42 cuts per metre. This new machine also has a hand operated centrally positioned hand wheel for bottom blade to cutting cylinder adjustment, which gives an accuracy of 25 mm with each turn.

8.5 SPRAYERS

Chieftain Forge Ltd. (Bathgate, West Lothian, Scotland)

8.5.1 The *'Chieftain Metsa'* blower is for use mainly in forestry work for the broadcasting of granulated or powdered weedkiller, insecticide, fertiliser or lime. This machine weighs 152 kg, is tractor driven and

8.5.1 (cont'd) mounted on a three-point linkage. All adjustments can be made from the driver's seat. The hopper capacity is 508 kg to 558 kg. The working radius is approximately 31 m to 41 m and the spreading height is 1.524 m. The blowing tube is adjustable vertically and turns 360 degrees, allowing the blower to spread over 5000 m^2 from one position.

Cooper, Pegler & Co. Ltd. (Burgess Hill, Sussex)

8.5.2 The *'Mini Trailer Unit Sprayer'* has been specifically designed for towing behind small tractors, lawnmowers etc. It has a pin-type linkage and by fitting different booms it can be adapted for spray application of various types of materials including selective weedkillers. The 91 litre nominal capacity galvanised steel tank has a large filler opening with a sieve-type strainer. Hydraulic agitation is provided within the tank and a sump plug is fitted for cleaning purposes and complete drainage. The 2-stroke petrol engine drives a Minar pump and is able to deliver up to 14 litres/minute at pressures of up to 140 tonne/m^2. A two piece spray boom can be adjusted for height from 304 mm to 609 mm and allows a coverage of 2.743 m width. Optional extras include a high pressure gun for use with up to 30.500 m of hose and a spray lance to give multi-use of the spray unit.

The Dorman Sprayer Co. Ltd. (Ely, Cambridgeshire)

8.5.3 The *'Rota Sprayer'* has been designed to fit on the Howard 'E' range of rotavators and is intended for use with the rotavator to combine the spraying and cultivating operations in one to give a more effective control of perennial grass weeds, in particular couch grass. The spray equipment consists of 273 litre front mounted tank, and a rollervane pump and spray boom are mounted on the rotavator. The spraybar is protected by a heavy shield from flying stones and the angle of the boom can be adjusted to give maximum cover in different types of soil.

8.5.4 The *'Auto-Sprayer'* is based on the Dorman Plastic Piston Knapsack. The tank has a capacity of 18 litres and is fitted with an agitator. The knapsack is mounted on a single wheeled chassis with a pneumatic tyred wheel. A solid rubber or cage wheel can be supplied as an alternative. A single lever pump is driven from the axle and a valve is incorporated to ensure even application irrespective of forward speed. Six nozzles at 333 mm centres on the sprayboom give a cover of 2.000 m width and are available for application rates of 56 or 112 litres per hectare. A row crop boom is available as an optional extra.

8.6 SWEEPERS

Horwool (Holdings) Ltd. (Romford, Essex)

8.6.1 The *Horwool 'Self-Propelled Sweeper'* has been designed for the purpose of simplifying most cleaning-up operations on turf, e.g. removal of debris after scarifying, picking up hollow tine cores, sweeping up leaves etc. The machine is powered by a Briggs & Stratton

8.6.1
(cont'd)
3 h.p. engine and separate clutches are also provided for machine drive and power to the nylon brushes. The nylon reinforced collecting bag is removable and is situated at the rear of the machine. A cover for the collecting bag, made from the same material, is also provided. The nylon sweeping brushes can be replaced quite easily when necessary. This machine is available with sweeping widths of 635 mm and 914 mm.

The Toro Manufacturing Corporation (Minneapolis, Minnesota, U.S.A.)
8.6.2
The Toro 'Rake-o-Vac' is now available through Flymo Ltd. (Watford, Herts.) This is a tractor drawn sweeper with a width of 1.524 m and a hopper capacity of 3.220 m^3. The machine is complete with three attachments for cleaning-up operations on grass and hard surfaces. These three attachments consist of a nylon fingered rotary rake for use on turf, a rotary sweeper reel for lifting litter from hard surfaces and a renovator reel. The latter has three rows of ten shock absorbing blades which can be used for cutting through matted grass and other tough vegetation which is then vacuumed into the hopper. The unit can be drawn by a tractor or a light truck at speeds of up to 64 km/hr.

9 Research report

9.1 SOURCES OF INFORMATION ON RESEARCH

9.1.1 Landscape research or work related to it is going on all over Great Britain and abroad, especially in universities and colleges.
The Countryside Commission now publishes, each autumn, a 'Research Register' which is available, free of charge, from
Countryside Commission,
1, Cambridge Gate,
Regents Park,
London NW1 4JY.
This covers countryside research only; urban projects are to be found in the Town Planning Institute's Register of Research. It would be invidious to select typical research projects from the Countryside Commission Register for inclusion in this publication, but as an indication of the scope covered, it is useful to list some of the subjects which are detailed in the 1971 edition:
Air surveys, bridleways, canals, common land, country parks, derelict land, disused railways, dunes, ecology, footpaths, forests, gravel pits, green belts, historic houses, information centres, landscape evaluation, litter, moorland, nature trails, open spaces, pollution, reservoirs, roads, scenic drives and routes, skiing, sports, structure plans, tourism, upland areas, vandalism, viewpoints, visitor survey, wilderness, wildfowl and youth hostels.

9.1.2 In 1971 C.R.R.A.G. (Countryside Recreation Research Advisory Group) produced a report for the Countryside Commission called 'Research Priorities'.

9.1.3 At the time of going to press we learn that a report on 'Landscape Evaluation Techniques' by Ian Laurie for the Countryside Commission will be published during 1972.

9.1.4 News of other research work, meetings, symposia and publications can be obtained from 'Landscape Research News' published by the Landscape Research Group which is administered from the Institute of Advanced Architectural Studies, The King's Manor, York.

9.1.5 N.E.R.C. (Natural Environment Research Council) supports many research projects with grants.

9.1.6 C.E.S. (Centre for Environmental Studies) has a Research Grants Committee which is responsible for allocating C.E.S. grants to externally based projects and for approving work financed from outside

9.1.6 resources for which C.E.S. assumes responsibility. The Centre Advisory
(cont'd) Committee is responsible for the development of in-house research and for the general programme of work done from 5, Cambridge Terrace, London N.W.1.

9.1.7 The Sheffield Centre for Environmental Research was established in 1970 with initial financial assistance from C.E.S.

Bibliography

BOOKS REFERRED TO IN THE TEXT OR USEFUL FOR ADDITIONAL INFORMATION

Arboricultural Association. *The Care of Trees on Development Sites.* Arboricultural Association.
Architects' Journal. *Metric Handbook.* Architectural Press.
Barr, J. *Assaults on our Senses.* Methuen.
Barr, J. *Derelict Britain.* Penguin.
Baver, L. D. *Soil Physics.* Chapan and Hall.
Bean, W. J. *Trees and Shrubs Hardy in the British Isles.* John Murray.
Beazley, E. *Design and Detail of Space Between Buildings.* Architectural Press.
Beazley, E. *Designed for Recreation.* Faber & Faber.
Bedall, J. L. *Hedges for Farm and Garden.* Faber & Faber.
Bengtsson, A. *Environmental Planning for Children's Play.* Praeger, New York.
Bonham-Carter, V. *The Survival of the English Countryside.* Hodder & Stoughton.
Brett, L. *Landscape in Distress.* Architectural Press.
Brookes, J. *Room Outside.* Thames & Hudson.
Caborn, J. M. *Hedges.* Ministry of Agriculture, Fisheries & Food.
Caborn, J. M. *Shelter Belts and Windbreaks.* Faber & Faber.
Carson, R. *Silent Spring.* Penguin.
Chadwick, G. F. *The Park and the Town.* Architectural Press.
Civic Trust. *Derelict Land.* Civic Trust.
Clapham, A. R., Tutin, T. G., Warburg, E. F. *Excursion Flora of the British Isles.* Cambridge University Press.
Clouston, D. *The Establishment and Care of Fine Turf for Lawns and Sports Grounds.* Clarke & Hunter.
Colvin, B. *Land and Landscape.* John Murray.
Colvin, B., Badmin, S. R. *Trees for Town and Country.* Lund Humphries.
Conover, H. S. *Grounds Maintenance Handbook.* McGraw-Hill.
Crowe, S. *Forestry in the Landscape.* H.M.S.O.
Crowe, S. *Landscape of Power.* Architectural Press.
Crowe, S. *Landscape of Roads.* Architectural Press.
Crowe, S. *Tomorrow's Landscape.* Architectural Press.
Cullen, G. *Townscape.* Architectural Press.
Daumel, G. *Concrete in the Garden.* Elsevier.

Dawson, R. B. *Lawns for Garden and Playing Fields.* Penguin.
Eckbo, G. *Urban Landscape Design.* McGraw-Hill, New York.
Fairbrother, N. *New Lives, New Landscapes.* Architectural Press.
Fish, M. *Ground Cover Plants.* Collingridge.
Forestry Commission. *Grants for Woodland Owners.* H.M.S.O.
Fox, C. *The Countryside and the Law.* David & Charles.
Fryer, J. D. & Makepiece, R. J. *Weed Control Handbook.* Blackwell Scientific Publications, Oxford.
Gibberd, F. *The Landscape of Reservoirs.* The Institution of Water Engineers.
Greenfield, I. *Turf Culture.* Leonard Hill.
Hackett, B. *Landscape Planning.* Oriel Press.
Harrison, D. (Editor). *Specification* (section on landscape—J. St. Bodfan Gruffydd). Architectural Press.
Hartwright, T. U. *Planting Trees and Shrubs in Gravel Workings.* Sand & Gravel Association.
Haworth-Booth, M. *Effective Flowering Shrubs.* Collins.
Hesse, P. R. *Soil Chemical Analysis.* John Murray.
Hillier, H. G. *A Tree for Every Site.* Arboricultural Association.
Holme, A., & Massie, P. *Children's Play.* Michael Joseph.
Hubberd, C. F. *Grasses.* Penguin.
Hurtwood, Lady Allen of, *Design for Play.*
Iliffe Science & Technology Publications. *Proceedings of the Derelict Land Symposium, Leeds 1969.*
Institute of Landscape Architects. *Techniques of Landscape Architecture.* Heinemann.
Institution of Civil Engineers. *Standard Method of Measurement.*
Jellicoe, G. A. *Studies in Landscape Design.* Vols. 1-3 Oxford University Press.
Jellicoe, S. & G. *The Use of Water in Landscape Architecture.* A & C Black.
Kendall, R. G. *Land Drainage.* Faber & Faber.
Kendrew, W. G. *Climatology.* Clarendon Press.
Livesley, M. C. *Field Drainage.* E. & F. N. Spon.
Lynch, K. *Site Planning.* M.I.T. Press, Cambridge, Mass.
Makins, F. K. *British Trees in Winter.* Dent.
Makins, F. K. *The Identification of Trees and Shrubs.* Dent.
Mansfield, T. C. *Shrubs in Colour and Cultivation.* Collins.
McHarg, I. *Design with Nature.* Natural History Press.
Miles, R. *Forestry in the English Landscape.* Faber & Faber.
Muirhead, D. *Green Days in Garden and Landscape.* Mirimar, Los Angeles.
Musser, H. B. *Turf Management.* McGraw-Hill, New York.

Nicholson, H. H. *Field Drainage*. Cambridge University Press.
Perry, F. *Water Gardens*. Penguin.
Pfarm Schmidt, Ernst-Erik. *Fountains and Springs*. Harrup.
Pirone, P. P. *Tree Maintenance*. Oxford University Press.
Ranson, F. *British Herbs*. Penguin.
Reed, F. J. *Lawns and Playing Fields*. Faber & Faber.
Royal Institute of British Architects. *Handbook of Architectural Practice and Management*.
Royal Institution of Chartered Surveyors. *Standard Method of Measurement*.
Roper, L. *Hardy Herbaceous Plants*. Penguin.
Royal Horticultural Society. *Dictionary of Gardening*.
Sharp, T. *Town and Townscape*. John Murray.
Skinner, H. T. *Garden Plants in Colour*. Sweeny, Krist, & Dimm, Portland, Oregon.
Smith, P. W. *Planning, Construction and Maintenance of Playing Fields*. Oxford University Press.
Sports Council. *Planning for Sport*. Central Council for Physical Recreation.
Somerville, W. *How a Tree Grows*. Oxford University Press.
Stamp, L. Dudley. *Nature Conservation in Britain*. Collins.
Tansley, A. G. *British Islands and their Vegetation*. Cambridge University Press.
Tansley, A. G. *Introduction to Plant Ecology*. Allen & Unwin.
Thomas, G. S. *Plants for Ground Cover*. Dent.
Trueman, A. E. *Geology and Scenery*. Penguin.
Turner, A. L. *Sports Field Drainage*. National Association of Groundsmen.
Weaver, S. *Flowering and Ornamental Shrubs*. Faber & Faber.
Willis. *Elements of Quantity Surveying*. Crosby Lockwood.
Willis. *Specification Writing for Architects and Surveyors*. Crosby Lockwood.

PUBLICATIONS

Agricultural Research Council
Effects of Air Pollution on Plants and Soil.
Pest Infestation Research 1968.
Soil Survey Research Board: Soil Survey of Great Britain Report No. 19.
Weed Research Organisation: 1st Report 1960-64
                              2nd Report 1965-66
                              3rd Report 1967-68

Central Electricity Generating Board
C.E.G.B. Newsletters:—
Generating Board in the Role of Beautifier (P.F.A.)
P.F.A.—a 20th Century By-Product.
Design Memorandum on the use of fences.
Win Back the Acres—Ash and Agriculture.

Countryside Commission

Papers obtainable through the Countryside Commission
Demand for Outdoor Recreation in the Countryside.
Digest of Countryside Recreation Statistics.
Leisure; Problems and Prospects for the Environment.
Llyn Tegid and Llyn Celyn, Merionethshire: Development for Recreation.
Northern Burrows: A Study in Conservation and Management.
Planning for Leisure and Recreation.
Policy on Country Parks and Picnic Sites.
Research into Planning for Recreation.
Research Register No. 5.
Resource Planning.
Rural Planning Methods.
Schemes for the Recreational Use of Disused Railways.
The Wash Desk Study 1969—Recreation and Amenity.

Publications in conjunction with H.M.S.O.
Coastal Heritage.
Coastal Recreation and Holidays.
Coasts of England and Wales: Measurement of Use, Protection and Development.
Disused Railways in the Countryside of England and Wales.
Guide Books to Long Distance Footpaths.
Guide Books to National Parks.
Picnic Sites.
Planning of the Coastline.
Reports on Coastal Preservation and Development.

Design Council (formerly Council of Industrial Design)

C.O.I.D. publications.
Gardens (Peter Shepheard)
Street Furniture Catalogue (revised annually)

Bibliography

Publications from other sources obtainable from the Design Centre.
Frank Lloyd-Wright: Architecture & Space (P. Blake).
Garden Design & Layout (John Brookes).

Electricity Council
Electricity in Your Garden.
Electric Growing.

Greater London Council
Colne Valley; Studies for a Regional Park.
Future of London Transport
Greater London Development Plan—under consideration.
  North East London—some implications of Greater London Development Plan.
  The Report of Studies; facts and forecasts on which the policies are based.
  The Statement—explanation of the policies and proposal within the Plan.
  Tomorrow's London—background to the Development Plan.
Kensington Environmental Management Study
London's Canal—its past, present and future
London Traffic Survey Vol. I & II
Movement in London
Parks, Gardens and Open Space By-Laws
Planning for a New Town
Surveys of the Use of Open Spaces Vol. I.
London—a study for further expansion
Thamesmead; a riverside development
Thames-side Environmental Assessment
Thames-side Survey 1967

H.M.S.O.

Building Research Station
Children's Play on Housing Estates

Department of Economic Affairs (Former)
Challenge of the Changing North
Challenge to Northerners
Development Areas
East Midlands Study
National Plan

North-West Economic Planning Council: Strategy II
Opportunity in the East Midlands
Problems of Merseyside
Region with a future—Draft Strategy for the South-West
Review of Yorkshire and Humberside
Strategy for the South-East

Also area studies and feasibility reports on the following:—
  Doncaster
  East Anglia
  Halifax and Calder Valley
  Huddersfield and Colne Valley
  Humberside
  The North-West
  The West Midlands

Government Social Survey
Planning for Leisure
Play Spaces for Children on Estates

Ministry of Agriculture and Fisheries
Agricultural Chemicals Approval Scheme
Capillary Watering of Plants in Containers
Chemicals for the Gardener
Concrete Roads
Control of Aquatic Weeds
Farm and Estate Hedges
Farm Gates
Farm Roads
Field Drainage Grants
Grants for Farm Water Supply Schemes
Guide to the Land Drainage Act 1961
Identification of Common Water Weeds
Irrigation
Lime and Liming
Mole Drainage for Healthy Land
Permanent Farm Fences
Soil Analysis for Advisory Purposes
Soil—Cement Roads
Tree, Bush and Stump Clearance
Use of Concrete on Farm and Estate

Bibliography

Ministry of Housing and Local Government (former)
Caravan Parks
Coasts of England and Wales
Explanatory Memorandum on Planning Grants under the Town & Country Act 1947
Footpaths and Access to the Countryside
Greater London Plan
Green Belts
Landscaping for Flats
Leisure in the Countryside: England and Wales
Memorandum on the Preservation of Trees and Woodland
National Parks and Access to the Countryside
National Parks in England and Wales
New Life for Dead Lands
Restoration of Land Affected by Iron Ore Working
South East England
South East Study, 1961-81
South Wales Outline Plan
Strategic Plan for the South-East
Streets
Swimming Pools
Trees in Town and City

Ministry of Public Buildings and Works (former)
Official Guides to Ancient Monuments and Historic Buildings
Royal Botanic Garden, Edinburgh
Royal Parks of London

Ministry of Transport (former)
Specification for Road and Bridge Works

Nature Conservancy
Countryside in 1970
Monograph Series:
    No. 1. *Plant Communities of the Scottish Highlands*
    No. 2. *The Geology of Moor House (Westmorland)*
Nature Conservancy Handbook

Road Research Laboratory
Bituminous Materials in Road Construction
Compaction of Concrete Road Slabs
Compaction of Soil

Concrete Roads: Design and Construction
Design of Concrete Mixes
Durability of Road Tar
Effect of Soil Organic Matter on the Setting of Soil-Cement and Mixtures
Flexural Strength of Plain Concrete, Measurement and Use in Designing Concrete Mixes
Grading of Aggregates and Workability of Concrete
Guide to Engineers on the Making Up of Private Streets
Guide to the Structural Design of Flexible and Rigid Pavements for New Roads
Investigations to Assess the Potentialities of Lime for Soil Stabilisation in the United Kingdom
Prevention of Wet Weather Damage to Surface Dressings
Recommendations for Tar Surface Dressings
Soil Survey Procedure
Sources of Road Aggregates in Great Britain
Sources of White and Coloured Aggregate in Great Britain
Specifications for the Construction of Housing Estate Roads using Soil-Cement

Institute of Landscape Architects
Basic Plant List
Conditions of Contract with Quantities
Industry and Landscape
Information Sheets (horticultural and constructional)
Landscape Design in the Countryside
Landscape Maintenance
Landscape Treatment of Housing Estates
Landscape Treatment of Roads
Organisation of Space in Housing Neighbourhoods
Private Enterprise Housing and Landscape Design
Roads in the Landscape Conference Papers
Scale of Professional Charges
Standard Forms for landscape architects instructions and certificates
Urban Scene: Design for Pleasure and Hard Wear in the Landscape

National Playing Fields Association
Athletic Training Areas (Outdoor)
Community Sports Halls (Revised edition 1971)—G. Perrin
Cricket on Non-Turf Pitches
Disused Burial Grounds as Playgrounds and Playing Fields
Drainage Problems on Playing Fields

Floodlighting of Outdoor Sports Facilities
Grants and Loans for Recreation
Hard Porous and All Weather Surfaces for Recreation (Outdoor)
Land for Play
Lighting for Sport
Lollard Adventure Playground
Making the Most of School Playing Fields
Mounds for Playgrounds
New Playgrounds
Notes on Adventure Playgrounds
Notes on Choosing a Hard Tennis Court
Notting Hill Adventure Playground
Outdoor Playing Space Requirements
Planning for Play
Playgrounds for Blocks of Flats
Reclamation for Recreation-Levelling and Reinstatement of Land
Recreation and Play
Sandpits, Construction and Maintenance
Specification for Hard Surface Area
Sports Ground Maintenance

Royal Horticultural Society
Dictionary of Garden Plants in Colour
Dictionary of Roses in Colour
Gardening Chemicals
International Code of Nomenclature of Cultivated Plants
New Supplement to the R.H.S. Dictionary of Gardening
R.H.S. Dictionary of Gardening
Trees and Shrubs Hardy in the British Isles

Pamphlets
Annual and Biennial Flowers
Choice and Care of Trees for the Small Garden
Climber and Other Plants for Walls
Decorative Autumn Fruits and Berries
Ground-Cover Plants
Hardy Herbaceous Plants for the Garden
House Plants
Pruning Hardy Shrubs
Young Garden Lover and Some Plants He Should Love

Penguin handbooks prepared in conjunction and collaboration with the Royal Horticultural Society
Annual and Biennial Flowers
Garden Design
Hardy Bulbs—Parts 1 & 2
Hardy Herbaceous Plants
Rock Gardens
Roses

Timber Research and Development Association
Maintaining Timber Exposed to the Weather
Timber Fencing and Gates for Agricultural and Open Space Purposes
Timber Fencing and Gates for Housing and Other Buildings

Town Planning Institute
Changing the North
Decade—South Wales Enters the Seventies
Planning for the Changing Countryside
Planned London
Planning Research
Rees Jeffreys Triennial Lectures:
    Motorways—their landscaping, design and appearance
    Requirements of the Road User with reference to the design and layout of roads
    Safety as a factor in road design, construction and layout
    Urban Motorways and their environment
Research for Urban Planning
Safety Nets for Urban Planners
Techniques for Local Plans

British Standards Applicable to Landscape Works (current at time of going to press)

B.S. 12:1958	Portland cement (ordinary and rapid hardening).
B.S. 63	Single-sized roadstone and chippings.
Part 1:1951	Imperial units.
Part 2:1971	Metric units.
B.S. 65 & 540: 1966	Clay drain and sewer pipes including surface water pipes and fittings.
B.S. 76:1964	Tars for road purposes.
B.S. 340:1963	Precast concrete kerbs, channels, edgings and quadrants.
B.S. 368:1971	Precast concrete flags.
B.S. 381C:1964	Colours for specific purposes.

B.S. 435:1931	Granite and whinstone kerbs, channels, quadrants and setts.
B.S. 497:1967	Cast manhole covers, road gully gratings and frames for drainage purposes.
B.S. 539:1971	Dimensions of fittings for use with clay drain and sewer pipes.
B.S. 556:1966	Concrete cylindrical pipes and fittings including manholes, inspection chambers and street gullies.
B.S. 594:1961	Rolled asphalt (hot process).
B.S. 659:1967	Light gauge copper tubes (light drawn).
B.S. 706:1936	Sandstone kerbs, channels, quadrants and setts.
B.S. 743:1970	Materials for damp-proof courses.
B.S. 802:1967	Tarmacadam with crushed rock or slag aggregate.
B.S. 864:1953	Capillary and compression fittings of copper and copper alloy for use with copper tube complying with B.S. 659 or B.S. 1386 & B.S. 3931.
B.S. 873	The construction of road traffic signs and internally illuminated-bollards. Part 1. 1970. General traffic signs. Part 3. 1970. Internally illuminated bollards.
B.S. 882, 1201:1965	Aggregates from natural sources for concrete (including granolithic).
B.S. 892:1967	Glossary of highway engineering terms.
B.S. 913:1954	Pressure creosoting of timber.
B.S. 1010:1959	Draw off taps and stopvalves for water services (screwdown pattern).
B.S. 1014:1961	Pigments for cement, magnesium oxychloride and concrete.
B.S. 1162,1410, 1418:1966	Mastic asphalt for building (natural rock asphalt aggregate).
B.S. 1180:1944	Concrete bricks and fixing bricks.
B.S. 1185:1963	Guards for underground stopvalves.
B.S. 1194:1969	Concrete porous pipes for under-drainage.
B.S. 1196:1971	Clayware field drain pipes.
B.S. 1198-1200:1955	Building sands from natural sources.
B.S. 1217:1945	Cast stone.
B.S. 1222:1945	Battery operated electric fences.
B.S. 1241:1959	Tarmacadam and tar carpets (gravel aggregate).
B.S. 1242:1960	Tarmacadam 'tarpaving' for footpaths, playgrounds and similar works.
B.S. 1282:1959	Classification of wood preservatives and their methods of application.
B.S. 1286:1945	Clay tiles for flooring.
B.S. 1308:1970	Concrete street lighting columns.

Bibliography

B.S. 1324:1962	*Asphalt tiles for paving and flooring (natural rock asphalt).*
B.S. 1377:1967	*Methods of testing soils for civil engineering purposes.*
B.S. 1386:1957	*Copper tubes to be buried underground.*
B.S. 1446:1962	*Mastic asphalt (natural rock asphalt aggregate) for roads and footpaths.*
B.S. 1447:1962	*Mastic asphalt (limestone aggregate) for roads and footways.*
B.S. 1485:1971	*Galvanised wire netting.*
B.S. 1621:1961	*Bitumen macadam with crushed rock or slag aggregate.*
B.S. 1647:1961	*pH scale.*
B.S. 1690:1962	*Cold asphalt.*
B.S. 1722	*Fences.*
Part 1:1963	*Chain link fences.*
Part 2:1963	*Woven wire fences.*
Part 3:1963	*Strained wire fences.*
Part 4:1963	*Cleft chestnut pale fences.*
Part 5:1963	*Close boarded fences including oak pale fences.*
Part 6:1963	*Wooden palisade fences.*
Part 7:1963	*Wooden post and rail fences.*
Part 8:1966	*Mild steel or wrought iron continuous bar fences.*
Part 9:1963	*Mild steel or wrought iron unclimbable fences with round or square verticals and flat standards and horizontals.*
Part 10:1963	*Anti-intruder chain link fences.*
Part 11:1965	*Woven wood fences.*
B.S. 1831:1969	*Recommended common names for pesticides.*
B.S. 1840:1960	*Steel columns for street lighting.*
B.S. 1926:1962	*Ready-mixed concrete.*
B.S. 1972:1967	*Polythene pipe (Type 32) for cold water services.*
B.S. 2028, 1364: 1968	*Precast concrete blocks.*
B.S. 2040:1953	*Bitumen macadam with gravel aggregate.*
B.S. 2468:1963	*Glossary of terms relating to agricultural machinery and implements.*
B.S. 2660:1955	*Colours for building and decorative paints.*
B.S. 2760	*Pitch-impregnated fibre pipes and fittings, for drainage below and above ground.*
Part 1 1966	*Pipes and couplings.*
Part 2 1967	*Fittings.*
B.S. 2787:1956	*Glossary of terms for concrete and reinforced concrete.*
B.S. 2847:1957	*Glossary of terms for stone used in building.*

B.S. 3178	*Playground equipment for parks.*
Part 1 1959	*General requirements.*
Part 2A 1959	*Special requirements for static equipment (except slides).*
Part 2B:1960	*Special requirements for slides.*
Part 3	*Special requirements for swinging apparatus.*
Part 3A:1960	*Pendulum see-saws.*
Part 3B:1962	*Plane swings.*
Part 3C:1964	*Plank swings.*
Part 3D:1964	*Swings.*
Part 3E:1964	*Rocking boats.*
Part 3F:1964	*Rocking horses.*
Part 4:1965	*Rotating equipment.*
B.S. 3284:1967	*Polythene pipe (type 50) for cold water services.*
B.S. 3455:1961	*Field water troughs.*
B.S. 3470:1962	*Field gates and posts.*
B.S. 3505:1968	*Unplasticized P.V.C. pipe for cold water services.*
B.S. 3589:1963	*Glossary of general building terms.*
B.S. 3656:1963	*Asbestos cement pipes and fittings for sewerage and drainage.*
B.S. 3690:1970	*Bitumens for road purposes.*
B.S. 3798:1964	*Coping units (of clayware, unreinforced cast concrete, unreinforced cast stone, natural stone and slate).*
B.S. 3826:1969	*Silicone based water repellents for masonry.*
B.S. 3854:1965	*Farm stock fences.*
B.S. 3882:1965	*Recommendations and classification for topsoil.*
B.S. 3892:1965	*Pulverized-fuel ash for use in concrete.*
B.S. 3921:	*Bricks and blocks of fired brick earth, clay or shale.*
Part 2: 1969	*Metric units.*
B.S. 3936	*Nursery stock.*
Part 1:1965	*Trees and shrubs.*
Part 2:1966	*Roses.*
Part 3:1965	*Fruit.*
Part 4:1966	*Forest trees.*
Part 5:1967	*Poplars and willows for timber production.*
Part 7:1968	*Bedding plants grown in boxes or trays.*
Part 9:1968	*Bulbs, corms and tubers.*
B.S. 3969:1965	*Recommendations for turf for general landscape purposes.*
B.S. 3975	*Glossary for landscape work.*
Part 4:1966	*Plant description.*
Part 5:1969	*Horticultural arboricultural and forestry practice.*

B.S. 3989:1966 *Aluminium street lighting columns.*
B.S. 3998:1966 *Recommendations for tree work.*
B.S. 4043:1966 *Recommendations for transplanting semi-mature trees.*
B.S. 4428:1969 *Recommendations for general landscape work.*
B.S. 4357:1968 *Precast terrazzo units.*
B.S. 4483:1969 *Steel fabric for the reinforcement of concrete.*
B.S. 4729:1971 *Shapes and dimensions of special bricks.*

British Standards Codes of Practice Applicable to Landscape Work

Building
C.P. 121.101:1951 *Brickwork.*
C.P. 121.201:1951 *Masonry walls ashlared with natural stone or with cast stone.*
C.P. 121.202:1951 *Masonry Rubble walls.*
C.P. 122:1952 *Walls and partitions of blocks and of slabs.*
C.P. 123.101:1951 *Dense concrete walls.*
C.P. 202:1959 *Tile flooring and slab flooring.*
C.P. 221:1960 *External rendered finishes.*
C.P. 231:1966 *Painting of buildings.*
C.P. 301:1971 *Building drainage.*
C.P. 301:1965 *Water supply.*
C.P. 402:101:1952 *Hydrant systems.*

Electrical Engineering
C.P. 1004 *Street lighting.*
Part 1:1963 *General principles*
Part 2:1963 *Lighting for traffic routes.*
Part 3:1969 *Lighting for lightly trafficked roads and footways (Group B).*
Part 4:1967 *Lighting for single level road junctions including roundabouts.*
Part 6:1967 *Lighting for bridges and elevated roads (Group D).*
Part 7:1971 *Lighting for under-passes and bridged roads.*
Part 8:1967 *Lighting for roads with special requirements (Group F).*
Part 9:1969 *Lighting for town and city centres and areas of civic importance (Group G).*

Civil Engineering
C.P. 2001:1957 *Site investigations.*
C.P. 2003:1959 *Earthworks.*
C.P. 2005:1968 *Sewerage.*

Bibliography

Periodicals

Anthos,
Graf & Neuhaus, Bachtoldstrasse 4, 8044 Zurich.

Biological Conservation,
Elsevier Publishing Co. Ltd., Ripple Road, Barking, Essex.

Design & Environment,
6400 Goldsboro Road, Washington D.C. 20034, U.S.A.

Ekistics,
24 Strat, Syndesmou, Athens 136, Greece.

Espaces Verts,
20 Rue Delaunay, 91 Saint-Michel-sur-Orge, France.

Gardener's Chronicle,
9 Harrow Road, London W.2.

Garten und Landschaft,
Georg D. W. Callwey, 8 Munich 80, Streitfeldstrasse 35.

Journal & Bulletin of the Sports Turf Research Institute,
Sports Turf Research Institute, Bingley, Yorkshire.

Journal of the Royal Horticultural Society,
Royal Horticultural Society, Vincent Square, London S.W.1.

Journal of the Town Planning Institute,
The Royal Town Planning Institute, 26 Portland Place, London W.1.

Landscape Architecture,
American Society of Landscape Architecture, Schuster Building, 1500 Bardstown Road, Louisville, Kentucky 40205, U.S.A.

Landscape Design,
Institute of Landscape Architects, 12 Carlton House Terrace, London S.W.1.

Landscape Design & Construction,
Mirimar Publishing Co., 2048 Cotner Avenue, Los Angeles, California 90025, U.S.A.

Landschaft & Stadt,
Verlag Eugen Elmer, 7 Stuttgart 1, Postfach 1032, Germany.

Landskap,
Arkitekteus Forlag, Nyhavn 43, 1051 Copenhagen K.

Nature in Focus,
Countryside Commission, 1 Cambridge Gate, London N.W.1.

Nurserymen & Garden Centre,
Benn Bros. Limited, 154 Fleet Street, London E.C.4.

Parks & Recreation,
Journal of the Institute of Park & Recreation Administration, The Adelphi, John Adam Street, London W.C.2.

Parks & Sportsgrounds,
Clarke & Hunter (London) Limited, Armour House, Bridge Street, Guildford, Surrey.

Quarterly Journal of Forestry,
Royal Forestry Society, 102 High Street, Tring, Herts.

Recreation News,
Countryside Commission, 1 Cambridge Gate, London N.W.1.
Your Environment,
10 Roderick Road, London N.W.3.

Appendix

PROFESSIONAL BODIES AND ASSOCIATIONS CONCERNED WITH THE ENVIRONMENT

Agricultural Engineers Association,
6 Buckingham Gate, London S.W.1.

Ancient Monuments Society,
11 Alexander Street, London W.2.

Arboricultural Association,
59 Blythewood Gardens, Stansted, Essex.

Association of British Tree Surgeons and Arborists,
11 Wings Road, Upper Hale, Farnham, Surrey.

Association of County Councils in Scotland,
3 Forres Street, Edinburgh EH3 6BL.

Association of Municipal Corporations,
36 Old Queen Street, London SW1H 9JE.

Association for the Preservation of Rural Scotland,
39 Castle Street, Edinburgh 2.

Association of Tree Transplanters,
91a High Street, Great Missenden, Bucks.

British Road Federation,
26 Manchester Square, London W1M 5RF.

British Standards Institution,
2 Park Street, London W1A 2BS.

British Stone Federation,
37 Soho Square, London W.1.

British Waterways Board,
Melbury House, Melbury Terrace, London N.W.1.

Building Centre,
26 Store Street, London W.C.2.

    Building Centre of Northern Ireland,
    4 Arthur Place, Belfast BT1 4HJ.

    Engineering & Building Centre,
    Broad Street, Birmingham 1.

    Bristol Building & Design Centre,
    Colston Avenue, The Centre, Bristol BS1 4TW.

    Building Centre Cambridge,
    15-16 Trumpington Street, Cambridge CB2 1QD.

    Coventry Building Information Centre,
    Council House, Earl Street, Coventry CB1 5SE.

Appendix

The Building Centre of Ireland,
17 Lower Baggot Street, Dublin 2.

Building Centre of Scotland,
6 Newton Terrace, Glasgow G3 7PF.

Liverpool Building & Design Centre,
Hope Street, Liverpool L1 9BR.

Building & Design Centre Manchester Ltd.,
113-115 Portland Street, Manchester M1 6FB.

Midland Design & Building Centre,
Mansfield Road, Nottingham NG1 3FE.

Building Centre of Southampton Ltd.,
Grosvenor House, 18-20 Cumberland Place, Southampton SO1 2BD.

Building Information Centre,
College of Building & Commerce, Stoke Road, Shelton, Stoke-on-Trent ST4 2DG.

Building Research Station,
Bucknalls Lane, Garston, Watford, Herts.

Cement & Concrete Association,
52 Grosvenor Gardens, London SW1W OAQ.

Central Council for Rivers Protection,
Fishmongers' Hall, London EC4R 9EL.

Central Rights of Way Committee,
166 Shaftesbury Avenue, London W.C.2.

Centre for Environmental Studies,
5 Cambridge Terrace, London N.W.1.

Chartered Land Agents Society,
21 Lincolns Inn Fields, London W.C.2.

Civic Trust,
17 Carlton House Terrace, London S.W.1.

Commission for New Towns,
Glen House, Stag Place, London SW1 E5A.

Committee for Environmental Conservation,
4 Hobart Place, London SW1W OHY.

Commons, Open Spaces and Footpaths Preservation Society,
166 Shaftesbury Avenue, London W.C.2.

Concrete Society,
Terminal House, Grosvenor Gardens, London S.W.1.

Conservation Society,
34 Bridge Street, Walton-on-Thames, Surrey.

Council for British Archaeology,
4 St. Andrew's Place, London N.W.1.

Council for Nature,
c/o Zoological Society of London, Regents Park, London N.W.1.

Council for the Protection of Rural England,
4 Hobart Place, London S.W.1.

Council for the Protection of Rural Wales,
Meifod, Montgomeryshire.

Country Landowners Association,
7 Swallow Street, London W.1.

Countryside Commission,
1 Cambridge Gate, London N.W.1.

County Councils Association,
Eaton House, 66a Eaton Square, London SW1W 9BH.

County Naturalists Trusts (Headquarters in each county).

Crown Estate Commissioners,
13-15 Carlton House Terrace, London SW1Y 5AH.

Dartington Amenity Research Trust,
Skinners Bridge, Dartington, Totnes, Devon.

Department of the Environment,
2 Marsham Street, London SW1P 3EP.

Design Council,
The Design Centre, 28 Haymarket, London S.W.1.

Electricity Council,
30 Millbank, London SW1P 4RD.

Fauna Preservation Society,
c/o Zoological Society of London, Regents Park, London N.W.1.

Field Studies Council,
9 Devereux Court, Strand, London W.C.1.

Forestry Commission,
25 Savile Row, London W.1.

Her Majesty's Stationery Office,
P.O. Box 569, London S.E.1.

Highlands and Islands Development Board,
Bridge House, Bank Street, Inverness.

Historic Buildings Council for England,
25 Savile Row, London WIX 2PT.

Historic Buildings Council for Scotland,
Argyle House, Lady Lawson Street, Edinburgh EH3 9SF.

Historic Buildings Council for Wales,
Summit House, Windsor Place, Cardiff.

Horticultural Education Association,
c/o J. H. Glazebrook Esq., Pershore College of Horticulture, Pershore, Worcestershire.

Institute of Advanced Architectural Studies,
The Kings Manor,
York YO1 2EP.

Institute of Building,
Englemere, Kings Ride, Ascot, Berkshire.

Institute of Landscape Architects,
Nash House, 12 Carlton House Terrace, London S.W.1.

Institute of Park and Recreation Administration,
Lower Basildon, Reading, Berkshire.
Institute of Quantity Surveyors,
98 Gloucester Place, London W.1.
Institute of Water Engineers,
6/8 Sackville Street, London W1X 1DD.
Institution of Civil Engineers,
Great George Street, London SW1P 3AA.
Institution of Highway Engineers,
14 Queen Anne's Gate, London SW1H 9AF.
Institution of Municipal Engineers,
25 Eccleston Square, London SW1 1NX.
Men of the Stones,
The Rutlands, Tinwell, Stamford, Lincolnshire.
Men of the Trees,
Crawley Down, Crawley, Sussex.
Metropolitan Public Gardens Association,
58 Denison House, 296 Vauxhall Bridge Road, London S.W.1.
Ministry of Agriculture, Fisheries and Food,
Whitehall Place, London S.W.1.
Ministry of Agriculture, Government of Northern Ireland, Forestry Division,
Dundonald House, Upper Newtownards Road, Belfast BT4 3SB.
Ministry of Development, Government of Northern Ireland, Conservation Branch,
Parliament Buildings, Stormont, Belfast BT4 3SS.
National Building Agency,
NBA House, Arundel Street, London WC2R 3DZ.
National Caravan Council,
Sackville House, 40 Piccadilly, London W1V OND.
National Farmers Union,
Agriculture House, Knightsbridge, London S.W.1.
National Gardens Scheme,
57 Lower Belgrave Street, London S.W.1.
National Housing and Town Planning Council,
11 Green Street, London W1Y 4ES.
National Monuments Record (England),
Fielden House, 10 Great College Street, London S.W.1.
National Monuments Record (Scotland),
52/54 Melville Street, Edinburgh EH3 7HF.
National Monuments Record (Wales),
Edleston House, Queen's Road, Aberystwyth, Cardiganshire SY23 2HP.
National Playing Fields Association,
57b Catherine Place, London SW1 6EY.
National Society for Clean Air,
Field House, Breams Building, London, E.C.4.

National Trust for England & Wales,
42 Queen Anne's Gate, London S.W.1.

National Trust for Northern Ireland,
82 Dublin Road, Belfast BT2 7 JA.

National Trust for Scotland,
5 Charlotte Square, Edinburgh EH2 4DU.

Natural Environment Research Council,
Alhambra House, 27—33 Charing Cross Road, London W.C.2.

Nature Conservancy,
19 Belgrave Square, London S.W.1.

Noise Abatement Society,
6 Old Bond Street, London W.1.

Ordnance Survey,
Romsey Road, Maybush, Southampton SO9 4DH.

Pilgrim Trust,
Millbank House, 2 Great Peter Street, London S.W.1.

Prince of Wales's Committee,
15 Wellfield Court, Bangor, Caernarvonshire.

Ramblers Association,
124 Finchley Road, London N.W.3.

Road Research Laboratory,
Crowthorne, Berkshire.

Royal Commission on Ancient Monuments in Wales & Monmouthshire,
Edleston House, Queen's Road, Aberystwyth, Cardiganshire SY23 2HP.

Royal Commission on the Ancient and Historical Monuments of Scotland,
52/54 Melville Street, Edinburgh 3.

Royal Commission on Environmental Pollution,
Church House, Great Smith Street, London SW1P 3BL.

Royal Commission on Historical Monuments (England),
Fielden House, Great College Street, London S.W.1.

Royal Fine Art Commission,
2 Carlton Gardens, London S.W.1.

Royal Fine Art Commission for Scotland,
22 Melville Street, Edinburgh EH4 1PL.

Royal Forestry Society of England, Wales & Northern Ireland,
102 High Street, Tring, Hertfordshire.

Royal Horticultural Society,
Vincent Square, London S.W.1.

Royal Institute of British Architects,
66 Portland Place, London W1N 4 AD.

Royal Institution of Chartered Surveyors,
12 Great George Street, London S.W.1.

Royal Scottish Forestry Society,
26 Rutland Square, Edinburgh EH1 2BU.

Appendix

Royal Society for the Protection of Birds,
The Lodge, Sandy, Bedfordshire.

Royal Town Planning Institute,
26 Portland Place, London W1N 4BE.

Sand and Gravel Association,
48 Park Street, London W1Y 4HE.

Scottish Civic Trust,
24 George Square, Glasgow C.2.

Scottish Design Centre,
72 St. Vincent Street, Glasgow C.2.

Scottish Development Department,
St. Andrew's House, Edinburgh 1.

Scottish National Housing and Town Planning Council,
Council Chambers, Renfrew, Renfrewshire.

Scottish Rights of Way Society,
32 Rutland Square, Edinburgh 1.

Society for the Promotion of Nature Reserves,
The Manor House, Alford, Lincolnshire.

Society for the Protection of Ancient Buildings,
55 Great Ormond Street, London WC1N 3JA.

Soil Association,
Walnut Tree Manor, Haughley, Stowmarket, Suffolk.

Sports Council,
26 Park Crescent, London W1N 4AJ.

Timber Research and Development Association,
Hughenden Valley, High Wycombe, Buckinghamshire.

Town and Country Planning Association,
28 King Street, London W.C.2.

Ulster Society for the Preservation of the Countryside,
West Winds, Cragavad, Co. Down.

Water Resources Board,
Reading Bridge House, Reading, Berkshire.

Youth Hostels Association (England & Wales),
8 St. Stephen's Hill, St. Albans, Hertfordshire.

Index

Abacus Municipal Ltd.   160, 205, 208, 209, 297, 338, 341, 342
Abandoned vehicles   5
Abandoned work   23, 45, 50, 51
Acceptance of tenders   50, 73
Access orders   6
Accounts, certifying of   16, 20
   final   47, 49, 50, 59, 61, 63, 64, 65, 66, 70, 75, 77, 79
Acquisition of land   10
Acts, Agriculture Act   7
   Amenity Lands Act (Northern Ireland)   5
   Caravan Sites & Control of Development Act   13
   Civic Amenities Act   4, 9
   Countryside (Scotland) Act   6
   Forestry Act   7
   Industrial Development Act   10
   Local Employment Act   10
   National Parks & Access to the Countryside Act   5, 10, 11, 12
   Public Health Act   13
   Town & Country Planning Act   3, 4, 6, 9, 13
   Town & Country Planning (Scotland) Act   4
Additional services   25
Addresses   374
Adjustment to final cost   79
Advertising costs   26
Advice on contracts   34
Advisory work   18, 24
Aerators   346
Afforestation   7
After-care, permanent   79
Aggregate   181
   coarse   170, 173
   exposed   186
   fine   170, 173
Aggregation of fees   50
Agreements, forestry dedication   8, 9

I.L.A.   74
   with clients   15, 17, 46
Agricultural Chemicals Approvals Scheme   91
Agricultural Development & Advisory Service   7, 96
Agricultural Act   7
Allen & Sons Ltd., John   347
Allett, R. K.   348
Allsebrook & Co., Ltd., G.   204, 337
Alteration work   18, 37, 40, 55, 63, 65
Amalgamated Roadstone Construction Ltd., 197, 331
Amerliorants, soil   90, 98
Amenity Lands Act   5
Amenity lighting   205, 338
Annual Management Grant   8
Anti-desiccant spray   151, 294
Anti-intruder fencing   308
Appeals against refusals of planning permission   4
Applications for grants   12
   for planning   9
Appointment of contractor   31, 34
Approvals   36
   client's   31
   negotiations for   35
   R.I.B.A.'s and special agreements   30, 39
Approximate estimates   20, 56, 63, 64
Arbitration   17, 43, 46, 51, 67
Arbitrators, Institute of   18, 46
Architects, as clients   23
   consultant   43
   fees   30
   resident   33
Areas of Outstanding Natural Beauty   6
Art, works of   35
Artifacts, existing   84, 87
Artificial surfaces   196, 330
Asphalt, base for   174
   fine cold   173
   laying of   175, 314, 315
   materials for   173

382 Index

mixing of 174
rolled 173
transportation of 175
Associates, rates for 18
Association of British Tree Surgeons & Arborists 72
Association of Swimming Pool Contractors 72
Association of Tree Transplanters 72
Association, trade 72
Athletics 256
Atlas Stone Co., Ltd. 156, 189, 296, 319
Auger, hand 97
mounted mechanical 97
Authorities, local 3, 4, 5, 6, 9, 10, 12, 13, 71, 74, 79
park 6
planning 3, 6, 9, 13
statutory 3
Authority of landscape architect 16

Backfilling 111, 152, 268
Bankruptcy of contractor 33
Banks 102
seeding to 118, 274
turfing to 128, 277
Barriers, crash 159, 297
traffic 159, 296
Base for asphalt 174
for in-situ concrete 182
Basis I provisions 8
Basis II provisions 8
Basketball 256
Battenhurst Developments 210, 343
Beating up 147
Bedding out 221, 345
Bell & Webster Ltd. 164, 306
Bibliography 358
Bills of approximate quantities 61, 64
Bills of quantities 25, 34, 49, 52, 55, 56, 69, 70, 72, 73, 77
copyright of 47
division of 70
planting section of 70
setting out of 70
Binder 171
Bins, litter 208, 340
Blasting 89
Blinding 168, 310
Blocks, paving 191, 253, 322, 328

Bloc Products 159, 296
Board of Trade 8
Bollards, fixed 159, 296
lighted 206, 339
moveable 159, 296
Bonfires 83, 85
Books, reference 358
Borer Engineering Co. 159, 296
Boundary ditches 114, 271
Bowling greens 255, 330
Braby Group Ltd. 208, 341
Bracing 215, 216
Brackets, wall 207, 339
Brick paving 192, 247, 251, 252, 323, 324, 327
Bricks, lighting 207, 340
British Aluminium Co., Ltd. 160, 297
British Association of Sportsground & Landscape Contractors 72
British Standard for drawing office practice 68
British Standard for landscape drawing office practice 68
British Standard specifications 69
British Standards 367
British Standards Codes of Practice 69, 371
British Standards for fencing 161
British Steel Corporation 160, 297
B.S. 340. 168
B.S. 368. 188
B.S. 594. 173
B.S. 1242. 170
B.S. 1377. 97
B.S. 3882. 92
B.S. 3921. 192
B.S. 3936. Part 1. 133
B.S. 3936. Part 4. 136
B.S. 3969. 125
B.S. 3998. 211
B.S. 4043. 147
B.S. 4428. 85, 96, 105, 117, 127, 137
Budget estimates 47
Building development 3, 4
Building paper 317
Building Preservation Orders 4
Building regulations 35, 36
Building surveys 41
Building systems and components 42
Buildings, historic 4, 37
Buildings of architectural merit 4

Index

Buildings, preservation of 4
Built-in furniture and equipment 36
Bulbs 142, 291
Bulkhead fittings 207, 340
Bulking 89
Burnham & Co., Ltd. 208, 341
Burning 83

Calculation of earthworks 100
Calculation of fees 20, 21, 36, 49, 54, 56, 57
Camping sites 6, 13
Caravan sites 13
    and Control of Development Act 13
    holiday 14
    licenses for 13
    permanent residential 13
    standards for 13, 14
Car parks 6, 170, 314
Catchwater drains 112, 269, 270
Ceiling figure 23
Certificates 50, 77
    final 50, 79
    I.L.A. 77
    interim 59, 61, 64, 66, 77
Certifying of accounts 16, 20
Chain link fencing 85, 163, 165, 258, 305, 306
Chambers, inspection 108, 112, 270
Changes in instructions 33
Channels 242, 312
Charge, percentage 19, 20, 21
Charges for mileage 26
    post 26, 44
    staff 19
    telephone 26, 44
    time 18, 30, 31, 41, 43, 56, 67
Charles Wicksteed & Co., Ltd. 201, 334
Checking of tenders 47, 73
Chemical fertilisers 91
Chemical sprays 91
Chieftain Forge Ltd. 353
Child's World Agency 199, 332
Chippings 180, 316
Churchouse Ltd., C.M. 205, 206, 207, 338, 339, 340
Circular 17/70. 11
Circular 68/65. 10
Civic Amenities Act 4, 9
Clay tiles 193, 324

Clayware drains 110, 111, 265, 266, 267
Cleaning out 213
Clearance areas, derelict land 11
Clearance of site 83, 84, 86, 143, 144, 258
Cleft chestnut fencing 85, 258
Clerk of Works 16, 26, 32, 33, 44, 76
Clent, agreements with 15, 17, 46
    requirements 15, 20, 24
Client's approval 31
    instructions (deviations from) 16, 20
    supplying material, labour or carriage 37
    who are builders 37
    work done by 39
Climate, micro- 69
Climbers 141, 142, 290, 291
Climbing equipment 199, 200, 201, 332, 333, 334
Close boarded fencing 162, 236, 302, 304
Coarse aggregate 170, 173
Cobbles, fixed 194, 251, 253, 325, 327, 329
    loose 180, 316
Code of Conduct 15, 27
Code of Practice 303. 109
Codes of Practice 69, 371
Coefficients 20, 21
Collaborative work 18, 26
Colourguard Ltd. 165, 307
Columns 205, 338
Commissions, resumed 45
Common fees 27
Compacting plant 182
Compaction of concrete 184
    of tarmacadam 172
Completion 34, 77, 78
Components 42
Compost 91
Compounding of expenses 44
Concrete, base for 182
    compaction of 184
    curing of 184
    exposed aggregate 186
    fencing 162, 164, 303, 306
    in-situ 180, 250, 252, 316, 326, 327
    kerb 168, 310, 311
    materials for 181
    parking blocks 210, 344
    paving slabs 188, 245, 246, 250, 252, 317, 327, 328
Concrete, spreading of 183
    sub-grade for 182

Utilities Ltd. 159, 206, 297, 339
  weather effects on 184
Condition of contract 69, 74
  of plants 133, 137
  of turf 126, 128
Conifers 133, 135, 283, 284, 291, 292
Conservation areas 4
Consolidation 102
Consortia 31
Construction cost 36
Consultancy work 18, 24
Consultant architects 43
Consultants 30, 34, 36
  specialist 16, 24
Containers, plant 210, 343
Content, stone 93, 95, 97
Contract, conditions of 69, 74
  documents 20, 69
  extension or reduction of 22
  form of 20, 71, 74, 77
  management 24, 76
  procedure 68, 75
  services, post- 57
  services, pre- 52
  variations 16, 31, 47, 60
Contraction joints 186
Contracts 49, 71
  advice on 34
  lump sum 52
  negotiated 47, 70, 73
  phased 3, 23, 33, 34, 70, 71
  programming of 74, 75
Contracts, seasonal effects on 75, 76
  separate trades 42
  sub- 47, 74, 76
  sub-letting of 74, 75
  supervision of 75
Contractor, appointment of 31, 34
  bankruptcy of 33
  disputes with client 16
  information for 34
  liability of 16
  liquidation of 33
  selected 74
  sub- 31, 34, 36, 42, 49, 74
Control of development 6
Cooper, Pegler & Co., Ltd. 354
Copings to freestanding walls 228, 295
  to retaining walls 229, 295, 296
Copyright 17, 32, 42, 47

Cost, control of 60, 63, 66, 77
  estimates of 65, 66
  final 47, 79
  planning 47, 56, 63, 64, 65
  preliminary 70
  printing 26, 44
Country parks 6
Countryside Act 5, 10, 11, 12
Countryside (Scotland) Act 6
Countryside Commission 6, 7
Countryside Commission of Scotland 7
County Councils 6
Covenants, forestry dedication 8, 9
Crash barriers 159, 297
Cricket 255
Crown, lifting of 213
  thinning 213
Cubes, play 199, 332
Cultivation 90, 98, 127, 129, 144, 263, 264, 277
Culverts 115, 272, 273
Cumberland turf 126, 277
Curing of concrete 184
Currency 28
Cut, final 212.
  initial 118, 129, 276
Cutting back 143
Cycle stands 210, 344

Dedication agreements 8, 9
  covenants 8, 9
  of land to forestry 8
  of woodland 8
Defects liability 69, 75, 77, 79, 83, 84, 116
Defence Regulation No. 68. 8
Delay and changes in instructions 33
Delayed work 17, 23
Delivery of turf 126, 127
Demolition 87, 261
Dendix Brushes Ltd. 197, 331
Dennis Bros., Ltd. 349
Department of the Environment 6, 12
Departments, government 9, 71, 74
Derelict land 6, 10, 11, 12
Derelict Land Clearance Areas 11
Description of work/specification 16, 17, 20, 34, 69, 72, 73, 77
Design, interior 42
  landscape 41
Design of furniture 25

of ornaments 25
Detail design stage 34
Detailed estimates 25
Development areas 11
  building 3, 4
  control of 6
  improvements 10
  industrial 10
  notification of 4
  objections to 4
  of land 4, 6
  of systems 42
  plans 25, 34
  studies 34
Diggers, tractor mounted 97
Digging by hand 90
Dilapidations 41
Dimensions of plants 134, 136
Dimensions of turf 126
Disbursements 44
Discount 74
Discus 256
Disposal 4, 5, 261, 262
Disputes 16, 17, 46
Disused vehicles 4
Ditches 114, 271
  boundary 114, 271
  piped 114, 272
Division of bills of quantities 70
Documentation, tender 47, 69, 72
Dorman Sprayer Co., Ltd. 354
Drainage 11, 69, 105, 144, 147, 150, 265
  mole 108, 114, 271
  preliminaries 110
Drainage, subsoil 107
  systems, design of 106, 108
  tile 108, 109, 114, 265
Drains, catchwater 112, 269, 270
  clayware 110, 111, 265, 266, 267
  excavations for 108, 110, 266
  field 109
  flexible plastic perforated 110, 266, 268
  french 269
  lateral 108, 109, 265
  laying of 111, 267
  main 108, 109, 265
  porous concrete 110, 268
  rigid plastic perforated 110, 265, 268
  testing of 111
Drawing office practice 68

Drawings 16, 17, 20
  drainage 34
  marked up 78
  record 34
  services as executed 34
  sketch plan 68
  special 35
  working 68, 72
Drilling rigs 97
Driveways 250, 251, 326, 327

Earthmoving 11, 74
  machines 101, 347
Earthworks, calculations of 100
Ebor Fencing Ltd. 164, 307
Edgings 117, 168, 240, 241, 274, 310, 311, 312
Electrical services 54, 57, 59, 63, 65
Ellis & Sons Ltd., John 189, 319
Enclosure 81, 85, 158, 258, 295
Engagement, termination of 17, 45
Engineering schemes 4, 69
  services 30
Enquiries, public 4
En-Tout-Cas Ltd. 121, 196, 197, 198, 275, 330, 331
Equipment 37, 346
  climbing 199, 200, 201, 332, 333, 334
  play 199, 332
Esplana 210, 343
Estimates, approximate 20, 56, 63, 64
  budget 47
  detailed 25
  of cost 65, 66
  of expenses 28
  of fees 16, 27, 28
Excavation 70
  for drains 108, 110, 266
  hand 97, 261
  major 101
  mechanical 261
  mineral 3, 10
Excavations 88, 167
  liability for 166
  water in 167
Exhibition work 42
Existing artifacts 84, 87
  buildings, works to 37, 40
  services 81, 86
  vegetation 83, 86

Index

Expansion joints 185, 317
Expenses 26, 27, 28, 39, 44
   compounding of 44
   estimate of 28
   hotel 26, 44
   meals 26
   out of pocket 26, 44, 47
   travelling 26, 44, 47
Expert witness, fees for 43
Exposed aggregate 186
Extension of contract 22
Extensions to existing buildings 37
Extra fees 17, 20
Extra work and expense 33
Extraction of sand and gravel 3

Facilities, sports 196, 254, 330
Fallow 104
Farm Institutes 96
Feasibility studies 25, 33
Fees 15
   aggregation of 50
   apportionment between stages of service 40
   arbitration 43, 67
   architect's 30
   calculation of 20, 21, 36, 49, 54, 56, 57
   common 27
   expert witness 43
   estimate of 16, 27, 28
   extra 17, 20
   for quantity surveying services 52
   forward forecasting of 23
   I.L.A. graph 225
   landscape architect's 15
   limited stages of work 22
   lump sum 23, 24, 26, 27
   minimum 16
   mode and time of payment 26, 39
   negotiation of 20, 25
   new works 37, 40
   order of costs 17, 27
   out of pocket expenses 26, 44, 47
   overseas work 28
   paid in instalments 27, 50, 64
   partial services 35, 38
   percentage basis for 19
   rebatement of 25
   reductions in 37, 38, 39
   revision of 17

   time charges 18, 30, 31, 41, 43, 56, 67
   works to existing buildings 37, 40
Felling 8, 83, 86, 216, 258, 259, 260
Fencing 158, 295
   anti-intruder 308
   British Standards for 161
   chain link 85, 163, 165, 258, 305, 306
   cleft chestnut 85, 258
   close boarded 162, 302, 304, 336
   concrete 162, 164, 303, 306
   metal 237, 238, 304
   picket 162, 303, 304
   protective 86, 122, 141, 144, 258, 276
   P.V.C. 164, 307
   strained wire 163, 258, 305
   temporary 81, 85, 86, 122, 141, 258, 276
   tennis court 164, 306, 308
   timber 233, 234, 235, 236, 300
   timper panel 162, 304
   wrought-iron 163, 305
Fertilising 91, 117, 122, 129, 130, 146, 216, 218, 274, 276, 277
Field drains 109
Fields, playing 254, 255, 256, 330
Filler 171, 174
Filling 111, 152, 268, 269
Final accounts 47, 49, 50, 59, 61, 63, 64, 65, 66, 70, 75, 77, 79
   certificate 50, 79
   cost 47, 79
   cut 212
   handover 77
Financial account, settlement of 16
   bond 75
Fine aggregate 170, 173
   cold asphalt 173
Fire paths 191, 322
Fisons 129, 130, 277, 278
Fittings, bulkhead 207, 340
Fixed bollards 159, 296
   cobbles 194, 251, 253, 325, 327, 329
Flags 192, 322
Flats 38
Flexible plastic perforated drains 110, 266, 268
Flexible surfaces 170, 314
Floodlighting 206, 338, 339
Flymo Ltd. 353, 355
Football 254, 330
Forest trees 136, 143, 291

Index

Forestry 3, 7
  Acts 7
  Commission 7, 8
  Commissioners 7
  dedication agreements 8, 9
  dedication covenants 8, 9
  dedication of land to 8
  grants 7, 8
  planting 70
Form of contract 71, 74, 77
Form, instruction 76
Forms, removal of 185
  setting of 183
Formwork 317
Forward forecasting of fees 23
Fountain nozzles 204, 337
Fountains 204, 336, 337
Frames, climbing 199, 200, 201, 332, 333, 334
Freestanding walls 228, 295
French drains 269
Funds, retention 77
Furniture and fittings 25, 35, 36, 37, 42

Garden and landscape design 41
Gates 239, 303
G.E.C. (Street Lighting) Ltd. 206, 207, 338, 339
General conditions 15
Geometric Furniture 209, 343
Germination 116
Glasdon Ltd. 210, 344
Glenlivet 197, 331
G.L.T. Products and Engineering Ltd. 199, 332
Golf courses 330
Government departments 9, 71, 74
Government grants 6
Gradients 96
Grading 87, 90, 263, 264
  major 100
  minor 99
Graders 347
Granite kerbs 168, 311
  paving 192, 323
  setts 193, 248, 251, 253, 311, 325, 327, 329
Grants 6, 8, 35
  Annual Management 8
  applications for 12

forestry 7, 8
government 6
planting 8
reclamation 10, 11, 12
Graph, I.L.A. fees 225
Grasses 125
Grass maintenance 220, 345
  seeding 116, 274
Gratuities 26
Gravel 178, 251, 315, 327
Gravel extraction 3
Grids, tree 249, 325
Ground cover 289
Ground finishes, hard 166, 309
Groundworks 88, 261
Grubbing 84, 259
Guard rails, pedestrian 160, 297
Guards, tree 139, 284
Guarantee for plants 70
Guying 153, 155, 292

Hammer 256
Hand auger 97
  digging 90
  excavation 97, 261
Handover 77
Hardcore 167, 309, 310
Hard ground finishes 166, 309
Harrowing 117, 274
Haunchwood Lewis Brick & Tile Co., Ltd. 193, 324
Hayter Ltd. 350
Heaps, spoil 84, 101
Heating services 54, 57, 59, 63, 65
Hedges 142, 288, 289
Heeling in 145
Herbaceous plants 142
Highfield Engineering Co., Ltd. 160, 297
High jump 256
Historic buildings 4, 37
Hockey 254, 330
Hoggin 179, 315
Holiday caravan sites 14
Holton Builders Ltd. 209, 342
Horwool Ltd. 354
Hotel expenses 26, 44
Housing, repetitive 37
Hulland Products Ltd. 189, 319
Hydro-seeding 123

I.L.A. Agreements and Conditions of Contract 71, 74
I.L.A. Certificates 77
I.L.A. fees, graph 225
Imperial Chemical Industries 123, 129, 276, 277
Inception stage 33
Indemnity 75
Industrial development 10
Industrial Development Act 10
Industries, nationalised 9
Information centres 6
Information for contractor 34
Initial cut 118, 129, 276
Inquiries, planning 43
Insecticide 129, 277
In-situ concrete 180, 250, 252, 316, 326, 327
   base for 182
   compaction of 184
   curing of 184
   exposed aggregate 186
   materials for 181
   spreading of 183
   sub-grade for 182
   weather effects on 184
Inspection 25, 31, 32, 34, 35, 78
Inspection chambers 108, 112, 270
Instalment payments 27, 50, 64
Institute of Arbitrators 18, 46
Institute of Landscape Architects 72
Institutions 9
Instructions 16, 20, 33, 76, 77, 79
Interim certificates 59, 61, 64, 66, 77
   payment 47
Interior design 42
Intermediate (Land Clearance) Areas 11
Intermittent work 18
Investigations, site 86, 88, 96, 97, 98, 105
   soil 35, 94, 97
   structural 41
Invitation to tender 71
Ireland, Northern 4, 5, 28

Javelin 256
Johnsons 121, 275
Joints 172, 177
   contraction 186
   expansion 185, 317
Junctions 267, 268

Kerbs 168, 310
   concrete 168, 310, 311
   granite 168, 311
   granite sett 311
   precast concrete 168, 310, 311
   sandstone 169, 311
   setting of 169
Killing of roots 216, 218
Killing of stumps 216, 218

Labelling of plants 134
Lacrosse 254, 330
Lakes 203, 335
Lamflex 110
Land, acquisition of 10
   derelict 6, 10, 11, 12
   development of 4, 6
   Drainage Division 106
   use 3, 4
Landscape architect, as consultant 17
   authority of 16
   fees for 15
   nomination of deputy 16
Landscape Design 72
Landscape design 41
Lateral drains 108, 109, 265
Laying asphalt 175, 314, 315
   drains 111, 267
   tarmacadam 172, 314
   turf 124, 127, 128, 277
Layouts 35, 41
Layouts, parking 244, 313
Le Bas Tube Co., Ltd. 159, 210, 296, 344
Legal advice 44
Legal considerations 3
Legislation 3
Legislation, Scottish planning 4
Liability 69, 75, 77, 79, 83, 84, 116
   for excavations 116
   of contractor 16
Licences 35, 36
Licences for caravan sites 13
Licensing of felling of trees 8
Lifting of crown 213
   semi-mature trees 151
   turf 86, 124, 126, 258
Lighted bollards 206, 339
Lighting, amenity 205, 338
   bricks 207, 340
   low level 207, 340

Limited stages of work, fees for 22
Limmer & Trinidad Co., Ltd. 198, 331
Liquidation of contractor 33
Lists of tenderers 71, 72
Litigation 43, 51, 67
Litter bins 208, 340
Local authorities 3, 4, 5, 6, 9, 10, 12, 13, 71, 74, 79
Local Employment Act 10
Local scales and conditions 28
Long jump 256
Long term engagements 17
Lopping 5
Loose chippings 180, 316
    cobbles 180, 316
Low rails, metal 232, 299
    timber 230, 231, 298
Lump sum contracts 52
Lump sum fees 23, 24, 26, 27

Machinery 346
Machines, earthmoving 101, 347
Main drains 108, 109, 265
Maintenance 34, 69, 70, 74, 75, 78, 79, 116, 122, 129, 132, 147, 211, 276, 277, 284, 285, 288, 345
Major excavation 101
    grading 100
Management of contracts 24, 76
Managerial capacity of principals 18
Manufacture of tarmacadam 171
Manure 191
Marked up drawings 78
Marking of car parks 170, 314
Marley Buildings Ltd. 164, 190, 307, 320
Marshall & Sons Ltd., S. 190, 320
Marsh land 10
Master plan 68
Materials 69
    arising from site works 85
    for asphalt 173
    for in-situ concrete 181
    for tarmacadam 170
    old 37
    plant 25, 131
    re-use of 84, 87, 260
    supplied by building owner 49
Mather & Smith Ltd. 159, 297
Maxwell Hart Ltd. 119, 196, 274, 275, 331
May & Baker 123, 276

Meals expenses 26
Measurement of work 20, 25, 47
Mechanical excavation 261
Merchant Adventurers Ltd. 207, 339
Metaliform Ltd. 209, 341
Metal fences 237, 238, 304
Metal low rails 232, 299
Methods of staking 138
Micro-climate 69
Mileage charges 26
Mineral extractions 3, 10
Minimum fees 16
Mining operations 4
    subsidence 10
Minister of Agriculture 7
Minister of Agriculture in Wales 8
Minister of Housing & Local Government 10
Minister of Technology 10
Ministry of Housing & Local Government circulars 10, 11
Minnesota Mining & Manufacturing Co., Ltd. 197, 331
Minor grading 99
Mixes, seed 117, 119, 274
Mixing of asphalt 174
Models 35
Mode of payment 26, 39
Mole drainage 108, 114, 271
Mono Concrete Ltd. 159, 190, 191, 204, 208, 210, 297, 321, 322, 326, 336, 341, 344
Monsanto 196, 331
Mounted mechanical augers 97
Mountfield Ltd., G. D. 350
Moveable bollards 159, 296
Moving play equipment 200, 201, 202, 333, 334
Mowers 117, 347
Mowing 70, 118, 122, 129, 220, 276, 277, 345
Mowing margins 243, 313
Mulching 70, 152, 221, 284, 288, 294, 345

National Agricultural Advisory Service 7
National Association of Agricultural Contractors 72
National Parks 5, 11
National Parks & Access to the Countryside Act 5, 10, 11, 12
National Parks Commission 5, 6

Nationalised industries 9
Natural stone paving 192, 322
Nature Conservancy 6
Nature reserves 6
Negotiated contracts 47, 70, 73
Negotiation 20, 24, 25, 35, 36, 41
Neptune Concrete Ltd. 200, 209, 332, 342
Netball 256
New works, fees for 37, 40
Neolite Ltd. 191, 321
Nomenclature 69
Nominated suppliers 49
Nomination of deputy 16
Non-chargeable staff 18
Normal services 30, 33, 36
Norman & Sons Ltd. 160, 298
Northern Ireland 4, 5, 28
North point 68
Notching 146
Notification of development 4
Nozzles, fountain 204, 337
Number of tenders 72
Nursery stock 139, 279

Objections to development 4
Occasional visits 24
Old materials 37
Omitted works 36
Open spaces 5
Open tenders 71
Operations, preparatory 81, 258
Orchard Seating 209, 343
Order of costs 17, 27
Orientation 68
Origin of plants 133, 136
Ornamental pools 203, 335, 336
Ornaments, design of 25
Other services 30, 41
Outdoor seats 12, 209, 341
Outfall 112, 270
Outlets 107, 112
Outline proposals 34
Out of pocket expenses 26, 44, 47
Outstanding Natural Beauty, Areas of 6
Overheads 18, 24
Overseas work 28

Panels, timber 162, 304
Paper, building 317
Park authorities 6

Parking blocks, concrete 210, 344
Parking layouts 244, 313
Parks, country 6
  national 5, 11
Partial services 35, 38
Party walls 35
Paths 11, 191, 245, 246, 247, 317, 322, 323
Pattisson & Co., H. 346
Paving 12, 74, 166, 240, 309
  blocks 191, 253, 322, 328
  brick 192, 247, 251, 252, 323, 324, 327
  cobble 180, 194, 251, 253, 316, 325, 329
  granite 192, 323
  natural stone 192, 322
  Portland stone 192, 322
  precast concrete 188, 245, 246, 250, 252, 317, 327, 328
  preparation for 166, 309
  rigid 180, 316
  slate 192, 322
  unit 188, 317
  Yorkstone 192, 322
Payment 75, 77
  by installments 27, 50, 64
  interim 47
  mode of 26, 39
  terms of 74
  time of 26, 39
Pea shingle 178, 315
Peat 91
Pedestrian guard rails 160, 297
Percentage basis for fees 19, 20, 21
Periodicals 372
Permanent after-care 79
Permanent residential caravan sites 13
Phased contracts 3, 23, 33, 34, 70, 71
Photographs 44
pH value 93
Picket fencing 162, 303, 304
Picking, stone 91, 98, 104, 117, 118, 220, 263, 276
Picnic sites 6
Pipaway 110
Piped ditches 114, 272
Pitches 254, 330
Pit planting 146
Pits, tree 70, 132, 134, 150, 262
P.J.P. Trading Ltd. 164, 307
Planning, Acts 3, 6, 9, 13

Index

applications 9
authority 3, 6, 9, 13
cost 47, 56, 63, 64, 65
permission 2, 4, 5, 9, 13
submission 3
Plans, development 25, 34
  master 68
  reproduction of 26
  site 68
  structure 3
Plant containers 210, 343
  guarantee 70
  material 25, 131
  Protection 274
Planting 5, 10, 11, 70, 74, 131, 137, 139, 141, 145, 152, 279, 292
  Grant 8
  on ploughed land 146
  on turf 145, 146
  pit 146
  plans 3, 68, 70, 226, 227
  preparation for 140, 143, 261, 262, 263, 264
Planting schedule 68, 69, 70
  season 137, 140, 145, 148
  sections of bills of quantities 70
  weather conditions for 140, 149
Plants, condition of 133, 137
  dimension of 134, 136
  herbaceous 142
  labelling of 134
  origin of 133, 136
  packaging of 134, 137
  replacement of 79
  specification of 69
Plastic perforated drains 110, 265, 266, 268
Play, cubes 199, 332
  equipment, moving 200, 201, 202, 333, 334
  sculpture 200, 332, 333
Playground equipment 199, 332
Playing fields 254, 255, 256, 330
Ploughing 98, 268
Pole vault 256
Ponds 203, 335
Pools, ornamental 203, 335, 336
  swimming 203, 336
Porous concrete drains 110, 268
Portec (U.K.) Ltd. 351
Portland stone paving 192, 322

Postage charges 26, 44
Post-contract services 57
Postponed works 45
Practical completion 34, 77, 78
Precast concrete kerbs 168, 310, 311
Precast concrete paving 188, 245, 246, 250, 252, 317, 327, 328
Precautions, safety 216
Pre-contract services 52
Pre-emergent weedkiller 118, 274
Preliminary cost 70
  services 25
Preliminaries 69
  drainage 110
Preparation for paving 116, 309
  for planting 140, 143, 261, 262, 263, 264
  for seeding 116, 117, 122, 274
  for semi-mature trees 149, 151
  for turfing 127, 129, 277
Preparatory operations 81, 258
Preservation 84
  of buildings 4
  of topsoil 261, 262
  of townscape 5
  of trees 4, 5, 83
  orders, building 4
  orders, tree 5, 9
Prices, schedule of 64
Pricing of variations 77
Principals 18, 19
Printing costs 26, 44
Procedure, contract 68, 75
Procedure, tendering 47, 72
Production information stage 34
Production of timber 7, 8
Programmes 25
Programming of contracts 74, 75
Protection 82, 116, 137
Protective fencing 86, 122, 141, 144, 258, 276
Prototypes 35, 42
Pruning 132, 143, 149, 152, 212
Publications 6, 360
Public enquiries 4
  Health Act 13
  open space 5
Pugh Ltd., Charles H. 348
Purchase of materials and documents 26
P.V.C. fencing 164, 307

Index

Quantity surveying 30, 41
Quantity surveying services, fees for 52
Quantity surveying work 25
Quarry tiles 193, 250, 324, 327

Railings, wrought-iron 163, 305
Rails, guard 160, 297
   low metal 232, 299
   low timber 230, 231, 298
Railway sleepers 253, 329
Raking 117, 274
Ransomes, Sims & Jefferies Ltd. 351
Rate for associates 18
Rate for principals 18, 19
Reaction of soil 93, 95
Rebatement of fees 25
Reclamation 3, 10
Reclamation grants 10, 11, 12
Record drawings 34
Record of time 18
Recreation 3, 196, 254, 330
Redecoration 55, 63, 65
Redland Tiles Ltd. 191, 321
Reducing 213
Reduction of fees 37, 38, 39
   of contract 22
   of tenders 55
Reference books 358
Refuse 4, 5, 261, 262
Regulating 99
Reinforcement 181, 317
Reinstatement 82
Rejction of tenders 50, 73
Remedial work 83, 86
Removal of forms 185
Remuneration 14, 18, 30
Rental Equipment Manufacturing Co. 347
Repair work 41, 55, 63, 65, 214
Repetitive housing 37
Repetitive work 23
Replacement of plants 79
Replacement of topsoil 111, 152, 264, 268
Reports 35
Reproduction of plans 26
Research 34, 35, 356
Resident architects 33
Resident staff 19, 26, 28
Responsibilities 31
Restoration 3, 213
Resumed commissions 45

Retainers 24, 43
Retaining walls 229, 295, 296
Retention funds 77
Re-use of materials 84, 87, 260
Revision of agreements with clients 17
Revision of fees 17
R.I.B.A.'s approval 30, 39
R.I.B.A. standard form of contract 74
Rights of way 6
Rigid paving 180, 316
Rigid plastic perforated drains 110, 265, 268
Rock 89, 103
Rolled asphalt 173
Rolling 90, 118
Root pruning 149
Root systems 133, 136, 153
Roots, killing of 216, 218
Royal Fine Art Commission 35
Royalties 42
Rubbish 85, 87, 102
Rub-Kor U.K. Ltd. 197, 331
Rugby 255, 330
Running silt and sand 88

Safety precautions 216
Salaries of site checkers 47
Sand extraction 3
Sandstone kerbs 169, 311
Scale 36, use of 47
Scale 37, use of 47, 52
Schedule of planting 68, 69, 70
Schedule of prices 64
Schedule of substitutions 71
Scheme design stage 34
Scotland 4, 5
Scottish Countryside Commission 7
Scottish planning legislation 4
Screefing 145
Screen walls 158, 295
Scrub clearance 83, 84, 86, 143, 144, 258
Sculpture, play 200, 332, 333
Seasonal effects on contracts 75, 76
Season, planting 137, 140, 145, 148
Season, tree work 217
Seats, outdoor 12, 209, 341
Secretary of State for Scotland 4, 5, 7, 8
Secretary of State for the Environment 4, 5, 6, 13
Secretary of State for Wales 6, 8
Securing underground 155, 293

Index

Seed, mixtures 117, 119, 274
    protection of 116
    sampling 117
Seeded areas, turf edging to 117, 274
Seeding 116, 118, 274
    hydro- 123
    preparation for 116, 117, 122, 274
    to banks 118, 274
Seedling 136
Selected contractors 74
Selection of plant material 25
Selection of site 25
Selection of tenderers 71
Selection of trees 148
Selective weedkiller 123, 130, 276, 277, 278
Semi-mature trees 70, 147, 292
    lifting 151
    planting 152, 292
    preparation for 149, 151
    transporting of 151
Separate trades contracts 42
Services 168
    additional 25
    electrical 54, 57, 59, 63, 65
    engineering 4, 69
    existing 81, 86
    heating 54, 57, 59, 63, 65
    normal 30, 33, 36
    other 30, 41
    partial 35, 38
    post-contract 57
    pre-contract 52
    preliminary 25
    ventilating 54, 57, 59, 63, 65
Setting of forms 183
Setting of kerbs 169
Setting out of bills of quantities 70
Settlement of financial account 16
Setts, granite 193, 248, 251, 253, 311, 325, 327, 329
Shale 179, 316
Shaping 213
Shingle 178, 315
Shot putt 256
Shrub bed maintenance 220, 345
Shrubs 133, 135, 220, 345
    dimensions of 134
    planting of 139, 285
Silt or sand, running 88
Silt pits 112, 270

S.I.P.A. 197, 331
Sisis Equipment Ltd. 347
Site clearance 83, 84, 86, 143, 144, 258
    enclosure 81, 85, 258
    inspection 25, 78
    investigations 86, 88, 96, 97, 98, 105
Site licence 13
    plans 68
    selection 25
    surveying 25
    visits 76
Sites and buildings 35
Size of stones 94
Sketch plan drawings 68
Slate paving 192, 322
Sleepers, railway 253, 329
Slides 200, 332, 333
S.M.P. Landscapes Ltd. 200, 333
Soakaways 113, 270
Soil 126, 138
    ameliorants 90, 98
    investigations 35, 94, 97
    reaction 93, 95
    sampling 94, 96
    stripping 84, 87
    surveying 25
    texture of 92, 94
Sowing 118, 274
Spacing 145
Specialisation 18, 19
Specialist consultants 16, 24
    services 16, 24
    suppliers 16, 31
Specifications 16, 17, 20, 34, 69, 72, 73, 77
Speculative builders 37
Spiking 220
Spoil heaps 84, 101
Sports facilities 196, 254, 330
Sports pitches 254, 330
Sports Turf Research Institute 96
Sportsmark Equipment Ltd. 201, 333
Sprayers 353
Sprays, anti-desiccant 151, 294
Sprays, chemical 151, 294
Spreading concrete 91
    topsoil 183
Stabilised hoggin 179, 315
Staff, charges for 19
    non-chargeable 18
    resident 19, 26, 28

Staking 70, 138, 153, 279, 280, 281, 282, 283
　methods of 138
　out 69
Standard form of contract 20, 71, 74, 77
Standard instruction forms 76
Standards for caravan sites 13, 14
Standards of workmanship 69, 76
Stands, cycle 210, 344
Statutory authorities 3, 9
Stelcon Ltd. 210, 344
Stemport Marketing Co., Ltd. 352
Steps 252, 253, 327
Stone content 93, 95, 97
　paving, natural 192, 322
　picking 91, 98, 104, 117, 118, 220, 263 276
　Portland 192, 322
　size of 94
Strained wire fencing 163, 258, 305
Street furniture 205, 338
Street Furniture Ltd. 160, 298
Stripping 84, 87
Structural investigations 41
Structure plans 3
Stumps, killing of 216, 218
Sub-contractor 31, 34, 36, 42, 49, 74
Sub-contracts 47, 74, 76
Sub-grade for concrete 182
Sub-letting of contracts 74, 75
Submission for planning 3
Subsidence, mining 10
Subsoil 97
Subsoil drainage 107
Subsoiling 98, 103, 264
Substitutions 71, 73
Supervision of work 16, 20, 22, 75, 76
Suppliers 16, 31, 34, 49
Supply of turf 124, 127, 277
Surfaces, artificial 196, 330
Surfaces, flexible 170, 314
Surveys 7, 25, 35, 41
Sutcliffe Moulded Rubber Co., Ltd. 201, 333
Sweepers 354
Swimming pools 203, 336
Swings 200, 202, 333, 334
Systems, building 42
　drainage 106, 108
　root 133, 136, 153, 216, 218

Tack coat 174
Tarmacadam 170, 314
　compaction of 172
　joints in 172
　laying of 172, 314
　manufacture of 171
　materials for 170
　transport of 171
Telephone charges 26, 44
Temporary fencing 81, 85, 86, 122, 141, 258, 276
Temporary works 82
Tender, action to completion stage 34
　documentation 47, 69, 72
　invitation to 71
　willingness to 71
Tenderers, list of 71, 72
　number of 72
　selection of 71
Tendering procedure 47, 72
Tenders, acceptance of 50, 73
　checking of 47, 73
　negotiated 47, 70, 73
　open 71
　reduction of 55
　rejection of 50, 73
Tennis court fencing 164, 306, 308
Tennis courts 256, 330
Termination of engagement 17, 45
Terms of payment 74
Testing of drains 111
Texture of soil 92, 94
Thinning 152, 213
Thorn Lighting Ltd. 206, 207, 338, 339, 340
Tile drainage 108, 109, 114, 265
Tiles, clay 193, 324
　quarry 193, 250, 324, 327
Timber fences 233, 234, 235, 236, 300
Timber low rails 230, 231, 298
Timber panels 162, 304
Timber production 7, 8
Time charges 18, 30, 31, 41, 43, 56, 67
Time of payment 26, 39
Time, record of 18
　travelling 18, 19, 43
Top dressing 122, 129, 130, 276, 277
Topping 118, 129, 276
Topsoil 90, 92, 96, 262, 264
　preserving 261, 262

Index

replacement of 111, 112, 152, 268
  spreading of 103, 128, 262, 264
  texture of 92
Topsoiling 90, 103, 127, 128, 262, 264
Toro Manufacturing Corporation 353, 355
Total construction cost 36
Town & Country Planning Act 3, 4, 6, 9, 13
Town & Country Planning Order 4
Town & Country Planning (Scotland) Act 4
Town & Country Planning (Scotland) Order 4
Town planning 30, 33, 35, 36, 41, 43
Townscape, preservation of 5
Tractor mounted diggers 97
Trade association 72
Traffic barriers 159, 296
Transplants 136, 137
Transport of asphalt 175
  of semi-mature trees 151
  of tarmacadam 171
Travelling expenses 26, 44, 47
Travelling time 18, 19, 43
Tree felling 8, 83, 86, 216, 258, 259, 260
  grids 249, 325
  guards 139, 284
  pits 70, 132, 134, 150, 262
  Preservation Orders 5, 9
  staking 70, 138, 153, 279, 280, 281, 282, 283
  ties 70, 139, 279, 280, 281, 282, 283
  work 211
  work, season for 217
Trees, 131, 133, 134, 279
  dimensions of 134, 136
  for anchorage 218
  forest 136, 143, 291
  lopping of 5
  planting of 5, 10, 11, 137, 139, 145, 152, 279
  preservation of 4, 5
  selection of 148
  semi-mature 70, 147, 292
  work near 98
Trenching 108, 110, 266, 267
Triple jump 256
Turf, condition of 126, 128
  Cumberland 126, 277
  delivery of 126, 127
  dimensions of 126
  edging to seeded areas 117, 274
  laying of 124, 127, 128, 277
  lifting of 86, 124, 126, 258
  planting 145, 146
  supply of 124, 127, 277
Turfing 124, 277
  preparation for 127, 129, 277
  to banks 128, 277
Tying 139
Type of job 20

Undercutting 136, 137
Underground securing 155, 293
Unit paving 188, 317
Universal Graders Ltd. 347
Use of Scale 36. 47
Use of Scale 37. 47, 52

Valuation 16, 20, 25, 41
Variations in contract 16, 17, 31, 47, 60, 76, 77
  in expenditure 31
  pricing of 70, 76, 77
Vegetation, burning of 83
  existing 83, 86
  to be cleared 83, 86, 143, 258
Vehicles, abandoned 5
  disused 4
Ventilating services 54, 57, 59, 63, 65
Visits, occasional 24
  site 76

Wall brackets 207, 339
Walley Thurock Ltd. 180, 318
Walls, freestanding 228, 295
  party 35
  retaining 229, 295, 296
  screen 158, 295
Water features 203, 335
Water in excavations 167
Watering 70, 129, 132, 153
Waterways 6
Weather conditions for planting 140, 149
Weather effects on concrete 184
Weeding 70, 147, 284, 285, 288, 345
Weedkiller, pre-emergent 118, 274
  selective 123, 130, 276, 277, 278
Whinstone kerbs 168, 311
White & Carter Ltd. 208, 209, 341
Willingness to tender 71
Woodland 3, 7, 8, 9, 10

Woodland Dedication Scheme 8
Work, abandoned 23, 45, 50, 51
  advisory 18, 24
  alteration 18, 37, 40, 55, 63, 65
  collaborative 18, 26
  consultancy 18, 24
  delayed 17, 23
  done by client 39
  extra 33
  intermittent 18
  measurement of 20, 25, 47
  near trees 98
  omitted 36
  overseas 18, 24
  postponed 45
  remedial 83, 86
  repair 41, 55, 63, 65, 214
  repetitive 23
  stage 30, 31, 33
  supervision of 16, 20, 22, 75, 76
  temporary 82
  to existing buildings 37, 40
Works of art 35
Working drawings 68, 72
Workmanship, standards of 69, 76
Wrapping 153, 284, 294
Wrought-iron railings 163, 305

Yorkstone paving 192, 322

INDEX TO ADVERTISERS

The Atlas Stone Company Ltd.	*facing page* 319
Battenhurst Developments	*page* 343
Bernhard's Landscapes	*facing page* 281
Blakedown Landscapes Ltd.	*facing page* 318
The British Association of Landscape Industries	*facing page* 280
British Association of Sportsground & Landscape Contractors	*facing page* 294
Burnham Signs	*page* 340
Camland Advisory and Analysis Service	*facing page* 302
C. M. Churchouse Ltd.	*facing page* 339
Civic Trees (Tree Movers) Ltd.	*facing page* 293
Coblands Nurseries Ltd.	*facing page* 287
G. S. Daniels (Contracts) Ltd.	*facing page* 122
E. T. S. Landscaping Services	*facing page* 332
Geometric Furniture Ltd.	*page* 342
Griffin and Legg	*facing page* 303
Maxwell M. Hart	*facing page* 274
Highfield Engineering (Telford) Co. Ltd.	*facing page* 302
Gavin Jones Nurseries Limited	*facing page* 295
Charles Lambert (Lawns) Ltd.	*facing page* 274
L. & P. Peat Ltd.	*facing page* 122
Landscape and Sportsground Development Ltd.	*facing page* 123
Lord's Tree Services Ltd.	*facing page* 292
Mommersteeg Seed Co. Ltd.	*facing page* 275
Neptune Concrete Ltd.	*page* 332
Nickersons Seed Specialists Ltd.	*facing pages* 118, 119
Notcutts Nurseries Ltd.	*facing page* 286
R. G. Pawsey	*page* 279
Playstyle Ltd.	*jacket & cover*
SMP (Landscapes) Ltd.	*facing page* 333
Spearman Construction Ltd.	*facing page* 332
E. & F. N. Spon Ltd.	*facing pages* 281, 338, 349
Tacchi's Nurseries	*facing page* 287
Tilhill Landscaping Services	*facing page* 295
Gerald Williams	*facing page* 292
Wright Rain Ltd.	*facing page* 348

Advertisement Department:

T. G. Scott & Son Ltd, 1 Clement's Inn, London WC2A 2ED